ECOLOGICAL NUMERACY

ECOLOGICAL NUMERACY

Quantitative Analysis of Environmental Issues

Robert A. Herendeen
Illinois Natural History Survey
University of Illinois

JOHN WILEY & SONS, INC.

New York · Chichester · Weinheim · Brisbane · Singapore · Toronto

Copyright © 1998 by John Wiley & Sons, Inc. All rights reserved.

Published simultaneously in Canada.

Library of Congress Cataloging-in-Publication Data:
Herendeen, R. A.
    Ecological numeracy : quantitative analysis of environmental
issues / Robert Herendeen.
        p.   cm.
    Includes index.
    ISBN 0-471-18309-1 (alk. paper)
    1. Environmental management—Mathematical models.   2. Numeracy.
3. Environmental economics.   I. Title.
GE300.H47   1998
363.7′001′5118—dc21   97-31201

Printed in the United States of America.

10 9 8 7 6 5 4 3 2 1

To my father, Lemuel A. Herendeen,
my mentor, Daniel Alpert,
my children, Laurel and Paul Herendeen.

CONTENTS

FOREWORD

A decade ago a joke made the rounds about a man who purchased an energy-efficient furnace and thereby cut his energy bill by half. Delighted with his savings and thinking that he could reduce his costs to zero, he bought another. We laugh, but daily make mistakes only slightly less daffy. Illogic of this kind is evident all around us. Members of Congress routinely confuse resource stocks and flows. Technophiles talk glibly about rocketing excess human population off into space colonies without appraising the magnitude of the problem or the feasibility of the solution. Corporate leaders daily demonstrate their ignorance of the ecological consequences of exponential growth. Economists rigorously discount the prospects of future generations. Others believe that a global population of 15 billion people or more would be a great thing. And few of us pay attention to carrying capacity or "ecological footprints."

The scale of the human enterprise on earth is growing rapidly and the speed of human history is still accelerating. As a result, the lead time necessary to organize our affairs in more sustainable and desirable ways is shrinking. In matters having to do with our use of energy, land, biotic capital, and resources, which is to say the material underpinnings of civilization, good intentions are necessary but hardly sufficient. We will also have to be a great deal smarter about how the world is stitched together in patterns and systems, how ecologies work relative to various levels and kinds of human activity, and the design of incentives, both economic and cultural, that calibrate good intentions and desirable ecological outcomes.

My hunch is that we stand at the edge of a sea of change in human consciousness driven by dire necessity as well as the opportunity to create something far better than what lies in prospect. We are becoming aware that we are part of the biotic community, but have not yet reckoned with what ecological citizenship will require of us. To do so, we will have to discern what counts on a planet governed by the laws of thermodynamics and ecology and we will have to learn how to count ecologically. In large measure our facility with numbers has been put to the task of extending human domination over the earth. Ecological numeracy, as Robert Herendeen explains in this book, is intended to help us build ecologically smarter communities and a more durable culture.

Ecologically numerate people would not be easily bamboozled by those who would exploit them. They would be able to comprehend relative magnitudes, rates of change, multiplier effects, lead times, lag effects, ecological limits, life-cycle costs, and least cost ways of doing things. They would pay less attention to the Dow Jones averages and more to resource stocks and flows, emission of greenhouse gases, species loss, and ecological bookkeeping in their communities. They would not discount their children's prospects for any short-term gain. They would know that honest calculations of economic wealth require us to subtract the loss of soils, trees, wildlife, open space, and the drawdown of biotic capital caused by economic growth. Prices in an ecologically numerate society would tell the truth as Amory Lovins puts it. Ecologically numerate people would not only care about the ecological underpinnings of a decent future, but would be equipped with the analytic wherewithal to do so competently.

If this sounds unrealistic, it should not. When we put our minds to it, we learned how to measure the world down to parts per billion.[1] Most graduates of high schools and colleges can count and do basic math. An increasing percentage of the public has become computer literate. And in a relatively short time a significant fraction of the public has learned the rudiments of ecology. Ecological numeracy is a marriage of ecology and mathematics in the service of a smarter, more just, and more durable society. And where is this revolution in basic analytic competence to begin?

The obvious answer is in schools, colleges, and universities. School superintendents and college deans would be greatly embarrassed if a large percentage of their graduates did not know how to read or count. They should be no less embarrassed when their graduates lack the basic skills necessary for navigating their way on a planet with a biosphere. To be blunt: No student should complete 12 or 16 years of formal schooling without mastering the basics of ecological numeracy as a prerequisite for our dual citizenship as members of political communities and ecological communities. Numeracy in this sense means not only taking numbers seriously, but taking time, magnitude, thermodynamics, ecology, and systems dynamics seriously as well.

Garrett Hardin has taught us to ask "then what?" Ecological numeracy like ecological literacy and good intentions eventually will prove to be necessary but insufficient. It is entirely possible, perhaps probable, that ecological numeracy would be used by some to do more of the same, but more cleverly, in which case we will only delay the inevitable. Accordingly, it must be hitched to the goal of building a society that is both ecologically and morally sustainable. And then there is the problem of ignorance and human cussedness. There are numbers we cannot know, and others we will know only too late, and some things that should not be counted at all. The art of counting ecologically, I think, is understanding numbers relative to the things we ultimately value.

One of the great strengths of *Ecological Numeracy* is that it aims to equip people to be responsible citizens in their communities. A large fraction of the examples and exercises herein are aimed at problems and issues people face each day. The result is a practical and useful book. Widely used and studied,

---

[1]Alfred Crosby (1997). *The Measure of Reality.* Cambridge University Press, New York.

it can also be an influential book, helping us become wiser about the numbers that influence our future and some that dictate our options.

DAVID W. ORR

Professor of Environmental Studies
Oberlin College

INTRODUCTION

THE NUMBERS

There are many ways of knowing; knowing the numbers is one of them. In environmental issues, knowing the numbers means having a sense of the relative magnitudes of things and of the way these vary as systems change dynamically over time . . . and how what humans do, or do not do, affects that. If one does not know the numbers, one is sooner or later cut out of the discussion—and likely mystified by what is happening. Even more likely, one is held in thrall by someone who does know the numbers, or purports to . . . perhaps with aid of an intimidating computer presentation.

The idea behind this book is that relatively basic mathematics—no more than first-semester calculus, and usually just advanced high school math—allows one to understand the essential quantitative aspects of a wide range of environmental issues. Basic mathematics *and* careful thinking. The way to develop and strengthen this facility is to perform simple calculations covering diverse environmental issues. It will turn out that several general principles tend to emerge from the examples, but merely hearing about that is not adequate. The trick is to *do the calculations,* and that is the basis for a course on which this book is based. The book features many simple example calculations and contains problems, some with answers, for the reader to work him/herself.

The tradition of doing quick estimates and calculations to get a handle on things has already been crystallized for environmental work in John Harte's *Consider a Spherical Cow,* an inspiration for me. This book differs from Harte's in (1) covering a much wider range of topics (ranging to economics, trophic ecology, electricity forecasting, and sustainability issues) and (2) operating at a slightly lower level of rigor. It also explicitly introduces modeling concepts and allows for problems to be done—sometimes—on spreadsheets.

THE NUMBERS VERSUS THE REST OF THE PICTURE

At the outset we should acknowledge the duality inherent here: The numbers sometimes seem to clash with the rest of the picture. I was a graduate student in the 1960s when I learned of the plans to dam the Grand Canyon. Although I was studying physics, it was not the numbers that mobilized me. It was the Sierra Club images of time, silence, desert light, the song of the canyon wren, and memories of my own natural and wilderness experiences. Only later was I exposed to an astonishingly wide list of quantitative issues that were important—the demand for water, electricity, and lake and river recreation; reservoir evaporation and siltation rates; population and economic growth projections; political time horizons; institutional lag times; discount rates; profits and losses to diverse groups. This led me, 20 years later, to the LIEDQO framework I use to classify environmental issues in this book. By that time the purview had grown to include automobiles, urban planning, world food, Third World development, and—especially—the common aspects of their impacts and dynamics. I still return to the nonnumerical side; even Illinois sunsets can be stunning, and the daily news images of ravaged landscapes or peoples are arresting. But I know how to pull up the numbers when I need to.

ENERGY EMPHASIS

Readers will notice an emphasis on energy throughout the book. There are three reasons:

1. It is an excellent organizing concept, and using it allows drawing many parallels between ecological and economic systems. In some ways it is the universal currency of these two systems (but one must be very careful in converting the *analogies* into equivalences).
2. Energy is a good first-order indicator of overall environmental impact. The impact includes mining, processing, transport, conversion (burning, in the case of fossil fuels), transmission, disposal of waste, and so on. Detailed impacts are not simply proportional to energy, of course, but the approximate equivalence is often used. With increased interest in the climate-changing potential of CO_2 releases, much of it from burning fossil fuels, this approximation has renewed relevance.
3. As a trained physicist, I used energy as my entry to environmental work. It is what I did, and do, personally.

PREREQUISITES

This book is based on a one-semester course I have taught for several years at the University of Illinois. Typically, it is taken by juniors, seniors, and beginning graduate students in urban and regional planning and ecology, with a smattering of engineering. The course's roots go back to one I taught at Illinois with economist Richard Parker; it contrasted the physical and economic views of resource use and depletion. The student/reader preparation I assume is approximately one semester of calculus, up through simple integration, and one college science course. I look not so much for the content of those courses as for the inquisitiveness and tolerance for concepts and the numbers they imply. We will mostly use high school mathematics, but intensively. For example, there is one important formula (of four I will stress), the sum of a geometric series. It has application in:

1. Depletion of resources under exponential growth of consumption,
2. Benefit–cost analysis,
3. Mortgage payments.

I learned it in 11th-grade algebra, forgot it, and had to relearn it after I had my doctorate and found myself studying the economics of efficient air conditioners. In case you too have forgotten that formula, we will derive it. Then we will use it in several applications. If you are comfortable with this, you will have fun with this book. If it sounds difficult, you will have to work some before it is fun. If it sounds like the kiss of death, you will have to dedicate serious effort. I invite and challenge you to exert that effort. My purpose is to make the going interesting, but you must take the first and subsequent steps.

Fairly technical students will also find useful material here, in terms of an integration of several fields under one approach and in a deeper treatment of concepts that they know in their heads but quite possibly not in their guts. I have found that these subjects often have not jelled even in engineers or physical or natural scientists who have studied them:

1. Stocks and flows in interacting entities (such as pollution flows in lakes and the atmosphere) as a fundament to simulation modeling (and the importance of keeping dimensions straight to facilitate this),
2. The real consequences of exponential growth,
3. The consequences of time discounting,
4. The consequences of time lags.

As an example of the head–viscera disconnect, here is an apocryphal claim: The person most astonished by the result of the pond lily problem tends to be highly mathematical. That problem asks "If a pond is being covered by lily pads that double their area every day, and is first covered on day 23, on what day was it half-covered?" If you didn't fall for that, consider an alternate statement: During the next period (1998–2025), humans will likely consume an amount of fossil energy equal to all that consumed from the beginning of time until 1998. Conceptually, it is the same problem. We aim to *feel* what it means.

At the end of Chapter 1 I include a few diagnostic problems to give the reader a feeling for what to expect.

IS THIS APPROACH REALLY USEFUL TODAY?

My answer is yes. My hypothesis is that a shortcut from relative innumeracy to computer software package mastery is often a dead end requiring one to backtrack, because fundamental understanding is also shortcut. In this book I therefore do not use modeling software such as STELLA, though I like and use such software in my work. That is a reasonable next step after this book. In particular, Chapter 7 introduces the basic stock–flow mechanism of much simulation modeling.

I do embrace two aspects of computer technology. The first is the spreadsheet, such as EXCEL or Lotus 1-2-3, which I recommend for certain problems. Spreadsheets make bookkeeping easier, and ecological numeracy is often essentially bookkeeping or account keeping. Also, spreadsheets make it relatively easy to produce graphical output, which is often a forceful teacher. The second is using the Internet to obtain data. I came to this only late in the writing of this book and have found it extremely useful.

SUGGESTIONS FOR USING THIS BOOK

When *Ecological Numeracy* is used in a course, I expect the instructor will use it as he/she wishes. For a reader outside a formal course setting, I offer these guidelines. The material can be addressed at several levels, as follows.

Level 1. Basic Conceptual Meat of the Book   This is contained in Chapter 1 plus the four chapters covering the four important equations, which are discussed in:

Chapter 2	$I = PAT$	Analyzing components of change
Chapter 3	$1 + x + x^2 + x^3 + \cdots + x^{t-1}$ $= (1 - x^t)/(1 - x)$	Exponential (geometrical) growth
Chapter 7	$\Delta M/\Delta t = F_{in} - M/\tau$	Stocks and flows
Chapter 8	$\sum_{i=1}^{N} \epsilon_i X_{ij} + E_j = \epsilon_j X_j$	Indirect effects

Level 2. Quantitative Applications

Chapter 4	End-use analysis and predicting future demand
Chapter 5	Economic considerations
Chapter 9	Shared resources and the tragedy of the commons

Level 3. The Automobile plus Broader Applications

Level 4. Thermodynamics and Energy Efficiency

In a one-semester upper-level college course, I have usually covered all of Levels 1 and 2 and about half of Level 3. Level 4 has usually been optional and of more interest to students with a technical background. It does not assume that background, however. I feel that to get the essence and flavor of ecological numeracy in context, one should complete at least Levels 1 and 2. In any case, doing the problems, privately—or better, with other people—is critical.

ACKNOWLEDGMENTS

Many people have helped me in my wiggly path through environmental issues and connections, over many years . . . most of them by challenging me. Thanks to them all: Daniel Alpert, Urbana, IL; Clark Bullard, Urbana, IL; Ann Burke, Champaign, IL; Roger Carlsmith, Oak Ridge, TN; John Cender, Foosland, IL; Cutler Cleveland, Boston, MA; Paul Craig, Davis, CA; Robert Curry, Santa Cruz, CA; Scott Fawley, Carbondale, IL; Donna Fathke, Dothan, AL; Peter Fox-Penner, Washington, DC; Charles Goodall, Sidell, IL; Stewart Graham, Champaign, IL; John Grubman, Champaign, IL; Bruce Hannon, Champaign, IL; Eric Hirst, Oak Ridge, TN; Paul and Ellen Hofseth, Oslo, Norway; Timothy Kramer, Auburn, AL; Spencer Landsman, Urbana, IL; Richard and Elizabeth Parker, Camden, ME; Daniel Phelps, Vancouver, BC; Sergei Prokofieff, out there somewhere; Timothy Richards, Janesville, WI; John Taylor, Monticello, IL; Blair Tuttle, Urbana, IL; Scott Wyatt, Champaign, IL.

1 Context and Acclimatization

If there is magic on this planet, it is contained in water.
—Loren Eiseley, *The Immense Journey*

. . . we, compounded of dust, and the light of a star.
—Loren Eiseley, *The Immense Journey*

A horse! A horse! My kingdom for a horse!
—Shakespeare, *Richard III*

Earth provides enough for every man's need, but not every man's greed.
—Ghandi

The human world is beyond its limits.
—Meadows et al., *Beyond the Limits*

A sustainable society is still technically and economically possible.
—Meadows et al., *Beyond the Limits*

These quotes offer six perspectives on environmental issues. The first is about the poetry and magic of nature: The sun is dancing on the water, even if the water is polluted, dammed, overfished, or running out. This can be where one's environmental concern begins, and returns.

The second refers to the thermodynamic basis for life and its dependence (almost always) on the sun as the energy source.

The third conveys a sense of the economic reality of human activities: There are times when treading lightly, conserving stuff, and looking far into the future simply will not deal with immediate real (or perceived) survival problems. Such as King Richard's being cornered in battle. Ultimately, we decide what is important to us.

The fourth raises the issue of equity and the relative impact on poor and rich. Who wins, who loses?

The fifth is "hard" biological and physical thinking . . . though the conclusion is rabidly debated. Are there really limits?

Finally, the sixth, while tacitly admitting the limits issue that these same authors spearheaded a quarter-century ago (Meadows et al., 1972), offers technical and economic hope.

These statements encompass several of the many ways to view environmental issues, or the world at large. They touch on basic themes and contradictions . . . and they mix metaphors.

Environmental issues are broad and controversial. The debate is often qualitative instead of quantitative, and when it turns quantitative, the numbers are often uncertain, fuzzy, and actively challenged. We will, nonetheless, place ourselves on the quantitative side, so that we do not just throw our hands in the air and our thoughts in the clouds. We will work with a wide range of resource and environmental questions. Here are some examples:

- China has 1 car per 670 persons (Tunali, 1996). The United States has 55 cars per 100 persons. What is the CO_2 implication of China's rising to the U.S. per capital level?
- How long will Illinois' topsoil, or coal, last?
- What is the human carrying capacity of Chicago/Illinois/Japan/World, especially when the many indirect impacts and dependencies are accounted for?
- What is the total environmental cost of electricity from coal/oil/natural gas/hydropower/nuclear/solar sources? In parallel, what is the environmental cost of instead saving the electric energy through more efficient use?
- Can all humans be as rich as a Swede?
- Is there enough land in Illinois to produce ethanol for vehicle fuel from grain crops? Is there enough to plant trees to grow and sequester statewide CO_2 releases?
- For how long?
- How much grass is required to produce a hawk? How much energy is required to produce a desk? A trip to Europe?
- How much land is required (directly and indirectly) to support you?
- How long will it take to stabilize China's population, even if each female has only approximately two children. The United States, assuming different immigration policies?

We will use calculations, graphs, and simple models. We will toss numbers around, being careful, but also being adventurous enough to estimate what we do not know exactly. We will get to know the numbers well enough so that we can laugh when someone numerate attempts to use them as weapons against those who are not numerate. In the long run we hope to be (Hardin, 1985)

1. *Literate.* What do the words mean?
2. *Numerate.* What do the numbers mean?
3. *Ecolate.* What then should we do?

We approach goal 2 by working problems: by *doing them.*

The "logo" for the book contains a wide, unspoiled waterfall, which could be dammed to produce hydropower for an estimated 5000 electric toasters. (see Fig. box).[1]

SOME MOTIVATIONAL GRAPHS

The graphs in Figure 1.2 are presented with no axis labels. I ask you to decide what labels to place there, what phenomena the labeled graph describes, and what profession, group, or constituency might use this graph—explicitly or implicitly—in analyzing what they do and—especially—*planning* what they do. Remember to specify the range. In the following discussion I give my own response to these questions.

Figure 1.2*a*. (y = constant.) Phenomena: Solar power striking earth versus year; yield versus year for a sustainably harvested fishery or forest; the land area of Sri Lanka. As planning metaphor for: Canadian Fisheries Commission, regarding the collapsed Atlantic fishery.

Figure 1.2*b*. (Rapidly rising. Example: exponential growth, $y = e^{ax}$, with $a > 0$.) Phenomena: California population versus time (1850–1990); world population (same time period); year sales of McDonalds hamburgers versus year (1960–1995); world energy consumption (1940–1990); yearly micro-computer sales versus year (1980–1995). User: Almost any investor or economist, politician, transportation planner, or U.S. electric utility forecasting department between 1935 and 1978 (discussed in Chapter 4). The exponential growth curve is the metaphor for our culture and has been applied to many aspects of it. See R. Lapp (1973).

Figure 1.2*c*. [S-shaped curve. Example: logistic, $y = e^{ax}/(1 + e^{ax}/b)$, with a and $b > 0$; has value $b/(b + 1)$ at $x = 0$, and value b as $x \rightarrow \infty$. If y is population, the asymptote b is often interpreted as the carrying capacity.]

---

[1]Details of the calculation:

I estimated the river to be 100 ft wide by 4 ft deep and traveling at 3 mph (moderate walk).

I know that 60 mph is exactly 88 ft/sec, so 3 mph is $\frac{1}{20}$ of 88 $\approx$ 4 ft/sec. Then the flow is (4 ft)(100 ft)(4 ft/sec) = 1600 cu ft/sec.

I know a cubic foot of fresh water weighs about 62 lb.

The drop is 40 ft, so the power of the falling water is (40 ft)(62 lb/cu ft)(1600 cu ft/sec) $\approx$ 4 × 10^6 ft lb/sec.

I know that 550 ft lb/sec = 1 hp, so the power is 4000 × 10^6/550 $\approx$ 8000 hp.

I know that 1 hp is about $\frac{3}{4}$ kW, so the power is about 5000 kW.

Commercial turbines/generators can convert 95+% of the mechanical power to electricity.

Verification: Ontario Hydro estimates the potential of Thunderhouse Falls as at least 1.9 MW (available 95% of the time), and at least 8.2 MW (available 50% of the time) (Larry Onisto, Ontario Hydro, personal communication, August 1996).

Figure 1.1 Thunderhouse Falls.

Rapids That Shake the Earth/5000 Toasters

At Thunderhouse Falls in Ontario the Missinaibi River begins its descent off the Canadian Shield to the tidal lowlands of Hudson Bay. Two hundred river miles' worth of water drops 40 feet in three steps over a distance of perhaps 600 feet. The portage trail has been used by natives, fur traders, and adventurers for several thousand years. It is 50 miles to the nearest paved road. The water is thrashed by the fissured bedrock into a seething brown explosion.

Laying over at Thunderhouse, my children and I estimated the hydroelectric potential: 5000 1000-W toasters, or 5 MW of electric power. We needed to know—roughly—a couple of conversion factors, but the exercise is standard ecological numeracy: Estimate the drop by comparing with our heights, the river's speed by watching bubbles, its width by visually comparing with a familiar football field, its depth by how close the rocks had been as we paddled over them, the efficiency of turbines by guesswork. Our estimate is therefore uncertain, but useful. Sitting where Figure 1.1 was taken, we tried to put the result into perspective [compare a nuclear plant at Clinton, Illinois: maximum power 955 MW; Bonneville and Grand Coulee dams on the Columbia River, 1147 and 6448 MW, respectively; Hoover and Glen Canyon Dams on the Colorado River, 2078 and 1288 MW, respectively; Three Gorges Dam (proposed in China, 18,200 MW)]. We did this knowing that 30 years earlier Ontario Hydro Company had evaluated the site and decided not to touch it. Now Thunderhouse is protected as part of an Ontario provincial park.

Phenomena: Insect numbers versus time in confined space with unlimited food; standing biomass versus time in cleared area undergoing succession (time range 100–200 years for temperate hardwood forest); population versus time of community with strict greenbelt zoning (e.g., Boulder, Colorado, 1930–1990); height versus time for a human (up through age 40 years); weight versus time for a chicken (up through age 1 year). User: Certain communities, timber analyst, farmer.

Figure 1.2*d*. [Peaked. Example: slope of logistic, $y = ae^{ax}/(1 + e^{ax}/b)^2$.] Phenomena: Insect numbers versus time in bottle with fixed food stock; consumption per year versus year for a fixed-stock resource such as oil [width of peak at half-height approximately 50 years (Hubbert, 1971)]; yearly height gain versus year for a human (width at half-height approximately 10 years). User: Academics, analysts, but few people in everyday life.

TIME SCALES (CHARACTERISTIC TIMES)

Time scales are important in all dynamic phenomena, including those characterized by Figure 1.2*b–d*. A system can often be characterized by a time scale that will govern its speed of change, for better or worse. Table 1.1 lists some time scales.

To turn the question around, what are the characteristics times for these entities:

Refrigerator
House
Human sewage
Pet dog
Oil reserves
United States
Student apartment building
Electronic equipment
You
What you hold dear

In responding, you likely came up against the question of what time scale means. It can be a lifetime, a time to recover from disruption, a holding or residence time given a leakage or removal rate, or how far into the future or past one chooses to look. These possibilities point out that the time scale of interest depends on the question asked . . . a fairly universal problem.

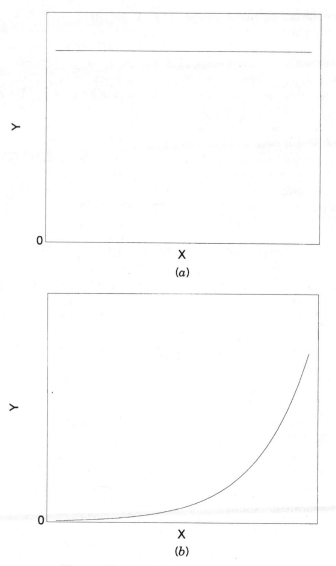

Figure 1.2 Four motivational graphs.

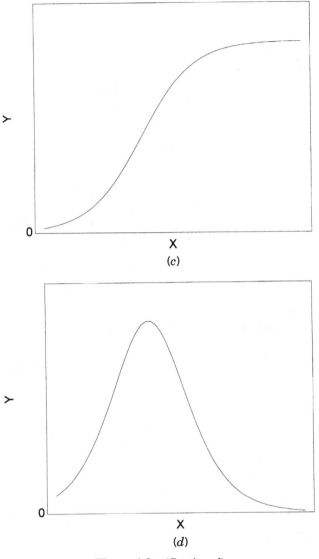

(c)

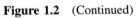

(d)

Figure 1.2   (Continued)

TABLE 1.1   Time Scales

Characteristic Time	Phenomenon
10^{-9} second	Light travels 30 cm: limits to computer's speed
10^{-2} second	Fly wingbeat
10^{0} second	Human heartbeat; reaction time
10^{2} seconds (≈ 1 minute)	TV sound bite
10^{4} seconds (≈ 3 hours)	Bacterial division
10^{7} seconds (≈ 1 year)	Lifetime of birds; political time horizon
10^{8} seconds (≈ 10 years)	Lifetime of car; human generation time; residence time of CH_3CCl_3 in the atmosphere
10^{9} seconds (≈ 100 years)	Lifetime of humans, housing, forests, old sea turtles, United States; residence time of CO_2 in the atmosphere
10^{11} seconds ($\approx 10,000$ years)	Time since Wisconsinian glaciation and arrival of humans in Western Hemisphere
10^{17} seconds ($\approx 10 \times 10^{9}$ years)	Age of solar system

LIEDQO: A FRAMEWORK FOR CLASSIFYING QUANTITATIVE ENVIRONMENTAL ANALYSIS

To integrate the preceding ideas, I will use a six-part framework to classify and organize what we do. Like all classification schemes, it is imperfect, and there is overlap between its (theoretically) distinct parts, but I have found it useful.

LIEDQO:

*L*imits
*I*ndirect effects
*E*fficiency
*D*ynamics and lags
e*Q*uity
*O*ther

L (*Limits*)   Resources of various types are limited. While this is still argued, it is sufficiently possible to be a starting principle and a fundamental issue. In Chapter 11 we discuss the emerging field of ecological economics, which differs from standard (neoclassical) economics in explicitly and proactively dealing with limits (Daly, 1992). Limits are discussed in more detail in Chapter 6. Here are just a few examples:

- Water is scarce in Israel and Arizona.
- Space per capita is scarce in Bombay and New York City.
- Oil is finite, with an expected global lifetime (depending on the rate of use) of several decades.
- Old-growth forests are few and diminishing in North America.
- Fisheries' sustainable catch has been exceeded in eastern Canada and fishing is now banned.
- Soil is eroding faster than it is forming in Illinois and Nepal.
- Water is being pumped out faster than it flows into the Ogalalla aquifer in Nebraska.
- Wood growth in the United States exceeds harvest (this argues *against* limits).

The difference between renewable and nonrenewable resources is often not clean. For all resources, the difference results from the competition between consumption and regeneration. For example, water is being used faster than its recharge rate in western Nebraska (hence nonrenewably), slower in most parts of Norway (hence renewably).

I (Indirect Effects)   The environmental literature is rich with surprises resulting from indirect linkages in concept, time, and space.

- The ozone layer is affected by residential, commercial, and transportation refrigeration (through the release of CFCs).
- Smog is produced by suburban transportation (e.g., through auto emissions).
- Clearing land for exports like bananas leads to global warming (it increases atmospheric CO_2; the effect on climate is controversial but seems real).
- War has been caused by transportation policy (to protect foreign oil suppliers).
- Controlling insect pests threatened raptorial birds (the well-known DDT story).
- Roads built to accommodate traffic stimulated still more traffic.
- A night at the opera increases atmospheric CO_2 (because all activity requires fossil fuel burning somewhere).
- Dam building on the Nile has reduced soil fertility in the Nile delta (by stopping sediment-laden seasonal floods).

- Air conditioning in New England could lead to inundation of wide expanses of Quebec (through hydroelectric development).
- Industrial production in Germany results in fishless lakes in Norway (through acid precipitation).

Indirect effects is a relative term; with increased understanding, the effects will not seem so indirect and surprising. There are two basic types: static indirect effects, at a single point in time; and dynamic indirect effects, in which time lags operate. Again, the separation is not clean.

Temporal indirect effects are essentially the same issue as dynamics and lags, which will be discussed later in this chapter. Characteristic times are experienced as lags and lead to a violation of our common preconception that effects should have prompt causes.

E (*Efficiency, Typically Physical*)   Environmental impacts usually result from the production of an environmental bad in the pursuit of a human good. The question is "how much of good y is produced when an amount of bad x is produced?" If the amount of bad x can be reduced to zero, there is no *environmental* reason not to produce as much good y as anyone wishes. In this case the efficiency of producing y "from" x is infinity.

Efficiency is usually, but not always, defined such that the best case corresponds to 100% efficiency. In terms of the preceding example, we could consider a device that reduces the amount of x released to the environment. Then no removal represents an efficiency of 0%, and complete removal, an efficiency of 100%.

Efficiency cuts two ways in environmental analysis. Where there is good potential for efficiency increase, we can—at least for a while—satisfy our desires for the growth of output of y, while not increasing the environmental burden caused by x. The much-touted opportunities for energy use efficiency are extremely promising, for example, and are discussed in Chapters 4, 5, and 12, as well as serving as an undercurrent to the entire book. On the other hand, there are absolute thermodynamic limits to efficiency and practical technological barriers to approaching the thermodynamic limits (discussed in Chapter 12), so that efficiency cannot be improved indefinitely.

Some examples include:

- Fluorescent light bulbs use about one-fourth as much electricity as incandescents to produce the same light.
- Reduced tillage practices in agriculture maintain crop yields while reducing soil erosion.
- Recycled aluminum requires only about 4% as much energy as new.
- Some new toilets use 3% as much water as conventional ones.
- Electronic communication (perhaps) accomplishes the same end as a much more input-intensive business trip.

- Carefully designed, but not more expensive, cooking stoves use half as much wood as conventional ones.
- New building energy efficiency [measured, say, in (conditioned square footage)/(energy used per year)] has increased severalfold in the last 20 years. Buildings can be constructed to be much more energy efficient than standard practice.

D (*Dynamics and Lags*)   Different parts of natural and human systems have different characteristic times, which produce delays, surprises, overshoots, miracles, and disasters. In addition, group dynamics often produces results that are collectively unsatisfactory, although they are the product of sensible individual strategies. Our reaction to this is confounded by our strong tendency to assume that events have temporally prompt causes:

- We are surprised that the Chinese population will grow for 40 years even if from today women adhere to the two-child rule; the reason is that at present the Chinese population is young, with a disproportionately high percentage of women of child-bearing age.
- The latency time for some cancers is on the order of 20 years.
- We are abashed when a highway, built to easily accommodate heavy traffic, is jammed the day it opens . . . even though we know it took 6 years to plan and build and regional development occurred in anticipation.
- We are disappointed to find that the pollution reduction from cleaner cars will take around 10 years to be felt significantly, because it takes that long for the old dirty cars to die natural deaths and get off the road.

Realistic environmental policy must deal with such dynamic, sometimes transient effects, because human expectations for stability and predictability usually carry an annual or shorter time scale. We want to know not only what a future state looks like, we also wonder what the path from here to there will entail.

Other examples of dynamics and lags include:

- Radio news item dated August 30, 1995: World-scale reduction in the production of CFCs will result in a decrease of stratospheric ozone toward preindustrial levels during the next century, but the present increasing trend will persist until the year 2000.
- The residence time of carbon dioxide in the upper atmosphere is approximately 100 years.
- Common resources such as fisheries and airsheds tend to be overexploited because of competition.

Q (Equity)   Who wins, who loses, or who thinks he/she wins or loses from environmental (or any) policy? No advanced mathematics is needed to realize that if there are limits to growth, at some point the poor get richer only if the rich get poorer. Likewise, one need not be a motivational psychologist to realize that this is *very* important to almost everyone. Furthermore, it is a volatile political issue. We will touch on this issue repeatedly.

Some examples include:

- Pollution is often heavier where the poor live than where the rich live ("environmental justice").
- The Clean Air Act reduced coal miner jobs and increased pollution control equipment jobs.
- The North American Free Trade Agreement (NAFTA) was felt by some to cost American workers their jobs and to produce jobs in Mexico.
- Immigration is felt by some to threaten American jobs.
- Legislation requiring deposits on beverage containers would produce jobs in handling bottles in markets and reduce jobs in producing bottles in glassworks (because the bottles would make many trips).
- Apocryphal tale: During the 1970s, it was proposed to increase thermostat settings and relax dress codes in summer in U.S. government offices to save energy. Protests were received from both shirt and tie manufacturers, who claimed that employment in both was threatened by no ties and short, rather than long, sleeves.
- China's fossil energy resources are dominated by coal, which therefore should be a major fuel driving economic growth. Coal is the most carbon intensive of the fossil fuels, and an international carbon treaty limiting new carbon dioxide emissions would discriminate against China.
- From the book *Material World* (Menzel, 1994):

    Kuwait. Household of 7 people owns 4 automobiles, 5 telephones, and 2 TVs. Their 4850-ft^2 house contains a modular sofa 45 ft long and a swimming pool.

    Bhutan. Household of 12 people has 0 automobiles, 0 telephones, and the members have never seen a TV. They live in the 726-ft^2 second floor over 1134-ft^2 basement/barn housing their cows and draft bulls.

    Japan. Household of 4 people owns 1 automobile, 1 telephone, and 1 TV. House is 1421 ft^2.

    Haiti. Household of 6 people owns 0 automobiles, 0 telephones, 0 TVs. House is 325 ft^2.

O (Other)   This has been added by my students, who rightly claim that there are issues and items not covered by LIEDQ. Therefore, LIEDQO is appropriate. For example, statistical questions, such as the human health effects of pollution, while important, are "other," outside the scope of this book.

To reiterate, the elements of LIEDQO are not necessarily independent and distinct. On balance, the framework that breaks things down this way is useful, but we must be wary of the exceptions.

THE LIEDQOMETER

Sometimes I find it useful to sketch a bar graph I call the LIEDQOmeter to indicate how important the components of LIEDQO are in a given application (see Fig. 1.3). In a few examples in Chapters 1 and 2 I will present a LIEDQOmeter. After that, I use it rarely, but we should keep it in mind.

ESTIMATING

Making and using rough estimates is invaluable in the active discussion of issues of any type. The day I wrote this I used a quick estimate to realize that all the on-site jobs touted for a proposed scrap recycling plant are for

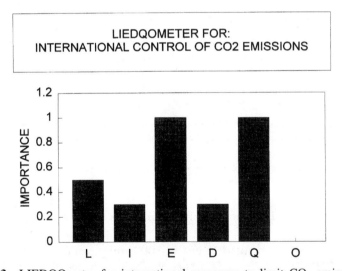

Figure 1.3 LIEDQOmeter for international measures to limit CO_2 emissions. The atmosphere's ability to absorb CO_2 without affecting global climate is *L*imited. Climate change is an *I*ndirect effect of burning fossil fuels to support economic activity. *E*fficiency of energy use and of producing energy from carbon are major factors connecting human activity and atmospheric carbon emissions. Dynamics and lags (*D*) are important in relating emissions (a flow) to the climate effects of CO_2, which are a function of the atmospheric stock; CO_2's atmospheric residence time is approximately 100 years. Deciding what countries will limit CO_2 emissions, especially developing countries like China, is a major e*Q*uity issue. The weightings in the LIEDQOmeter should not be taken too seriously, as they are based on judgment.

minimum wage, which makes them less desirable. All I did was divide the expected annual revenues (from one table in the report) by the expected number of workers (from another table) to obtain about $10,000/year per worker as an upper limit. (Because revenues are used for other expenses besides labor, the actual average annual earnings are even lower.) A work-year is (40 hours)(52 weeks) $\approx$ 2000 hours, so $10,000/year is about $5/hour. At that time minimum wage was $4.75/hour.

Most estimations are more complicated, but the idea is the same. We want an answer for a problem for which we lack complete information, and we have decided that an imprecise answer is useful. Doing estimates is like high diving—the first one is the toughest, and subsequent ones quickly become easier, but it takes many repetitions to become graceful. John Harte stresses that there are times when, for the purpose at hand, it is perfectly reasonable to assume a cow is spherical.[2] For everyone, it takes significant work to become a bold estimator. True wisdom couples that skill with the ability to recognize when the quick estimate is not adequate, and when more detail is warranted: Sometimes sphericality is too simple. The skills are developed by *doing* estimates, *often*. I know of no other way.

Four examples of estimating follow.

Hands Across America

On May 25, 1986 a publicity and public consciousness-raising exercise was for Americans to join hands to span the country from coast to coast. My son and I participated in Urbana, Illinois. We could see a ragged line of people trailing down Cunningham Road to a turn at University Avenue. We wondered how far it went without being broken, and if there were enough people to reach from the Atlantic to the Pacific. Later, we heard that the organizers claimed that between 5.4 and 7 million people participated. Were there enough?

Before you read further, make a stab at the answer right now. Remember it.

For our estimate, we first need some facts . . . approximately. There are some we will know from our general knowledge and some more specialized:

1. We say that the United States is 3000 miles wide; it is actually more like 2500, but it depends where you measure and anyway the line of people will wiggle. (The actual route was significantly longer, zigzagging through New York, Washington, DC, Cleveland, Dayton, Chicago, St. Louis, Dallas, and west to Los Angeles.)
2. A mile is 5280 feet; call it 5000 for short.

---

[2]For a real-life example (!), see Dincer (1994). Unsteady heat-transfer analysis of spherical fruit to air flow.

3. Finally, we need the U.S. population. It was then about 240 million.

Next is a number that can be measured or estimated close up:

4. I have never measured my arm span, but it is approximately my height, which is 6 feet. Let us call it 5 feet to be conservative and to account for children in the line.

This is all we need. It takes 5000/5 = 1000 people to span a mile, and 3000 * 1000 = 3 million people to span 3000 miles. Given the tortuous route, it might have required 4 or 5 million people. The reported 5.4 to 7 million therefore likely sufficed, though the organizers admitted some gaps, particularly in desert areas. If all 240 million Americans had participated, some 40 to 50 such lines could have formed.

How does this compare with your initial guess?

How Many Bagels Are Eaten in Champaign-Urbana, Illinois, per Day?

Before you read further, make a stab at the answer right now. Remember it.

Together the two towns have about 125,000 people, of which 35,000 are university students. Assume that one-third of the students eat an average of 1 bagel each day, while only one-tenth of the rest of the population eats 1 bagel each day. The total is $\frac{1}{3} \times 35,000 \approx 12,000$ student bagels, and $\frac{1}{10} \times 90,000 = 9000$ nonstudent bagels, for a total of 21,000 bagels/day. Averaged over the entire population of 130,000, this is about 1 bagel per person every 6 days.

How does this compare with your initial guess?

What about bagel data? From several sources accessed through the American Institute of Baking web page (http://www.bakery-net.com/rdocs/aiblbfcs.html), I find that U.S. per capita bagel consumption averages almost 4 pounds per year, or about 25 bagels/yr, which is about 1 per person per 15 days. (Even this datum is suspect, because bagel sales have increased fivefold between 1994 and 1997, according to the University of California Wellness Newsletter of 8 May 1997, p. 1.) Our estimate is thus $2\frac{1}{2}$ times the national average. One might expect a college town to eat more bagels than average, but the rough nature of our calculation implies that we can attach no significance to the difference.

How Significant Are the Oil Reserves under the Arctic National Wildlife Refuge?

News item dated August 1995: A draft study by the U.S. Geological Survey estimates the crude oil reserves in the Arctic National Wildlife Refuge (ANWR) in Alaska at 148 million to 5.15 billion barrels. (In 1989 the estimate was 697 million to 11.66 billion.) How big is this?

Before you read further, make a stab at the answer right now. Remember it.

The crux of this question is to ask "How big compared to what?" and to estimate how big "what" is. Here I will define "what" as the amount of oil used by the U.S. automobile fleet in a year.

How much fuel does a typical car use in a week? From experience, you may know that:

1. Weekly use is about a tankful, which is roughly 10 gallons. Another way to obtain this is to know that U.S. cars average 10,000 miles per year and to know that the U.S. auto fleet gets roughly 20 miles per gallon. This gives 500 gallons/year, or about 10 per week.

Unless you work in energy issues, you probably are unfamiliar with the conversion factor for gallons to barrels. You could look it up:

2. It is exactly 42 gallons per barrel.

Then a car uses $500/42 \approx 12$ barrels per year.

The lower limit for the ANWR is then enough to fuel 148×10^6 barrels/ $(12 \text{ barrels car}^{-1} \text{ year}^{-1}) \approx 12$ million cars for a year. Note that this is not a yearly oil flow from the find, which might persist for some time, but all the stock in the ground. All of it will fuel at least 12 million cars for 1 year. Then it is gone. On the other hand, the upper limit gives 5.15×10^9 barrels/ $(12 \text{ barrels car}^{-1}) \approx 400$ million cars for a year.

We now ask what fraction of the U.S. auto fleet these 12 to 400 million cars represent.

3. We need to know that there are about 130 million registered automobiles. We could also get this by knowing that there are about 0.55 registered autos per capita and knowing the U.S. population is about 250 million.

Thus estimated ANWR oil could keep the U.S. auto fleet running for 12/130 to 400/130 years, that is, from about 1 month to about 3 years.[3] Whether that is big or small still depends on the context one chooses.

How does this compare with your initial guess?

How Many Piano Tuners Are There in Chicago?

Scientists are heirs to several apocryphal stories about outrageous questions asked by famous scientists. This one is attributed to Enrico Fermi, nuclear

---

[3]This calculation ignores the oil used in extraction, refining, transportation, and so forth. Detailed studies show that 10 to 15% of the oil is consumed in this chain from well to gas tank (Bullard and Herendeen, 1975).

physicist, Nobelist, at the University of Chicago, who asked a graduate student during a qualifying examination, "How many piano tuners are there in Chicago?" The goal is to come up with an estimate of the number and an estimate of the uncertainty of that number.

By now you know enough not to say "I have no idea." On the other hand, you could offer a correct but flip answer of "half Chicago's population, plus or minus 100%." We can do better than that.

Before you read further, make a stab at the answer right now. Remember it.

What percentage of households have a piano? In Champaign-Urbana, a university town, I would estimate 1 in 10. In Chicago, I suspect it is lower . . . say, 1 in 15.

How often is a household piano tuned? Twice a year for serious players, but I suspect once a year on average.

How many households are there in Chicago? The population is roughly 3 million, and a household today is about 2.7 people . . . call it 3. So, 1 million households.

$\frac{1}{15}$ of 1 million = 70,000 household pianos, resulting in 70,000 tunings per year.

How many tunings does a full-time tuner do in a year? Assume the job takes 1 to 2 hours, so that a tuner does 4 per work day. A work year is 200 days, so a tuner can do $4 \times 200 = 800$ tunings per year, which requires $70,000/800 \approx 90$ full-time tuners.

This is just for residences. Schools, churches, bistros, and so forth also have pianos. We can get at this as follows: The school age population in Chicago, say 5 through 17 years, would be $(17 - 4)/65 = \frac{1}{5}$ of the total if all ages were equally represented and if all people die at age 65. This is a reasonable start; there are therefore 3 million/5 = 600,000 students. A school has about 500 students, so there are 600,000/500 = 1200 schools, and each school has approximately 2 pianos. Then there are 2400 school pianos. To this we might add symphonies, music teachers, bars, cabarets—which might sum to a few thousand pianos. The total of household and others might be raised to 80,000.

This would result in increasing the estimate of 90 tuners to about 100. Does this sound reasonable?

We can review some of the assumed factors and ask what happens to the estimate if we change those factors. Formally, this is called sensitivity/uncertainty analysis (see Appendix 1), but we proceed informally.

Let us stick with the assumption of 1 million Chicago households, but assume

- One piano in 20 households
- The average piano is tuned every 2 years
- A tuner can tune 1000 times per year

This yields an estimate of $(1 \times 10^6)/(20 * 2 * 1000) = 25$ full-time tuners. Correcting for the institutional pianos might push this up to 30 or 40.

Other corrections are, of course, possible, but we are getting to a point of closure. In 10 minutes' time we have estimates that are in the range of 25 to 100 tuners in Chicago, and in the process we have specified a range of uncertainty. To be a bit safer, we might increase the upper limit to 150. So, to Enrico Fermi we say "25 to 150 piano tuner equivalents in Chicago. If you want a better number, we will need significantly more time to improve our estimate."

How many piano tuners *are* in Chicago?

- In Chicago proper, there are 25 to 40 Yellow Page phone numbers under "piano tuning–repair–refinishing" and at least 4 more in the suburbs. Of course, more than one tuner could use a common phone.
- The Chicago Piano Tuners' Guide has 66 members. The University of Illinois Music Library estimates that there are two active tuners not in the guild for every tuner that is a member; this would yield 198 tuners.

The agreement with our estimate is good. But even these facts are fuzzy and open to difference in definition and interpretation, and we could continue to improve our estimation and our data gathering—if we wished. For our purpose here, we have done enough. There are approximately 100 piano tuners in Chicago.[4]

How does this compare with your initial guess?

PROBLEMS (INCLUDING PRELIMINARY DIAGNOSTICS)

Level of difficulty is indicated as Easier/Moderate/Harder. Problems marked "(Spreadsheet?)" can be fruitfully approached using a spreadsheet. They need not be, however.

Problems 1.1 to 1.6 are for practice in estimation and to learn how comfortable you are with manipulating numbers. Do not spend any significant time looking up numbers: Estimate or guess (and identify your guesses as such) and move on.

1.1. Express the miles driven annually by U.S. cars in round trips to the sun.

---

[4]Further reality check: To me 100 tuners initially sounded too big. With that many, I would think I would know some personally, but I don't know a single one. We can see what fraction of the labor force that would be. If Chicago has 1 million households, there are probably 1.3 million full-time equivalent jobs. $100/(1.3 \text{ million}) \approx 1/13{,}000$; one out of every 13,000 jobs is for tuning pianos. Given that number, it's reasonable that I personally don't know any.

1.2.   Estimate your home state or country's area in square miles, acres, hectares, square yards, U.S. area, world area, twin beds, 14-inch deep-dish pizzas.

1.3.   **(a)** What does it cost to light a 100 W bulb continuously for a year?

(b) What does it cost for all lighting in Room 109 at 907-1/2 W. Nevada, on the University of Illinois campus, which has nine fixtures each containing four fluorescent bulbs of approximately 50 W each.

(c) In the enclosed *Daily Illini* (student newspaper) article on efficient light bulbs, are the numbers consistent with each other and with what you found in (a) and (b)?

> The University had a bright idea on energy conservation when it recently replaced light bulbs in 8,000 student room desk lamps with more cost and energy efficient bulbs. Stan Kiser, associate director of housing for residential services, said workers replaced the usual 75 watt incandescent bulbs with 25 watt compact fluorescent lights, which produce as much light as 90 watt incandescent bulbs.
>
> Kiser said workers installed the new fluorescent light bulbs in the student room lamps of most undergraduate dorms during Winter break. Total cost for bulbs and labor came to $100,000, he said.
>
> Kiser said the fluorescent bulbs are an investment in energy conservation because they use "less electricity to make the same amount of light." The University hopes to save $50,000 a year on electrical energy as a result of the replacement, he said.
>
> Because the fluorescent bulbs have an average life expectancy of 10,000 hours, Kiser said students will not have to worry about light bulbs burning out for the next few years. The old incandescent bulbs typically lasted only 750 hours, he said.
>
> Kiser said the fluorescent bulbs are also slightly brighter than the former bulbs.
>
> Busey-Evans Hall is the only undergraduate residence hall that will not receive the new bulbs because the bulbs do not fit in the room lamps of this residence hall, he said. The Housing Division plans to install the new bulbs in Daniels Hall, a graduate student residence hall, next week.
>
> Donald Wendel, vice chancellor for administrative affairs and Energy Conservation Advisory Committee chairperson, said the fluorescent bulbs are "definitely a step in the right direction and will save a great deal of energy and dollars."
>
> Kiser said funding for the new bulbs came from $350,000 designated by the Housing Division for conservation improvements.
>
> Kiser also said the division is concerned about the increase in the use of energy in residence halls. In a survey, housing officials found the average student room contained 17 electrical appliances, he said.
>
> Eric Drake, a current resident of Weston Residence Hall, said he noticed the lamps are "definitely brighter." Drake, a junior in LAS,

said one problem with the bulbs is that they flicker for some time when first switched on.
—M. Mlynski (1994). University turning conservative. Better bulbs: New lights could save UI thousands. *Daily Illini* (10 January). © 1994 The Daily Illini. Reprinted with permission.

1.4. Compare the CO_2 released to the atmosphere from (a) your diet of food and (b) your car's diet of fuel. Consider only on-site emissions.

1.5. The Illinois coal extraction rate is about 25×10^6 tons/year. Its coal reserves are approximately 20 billion tons. (These are fairly correct numbers.) Assume Illinois consumes only Illinois coal and that Illinois exports no coal (not correct).

   (a) At the present consumption rate, how long will the coal last?

   (b) How long will it last if the consumption rate is increasing exponentially at 5%/year? Decreasing exponentially at 5%/year?

1.6. Figure 1.4 shows the flow in and out of a reservoir during 1993.

   (a) When in 1993 did the reservoir contain the most water? The least?

   (b) When was the amount of water in the reservoir decreasing at the greatest rate?

1.7. (Easier) In the following article identify all instances of LIEDQO:

   Advocates of controls on greenhouse gas emissions received some potent ammunition last week when the United Nations–sponsored Intergovernmental Panel on Climate Change (IPCC) released a major report in Washington. The panel concluded that global warming could affect everything from ocean fisheries to human health, generally for the worse. And it

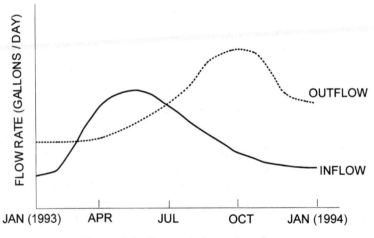

Figure 1.4   Reservoir in- and outflows.

declared that the warming and its effects could begin to be mitigated at a surprisingly low cost.

"Our first major conclusion is that climate change is an important new additional stress" on global systems both natural and human, said Robert Watson, associate director for environment in the White House's Office of Science and Technology Policy and co-chair of the study group. "Nearly every system we looked at is vulnerable. Climate change will affect all countries in one way or another—some beneficial effects and many adverse effects," among them the spread of tropical diseases including malaria (*Science,* 17 February, p. 957). And because of the cost and technological challenge of coping with these changes," he said, "the developing world in general is more vulnerable than the developed countries."

But in a second, more controversial conclusion, the group found, as Watson put it, that "significant decreases in greenhouse gas emissions are technically and economically feasible. Now it's up to the policy-makers," he said: "The challenge [they] have is to take our best estimates [of impacts and alternatives] and make decisions about how they want to deal with climate change."

The new assessment of impacts and alternatives is part of a massive international effort by the IPCC to sum up the current status of climate change science. Organized under the United Nations Environment Program and the U.N.'s World Meteorological Organization, IPCC is issuing its first full, three-part assessment in 5 years. The 1800-page report on impacts, mitigation, and adaptation has been 2 years in the making, involving about 500 scientist authors and another 500 reviewers from more than 70 countries.

The group, known as Working Group II, took as its starting point the conclusions of another IPCC group, Working Group I, on the likely magnitude of climate change. Its report, due out at the end of November, concludes that the world could warm between 1°C and 3.5°C by the year 2100. The exact figure will depend on how much carbon dioxide and other greenhouse gases humankind pumps into the atmosphere and how sensitive climate is to the added greenhouse gases.

The new upper limit of warming is lower than the 5°C the IPCC had forecast 3 years ago in an interim report, largely because of the newly appreciated cooling effect of pollutant aerosols (*Science,* 16 June, p. 1567). But a warming near the upper limit of the new range could still have dramatic impacts, Working Group II concluded. Midlatitude climate zones, for example, would shift northward by a hefty 550 kilometers over the next century. At that rate, some species of trees might not be able to keep up and might simply die out. In eastern North America, the panel says, a high-end warming would wipe out much of the eastern hardwood forest, opening the way for grassland and scrubland.

For human health, too, the effects at the high end of the temperature scale look disturbing—all the more so, perhaps, because the experts assessing health effects considered only a 3° to 5°C warming in their preliminary analysis. The expansion of the tropical and subtropical areas that favor malaria-transmitting mosquitoes would lead to an additional 50 million to 80 million cases of malaria each year late in the next century, said the report—a 10% to 15% increase. Dengue, yellow fever, and viral encephalitis would presumably increase as well as the high end of warming, the group found.

All of these effects and a litany of others—increased coastal flooding due to sea level rise, loss of mountain glaciers, shifting agricultural areas, land losses on low-lying coasts—could be mitigated with the right technology, according to the report. "There is a 10 to 30% greater-than-present level of efficiency [in energy consumption] that could be attained at little or no additional cost" over 3 decades, said James Edmonds of Battelle Pacific Northwest Laboratories' office in Washington, D.C., who contributed to the report. The savings could come from everything from more efficient heating and lighting to super-lightweight motor vehicles.

Not everyone agrees with the technologically upbeat tone of the report. John Shlaes, executive director of the Washington-based industry lobby group Global Climate Coalition, calls many of the proposed mitigation options "speculative technologies and wishful thinking." He also disputed the working group's optimistic view of how much mitigation would cost, arguing that the group overlooked macroeconomic factors. In the long run, for example, an energy-efficient light bulb might more than pay back its high initial cost, but, macroeconomists might ask, will consumers buy it without a costly incentive? Michael Oppenheimer of the Environmental Defense Fund in New York believes "the truth is probably somewhere in between" the technological optimism of the report and the pessimism of macroeconomists.

But there seems to be little debate over another point made in the report: Developing countries will suffer the most from any effects of global warming. "At the low end [of the projected warming], a country like the United States faces costly adaptation . . . but I don't think it will wreck the country," say Oppenheimer. "But some developing countries, even at the low end of warming, are facing a grim future." As the report notes, countries lacking large social and economic resources, especially those in semiarid, tropical to subtropical regions where agriculture is already marginal, will be hard-pressed to adapt to warming by changing crops, say, or improving irrigation systems.

On the other hand, says Oppenheimer, "at the high end of projected warming, all societies face substantial disarray." Adds Watson: "The message of this report is that we all must be concerned about climate."

—R. Kerr (1995). Greenhouse report sees growing global stress.
Science 270:731. © 1995 American Association for the
Advancement of Science. Reprinted with permission.

1.8. (Easier) Specify in a few words issues under each of the categories of LIEDQO that (1) are important to you on a continuing, long-term basis; and (2) you observed or experienced in the last 24 hours. (The latter is instructive if repeated for 10 days or more.) For example, long term, dynamics and lags: Automobiles knock out competing transport modes and make it even harder to get along without one; 24 hours, efficiency: In the building where I work, the space conditioning malfunctions at seasonal changes and it is necessary to open the doors to cool over-heated rooms.

1.9. (Easier) More motivational graphs. Figure 1.5 shows four graphs with no axis labels. As in the text, decide what labels to place on the axes,

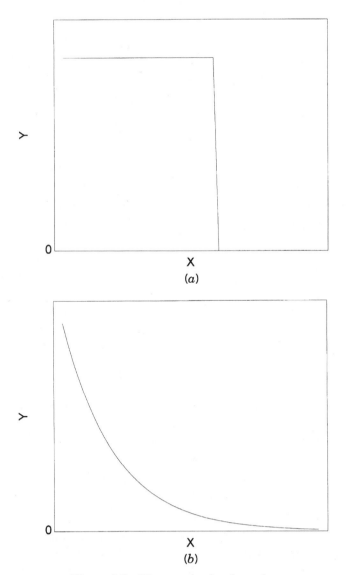

Figure 1.5 More motivational graphs.

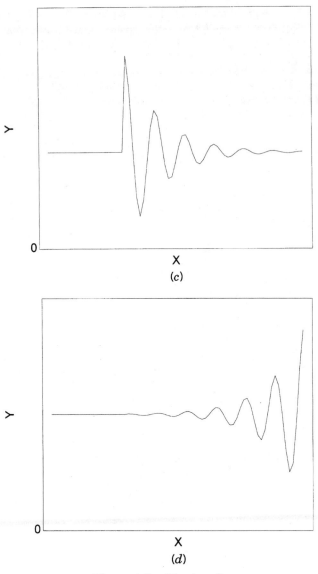

Figure 1.5   (Continued)

what phenomena the labeled graph describes, and what profession, group, or constituency might use this graph—explicitly or implicitly—in analyzing what they do and—especially—*planning* what they do.

1.10. (Easier) What is the average population density (people per unit of land area) in the United States? The world? Your present town/city/place?

1.11. (Easier) One reason given for the development of drug resistance in disease bacteria is that they can divide every half hour and hence can go through many "generations" in a short time compared with a human lifespan. How long a period in human time would correspond to a year in bacteria time?

1.12. (Easier) Energy use in air travel. On a 1995 trip to Scandinavia I received from the cockpit the following energy use data:

Origin–destination:	Champaign, IL–Chicago
Plane type:	Saab 340
Number of seats:	32
Number of passengers:	23
Trip distance:	120 nautical miles
Fuel used:	940 pounds

Origin–destination:	Chicago–Amsterdam
Plane type:	Boeing 747-300*
Number of seats:	297
Number of passengers:	284
Trip distance:	3696 nautical miles
Fuel used:	199,690 pounds

Origin–destination:	Amsterdam–Göteborg, Sweden
Plane type:	Boeing 737-300
Number of seats:	109
Number of passengers:	72
Trip distance:	462 nautical miles
Fuel used:	8100 pounds

Origin–destination:	Oslo, Norway–Amsterdam
Plane type:	Boeing 737-300
Number of seats:	109
Number of passengers:	101
Trip distance:	564 nautical miles
Fuel used:	7260 pounds

Origin–destination:	Amsterdam–Chicago
Plane type:	Boeing 747-300*
Number of seats:	211
Number of passengers:	211
Trip distance:	3715 nautical miles
Fuel used:	219,670 pounds

*Fewer seats than maximum because plane was a combined passenger and freight hauler.

Origin–destination	Chicago–Champaign, IL
Plane type:	ATR
Number of seats:	46
Number of passengers:	28
Trip distance:	119 nautical miles
Fuel used:	868 pounds

(a) For each of the six "hops," calculate seat-miles/gallon and passenger-miles/gallon. (A nautical mile is about 1.2 statute miles, and jet fuel, which is essentially kerosene, weighs about 6.7 pounds per gallon.)

(b) Comment on how these compare with auto fuel efficiency.

(c) How many barrels of oil did I use on this trip? Is this a large number?

(d) The Amsterdam–Chicago flight used about 10% more fuel than the trip from Chicago to Amsterdam. Why?

1.13. (Moderate) News item by Ed Kane on radio station WBBM, Chicago, September 21, 1996: Natural gas–burning vehicles produce 90% less pollution (than petroleum-burning vehicles). Is this correct if the pollutant in question is CO_2? Chemical formulas: natural gas (methane), CH_4; gasoline, $CH_{1.5}$. See also Appendix 2. What additional information do you need?

1.14. (Moderate) In a speech in March 1995 at Lewis and Clark College, Portland, Oregon, Helen Caldicott said (approximately): The U.S. has 110 nuclear power plants, and if everyone hung clothes out to dry instead of using mechanical drying, all 110 could be shut down. (A residential electric clothes dryer has a power use of about 4000 W.)

(a) Do you agree?

(b) Whatever the answer to (a), perform the following rough sensitivity/uncertainty analysis (see Appendix 1): Define R = (summed power of the 100 nuclear plants/average power of all electric clothes dryers). R is thus an indicator of the adequacy of the nuclear plants to power the dryers. How will R change (specify sign and magnitude) when these additional possibilities/factors are included in the calculations?

1. The fraction of dryers that are electric is greater than you originally estimated.

2. Dryer use peaks at 8 P.M. each day instead of being evenly distributed over 24 hours.

3. Not all nuclear power plants have as high a maximum capacity as the one you assume.

4. Power plants have a capacity factor of 0.6, not 1 (i.e., over a year they produce 60% of the energy they could if they operated at full power every minute).

5. Distribution losses in a typical electric grid are about 10%.

1.15. (Moderate) The following is excerpted from a letter to the editor of the Champaign-Urbana *News-Gazette* in June 1991:

> Energy policy affects all aspects of our lives. A prime example (besides the Gulf War) is the connection between drilling for oil in the Arctic National Wildlife Refuge (ANWR) in Alaska and the lack of higher miles-per-gallon standards for new automobiles. Currently in the US Congress there are proposed bills to 1. start the drilling, 2. to give the ANWR wilderness status and thereby forbid drilling, 3. to increase corporate average fuel economy (CAFE).
>
> What is clear to almost everyone except the Bush administration is that these bills are interrelated, and that by increasing CAFE in a progressive and attainable manner, we can bypass the need to drill in the ANWR, which, in addition to being a priceless national, natural treasure, may not have any oil, anyway. For example, the US Geological Survey estimates that the ANWR may produce 290 thousand barrels per day for 30 years, and that there is a 19 out of 100 chance that this much will be found. This is about 2% of current US oil use. In contrast, the improved auto fuel efficiency in Senate Bill 279, the "Bryan Bill" (40 mpg for new cars by the year 2001) would save 10% of current oil use, not for 30 years, but forever. The Bryan Bill hence does away, five times over, with the need to drill in the ANWR.
>
> The only serious objection to the higher-mpg cars is their safety: are they powerful and crashworthy enough? The answer is yes, according to the US Environmental Protection Agency, researchers at Princeton University, and to Volvo and Volkswagen, which have already built and demonstrated prototypes in the 60–70 mpg range. These fuel-efficiency cars are affordable, at least as safe as today's cars, and as fast.

(a) Check the veracity of the quantitative claims. Possibly useful information: 1 barrel = 42 gallons, current CAFE = approximately 27 mpg. Some other information may need to be estimated.

(b) Criticize this kind of argument (150 words max.).

1.16. (Harder) The following is from *Time* magazine, July 15, 1996, p. 46 (Kinsley, 1996). The standard fatality statistic for U.S. air transport is that you would have to fly every day for 21,000 years before dying in an air crash. Today using a discount airline can save a flyer $54 to $70/flight. Why shouldn't discount flights be less safe? For example, suppose flight safety were reduced by a factor of 10. Kinsley claims this would "increase your chance of a fatal crash by 1 in 855,000." Justify or debunk the figure of 1 in 855,000.

2 Contributions to Environmental Impact: Analyzing the Components of Change

[Lutz] also presented results of a recent study on population trends, showing that the growing number of households has a greater effect on the growth of CO_2 emissions in developed countries than the growing number of individuals.

—IIASA (1996)

IT'S SIMPLE MATH BUT REQUIRES CLEAR THINKING

In this book there are four equations to learn, master, and almost forget, so you can recall them reflexively when needed. This is Important Equation 1:

IMPORTANT EQUATION 1

$$I = PAT \tag{2.1}$$

---

where I = impact
P = population
A = in loose terms, affluence
T = technology

Affluence, also known as wealth, is a stock (e.g., how much one owns). Consumption is a flow (e.g., how much one consumes or acquires per unit time). Equation 2.1 can be written in terms of either stock or flow.

For example, the fuel used by all the cars in the United States may be thought of as a compounding of the human population, the number of cars per capita, and the fuel use per car:

Fuel use = (Population)(Number of cars per capita)(Fuel use per car)

There are at least three good reasons to analyze environmental problems using $I = PAT$:

1. It shows how contributing factors compound to produce a total effect. This is especially important in analyzing change. Because the effect is multiplicative, the total effect changes differently than would be implied by merely adding the changes. For example, in the United States between 1970 and 1990 (the 20 years following the first Earth Day), the human population increased 22% while per capita registered automobiles increased 32%. The automobile population increase is not the sum of the two individual increases (54%), but rather 61%. This can be seen from

$$(1 + 0.22)(1 + 0.32) = 1.61$$

2. It allows assignment of blame or praise to important factors. This is the thrust of the quote about the growth of CO_2 emissions that opens this chapter. In the preceding auto example, we can say that growth in per capita car ownership was more important than human population growth in the growth of the auto population from 1970 to 1990—assuming that the two factors are independent, an important assumption that we will discuss later in this chapter. We will also discuss the Ehrlich/Holdren–Commoner debate on "The Causes of Pollution" in the early 1970s, which centered on whether the T in $I = PAT$ was the dominant factor in environmental degradation.

3. It guides access for policy and action. The factors will differ in their technical and social accessibility. Scrutinizing the factors tells where there is real potential and where one should not waste one's time. For example, consider energy use for household refrigeration in a developing country. We likely would not challenge that there will be high growth in the number of per household refrigerators (the A term) until the average approaches one per household; that is given. On the other hand, recent advances in the energy use efficiency of refrigerators (the T factor) make the *kind* of refrigerator an important policy issue. The best available new model mass-market efficiency exceeds that of new models 20 years ago by a factor of 3 (Wilson and Morrill, 1996) and that of the average model now in use by at least a factor of 2. This means refrigeration energy can be only one-half, or less with continued efficiency improvement, of "business as usual" if the other factors remain constant. Energy-efficiency refrigerators could proliferate immediately in a developing country because there is no developed-country 15-year lag while older, less efficient models wear out. (Note how lags have crept into an efficiency discussion; the elements of LIEDQO are not totally independent.) As a first example of using the LIEDQOmeter, let us apply it to this problem. Equity is moderately important, and the crux of the discussion is efficiency. Both of these elements of LIEDQO therefore receive significant weight. See Figure 2.1.

There are several fundamental, recurring issues associated with $I = PAT$:

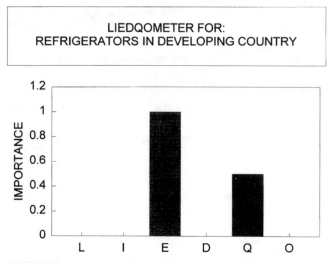

Figure 2.1 LIEDQOmeter for refrigerators in a developing country. Equity (Q) argues that refrigerators should proliferate in countries that essentially have none. Using
energy-efficient (E) units can reduce environmental impact.

1. The factors *PAT* are not the only possible ones in this generic approach
of breaking something into multiplicative factors. For example, in the car
example we used just P and A:

Cars = (Population)(Number of cars per capita)

The following two examples use four factors:

CO_2 = (Population)(Consumption of economic goods and services)

$\times$ (Energy per unit of economic goods and services)

$\times$ (CO_2 per unit of energy)

(A LIEDQOmeter for controlling CO_2 emissions is shown in Fig. 1.3)

Energy for a business transaction

= (Choice: travel for face-to-face meeting or use mail or phone)

$\times$ (If travel: what transportation mode: plane, train, bus, car)

$\times$ (If drive car: large or small car)

$\times$ (If drive car: travel alone or rideshare)

Other examples are given in Table 2.1.

TABLE 2.1 Examples of $I = PAT$ Analysis

Population		Affluence	Technology	
Population	$\times\ \dfrac{\text{Capital stock}}{\text{Person}}$	$\times\ \dfrac{\text{Material throughput}}{\text{Capital stock}}$	$\times\ \dfrac{\text{Energy}}{\text{Material throughput}}$	$\times\ \dfrac{\text{Environmental impact}}{\text{Energy}}$
Example: Coffee Cups				
Population	$\times\ \dfrac{\text{Cups}}{\text{Person}}$	$\times\ \dfrac{\text{Water + soap}}{\text{Cups/year}}$	$\times\ \dfrac{\text{Gigajoules or kilowatt-hours}}{\text{Kilogram water + soap}}$	$\times\ \dfrac{CO_2,\ NO_x,\ \text{land use}}{\text{Gigajoules or kilowatt-hours}}$
Applicable Tools				
Family planning Female literacy Social welfare Role of women Land tenure	Values Prices Full costing What do we want? What is enough?	Product longevity Material choice Minimum-materials design Recycle, reuse Scrap recovery	End-use efficiency Conversion efficiency Distribution efficiency System integration Process redesign	Benign sources Scale Siting Technical mitigation Offsets
Approximate Scope for Long-Term Change				
~2×	?	~3–10×	~5–10×	~10^2–10^{3+}×
Time Scale of Major Change				
~50–100 years	~0–50 years	~0–20 years	~0–30 years	~0–50 years

Source: Meadows et al. (1992). *Beyond the Limits*. © 1992 Chelsea Green. Reprinted with permission.

2. Emphasizing physical/technical factors such as *PAT* implicitly neglects other issues that may be important to other people. Donella Meadows relates how her use of *I* = *PAT* was disputed because it does not deal with the causality of growth and excludes the oppression of women (Meadows, 1995). That is true, and it may or may not be important, depending on what goals one has in using *I* = *PAT*.

3. *I* = *PAT* analysis requires keeping track of units. So far I have been purposely casual in the units of the quantities. Ecological numeracy requires dedicated, even slavish, attention to units. Units must be specified to keep the discussion clear and honest, and they also help the analyst to check the reasonableness of results. See the accompanying box.

Why be Attentive to Units?

1. *Christmas Tree Lights.* About a decade ago the home economics column in the Champaign-Urbana *News-Gazette* answered a question about the correct number of lights on a Christmas tree: Multiply the height by the diameter and triple it. No units were specified. Assume a tree 7 ft high and 4 ft in diameter. Depending on the choice of units, here is the recommended number of lights:

Units	Number of Lights
Yards	9
Feet	84
Inches	12,096
Centimeters	78,039

Note that because the formula uses the units twice, the result is proportional to the *square* of the conversion factor assumed.

2. *Limits to Speed.* In 1991 my two children and I entered Alberta, Canada by a 4-day hike and a ferry ride across the border on Waterton Lake. There we would pick up a car that had been left by friends and drive back to the U.S. As the ferry approached the dock, I told my 10-year-old son that he should appreciate the fact that he was entering a foreign country. He grumbled that it was no big deal; everyone spoke English and there was no difference. Shortly after we started back to Montana, he exasperatedly berated me for driving only 50 mph in an 80 zone. This continued past several speed limit signs of 80 and 90. Finally, we came to a sign that had another, smaller sign below the number. It said "km."

In the CO_2 example,

$$CO_2 = (\text{Population})(\text{Consumption/Person})(\text{Energy/Consumption unit})$$

$$\times (CO_2/\text{Energy})$$

A self-consistent set of units is

$$(\text{tons/year}) = (\text{persons})(\text{dollars/(person} * \text{year})(\text{joules/dollar})(\text{tons/joule})$$

One can verify that canceling units from the numerator and denominator on the right-hand side of the equation yields tons/year, which agrees with the units of the left-hand side, as it must. If it does not agree, check for a lost factor or inconsistent units.

Another example concerns refillable 12-oz beer bottles:

$$\text{Beer bottles} = (\text{Population})(\text{Beer/Person})(\text{Bottles/Beer})$$

A self-consistent set of units is

Number of bottles made/year

$$= (\text{persons})(\text{gallons/(person} * \text{year}))(12\text{-oz fills/gallon})$$

$$\times (1/\text{fills per bottle made})$$

The last factor is the number of times a bottle is filled/refilled before it is discarded, broken, or recycled. The factor is 1 if bottles are throwaway or smash and remelt types. Refillables made 8 to 15 trips in the 1960s. See Figure 2.2.

4. The factors P, A, and T may not be independent. For example, for P and A, with limits to economic activity a larger population could mean a smaller per capita affluence. Or, for A and T, efficient technology might cost more and be out of the reach of the less affluent. Often (not always), however, efficient technology has a lower cost, but there is still a problem: Although the *life* cost is less, the *first* cost is greater and the less affluent may not be able to afford the initial purchase.

NUMERICAL EXAMPLES OF $I = PAT$ ANALYSIS

The Components of Growth in Anthropogenic Atmospheric Carbon Emissions from Fossil Fuel Burning

Table 2.2 covers world carbon emissions resulting directly from fossil fuel combustion, which is approximately 3/5 of all carbon emissions. It does not

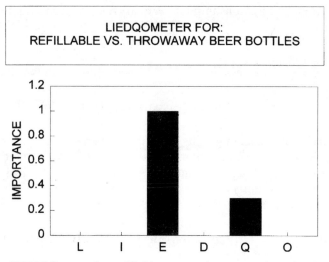

Figure 2.2   LIEDQOmeter for refillable versus throwaway beer bottles. The basic issue is the efficiency (*E*) of delivering beer to consumers. It can be done with many throwaways or fewer refillable bottles. Equity (*Q*) enters through the different employment impacts of the two options.

include, for example, nonenergy sources such as deforestation. The $I = PAT$ breakdown is

$$\text{C released} = \text{(Population)(Economic production per capita)}$$

$$\times \text{(C per unit of economic production)}$$

with units

$$\text{(kg C/year)} = \text{(person)(\$/(person} * \text{year))(kg C/\$)}$$

TABLE 2.2   World Fossil Fuel–Related Carbon Emissions and Economic Product, 1960–1990

Year	Human Population (10^9)	Gross Economic Product per Capita [\$(1987)/person year][a]	Carbon per Unit of Economic Product [kg C/\$(1987)]	World Carbon Release $(10^{12}$ kg C/year)
1960	3.04	2009	0.417	2.54
1970	3.70	2728	0.397	4.01
1980	4.45	3166	0.365	5.15
1990	5.29	3553	0.311	5.84

[a]Monetary data are given in constant 1987 dollars, indicated as \$(1987).

Source: Data from Brown et al. (1993), pp. 61, 73.

Note that this is measured in carbon, not carbon dioxide. The atomic weights of carbon and oxygen are approximately 12 and 16, respectively. Therefore, the carbon weighs $12/(12 + 2 * 16) = 12/44 = 0.27$ as much as the CO_2 of which it is a part.

We can use these data to analyze the components of growth for the three decades 1960–1990. For example, we have

$$P_{1970}A_{1970}T_{1970} = I_{1970}$$

$$P_{1960}A_{1960}T_{1960} = I_{1960}$$

We can divide the 1970 equation by the 1960 equation to obtain

$$\left(\frac{P_{1970}}{P_{1960}}\right)\left(\frac{A_{1970}}{A_{1960}}\right)\left(\frac{T_{1970}}{T_{1960}}\right) = \frac{I_{1970}}{I_{1960}}$$

All the multiplicative terms are now dimensionless and normalized to equal 1, the start of the decade. Doing this for 1960–1970, we get

$$\left(\frac{3.70}{3.04}\right)\left(\frac{2728}{2009}\right)\left(\frac{0.397}{0.417}\right) = \frac{4.01}{2.54}$$

or

$$(1.22)(1.36)(0.95) = 1.58$$

This says that during the decade 1960–1970 world energy-related carbon releases (I) increased 58%. Population (P) increased 22%, per capita economic product (A) increased 36%, and carbon released per unit of economic product (T) decreased 5%. The 5% reduction in T was overwhelmed by the growth in P and T. We can calculate these factors for the decades through 1990 also as shown in Table 2.3.

During the three decades we see these trends: The population growth rate decreased slightly but consistently from 22%/decade to 19%/decade (note the units). The growth of per capita consumption decreased from 36%/decade to 16%/decade between decades 1 and 2 and to 12%/decade in decade 3.

TABLE 2.3 $I = PAT$ Analysis for World Energy-Related Carbon Releases, 1960–1990

Decade	P_{end}/P_{start}	A_{end}/A_{start}	T_{end}/T_{start}	I_{end}/I_{start}
1. 1960–1970	1.22	1.36	0.95	1.58
2. 1970–1980	1.20	1.16	0.92	1.28
3. 1980–1990	1.19	1.12	0.85	1.13

(*Aside:* Searching for an explanation, one might note that the world oil price quadrupled between 1973 and 1980.) The technology of producing economic goods and services using processes that release carbon improved at an increasing rate through the three decades. Stated in terms of the factor T, the releases of carbon decreased during the three decades, with greater decreases coming in the later decades. For all three decades, the reduction of T was not enough to compensate for the growth of P and A, and I increased, though at a decreasing rate.[1]

One question raised by this analysis regards the decrease in T: We can write

$$T = \text{Carbon}/\$ = (\text{Energy}/\$)(\text{Carbon}/\text{Energy})$$

The first factor is the inverse of one kind of energy efficiency. The second factor is the carbon intensity of the fuel. Both of these potential access points have technical possibilities for improvement. Table 2.4 gives several examples.

Are 50-Year "Sustainable Development" Goals Self-Consistent?

In his elementary reality check (see Fig. 2.3), economist Paul Ekins asked if the environmental impact of all human activity 50 years from now is consistent with explicit or implicit goals we have for population, affluence, and pollution control technology (Ekins, 1993). Specifically, he said:

- *Population.* Will likely double.
- *Consumption per Capita.* A consensus of aspirations, especially stressing rapid growth in the underdeveloped world, is that the world average will

---

[1]In terms of calculus: Comparing the entries in Table 2.3 minus 1.0 corresponds to taking first-time derivatives. Comparing how these quantities change over time corresponds to taking second-time derivatives.

TABLE 2.4   Possible Changes in Energy Intensity of Services and in Carbon Intensity of Energy Sources

Energy/Service	Carbon/Energy
80 mpg auto (versus new car average of 27 in 1996)(1/3 as much energy per unit of service)	Fuel switch (e.g., coal to gas)(1/2 as much carbon per unit of energy)
Fluorescent light (1/4)	Solar energy (≈ 0)
Well-insulated building (1/6)	
More efficient refrigerator (1/3)	

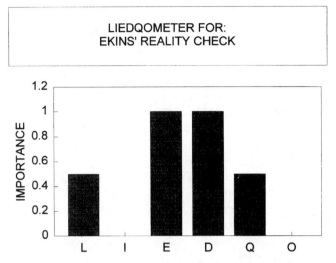

Figure 2.3 LIEDQOmeter for Ekins' reality check on the consistency of economic and environmental protection goals. Limiting environmental impact is advisable because of limits (*L*) to biospheric assimilative capacity. Efficiency (*E*) in making technology cleaner is a key issue. Dynamics (*D*) enters through the interaction of population, per capita affluence, and technology in determining impact. Ekins' investigation of different growth scenarios for developed and developing nations addresses an obvious equity (*Q*) issue.

quadruple in 50 years (this is an exponential growth rate of 2.8%/year, which we discuss in Chapter 3.)

- *Environmental Impact.* A reasonable goal is for it to diminish by a factor of 2.

Given these assumptions, how much cleaner does our technology have to be? Using the *I = PAT* framework,

$$\left(\frac{2}{1}\right)\left(\frac{4}{1}\right)\left(\frac{T_{now+50}}{T_{now}}\right) = \frac{1}{2}$$

which requires that technology 50 years from now be only 1/16 (7%) as impacting per unit of economic product, that is, 16 times cleaner. This is a remarkable reduction, equivalent to a halving every 12.5 years or an exponential decrease rate of 5.5%/year (as we will discuss in Chapter 3). Ekins felt that such improvement is so doubtful that this scenario for economic growth is unrealistic. He then created his own scenario in which the developed world (of about 0.8 billion people) experiences no growth in population or per capita affluence, while the developing world (of 4.3 billion) undergoes the population doubling and per capita affluence quadrupling assumed already. In this case average technology needs to be only 21% as polluting as today—a difficult but perhaps attainable goal.

IS TECHNOLOGY (ALONE) THE PROBLEM? THE ERLICH/HOLDREN–COMMONER DEBATE (1972)

Paul Ehrlich's 1968 book *The Population Bomb* stressed population growth as the major environmental worry. Barry Commoner's 1971 book *The Closing Circle* discussed all factors *P*, *A*, *T*, but implied, and stated, that population growth would take care of itself as people became richer and reduced their family size (known as the *demographic transition*), while the dominant factor in *I* was *T*. Commoner's examples from the industrial surge in the United States after World War II were compelling: cars, synthetic fertilizers and pesticides, throwaway containers, and so on.

Paul Ehrlich and John Holdren challenged both of Commoner's positions. Their challenge, and Commoner's response, were published in *Environment* magazine in April 1972. Besides attacking the validity of the demographic transition (which we do not discuss here), they used extensive *I = PAT* arguments to demonstrate the importance of *P* and *A* (the latter especially in the United States after World War II), and their multiplicative interaction, in the growth of *I*. They stressed that to blame technology alone was "uncomplicated, socially comfortable, and hence seductive" and that "[Commoner]" . . . misleads his readers into thinking that [curtailing resource depletion] can be accomplished by ecological reform alone, without population control or a reduction in what most Americans perceive as their high standard of living." See Figure 2.4.

The tone was hot and attacking, and Commoner's response was hot and defensive. Science, estimation arithmetic, politics, and opinions were intermixed. In my opinion, Ehrlich and Holdren won, but you are invited to read this debate and decide for yourself.

ASSESSING THE COMPONENTS OF CHANGE: A FURTHER ATTEMPT

As discussed previously, one use of *I = PAT* is to allocate "blame" for growth or decline: "Of the change in atmospheric carbon emissions 1960–1990, what percentages were due to population growth, per capita affluence growth, and change in technology?" One hopes the percentages add to 100. This does not work perfectly (as we saw in the auto growth example), because percentages are based on an additive view of how things interact, while *I = PAT* is a multiplicative interaction.

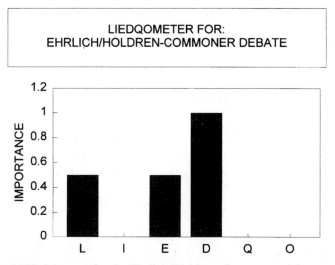

Figure 2.4 LIEDQOmeter for the Ehrlich/Holdren–Commoner debate on the causes of pollution. The debate was motivated by a perceived limit (*L*) to environmental pollution. Efficiency (*E*) arguments dominated discussions of new technologies such as chemical agriculture. The crux of the debate was the dynamic interaction (*D*) of population, affluence, and technology over time.

One initially attractive attempt to fix this is used by Commoner in *The Closing Circle.* A way to assure that the influence of all factors add to 100% is to take the logarithms:

$$I = PAT$$

$$\log I = \log P + \log A + \log T$$

$$\log(I + \Delta I) = \log(P + \Delta P) + \log(A + \Delta A) + \log(T + \Delta T)$$

In the last equation *P*, *A*, *T*, and *I* have changed. Subtracting the initial equation from the new gives

$$\log\frac{I + \Delta I}{I} = \log\frac{P + \Delta P}{P} + \log\frac{A + \Delta A}{A} + \log\frac{T + \Delta T}{T}$$

This says that the logs of the factors $(P + \Delta P)P$, and so forth, add up to the log of $(I + \Delta I)/I$. Because these are now additive, we can determine each factor's fraction of the total. For the car example,

Change in total cars: $\log 1.61 = 0.208$

Change in population: $\log 1.22 = 0.087 = 42\%$ of total

Change per capita cars: $\log 1.32 = 0.121 = 58\%$ of total

This method encounters a difficulty when factors are changing in opposite directions, however. If population is halved and per capita cars are doubled, the number of cars is unchanged and

$$\log(I + \Delta I)/I = 0$$
$$\log(P + \Delta P)/P = \log(0.5/1) = -0.302$$
$$\log(A + \Delta A)/A = \log(2/1) = 0.302$$

(There is no T in this example.) This shows that the two factors have equal and opposite effects, but we cannot express their individual effects as fractions of the total.

Let us also look at the previous carbon release data. From Table 2.3, for 1980–1990:

$$\log(P + \Delta P)/P = \log(1.19) = 0.076 = 136\% \text{ of total}$$
$$\log(A + \Delta A)/A = \log(1.12) = 0.050 = 92\% \text{ of total}$$
$$\log(T + \Delta T)/T = \log(0.85) = -0.071 = -128\% \text{ of total}$$
$$\log(I + \Delta I)/I = \log(1.13) = 0.054 = 100\% \text{ of total}$$

Here there is partial cancelation, and the change in I is nonzero and the method can be applied. During this decade population growth was the (barely) strongest factor, almost exactly canceling technology improvement.

This method should be used with caution. There are other ways to allocate causation for change in $I = PAT$. One method is comparable to the Commoner approach (see Problem 2.7), and others are more complicated (Schipper et al., 1992).

PROBLEMS

Level of difficulty is indicated as Easier/Moderate/Harder. Problems marked "(Spreadsheet?)" can be fruitfully approached using a spreadsheet. They need not be, however.

2.1. (Easier) Design a table like Table 2.1 to cover energy in transportation. Use as factors: population, miles per capita, mode choice, and energy efficiency of mode. Apply (speculatively) to China and the United States for 1990–2020. The idea is see the range of energy requirements relative to today's results from different assumptions about different factors.

2.2. (Easier) Another reality check from the literature (Jenkins, 1996). The goal is to reduce greenhouse gas (methane, CO_2, CFCs) emissions per year so that their heat balance impact is reduced by 60% over the next 35 years (a target of the Intergovernmental Panel on Climate Change). Assume the world population will grow from 5.3 to 8.3 billion.

(a) If average per capita consumption is unchanged, how much does technology (represented by greenhouse gas emissions per $ of production) have to change?

(b) If technology does not change, by how much does per capita consumption have to change?

2.3. (Moderate) $I = PAT$ for beer bottles, from the Ehrlich/Holdren–Commoner debate (1972). The purpose of the "beer delivery system" is to deliver beer to consumers. Between 1950 and 1967 the system's consumptive use of bottles changed.

(a) Complete Table 2.5. Assume exponential growth of each factor between 1950 and 1967 (this looks ahead to Chapter 3).

(b) Compare the roles of population growth, per capita beer intake, and beer packaging in the growth of beer bottle consumption.

(c) Suggest a reasonable explanation for what you conclude in (b).

2.4. (Moderate) If I is primary energy demand, the technology factor T in $I = PAT$ is considered changeable by a factor of 2 or 3 by a number of researchers. That is, energy efficiency can be increased by that factor over several decades. This problem draws from the energy future envisioned by Goldemberg et al. (1988). Here we will combine A and T into a single factor "power per capita." The baseline case is shown in Table 2.6.

(a) Calculate the total power for the industrialized countries, the developing countries, and the whole world. Compare the relative contributions of the two sets of countries in 1980 and 2020 and to the changes between the two years.

(b) Goldemberg et al. make a reasonable technical case for an energy future in which the industrialized countries in particular can improve energy efficiency. They claim that the lifestyle of western Europe in the 1980s can be supported by a power of approximately 1 kW per

TABLE 2.5

	Population	Beer per Capita (gallons/year)	Bottles Consumed per Gallon of Beer Delivered	Bottles Consumed per Year
1950	151.9×10^6	25.0	0.25	_____
1967	197.9×10^6	26.3	1.26	_____
Ratio 1967/1950	1.30	_____	_____	_____
r(exponential growth rate)(%/year)	_____	_____	_____	_____
τ(doubling time)(year)	_____	_____	_____	_____

TABLE 2.6

Year	Population (10⁹)	Per Capita Power (kW)	Total Power (10⁹ kW)
		Industrialized Countries	
1980	1.11	6.3	7.00
2020	1.52	11.3	_____
		Developing Countries	
1980	3.32	1.0	3.32
2020	5.88	1.9	_____

capita. (For comparison, in 1995 the United States used about 10 kW per capita.) They put forward the "efficient" scenario shown in Table 2.7. Repeat (a) for this case.

2.5. (Moderate) Energy-related CO_2 emissions can be thought of as a product of four factors:

$$(\text{Population})(\text{GDP per capita})(\text{Energy}/\text{GDP})(CO_2/\text{Energy})$$

Using the data in Table 2.8 (Laitner, 1995):
- **(a)** Set up a table for the years 1950, 1960, 1970, 1980, 1990, and 1994, which shows quantitatively the four factors for each year. Be sure to list units.
- **(b)** For the intervals 1950–1960, 1960–1970, 1970–1980, 1980–1990, and 1990–1994, calculate how much each factor, and the total emissions, changed during that interval. Normalize so that each factor is 1 at the start of the interval.

TABLE 2.7

Year	Population (10⁹)	Per Capita Power (kW)	Total Power (10⁹ kW)
		Industrialized Countries	
1980	1.11	6.3	7.00
2020	1.24	3.2	_____
		Developing Countries	
1980	3.32	1.0	3.32
2020	5.71	1.3	_____

TABLE 2.8

Year	U.S. Population (thousands)	Gross Domestic Product [billion/$(1987)]	Employment (thousands)	Energy use in Year (quadrillion Btu)	Carbon Emissions in Year (million metric tons)
1950	152,271	1,418.5	58,918	33.1	690.8
1951	154,878	1,558.4	59,961	35.5	711.0
1952	157,553	1,624.9	60,250	35.3	692.1
1953	160,184	1,685.5	61,179	36.3	708.4
1954	163,026	1,673.8	60,109	35.3	674.2
1955	165,931	1,768.3	62,170	38.8	738.8
1956	168,903	1,803.6	63,799	40.4	774.3
1957	171,984	1,838.2	64,071	40.5	768.0
1958	174,882	1,829.1	63,036	40.4	743.3
1959	177,830	1,928.8	64,630	42.1	773.3
1960	180,671	1,970.8	65,778	43.8	791.9
1961	183,691	2,023.8	65,746	44.5	794.2
1962	186,538	2,128.1	66,702	46.5	823.5
1963	189,242	2,215.6	67,762	48.3	867.2
1964	191,889	2,340.6	69,305	50.5	904.1
1965	194,303	2,470.5	71,088	52.7	939.4
1966	196,560	2,616.2	72,895	55.7	990.6
1967	198,712	2,685.2	74,372	57.6	1,030.4
1968	200,705	2,796.9	75,920	61.0	1,071.6
1969	202,677	2,873.0	77,902	64.2	1,122.5
1970	205,052	2,873.9	78,678	66.4	1,156.5
1971	207,661	2,955.9	79,367	67.9	1,163.5
1972	209,896	3,107.1	82,153	71.3	1,217.1
1973	211,909	3,268.6	85,064	74.3	1,264.8
1974	213,854	3,248.1	86,794	72.6	1,221.1
1975	215,973	3,221.7	85,846	70.6	1,170.6
1976	218,035	3,380.8	88,752	74.4	1,253.7
1977	220,239	3,533.3	92,017	76.3	1,260.8
1978	222,585	3,703.5	96,048	78.1	1,283.5
1979	225,055	3,796.8	98,824	78.9	1,293.4
1980	227,726	3,776.3	99,303	76.0	1,252.5
1981	229,966	3,843.1	100,397	74.0	1,204.5
1982	232,188	3,760.3	99,526	70.9	1,144.6
1983	234,303	3,906.6	100,834	70.5	1,149.1
1984	236,348	4,148.5	105,005	74.1	1,184.6
1985	238,466	4,279.8	107,150	74.0	1,208.0
1986	240,651	4,404.5	109,597	74.3	1,227.7
1987	242,804	4,539.9	112,440	76.9	1,273.8
1988	245,021	4,718.6	114,968	80.2	1,347.6
1989	247,342	4,838.0	117,342	81.3	1,360.4
1990	249,911	4,897.3	117,914	81.3	1,337.3
1991	252,643	4,867.6	119,877	81.1	1,336.7
1992	255,407	4,979.3	117,598	82.1	1,358.8
1993	258,120	5,134.5	119,306	83.9	1,386.7
1994	260,651	5,314.1	123,060	85.6	1,411.7

TABLE 2.9   Passenger Kilometers and Energy Use by Modes of Transportation in the United States,[a] 1970–1987

Mode	Passenger Kilometers					Energy Use			
	1970	1987	Growth	1970	1987	1970	1987	1970	1987
	(billion)		(%/year)	Share (%)		$(10^{15}$ J)		$(10^6$ J/pkm)	
Car	3,327	4,615	1.9	90.7	85.9	9,774	12,353	2.94	2.68
Bus	137	190	1.9	3.7	3.5	115	165	0.84	0.87
Rail	37	38	0.2	1.0	0.7	64	80	1.73	2.10
Air	168	530	6.8	4.6	9.9	1,002	1,478	5.96	2.79
Total	3,669	5,373	2.2	100.0	100.0	10,955	14,076	2.99	2.62

[a]Totals per capita in 1987: 22,020 pkm/capita and 57.7 GJ/capita. 1 GJ $= 10^9$ J.

TABLE 2.10   Passenger Kilometers and Energy Use by Modes of Transportation in West Germany,[a] 1970–1987

Mode	Passenger Kilometers					Energy Use			
	1970	1987	Growth	1970	1987	1970	1987	1970	1987
	(billion)		(%/year)	Share (%)		$(10^{15}$ J)		$(10^6$ J/pkm)	
Car	349	526	2.4	77.6	83.2	666	1,215	1.91	2.31
Bus	49	53	0.5	10.8	8.4	25	41	0.51	0.77
Rail	49	48	−0.1	10.9	7.6	32	29	0.64	0.60
Air	3	5	2.6	0.7	0.8	14	13	4.36	2.64
Total	450	632	2.0	100.0	100.0	737	1,998	1.64	2.05

[a]Totals per capita in 1987: 10,350 pkm/capita and 21.3 GJ/capita.

TABLE 2.11   Passenger Kilometers and Energy Use by Modes of Transportation in Sweden,[a] 1970–1987

Mode	Passenger Kilometers					Energy Use			
	1970	1987	Growth	1970	1987	1970	1987	1970	1987
	(billion)		(%/year)	Share (%)		$(10^{15}$ J)		$(10^6$ J/pkm)	
Car	55	79	2.1	82.4	80.0	108	159	1.95	2.02
Bus	6	9	2.9	8.2	9.1	5	9	0.92	1.03
Rail	6	8	1.8	8.5	7.9	3	4	0.50	0.52
Air	1	3	9.3	0.9	3.0	4	9	6.11	3.13
Total	67	99	2.3	100.0	100.0	119	182	1.79	1.84

[a]Totals per capita in 1987: 11,683 pkm/capita and 21.5 GJ/capita.

2.6. (Moderate) Tables 2.9 to 2.11 present an $I = PAT$ type analysis of energy in transportation in the United States, Germany, and Sweden, 1970–1987 (Schipper, et al., 1992). For each country:

(a) Was the change in average energy per kilometer dominated by changes in energy per kilometer of individual modes or by shifts between modes.

(b) Comment on the relative importance of the change in total kilometers traveled and of the change in average energy per kilometer. Do not spend a lot of words here; just show you understand how to interpret other people's use of $I = PAT$ thinking.

2.7. (Harder) Raskin (1995) proposes another approach to assigning causation for change in $I = PAT$. Assume just two factors, P (population) and C (consumption per capita): $I = PC$. Then $\Delta I/I = \Delta P/P + \Delta C/C + (\Delta P/P)(\Delta C/C)$. Assume the cross term $(\Delta P/P)(\Delta C/C)$ can be divided proportionally to $\Delta P/P$ and $\Delta C/C$:

$$\text{Population's share of cross term} = \left(\frac{\dfrac{\Delta P}{P}}{\dfrac{\Delta P}{P} + \dfrac{\Delta C}{C}} \right) \frac{\Delta P}{P} \frac{\Delta C}{C}$$

$$\text{Consumption's share of cross term} = \left(\frac{\dfrac{\Delta C}{C}}{\dfrac{\Delta P}{P} + \dfrac{\Delta C}{C}} \right) \frac{\Delta P}{P} \frac{\Delta C}{C}$$

(a) Derive the fractions of $\Delta I/I$ that are allocable to changes in population and consumption. Show that they add to 1.

(b) Commoner's approach in the text breaks down when $\Delta I = 0$. What about this method?

(c) Table 2.12 presents a CO_2 scenario from the International Panel on Climate Change (1992), reproduced in Raskin (1995). Using Com-

TABLE 2.12

		Year	
Region		1990	2050
More developed	Population (billion)	1.24	1.43
	CO_2 emissions (billion tons C/year)	3.92	5.91
	Per capita emissions (tons C/year)	3.15	4.12
Less developed	Population (billion)	4.08	8.60
	CO_2 emissions (billion tons C/year)	1.74	7.32
	Per capita emissions (tons C/year)	0.43	0.85
World	Population (billion)	5.33	10.03
	CO_2 emissions (billion tons C/year)	5.66	13.23
	Per capita emissions (tons C/year)	1.06	1.32

moner's method and Raskin's method, determine the percentage contributions of population growth and per capita emissions to the growth in total CO_2 emissions in this scenario. Do this for more developed and less developed areas and for the world.

(d) Of the growth in CO_2 emissions, what percentage occurred in more developed countries? Less developed countries?

3 Consequences of Exponential (Geometric) Growth

EXPONENTIAL AND GEOMETRIC GROWTH: PREVALENCE IN OUR WORLD VIEW, APPROXIMATE EQUIVALENCE

I have hinted that exponential increase is a dominant mindset of our culture. In our everyday affairs, we are bombarded by, and likely assume, exponential thinking: interest on money either borrowed or loaned, overall growth of "the economy," the academic model of one professor cloning him/herself 20 or more times to produce Ph.D.s who are supposed to get an academic job and do the same thing. See the accompanying box and Figure 3.1. Certainly in nature there are examples of exponential growth, for a time (especially when species are introduced to new territory where there are no natural enemies). But not forever.

Exponential Growth Language in the News

The Illinois economy, which is experiencing a strong 1995, will continue to grow next year and in 1997, posting solid gains in employment and personal income, UI economists predict.

Following a solid 3.2 percent inflation-adjusted growth rate so far this year, the Gross State Product (GSP) is expected to expand 4.7 percent in 1996 and then moderate to 3.1 percent in 1997. The GSP consists of the total dollar value of goods and services produced in Illinois.

This steady growth will boost "real" (inflation-adjusted) personal income in the state by 3.7 percent in 1996 and 3.4 percent in 1997, rates very close to this year's 3.5 percent pace.

Analysts at the UI Bureau of Economic and Business Research do not anticipate a recession in the foreseeable future. Instead, they suggest that Illinois will glide to a "soft landing" of more limited growth in 1996 and 1997.

If this proves to be true, the economy will repeat its performance of the 1960s when business enjoyed eight years of uninterrupted growth. Such expansion has not been recorded in the last 25 years.

The Illinois economy, which emerged from a sharp recession in fiscal 1990–91, has been outpacing the growth of the U.S. economy since 1994. The same pattern is generally true throughout the Midwest, which has outperformed both the Northeast and Pacific Coast economies in the last two years.

Some of the nation's strongest growth has been centered in the Chicago region, buoyed by an expanding service sector and greater international trade, especially in machinery and electronics.

The manufacturing sector has been a leading factor in Illinois' current economic expansion and is expected to grow 4.1 percent overall this year. Growth in the sector is expected to slow next year and in 1997. Construction and transportation are expected to remain strong through 1996, while downstate coal mining is expected to drop steeply as a result of industry-wide contraction.

The heightened economic activity is expected to produce more revenues for the state government. A 4.8 percent increase in general funds revenue is anticipated through the fiscal year ending June 30, 1997, Bureau analysts forecast. Smaller increases are expected in the growth of corporate income tax revenue and miscellaneous tax revenue.

Perhaps chastened by a tight employment market until recently, consumer spending is projected to expand only moderately. An increase of 3.3 percent is projected for this year, followed by about 2 percent growth rates in 1996 and 1997. The increases in consumer spending will be driven primarily by purchases of nondurable goods, according to the UI analysts.

Spending for durable goods such as automobiles and large appliances is expected to decline this year and in 1996 after a period of robust growth.

—M. Reutter (1995). Illinois economy to experience "steady growth" in 1996, '97. *Inside Illinois* 15(5):1. Reprinted with permission. *Inside Illinois* is the faculty-staff newspaper at the University of Illinois.

Here we will discuss how to think of this pattern in several alternative ways and how to perform useful, revealing, quick calculations about it. The reference example we will use is the lifetime of a finite resource being consumed at an exponentially increasing rate over time.

Exponential growth is defined thus: The change of gloof per unit time is proportional to the current amount of gloof.[1] Suppose the gross domestic product (GDP) grows exponentially at 2%/year this year, 2%/year next year. After 2 years the GDP is $(1.02)(1.02) = 1.0404$ times its starting value, and *not* $1 + 0.0200 + 0.0200 = 1.0400$ (the latter is linear, or arithmetic, growth). The result of exponential growth can be stated two ways:

---

[1]Throughout the book, "gloof" is my catchall term for the generalized quantity under discussion.

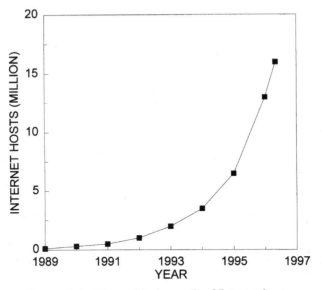

Figure 3.1 Geometrical growth of Internet hosts.

$$C = C_0(1 + r\Delta t)^N \qquad \text{(geometrical)}$$

$$C = C_0 e^{r\Delta t N} \qquad \text{(exponential)}$$

(3.1)

where C_0 is the value of gloof at the beginning of the growth period, r is the growth rate (which can be negative, implying decline), Δt is the chosen time step, and N is the number of time steps. Readers may see these in slightly different form; I use these to be careful about units. r is given in units of 1/time (e.g., r for world population is now about 0.014/year = 1.4%/year). Δt is in units of time, say years. N is the number of time steps, a dimensionless quantity. Then $r\Delta t$ is dimensionless and can be added consistently to 1 in the first expression, and e can be raised to a dimensionless power in the second.[2]

---

[2]This may be a case of misplaced rigor, but we should be careful with units. Often one sees these expressions written as

$$C = C_0(1 + r)^t$$

or

$$C = C_0 e^{rt}$$

where t is the elapsed time $N \Delta t$. This makes dimensional sense for the second expression, but not the first. Actually in the first expression the time step has been assumed and r is the fractional change in that time step. Another indication the problem is seen when $r\Delta t \ll 1$, when the two expressions should give the same result. For a given r, this occurs when Δt approaches zero and N approaches infinity. In an interest-bearing bank account, this corresponds to compounding infinitely often.

In this book we will usually treat the two forms of growth as equivalent. They are identical in the limit $r\Delta t \to 0$ or $N \to 0$. Table 3.1 compares them for nonzero values.

"RULE OF 70" CONNECTING GROWTH RATE AND DOUBLING TIME

Table 3.1 shows that as r increases, the difference between geometrical and exponential growth becomes large. We should remember this when using the well-known "Rule of 70," which says that

$$r\tau \approx 70 \tag{3.2}$$

where r is in % per time period and τ is the doubling time. (Being consistent about units is important!) Equation 3.2 is derived as follows. Assuming exponential growth, $C/C_0 = e^{r\tau}$. If $C/C_0 = 2$, $r\tau = \ln 2 = 0.693$. This applies if r is in units of 1/time. Multiplying both sides by 100 converts r to units of %/time. Then $r\tau = 69.3$, which is often estimated as 70.

TABLE 3.1   Comparison of Geometric and Exponential Equations for Different Time Periods and Growth Rates

	$(1 + r\Delta t)^N$	$e^{r\Delta t N}$
For $r = 0.1$/year		
$N\Delta t$ (years)		
0	1	1
1	1.1000	1.1052
2	1.2100	1.2214
5	1.6105	1.6487
10	2.5937	2.7183
100	13,781	22,024
For $N\Delta t = 10$ years		
r (year^{-1})		
0	1	1
0.05	1.6289	1.6487
0.10	2.5937	2.7183
0.25	9.3132	12.1825
0.50	57.6651	148.4133

Note: They are identical when $N\Delta t$ or $r \to 0$. Otherwise, the exponential result exceeds the geometric.

TABLE 3.2   Growth Rates and Corresponding Doubling/Halving Times for Exponential Growth

r (%/year)	τ (years)	Double or Halve?	Example
0	∞	NA	Mass of earth (C = constant)
1.4	50	Double	World population growth
2	35	Double	U.S. GDP growth in mid-1990s
7	10	Double	Chinese GDP growth in mid-1990s
10	7	Double	
18	4	Double	Interest on credit card balance
−0.0029	24,000	Half	Plutonium radioactive decay
−1.4−−0.35	50–200	Half	Loss of atmospheric CO_2 to, e.g., oceans
−2	35	Half	
−3	23	Half	
−5.8	12	Half	Loss of methane (CH_4) from atmosphere

This assumes r is positive. If r is negative, τ is the halving time or half-life.

This derivation uses the exponential form of growth. For $r\,\Delta t \ll 1$, the geometrical version gives an identical result.[3] For $r\Delta t$ not $\ll 1$, Equation 3.2 breaks down, as demonstrated in Problem 3.6.

The Rule of 70 is useful for getting a handle on the growth or decline impacts of a given interest rate, growth rate, and so on. Doubling or halving time is much more vivid and real to most people than growth rate. Table 3.2 lists some examples:

Reminder: The Rule of 70 applies only to exponential (geometrical) growth which is sustained over a long-enough time period to make the idea of doubling (or halving) time sensible.

INFERRING DOUBLING TIMES FROM EXAMPLES IN CHAPTER 2

Example: What Are Doubling Times in U.S. Auto Increase 1970–1990?

We saw that population grew 22% during that period, and per capita car ownership grew 32%. Population: Assuming exponential growth, $1.22 = e^{20r}$, ln $1.22 = 0.199 = 20r$, $r = 0.00993$/year $= 0.993$%/year. By the Rule of 70, $\tau = 70/0.993 = 70$ years. For per capita cars, solving $1.32 = e^{20r}$ yields $r = 1.38$%/year and $\tau = 50$ years.

[3] $2 = (1 + r\Delta t)^{N_{double}}$, ln $2 = N_{double}\ln(1 + r\Delta t)$. For $r\Delta t \ll 1$, ln$(1 + r\Delta t)$ is well approximated by $r\Delta t$, and ln $2 = r(N_{double}\ \Delta t) = r\tau$.

TABLE 3.3 Growth Rates and Doubling/Halving Times for the World Carbon Emissions Example in Table 2.3

Decade	P_{end}/P_{start} [$r(\%/year)$, $\tau(year)$]	A_{end}/A_{start} [$r(\%/year)$, $\tau(year)$]	T_{end}/T_{start} [$r(\%/year)$, $\tau(year)$]	I_{end}/I_{start} [$r(\%/year)$, $\tau(year)$]
1960–1970	1.22	1.36	0.95	1.58
	(2.01, 35)	(3.12, 22)	(−0.51, 135)	(4.68, 15)
1970–1980	1.20	1.16	0.92	1.28
	(1.84, 38)	(1.50, 46)	(−0.83, 83)	(2.50, 28)
1980–1990	1.19	1.12	0.85	1.13
	(1.75, 40)	(1.14, 61)	(−1.61, 43)	(1.23, 56)

Example: What Are Doubling/Halving Times in the World Carbon Emission Example?

In the decade 1960–1970 we found that P, A, T, and I changed by 22%, 36%, −5%, and 58%, respectively. Assuming exponential growth, the growth rate of carbon emissions, I, is obtained from $1.58 = e^{10r}$, where r is in units of year^{-1}. Solving gives ln $1.58 = 0.456 = 10r$, $r = 0.0456/year = 4.56\%/$year. By the Rule of 70, the associated doubling time τ is $70/4.56 = 15$ years.

Similarly, for technology T, ln $0.95 = -0.0511 = e^{10r}$, $r = -0.00511/$year, and *halving* time $\tau = 140$ years. In Table 3.3 the growth rate and doubling/halving times are given for some of the entries in Table 2.3.

Strictly speaking, there is no more information in Table 3.3 than in Table 2.3, but the growth rates or doubling/halving times may make the trends more vivid. The greatest growth in the factors *PAT* occurred in per capita consumption in the 1960s (3.12%/year), while the greatest decline occurred in the CO_2 intensity of technology in the 1980s (−1.61%/year).

SUM OF GEOMETRIC SERIES: IMPORTANT EQUATION 2

During roughly the last 20 years humans burned 50% of all the fossil fuel burned since the dawn of time. This is a consequence of rapid growth[4] and is rigorously true for continued exponential growth. This can be seen by using an even more useful version of the exponential equation $C = C_0 e^{rt}$. Rewrite the argument of the exponential as ln $2 * (r/\ln 2) * t$ and recall that ln $2/r = \tau$. Then

$$C = C_0 2^{t/\tau} \quad \text{(growth)} \quad (3.3)$$

This is just the exponential equation written in terms of base 2 and $1/\tau$ in-

---

[4]". . . more articles on chemistry have been published in the past two years than throughout history before 1900." Annual cost of *Chemical Abstracts*: 1940, $12; 1977, $3500; 1995, $17,400 (Noam, 1995).

stead of base e and r. It shows explicitly how C doubles every doubling time. To cover decline instead of growth, r is negative, which here means τ is negative $= -|\tau|$, and

$$C = C_0 2^{-t/|\tau|} = C_0(1/2)^{t/|\tau|} \quad \text{(decline)}$$

The fossil fuel statement given previously can be justified in three ways: (1) just writing down and scrutinizing some numbers, (2) mathematically integrating the expression for C over time, and (3) determining the sum of the geometric version of C over time.

Method 1: Writing Down and Scrutinizing Some Numbers Assume that a resource is consumed this year at a rate of 1 ton/year and that the rate is doubling every year. Table 3.4 shows the consumption each year (a removal flow) and the cumulative consumption up through that time (a reduction in stock). Compare the cumulative consumption at the end of any year to the consumption in the following year. For example, in year 8 the consumption rate is 128 tons/year, while 127 tons have already been consumed. As time goes on these are very nearly equal, which demonstrates the statement.

Method 2: Integrating (Using Calculus)

$$\text{Cumulative consumption} = \int_{t_1}^{t_2} C_0 e^{rx} \, dx = \frac{C_0}{r}(e^{rt_2} - e^{rt_1}) \quad (3.4)$$

Let us compare the consumption during the period $t \to t + \tau$ to that during the period $-\infty \to t$. Applying the integrated equation,

TABLE 3.4   Yearly Consumption Rate and Cumulative Consumption with a Doubling Time of 1 Year

Year	Consumption Rate (tons/year)	Cumulative Consumption at End of Year (tons)
1	1	1
2	2	3
3	4	7
4	8	15
5	16	31
6	32	63
7	64	127
8	128	255
9	256	511
10	512	1023

$$\frac{\text{Consumption during period } t \rightarrow t + \tau}{\text{Consumption during period } -\infty \rightarrow t} = \frac{e^{r(t+\tau)} - e^{rt}}{e^{rt} - 0}$$

This ratio reduces to $(e^{r\tau} - 1)$. But $r\tau = \ln 2$, so $(e^{r\tau} - 1) = 2 - 1 = 1$. This demonstrates the statement (exactly, because we looked back to $t = -\infty$).

Method 3: Determining the Sum of a Geometric Series   Suppose that there are M tons of a depletable resource. Today we are using it at a rate of C_0 tons/year. At today's rate of use, it would last M/C_0 years. [*Note units:* Divide a stock (tons) by a flow (tons/year) to get time (years).] M/C_0 is called the static lifetime. If, however, annual consumption is growing geometrically at a rate r per year, how long will the resource last?

Using a table like Table 3.4 and integrating as in Equation 3.4, are ways to answer this question. A table is cumbersome, but can be used: Just add up the yearly total consumptions until the sum reaches M. In fact, this would be the appropriate method if the yearly consumption rate were changing arbitrarily over time. Integration is elegant and acceptable, but not really needed; there is a simpler way using algebra to sum a geometrically increasing series. This equation has applications in resource use, bank accounts, mortgages, time discounting (in benefit–cost analysis), annuities, loan sharking, lottery payments, and many other forms of exponential grist for the U.S. (and world) economic mill. The results are contained in rate books used by bankers and lawyers and are burped out by multicolor, soundblasting computer packages. Many people assume the mathematics is intricate.

Not so. We will derive the equation. As with Important Equation 1 ($I = PAT$), your task is to learn how to do it, then almost forget it . . . subject to recall on demand.[5]

Starting in year 1, the summed consumption is $C_1 + C_2 + C_3 + \cdots + C_t$. Assuming geometric growth, this sum is $C_1 (1 + x + x^2 + \cdots + x^t)$, where $x = 1 + r$, r being the consumption growth rate.

We want the value of t for which the sum equals M, the initial amount of the resource. We use a trick for the sum: For a geometric series, define the sum at time t:

$$S_t = 1 + x + x^2 + x^3 + \cdots + x^{t-1}$$

Likewise, the sum one year later is

$$S_{t+1} = 1 + x + x^2 + x^3 + \cdots + x^{t-1} + x^t$$

S_{t+1} can be written two ways:

---

[5]This equation is also derived in Stokey and Zeckhauser (1978).

$$S_{t+1} = S_t + x^t$$

or

$$S_{t+1} = xS_t + 1$$

The first is obtained by adding the additional term x^t to S_t, while the second is obtained by multiplying S_t by x and adding 1. Note that the two formulas are equivalent:

$$S_t + x^t = xS_t + 1$$

Solve this equation to obtain

IMPORTANT EQUATION 2

$$S_t = 1 + x + x^2 + x^3 + \cdots + x^{t-1} = \frac{1 - x^t}{1 - x} \qquad (3.5)$$

In our case, $x = 1 + r$. Substituting, we obtain

$$1 + (1 + r) + (1 + r)^2 + \cdots + (1 + r)^{t-1} = (1 - (1 + r)^t)/(1 - (1 + r))$$
$$= (1 + r)^t - 1)/r$$

Then

$$M = C_0 \frac{(1 + r)^t - 1}{r} \qquad (3.6)$$

Solve this for t:

$$t_{\text{geometric}} = \frac{\ln\left(1 + \dfrac{rM}{C_0}\right)}{\ln(1 + r)} \qquad (3.7)$$

This expression works for positive and negative r. For $r = 0$, it seems to blow up, but if one performs the mathematical operation of taking limits carefully it reduces to $t = M/C_0$, as expected. It can be compared with the result from the integrated form (Eq. 3.4), which gives

$$t_{\text{exponential}} = \frac{1}{r} \ln\left(1 + \frac{rM}{C_0}\right) \tag{3.8}$$

For $|r| \ll 1$, $\ln(1 + r) \to r$, and Equation 3.8 also gives $t = M/C_0$.

The exponential growth of consumption shortens resource lifetimes dramatically. If the resource is depleted in n doubling times, a comfortable-feeling half of it was still there just one doubling time ago. We have manipulated the preceding numbers to get that notion into our brains, but it is difficult to get it into our hearts and guts.

RESOURCE LIFETIMES WITH EXPONENTIATING CONSUMPTION: ILLINOIS COAL AS EXAMPLE

Illinois has enough coal to last 800 years at current extraction rates. That is, the static lifetime is 800 years. This includes significant coal exports to neighboring states. There are environmental reasons not to burn it all, and the number 800 years is uncertain for many reasons, but let us forget all that and see how long it would last with consumption increasing exponentially at 5%/year. See Figure 3.2.

This is a consumption doubling time of $70/5 = 14$ years. If this rate of increase could be maintained for 800 years, the consumption rate would be about $2^{800/14} = 2^{57} \approx 10^{17}$ times today's. Therefore, long before 800 years, the resource would be gone. Substituting in Equation 3.8, we get

$$t_{\text{geometric}} = \ln(1 + (0.05)(800))/\ln(1 + 0.05) = 74.3 \text{ years}$$

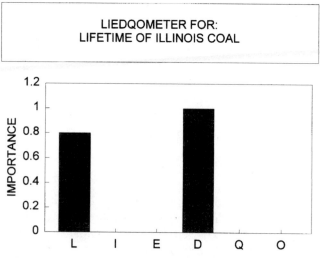

Figure 3.2 LIEDQOmeter for lifetime of Illinois coal.

TABLE 3.5   Resource Lifetime as a Function of Growth of Consumption Rate for Linear, Geometric, and Exponential Growth

r^a (%/year)	t_{linear} (years)	$t_{geometric}$ (years)	$t_{exponential}$ (years)
0.00^b	800.0	800.0	800.0
1.00	312.7	220.8	219.7
2.00	237.6	143.1	141.7
5.00	160.4	76.1	74.3
10.00	117.3	46.1	43.9
15.00	97.3	34.3	32.0
20.00	85.1	27.9	25.4

[a] r for linear growth is based on the first year; see the box on page 58.
[b] With no growth ($r = 0$), the (static) lifetime is 800 years.

more than a factor of 10 reduction from the static lifetime. Table 3.5 shows how resource lifetime depends on growth rate.

Besides the geometric case, we also include the exponential, which scarcely differs, even for $r = 20\%$/year, and the linear (see the box below), which is intermediate between the static (no-growth) value of 800 years and the geometric value.

Lifetime with Linear Growth of Consumption

In linear growth the change of gloof per unit time is proportional to the *initial* amount of gloof. Obtaining the lifetime here is also an application of algebra, this time for the sum of an arithmetic, rather than geometric series. For example, let consumption in succeeding years be 1.0, 1.1, 1.2, 1.3, 1.4, 1.5, etc. for 10%/year arithmetic growth. The yearly increment is a constant fraction of the original consumption rate. Then

$$M = C_0 + (C_0 + \Delta C) + (C_0 + 2\Delta C) + (C_0 + 3\Delta C) \cdots (C_0$$
$$+ (t - 1)\Delta C)$$
$$= C_0 t + \Delta C(1 + 2 + 3 + \cdots + (t - 1))$$

where ΔC is the annual increase.

The sum $1 + 2 + 3 + \cdots + (t - 1)$ is obtained by another trick: Rearrange the terms in pairs by taking one member from each end of the sum

$$(1 + (t - 1)) + (2 + (t - 2)) + (3 + (t - 3)) \cdots$$

Each pair has the same value ($= t$), and there are $(t - 1)/2$ pairs, so the sum $= t(t - 1)/2$. Then

$$M = C_0(t + rt(t - 1)/2) \quad \text{or} \quad t^2 + (2/r - 1)t - 2M/rC_0 = 0$$

where r is defined in reference to the initial consumption rate: $r = \Delta C/C_0$. The equation is solved using the quadratic formula to give

$$t_{\text{linear}} = \frac{1}{2}\left(-\left(\frac{2}{r} - 1\right) + \sqrt{\left(\frac{2}{r} - 1\right)^2 + \frac{8M}{rC_0}}\right)$$

This expression is used to calculate the linear growth resource lifetimes in Table 3.5.

Making a Resource Last Forever

If Illinois coal extraction were decreasing geometrically at 5%/year, how long would it last? Using Equation 3.7, we have $t_{\text{geometric}} = \ln(1 - (0.05)(800))/\ln(1 - 0.05)$. This requires taking the logarithm of a negative number, which is impossible. The interpretation is that the resource lasts forever. The threshold value for r is given when $1 + rM/C_0 = 0$. In our case this occurs for $r = -1/800 = -(1/8)\%$/year. This is a halving time of $70/(1/8) = 560$ years. Can you restate the requirement for infinite lifetime in terms of static lifetime and halving time?

PROBLEMS

Level of difficulty is indicated as Easier/Moderate/Harder. Problems marked "(Spreadsheet?)" can be fruitfully approached using a spreadsheet. They need not be, however.

3.1. (Easier) News item dated December 10, 1995: South Korea's 15-year plan calls for a tripling of GNP and auto population.
  (a) What is implied growth rate, assuming (1) linear and (2) exponential (geometric) growth? What is the doubling time in each case? In words, define the doubling time in each case.
  (b) Are the growth rates obtained in (a) large? Explain.

3.2. (Easier) Suppose a bank account doubles in value in a year. If we assume that $r = 100\%$ per year, then the Rule of 70 gives the doubling time as

0.7 years, which contradicts the premise. Alternatively, if we assume the doubling time is 1 year, the Rule of 70 gives $r = 70\%$ per year, which also seems to contradict the premise. Explain/demonstrate the problem here. It may be useful to compare the case when the interest is paid and reinvested every month, say.

3.3. (Moderate) World oil data for 1988 from Meadows et al. (1992), Table 3.2:

Cumulative production (i.e., extraction)	610	billion barrels
1988 production	21.3	billion barrels
Known reserves	922	billion barrels
Estimated undiscovered reserves	275–945	billion barrels

(a) Assume the undiscovered reserves are the mean of the range given. What is the remaining oil's lifetime assuming exponential growth of consumption with growth rates of 0, 2, and 5%/year and doubling times of 70, 23, and 10 years?

(b) What exponential growth rate results in an infinite lifetime?

(c) Suppose that there are no undiscovered reserves at all. Repeat (a) in this case.

(d) Suppose that the undiscovered reserves are the maximum of the range given. Repeat (a) in this case.

(e) Parts (c) and (d) ask for lifetimes with assumed reserves differing by roughly a factor of 2. Comment on the effect this has on lifetime for different geometric growth rates (150 words max.).

3.4. (Moderate) In the text, using a table and integration, we demonstrated that the next doubling time's consumption equals all previous consumption.

(a) Show this using Important Equation 2 (Eq. 3.5).

(b) State the analogous principle when consumption is exponentially declining.

3.5. (Moderate) Fixed-rate mortgage. Assume you borrow M dollars at a monthly interest rate of r, to be paid back in N equal monthly payments p. Use Important Equation 2.

(a) Determine p in terms of M, N, and r. *Hint:* Each month the unpaid balance is increased by the interest and then decreased by the payment p. That balance is M at the start and drops to 0 with the last payment.

(b) Check the expression for p when $r \to 0$. Does it make sense?

(c) Your total payments are Np. Compare this amount with the amount of the loan, M.

(d) A rule of thumb says that for a 30-year mortgage of value M at 10%/year interest, the monthly payment is about 1% of M. Do you agree?

3.6. (Moderate) This letter to the editor appeared in *Scientific American,* January 1996:

> In "Solar Energy" [*Scientific American,* September 1995], William Hoagland states that the solar energy reaching the earth yearly is 10 times total energy stored on the earth, as well as 15,000 times the current annual consumption. This seems to mean that we have a 1,500-year supply of energy. But the usual estimate is that existing reserves will last 50 to 100 years.
>
> Ralph M. Potter
> Pepper Pike, Ohio

Hoagland replies:

> The 50- to 100-year figure is for fossil energy in the mix that is currently used (oil, coal, natural gas); it is also dependent on many estimates of the future demand for energy. It does not consider, for example, the broader use of coal and nuclear energy to meet these needs. The issue is really whether we want to incur the economic and environmental consequences of this route given the opportunities of solar energy.
> —Reprinted with permission of *Scientific American*
> and Ralph M. Potter

Design a hypothetical future demand pattern that supports Hoagland.

3.7. (Moderate) (Spreadsheet?) A researcher wants to know the change in U.S. gross domestic product between 1977 and 1995. The only source he/she can find gives the following data. Calculate the change.

YEAR	PERCENTAGE CHANGE FROM PRECEDING YEAR
1977	4.9
1978	5.0
1979	2.9
1980	−0.3
1981	2.5
1982	−2.1
1983	4.0
1984	6.8
1985	3.7
1986	3.0
1987	2.9

1988	3.8
1989	3.4
1990	1.3
1991	−1.0
1992	2.7
1993	2.3
1994	3.5
1995	2.0

(Data from U.S. Bureau of Economic Analysis, http://www.bea.doc. gov/bea/sumnip-d.html.)

3.8. (Moderate) Champaign-Urbana *News-Gazette,* December 15, 1996: Mrs. Sallie Dorsey, 107, died December 12, 1996, in Champaign, Illinois. She was born in 1888 in Mississippi. Survivors include 2 sons, 3 daughters, 78 grandchildren, 125 great-grandchildren, and 9 great-grand children. She was preceded in death by her parents, 14 brothers and sisters, and 6 children.

- **(a)** What is the average (exponential) growth rate and doubling time for these generations:
  - **1.** Mrs. Dorsey's parents' generation
  - **2.** Mrs. Dorsey's generation
  - **3.** Her children's generation
  - **4.** Her grandchildren's generation
  - **5.** The average of the preceding four generations.
- **(b)** Qualitatively compare the answers from part (a).

3.9. (Harder) Exponential versus logistic growth:
  - **1.** $d(\text{gloof})/dt = r(\text{gloof})$ defines exponential growth and is solved to give $\text{gloof} = (\text{gloof})_0 e^{rt}$.
  - **2.** $d(\text{gloof})/dt = r(\text{gloof})(1 - (\text{gloof})/K)$ defines logistic growth.

For the second equation:
- **(a)** Qualitatively describe how gloof varies with time when it starts with $\text{gloof}/K \ll 1$. What happens when $\text{gloof} = K$?
- **(b)** Solve the second equation. Does the result for gloof behave over time as expected?
- **(c)** What has this got to do with carrying capacity?

4 End-Use Analysis and Predicting Future Demand

WHY END-USE ANALYSIS?

It is a sweltering July afternoon in the Midwest in the early 1970s. The temperature has gone over 90°F for the fourth day in a row and people's patience and tolerance are stretched thin. At the head office of the XYZ Power Company, an engineer has phoned the vice-president of operations to say that power now being delivered is at an all-time high and dangerously close to what the company *can* deliver. XYZ's power demands peaks in the summer, as shown in a typical bill in Figure 4.1. The vice-president calls the forecasting department and asks their opinion. As a result a meeting is set up with the forecasters, facilities planners, and top brass. The next day the heat wave breaks, and the meeting is held.

At the meeting, the forecasting chief starts the discussion by showing graphs of peak power demand versus time such as Figure 4.2. The logarithmic graph (Fig. 4.2*b*) shows an almost perfect straight line from 1935 to 1974, with only a little bend down beginning around 1970. A straight-line logarithmic plot indicates a constant growth rate, that is, exponential growth. For over 30 years starting in 1935, peak power demand has increased exponentially at 9%/year. This is a doubling time of 8 years, so 30 years is almost four doublings; during that period peak power increased almost $2^4 = 16$-fold. After 1967 the growth rate was 6%/year. See the accompanying box.

Energy versus Power: Stock versus Flow

Power is energy per unit time. If electricity is produced by burning coal, the company's coal pile (measured in tons, say) represents a stock of energy. When burned and converted, it will produce electrical energy (measured in kilowatt-hours). This electrical energy is also a stock; it could be stored in batteries. On the other hand, burning the coal at a given rate (measured in tons/hour, say) represents power, a time flow of energy. When converted, this flow produces electrical power (a flow measured in kilowatt-hours per hour, or kilowatts). The peak power on the sultry July day is a peak flow, and to produce that peak power requires a certain size

---

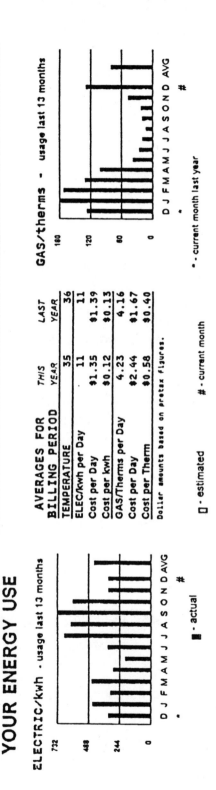

Figure 4.1 Sample residential electric and gas bill from central Illinois. This residence has a gas furnace, hot water heater, and clothes dryer, and an electric central air conditioner. Gas use peaks in winter; electricity use peaks in summer.

63

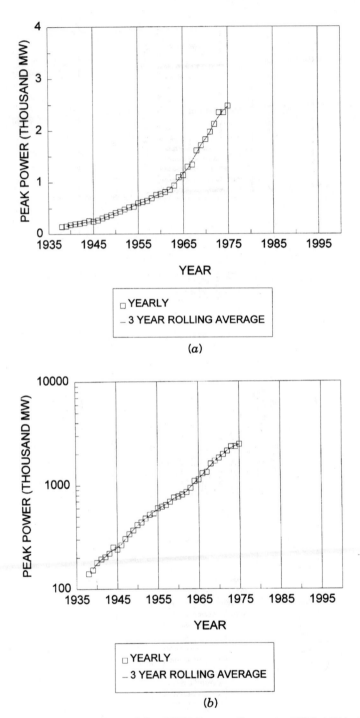

Figure 4.2 Peak power demand for XYZ Power Company 1938–1974. (*a*) linear scale, (*b*) logarithmic scale. Through 1958 the peak occurred in the winter (with one exception: 1944). In 1959 and following the peak occurred in the summer (with one exception: 1962).

of power plant . . . even if it only operates at that peak level for 30 minutes a year.

On that hot day, the power plant turbines are spinning at top speed (units = rotations/time). At the other end, a merciless sun is causing a peak flow of heat (units = calories/time) into a living room, and a window air conditioner is spinning a compressor at maximum (units = rotations/time) to cause a flow of heat (units = calories/time) *out* of the living room. The peak power is produced by a stock of turbines, and the peak air-conditioning rate is produced by a stock of air-conditioning equipment.

The question is raised: What about future demand? Two possibilities are as follows:

1. Straight-line logarithmic extrapolation of a 6 to 9%/year trend. In 8 to 12 years XYZ Power Company will need to double its capacity. Compared with other power sources, nuclear looks cheapest, and the company begins planning, applying to the Atomic Energy Commission for a license, for the Alpha Nuclear Power Plant. In 1974 the U.S. Atomic Energy Commission (now the Nuclear Regulatory Commission) predicts that between 1971 and 1980, XYZ Power Company's peak power demand will increase 110%.[1]

2. Prediction based on detailed analysis of how electric power is used and how those various demands should change over time. At 1975 hearings before the Atomic Energy Commission, the "need for power" is a mandatory criterion for approval. Some testimony challenges XYZ Power Company's use of extrapolation. The testifiers claim that peak power will grow at a yearly rate of 1 to 3%, not 6 to 9%, thus setting back the time that the power plant will be needed by at least 10 years.

The basis for this claim is that other factors besides *time* are important in predicting power growth. The fundamental trends that contributed strongly to sustained peak power increases between 1930 and 1960 would not continue in the 1970s and 1980s. For example:

- In contrast to baby boom growth years (1946–ca. 1970), local population growth would slow. The birth rate was dropping, and people were moving to Arizona, Texas, and California, not the Midwest.
- In the 1950s and 1960s, people were acquiring air conditioning; now most had it.
- Reversing a long trend, energy efficiency (i.e., the energy service per unit of energy) was going to increase.

[1]XYZ Power Company and Alpha Power Plant are pseudonyms. The issues, dates, and data are real.

This argument is shown semiquantitatively in the Table 4.1, based on an application of $I = PAT$:

$$\text{Energy} = (\text{Population})(\text{Affluence})(\text{Energy intensity})$$

This semiquantitative table assigns very approximate numbers to qualitative factors and justifies what we have already intuited. Peak power would not grow in the 1970s and 1980s (when the sum of factors = +1) as fast as it had between 1930 and 1960 (when the sum of factors = +5 to +7).

In 1975 the straight-line logarithmic extrapolation view prevailed and the Alpha Power Plant was authorized. It was constructed between 1976 and 1987 and is currently in operation. Figure 4.3 shows the peak power demand of XYZ Power Company through 1996. A clean break in the curve occurs around 1978, as predicted by the rough analysis given previously. Peak power growth has averaged 1.4%/year since then through 1996. The AEC's prediction that demand would increase 110% from 1971 to 1980 has still not been fulfilled: 1996's peak demand is 86% greater than 1971's. What was predicted to happen in 9 years' time has still not happened after 25 years. The more accurate end-use-based prediction differed from the straight-line extrapolation by disaggregating the demand into factors that could be analyzed in detail and that in this case could be expected to change. XYZ Power Company now makes forecasts incorporating end-use thinking.

The monetary consequences of the change in growth of peak power are somewhat more subtle. The Alpha Power Plant was under construction for 11 years and went through lengthy regulatory review, all of which added to its cost, which ultimately was about $4.3 billion, in unadjusted dollars between 1976 and 1987. Figure 4.3 shows that between 1971 and approximately 1987, peak demand had increased by about 1000 MW, roughly the output of the Alpha Power Plant. Thus Alpha came on line at about the right time, yet it seems to have been started early. XYZ Power Company had to pay $4.3 billion several years too soon. Because all costs are ultimately passed on, XYZ's customers had to pay $4.3 billion several years too soon. (This increased the price of electricity, which also reduced demand.) Given the choice, people prefer to pay bills later rather than earlier, so this is a wasteful consequence. In Chapter 5 we cover discounting, the formal process for comparing costs and benefits that occur at different times.

The process of disaggregating and analyzing on the consumption end is generally called end-use analysis. End use is a relative term; we could certainly study items closer to actual use, such as looking at industrial and commercial, as well as residential use, or breaking residential use into uses that are weather independent (say washing machines) and that are weather dependent (air conditioning), and so on. The level of breakdown depends on the problem.

End-use analysis is a careful way of restating the question "What do we want?" Table 4.2 lists some of the questions and concerns that we might have

TABLE 4.1 Semiquantitative (Population)(Affluence)(Energy Intensity) Factors in Electrical Demand in Central Illinois, 1930s–1980s

Time Period	Population (Number of people)	Affluence, Especially Regarding Electricity Use ($/person)	Energy Intensity (Inverse of Energy Efficiency) (energy/$)	Sum of Factors (a Rough Indicator of Growth Potential of Peak Electrical Power)
1930s & 1940s	Medium growth (+2)	High growth (+3) (Rural electrification)	No growth (0)	+2 + 3 + 0 = +5
1950s & 1960s	High growth (+3) (Baby boom)	High growth (+3) (Overall national economic growth, farm income boom from international grain market, increase in air conditioning, declining electricity prices)	Low growth (+1) (Low energy prices, lack of attention to energy costs)	+3 + 3 + 1 = +7
1970s & 1980s	Low growth (+1) (Midwest slower than national average)	Low growth (+1) (Oil price increases, international job drain, saturation of air conditioning)	Low decline (−1) (Increasing energy process, national appliance labeling, increased public environmental awareness, requirements by some state utility commissions that power companies encourage energy efficiency)	+1 + 1 − 1 = +1

The degree of change is roughly indexed: high growth = +3/high decline = −3, medium: +2/−2, low: +1/−1.

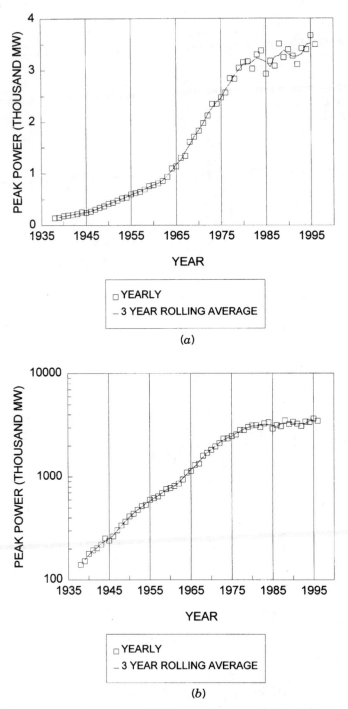

Figure 4.3 Peak power demand for XYZ Power Company 1938–1996, a continuation of Figure 4.2. (*a*) Linear scale, (*b*) logarithmic scale. All peaks between 1975 and 1996 occurred in the summer.

TABLE 4.2   Example Questions and Concerns Stimulated by End-Use Analysis

Issue/Item	Comment
Food System	
Calories	Too few or too many?
Vitamins	Enough?
Minerals	Enough?
Protein	Too little or too much?
Additives	Present? Harmful?
Fat	Too much?
Sugar	Too much?
Salt	Too much?
Health	How is food integrated into a total health program?
Social stability	What is consolidation in agriculture doing to rural communities in North Dakota? What happens to peasant self-sufficiency when land is taken and converted from staple crops to export luxuries like bananas?
Energy System	
Cheap energy versus clean energy	Cheap and clean are increasingly impossible together
Energy services	
1. Conditioned space	Buildings, refrigerators
2. Electron motion	Electronics
3. Mechanical motion	Labor-saving, transportation
Stable and functional transportation	To avoid social chaos
Economic growth (or "health")	Energy is a significant factor
International security	Wars are fought over energy, as recently as the Persian Gulf War in 1990
Transport/Communication System	
Transact business	Travel or teleconference?
Deliver health services	Doctor visit or wise diet choice at home?
Deliver health	Exercise program?
Commuting	Why commute? Mode choice
Pleasure	Recreational driving
Goods	Trucks have overtaken railroads; trucks use subsidized interstate highways
Cheap	
Fast	
Save	
Pleasant for nonparticipant	Traffic noise is serious
Convenient	

regarding the food system, energy system, or transportation/communication system. For example, we might say "We need more food." But this is vague and has the immediate rejoinder that for many people in rich countries, there is too much food.

As we have said, end-use analysis is often easily couched in the $I = PAT$ framework. For example,

Energy service = (Energy)(Service/Energy)

Refrigerated space = (Energy)(Refrigerated space/Energy)

A vacation: [Near/far][Transportation mode][Load factor][Hike/hotel]. The square brackets indicate that the factors are not strictly multiplicative.

A glass of beer: [Near/far][Package type][Recycle?]

Calories of protein food: [Animal/vegetable][Near/far][High/low intensity agriculture][Packaging type]

A spiritual experience: [Where (Nepal or Cleveland?)][When][Immediate surroundings][Alone?][Preparation]

A PREMIER EXAMPLE OF END-USE ANALYSIS: ENERGY EFFICIENCY

At the time of the Alpha Power Plant hearings (ca. 1975), energy efficiency was receiving increasing interest following the oil embargo in 1973. This concentration on T in $I = PAT$ was typified by detailed end-use analysis of the many ways energy services can be provided. There were three types of evidence that energy efficiency ($\equiv$ energy service/energy) could be increased dramatically over current U.S. practice. They were:

1. Thermodynamic arguments: The theoretical limits are often far off.
2. International economic comparisons.
3. Comparison of energy-using appliances, devices, and systems now on the market, based on the concept that if something exists, it must be possible!

First, thermodynamic arguments. There are fundamental limits to how much heat, for example, can be moved from a cold place to a hot place (which is what an air conditioner or refrigerator does) for a given amount of work (energy) input. Or, to how much iron can be separated from its oxide for a given amount of energy. Typically, today's technology falls short of that limit. How close we can expect to come is a two-step consideration. The first is theoretical; the usual thermodynamic limit is based on an idealized process occurring infinitely slowly. Of course, we want processes to occur faster than that, and there is a theoretical efficiency loss from this speed. The second consideration is more practical; designing a real machine to operate at the theoretical nonzero-speed limit is a difficult engineering problem. In Chapter 12 we return to the thermodynamic issue.

Second, international comparsions. Figures 4.4 and 4.5 tell a story. Figure 4.4 shows two things. First, in general terms gross domestic product (GDP) (units = $/year) and energy use (units = Btu/year) *are* related. The current German economy cannot run on current Bangladeshan per-capita energy consumption. Second, however, there is flexibility in the relationship. We can see at least a factor of 2 in the energy for a given GDP, especially for wealthier countries. Compare Canada and Germany or the United States and Sweden. This flexibility stimulated researchers to examine how energy is used in different countries. A classic study (Schipper and Lichtenberg, 1976) compared Sweden and the United States. In the early 1970s the two countries had nearly

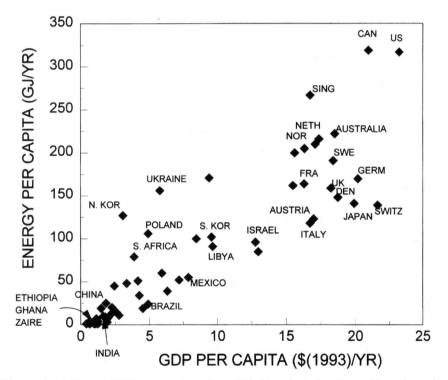

Figure 4.4 Energy/GDP comparison for 1993 for selected nations. Not all are labeled. A GJ (gigajoule = 10^9 joule) is about one million Btu, or the energy in 1/6 barrel of oil or 1/24 ton of coal. The U.S. per capita energy use is therefore about 55 barrels of oil equivalent, or 14 tons of coal equivalent, per year. GDPs are compared on the basis of purchasing power. *Source:* World Resources (1996), Tables 7.1 and 12.2.

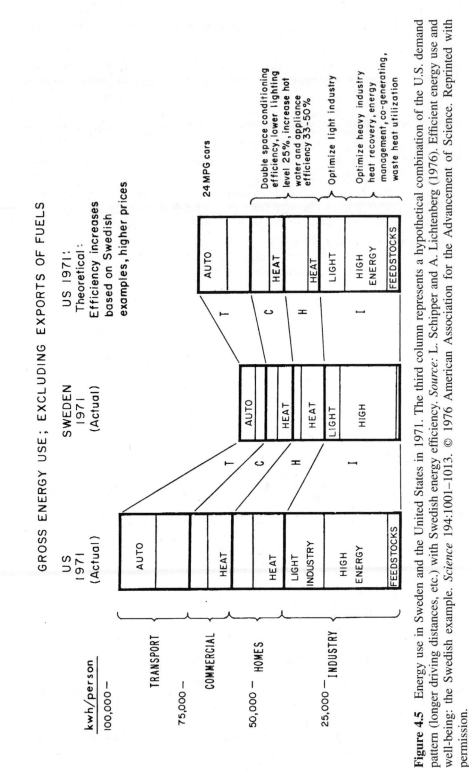

Figure 4.5 Energy use in Sweden and the United States in 1971. The third column represents a hypothetical combination of the U.S. demand pattern (longer driving distances, etc.) with Swedish energy efficiency. *Source:* L. Schipper and A. Lichtenberg (1976). Efficient energy use and well-being: the Swedish example. *Science* 194:1001–1013. © 1976 American Association for the Advancement of Science. Reprinted with permission.

identical per capital GDPs, yet Sweden used only 60% as much per capita energy (roughly true in 1993, also). Careful study of energy end use showed that, compared to the United States, Sweden had:

Major:

    Better buildings

    Fewer cars, with higher fuel efficiency (then 24 miles per gallon versus 13 in the United States)

    Heat-saving practices in industry

Minor:

    Fewer appliances

    More efficient small trucks

    More-used mass transit

Factors:

    Stronger building codes, colder climate

    Higher energy prices

    Better mass transit

    Better urban planning

Of course, Sweden and the United States differ in physical extent and culture, so this comparison was enriched by a lively debate about quality of life and those aspects not conveyed by the single quantity, GDP. However, Swedish efficiency was undeniable; though it has a colder climate, its housing used less energy per square meter than that of the United States (air conditioning is too small to swing it the other way). In fact, Swedish efficiency was partially a consequence of the colder climate, making insulation more economical. On the other hand, the relatively shorter distances in Sweden do favor reduced transportation energy. In 1971 Sweden used about 55% as much per capita energy annually as the United States. Schipper and Lichtenberg calculated what U.S. energy use would be if Swedish efficiencies were applied to the U.S. pattern of energy end uses. The result was about 70% of 1971 U.S. use, a real improvement but somewhat short of the 55% then true of Sweden. This is shown in Figure 4.5.

Third, Table 4.3 is one example of what is technically possible in terms of residential buildings and devices, in an economically cost-effective way. We know that one can purchase a new car that gets 40 miles per gallon; the average is 27. Today's new U.S. refrigerators are three times as efficient (i.e., cool the same space for a given time using one-third as much energy) as those sold in 1975 (Wilson and Morrill, 1996). Further improvements of the same magnitude are possible, with expectations (but not guarantees) that their costs will come down when they are mass produced. A skeptic will ask if the efficient devices are identical in all other respects and what they *do* cost. Often the answer is (approximately) "Yes, they are equivalent" and "the life

TABLE 4.3   1989 Energy Efficiency Potential

	Car (mpg)	Refrigerator (kWh/day)	Gas Furnace (10^6 J/day)	Air Conditioner (kWh/day)	Residence (10^3 J/m^2/ hour)
Current average	18	4	210	10	190
New model average	27	3	180	7	110
Best model	50	2	140	5	68
Best prototype	77	1	110	3	11

Source: Gibbons et al. (1989).

cost is no more than, and often less than, that of the less efficient model." We discuss this in more detail in Chapter 5.

These comparisons stimulated the idea of alternative energy demand futures, covering everything from subsidies for energy exploration to automobile miles per gallon standards to building codes. Detailed end-use analysis was an integral part, and results showed a wide range of energy demand possibilities. For example, Figure 4.6 shows the results of the Committee on Nuclear and Alternative Energy Systems (CONAES) of the National Academy of Sciences study on U.S. energy futures. All but one of the scenarios assume the same rate of economic growth between 1985 and 2010, yet different scenarios result in more than a factor of 2 difference in annual energy consumption in 2010. The scenarios are described in Table 4.4.

Figure 4.6 also indicates the actual U.S. energy use through 1995. It has grown dramatically less than the business-as-usual scenario C, another vindication of end-use analysis. Real energy prices averaged roughly constant, and real GDP growth averaged 2.6%/year between 1977 and 1995, so the CONAES prediction would be a bit below the line for Scenario B'. This is still a bit more than the observed energy use. Explaining this difference is more complicated.

Possible contributors are energy efficiency standards for automobiles and residential appliances and the move away from heavy industry and toward services. Between 1977 and 1994 the economic growth in construction and manufacturing (which are usually energy intensive) was below the average GDP rate of 2.6%/year, while the growth in services, wholesale and retail trade, and finance and insurance (usually less energy intensive) was above average. On the other hand, agriculture and transportation (energy intensive) grew faster than average (Yuskavage, 1996).

Also of note is the timing: Energy demand essentially remained the same between 1975 and 1985, but has grown quite fast since. Between 1975 and 1985 real oil prices doubled, and federal mile-per-gallon requirements for cars were established and increased. Since 1985 real oil prices have dropped and

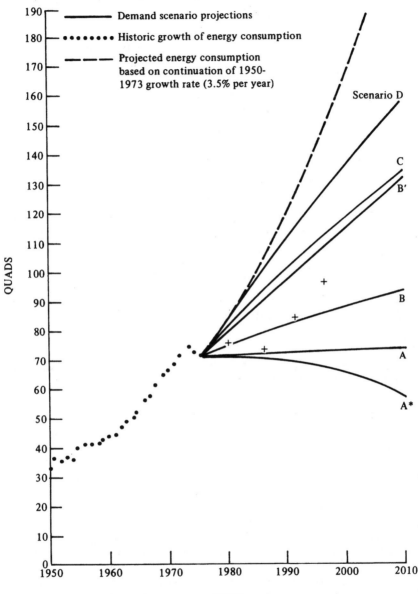

Figure 4.6   Possible annual energy demand futures in the CONAES study. All scenarios assume 2% annual GDP growth, except B′ (3%). The crosses (added by author) represent actual U.S. energy use in 1980, 1985, 1990, and 1995. A "quad" is a quadrillion (10^{15}) Btu. *Source:* National Academy of Sciences (1980). *Energy in Transition 1985–2010: Final Report of the Committee on Nuclear and Alternative Energy Systems.* © 1980 National Academy of Sciences. Reprinted with permission.

TABLE 4.4   Scenarios in the CONAES Energy Futures Study Shown in Figure 4.6

Scenario	Elements of Energy Policy	Energy Price Ratio, in Constant Dollars (2010/1975)	Average Annual Real GDP Growth[a]
A*	Very aggressive, requires some lifestyle changes	4	2%
A	Aggressive, aimed at maximum efficiency, minor lifestyle change	4	2%
B	Moderate, slowly incorporates efficiency improvement	2	2%
B'	Same as B, but with 3% annual GDP growth	2	3%
C	Current (1975) policies continue	1	2%
D	Energy prices lowered by subsidy	0.66	2%

[a]All assume 2% annual real economic growth except B', which assumes 3%.

the auto fuel economy standard has been frozen at 27.5 miles per gallon. Dynamic issues like this are discussed in Chapter 7.

EXAMPLE OF DYNAMIC END-USE ANALYSIS: RESIDENTIAL REFRIGERATION ENERGY IN SWEDEN

A recent example of detailed energy end-use analysis can be found in an article entitled "Dynamics of Appliance Energy Efficiency in Sweden" (Swisher, 1994). The abstract is reprinted verbatim:

We discuss the results of a time-dynamic analysis of household appliance electricity use and efficiency improvement in Sweden. We focus on refrigerators and freezers but also consider washing machines and other appliances. In our scenarios, we consider minimum performance standards that remove the least efficient products from the market, as well as public procurement (technology push) to accelerate the high-efficiency appliance market. The scenarios show that, while current efficiency trends are likely to keep appliance energy use roughly constant, progressive performance standards could reduce consumption by about 35% by 2010. This level of savings is based on new-model consumption savings of nearly 70%, but not all of the efficiency improvements are translated into energy savings because of an increased number of units and the time required to remove old units from service. Moving the high-efficiency end of the market via the public procurement process accelerates energy-saving potential earlier in time and is particularly effective in combination with energy performance standards.

The abstract formally states the process we outlined about electricity demand for the Alpha Nuclear Power Plant: Sum the end uses multiplied by their energy (or power) requirements, taking into account trends in efficiency, growth, and saturation. For example, Swisher explicitly considered a "technical procurement" option, which guarantees industry that if it brings out a more efficient model, at least a minimum number will be purchased (such industry/government/consumer agreements are more common in Sweden than in the United States).

This approach can be used for many impacts besides electricity [e.g., water (device = shower heads, toilets, or type of irrigation) or gasoline (device = automobiles), etc.]. With changing efficiencies for new devices, the total gloof requirement is

$$\text{Gloof per year} = \sum_{\text{all devices}} (\text{Device})(\text{Gloof per year per device})$$

In general, gloof use can depend both on when a device was produced and on how old it is. In fact, Swisher assumes that efficiency does decrease with age somewhat, but, for simplicity, we assume that age is unimportant. On the other hand, the production year is crucial because the efficiency of new devices may change dramatically, especially as a result of policy. Then the specific expression for electrical devices is

$$E_{\text{year } i} = \sum_{\text{prod. year } j} N_{\text{year } i, \text{ prod. year } j} \, E_{\text{prod. year } j} \tag{4.1}$$

where $N_{\text{year } i, \text{ prod. year } j}$ is the number of devices in year i that were produced in year j. This information is called age class or cohort data. In order to use information on how energy use by new models varies over time, Equation 4.1 requires age class data, either actual or predicted. (Using simple birth–death models to follow age classes through time is covered in more detail under dynamics and lags in Chapter 7.) A general observation is that because electrical appliances have lifetimes of 10 to 20 years, there will be delays of 10 to 20 years in the full impact of improved efficiency.

Tables 4.5 and 4.6 show some of the information used/assumed by Swisher to construct an end-use-based projection of energy use by Sweden's residential refrigerators and freezers through the year 2010. Especially important are the assumed efficiency improvements: Table 4.6 indicates a factor of 2 to 3 improvement for new models between 1996 and 2005. These are technically feasible and economically beneficial, but not guaranteed without specific policies. Studies like this one are often an important part of the debate about the impact of implementing such policies.

Before we look at Swisher's results, let us make a quick $I = PAT$ estimate of what to expect for the simplest case, where no further efficiency improve-

TABLE 4.5   Assumed Saturation Factors (Number of Devices per Household, Expressed in %) for Residential Refrigeration Appliances in Sweden

Dwelling Type	Single Family		Multifamily		Total	
Year	1987	2010	1987	2010	1987	2010
Population (million)					8.41	9.21
Households (million)	1.77	1.88	1.95	2.24	3.72	4.12
Saturation (%)						
Refrigerators	93	75	70	55	81	64
Freezers	111	80	40	60	74	69
Refrigerator-freezers	15	85	40	80	28	82
Total	219	240	150	195	183	215

Source: Swisher (1994).

ments occur and 1990's best efficiencies enter Swedish households completely by the year 2010. We can see that for the period 1986–2010:

1. From Table 4.5, the number of households will increase by a factor of 4.12/3.72 = 1.11.
2. From Table 4.5, the saturation of residential refrigeration devices will increase by a factor of 215/183 = 1.17.
3. From Table 4.6, the average energy intensity of residential refrigeration devices will decrease by a factor of 0.7/1.1 = 0.64 (this factor is approximately the same for all three appliance types).

TABLE 4.6   Assumed Standards for New Residential Refrigeration Appliances in Sweden

New Appliances	Average kWh/year (1990)	Best kWh/year (1990)	Energy Performance Standards (kWh/year per liter of Conditioned Space)			
			1996	1999	2002	2005
Refrigerator	1.1	0.7	1.1	0.7	0.5	0.35
Freezer	2.2	1.5	2.2	1.5	1.1	0.7
with technical procurement			2.2	1.1	0.8	0.6
Refrigerator-freezer	1.5	1.1	1.5	0.8	0.9	0.7
with technical procurement			1.5	1.1	0.6	0.45

Lifetime of devices, 15 years. Sizes: refrigerators, 270 l (10 cu ft); freezers, 220 l (8 cu ft); refrigerator-freezers, 200/100 l (7 cu ft/3.5 cu ft) for refrigerator/freezer compartments, respectively. Technical procurement is an agreement by industry to produce higher-efficiency devices in return for guaranteed sales of a minimum number of units.
Source: Swisher (1994).

Then the energy requirements in 2010 will be $(1.11)(1.17)(0.64) = 0.83$ times that in 1987. In this scenario, a decrease in T more than cancels the growth in P and A.

Figure 4.7 shows Swisher's results. There are several outcomes, depending on the strength of the efficiency measures taken. The reference case corresponds closely to our previous assumptions and shows a decrease of roughly 7% (estimated from Fig. 4.7), whereas we predicted a decrease of 17%. That is good agreement, given that we neglected the drop in efficiency with age and other details that Swisher included. One outcome ("1990 Efficiency") shows a dip until the mid-1990s as very old models are retired, but then with constant efficiency the growth in the units increases electrical requirements again. The other options show decreasing electrical requirements because new device energy efficiency increases throughout the whole period. In the most ambitious scenario, 2010 electricity use is reduced by about 38% from that in 1990.

Even this "clean" and vivid example is based on many assumptions and on time-consuming and expensive analysis. More important than the actual

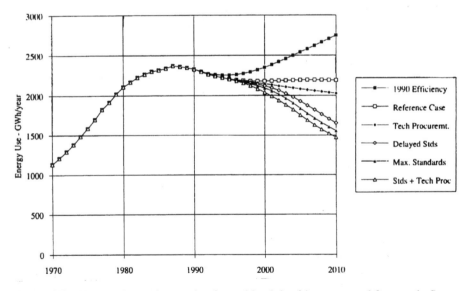

Figure 4.7 Energy demand scenarios for residential refrigerators and freezers in Sweden through 2010. Recent increases in efficiency produce a short-term decrease in energy. However, without continued efficiency increase the growth of households and of per household ownership causes a longer-term increase. Several scenarios incorporate continued efficiency improvement in new units, in which case electricity requirements continue to decrease. *Source:* J. Swisher (1994). Dynamics of appliance energy efficiency in Sweden. *Energy* 19:1131–1142. © 1994 Elsevier Science Ltd. Reprinted with permission.

numbers in any particular scenario is the range of possibilities and policies, or lack of policies, that affect them. The process of looking at end uses, of mechanistic projection, and of predicting with other independent variables besides time is valuable and increasingly used.

OBJECTIONS TO END-USE ANALYSIS: UNLIMITED WANTS AND INDIRECT EFFECTS

End-use analysis is physically based. In the energy examples used here, there are several assumptions such as:

1. A household will have no more than an assumed number of central air conditioners, televisions, or refrigerators. Household ownership of devices saturates.
2. Annual use per device is known; for example, a household in Illinois will use about 1000 kWh/year for lighting (with incandescent bulbs) or 100 kWh/year per clothes washer (not including the hot water). Such estimates are based on assumptions about how many bulbs are on how long or how many wash loads are done per year. It is then assumed that this use level is constant over time and across income and energy price levels.
3. There is new, energy-gobbling product just over the horizon (the so-called "phantom appliance").
4. In the CONAES study (National Academy of Sciences, 1980), it was concluded that Americans would not want to spend more than about 40 minutes in a car commuting each way, which can be used to estimate an upper limit on commuting energy.

If you are an economist, your heart rate just jumped 100 beats a minute. You know that there are major exceptions to all of these assumptions.

1. My relatives' house in Georgia has two central air-conditioning units; almost everyone I know has several televisions; and it is common for people who purchase a new refrigerator to keep the old one running in the garage for beer and soda. In 1980 refrigerator saturation in Illinois was 122%. Table 4.5 shows that in Sweden the single-family dwelling combined saturation for refrigerators, freezers, and combination refrigerator-freezers was 215%. The typical household had, on average, a refrigerator, a freezer, plus some extra.
2. Why should people limit the number of hours of "on" time for lighting or the number of bulbs? Daniel Luten wrote in the 1960s that he had never met someone under age 30 who had ever turned off a light switch. What pressure is there to limit the use of an appliance?

3. In 1981 the personal computer was unknown; today it is commonplace, along with the 40-inch TV, tanning booth, Jacuzzi, and microwave oven.

4. Air conditioning, bucket seats, quadraphonic sound, mobile telephones, and faxes make cars more tolerable and less disruptive of normal activities, so who is to say that the 40-minute commuting limit holds today?

Objections like this are covered by the economic view that says that the use of anything is dependent on its price and that any predictive method that does not account for price is incomplete and will fail. This view says roughly:

> If energy is cheap enough and/or people are rich enough, they will acquire more devices to use more of it. Human wants are unlimited. Why not? is the flip but telling question about consumption. In practice, the reason why not is price. Savings from efficiency improvements are subject to a rebound effect when consumers operate a device more because efficiency has made it less expensive to use. High prices could reduce use to below the amounts here, and low prices could lead to use exceeding them. In the medium and long terms, there must be price signals to control consumption, and these should be explicitly included in forecasting.

This view holds that in fact the increased price of electricity, much of it attributable to the Alpha's construction costs, was a major factor in XYZ Power Company's reduced demand growth in the 1980s. Electricity demand forecasting today also includes explicit price dependence.

The economic approach is valid to some degree, especially in the long term. See the accompanying box. End-use analysis remains a powerful tool in many applications, but it must be used carefully.

A second concern is that energy end-use analysis, as usually practiced, almost always ignores the energy to make things. It is especially important when changes are occurring and old equipment is being retired prematurely (another example of dynamics and lags). This problem can be solved by careful (physical) analysis, however. We will deal with this in detail in Chapter 8.

Quick Jokes to Vindicate the Economist's Skepticism

1. Questionnaire: A light switch is used to:
   a. Turn lights on
   b. Turn lights off
   c. Both
   d. Neither
   e. Unfamiliar with item

2. Apocryphal story from early days of energy research (ca. 1972): A questionnaire to assess residential energy use was being assembled by a team composed of engineers and physical and social scientists. A psychologist proposed this: "How often do you run the air conditioner with the windows open?" The engineers declared that a ridiculous question, and insisted that it be removed. When the team visited participating households, the first one was running the air conditioner with the windows open.

EXAMPLE OF END-USE ANALYSIS: GLOBAL ENERGY FUTURES

Four researchers, J. Goldemberg, T. Johansson, A. Reddy, and R. Williams (from Brazil, Sweden, India, and the United States, respectively), have applied end-use thinking to total global energy demand in the year 2020 (Goldemberg et al., 1988). (Problem 2.4 is based on this work.) They conclude that developing countries could attain a lifestyle equivalent to that of present western Europe with an average power of 1 kW per capita. (This is the total power, including all sources, and not just limited to electricity. In the United States the average is about 10 kW per capita.) In developing countries this is accomplished by acquiring efficient new energy devices and systems. Meanwhile the developing countries could reduce their per capita use from the present average of 5 kW to 2.5 kW. This is also accomplished by acquiring efficient energy systems, but the process is slow because of lags from waiting for present (inefficient) systems to wear out and be replaced. Figure 4.8 shows the schematic for the calculation. Their result, 11.2 TW in 2020, is only 9% greater than the 1980 world total of 10.3 TW, and significantly below "conventional" predictions. (TW = terawatt = 10^{12} W.) However, it is sobering to note that in 1995 world energy use was already at 12.1 TW, greater than their figure for 2020.

PROBLEMS

Level of difficulty is indicated as Easier/Moderate/Harder. Problems marked "(Spreadsheet?)" can be fruitfully approached using a spreadsheet. They need not be, however.

4.1. (Easier) There are several systems of units used in energy matters. There is little recourse but to learn how to convert one to another. As always, there is potential confusion between energy (a stock) and power (a flow). In this chapter we used power units of quads/year (10^{15} Btu/year) and terawatts (1 TW = 10^{12} W).

   (a) Use the information in Appendix 2 to obtain the conversion factor between quads/year and terawatts.

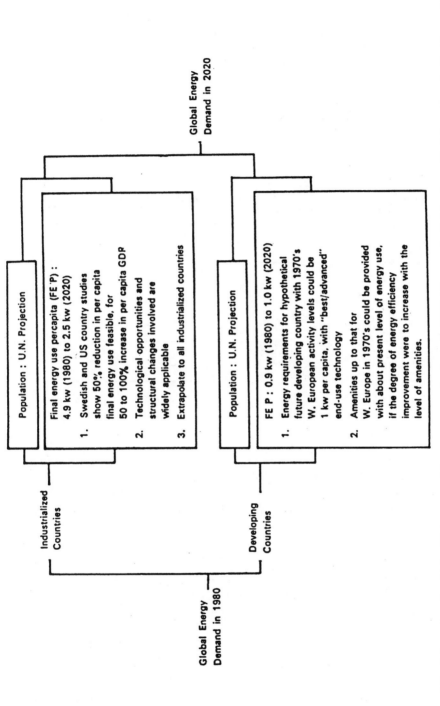

Figure 4.8 Schematic of a high-efficiency world energy scenario through 2020. *Source:* J. Goldemberg, T. Johansson, A. Reddy, and R. Williams (1988). *Energy for a Sustainable World.* © 1988 Wiley Eastern. Reprinted with permission.

The diagram contains the following text:

Global Energy Demand in 2020

Industrialized Countries

Population : U.N. Projection

Final energy use percapita (FE'P) : 4.9 kw (1980) to 2.5 kw (2020)

1. Swedish and US country studies show 50% reduction in per capita final energy use feasible, for 50 to 100% increase in per capita GDP
2. Technological opportunities and structural changes involved are widely applicable
3. Extrapolate to all industrialized countries

Developing Countries

Population : U.N. Projection

FE P : 0.9 kw (1980) to 1.0 kw (2020)

1. Energy requirements for hypothetical future developing country with 1970's W. European activity levels could be 1 kw per capita, with "best/advanced" end-use technology
2. Amenities up to that for W. Europe in 1970's could be provided with about present level of energy use, if the degree of energy efficiency improvement were to increase with the level of amenities.

Global Energy Demand in 1980

(b) In 1990 world energy use was 10.2 TW (i.e., the average power was 10.2 TW). U.S. energy use was 84 quads/year (i.e., the average power was 84 quads/year). What fraction of world use was U.S. use?

4.2. (Moderate) An end-use-based projection of your personal residential electricity time line: Determine how your per capita household electricity consumption (in kilowatt-hours/year) demand will develop over time by charting your acquisition of appliances and devices. Set up a table as follows:

Year Acquired	Device Name	kWh/year for Device	kWh/year for All Devices Acquired to Date

(a) Start by listing what you have now. Then fill in future plans and hopes. Use the following list. For uses not covered, estimate.

(b) Sketch a graph of your household kilowatt-hours/year against time.

(c) Using the 5-year points from (b) and assuming geometric annual growth, calculate the average annual growth rate for each period. Is this large?

(d) Criticize this approach. Include efficiency, number of people/household, geographic differences, other issues.

End Use	kWh/year
Space heating	
Electric (resistance)	10,000
Gas (fan only)	500
Refrigerator	1,000
Freezer	800
Water heater (electric)	4,500

Washing machine (not including hot water)	100
Electric stove	780
Clothes dryer	
Electric	1,000
Gas	70
Air conditioner	
Room	1,000
Central	2,000
Lighting	1,000
Other uses/devices (Meier et al., 1992)	
Aquarium/terrarium	548
Audio system	50
Black-and-white TV	40
Blanket	120
Bottled water cooler	300
Ceiling fan	50
Clock	25
Coffee maker	50
Color TV	250
Computer	130
Crankcase heater	200
Dehumidifier	400
Dishwasher	200
Exhaust fan	15
Engine heater	250
Furnace fan	500
Garbage disposer	10
Grow light and accessories	800
Hair dryer	40
Humidifier	100
Instant hot water	160
Iron	50
Microwave oven	120
Mower	10
Heat tape	100
Pool pump	1,500
Spa/hot tub	2,000
Sump/sewage pump	40
Toaster/toaster oven	50
Vacuum cleaner	30
VCR	40
Waterbed heater	900
Well pump	400
Whole house fan	80
Window fan	20

4.3. (Moderate) (Spreadsheet?) Assume that there are 500,000 residential refrigerators in the XYZ Power Company service area, each using 1200
kWh/year. A new, cost-effective model is available; it uses 700 kWh/
year. Assume the refrigerator lifetime is 15 years (exactly) and that the
present refrigerator population is evenly distributed across ages 1 to 15
years. For the following, the time horizon is 30 years.

(a) Plot relatively accurately the summed kilowatt-hours/year versus
time for all residential refrigerators under these assumptions:
   1. No change in number of units; no model change.
   2. No change in number of units; all units change instantaneously
      to new models.
   3. No change in number of units; all new units are new models, old
      units die a natural death.
   4. 2% annual growth (geometric) of number of units; no model
      change.
   5. 2% annual growth in number of units; all units change instanta-
      neously to new models.
   6. 2% annual growth of number of units; all new units are more
      efficient; old units die a natural death.

(b) The Alpha Power Plant has a peak capacity of 955 MW. Compare
this with the power not needed under option 1.

(c) Briefly compare the impacts of these scenarios for an audience of
your choice (e.g., city council, power plant sitting board, chamber
of commerce, environmental group). Note that compelling cases are
usually made relative to a base case, and assume your audience wants
to know *when* as well as what.

5 Economic Considerations, Discount Rates, and Benefit–Cost Analysis

EXAMPLE: ECONOMICS OF ENERGY-EFFICIENT LIGHT BULB. REDUCING T TO OFFSET INCREASES IN P

End-use analysis is used to generate scenarios; it is often used in a debate to convince policy-makers, or anyone, to "do it my way." Economic questions almost always arise: What does it cost? Who is going to pay for it? When must it be paid? The efficient light bulb is an example. These bulbs are in the limelight today. Typically, the compact fluorescent uses one-fourth as much electric power as an incandescent to provide the same light level. Table 5.1 shows how they compare.

The question is: How does saving energy by switching to these efficient bulbs compare in cost to building more power plants, and to whom? Let us pose the problem this way (there are other ways): suppose more residential lighting is required. This can be supplied with new power plants plus new light bulbs (we neglect the cost of new power lines, etc.). We will compare incandescent bulbs plus the portion of a power plant they require versus compact fluorescent bulbs plus the (smaller) portion of a power plant they require.

For now we consider only the cost of purchase of the bulbs and construction of the power plants, the first costs. Later we will include the cost of operation.

First (Capital) Cost of One Deliverable Kilowatt   A new power plant costs about $5000 to $7000 (1996) per kilowatt of capacity.[1] To deliver a kilowatt to the customer, we need to account for distribution losses (around 10%) and the necessity that a utility have a 20% reserve margin. Therefore we need

---

[1]This figure is controversial. It is correct for recently completed or soon-to-be-completed nuclear plants, but old nuclear plants were much cheaper, around $1000/kW. Coal-burning plants typically are listed round $2000/kW, though they are extremely hard to site today. Hydro projects, especially in places devoid of people, are even cheaper, though there also rages controversy about their "true" costs in terms of altered landscapes and dislocated local people, even if there are relatively few of them. Typically, these people have lived there a long time and are strongly linked to the land. Solar/wind is starting to penetrate sunny places, but not in most places. For all, there is the question of how the cost is changing over time.

Three Approaches to Energy Management on a Single Page

Figure 5.1   Newspaper advertisement, 1983.

Figure 5.1 is copied from a 1983 newspaper advertisement of a do-it-yourself home improvement store. It shows many options in residential energy management. Among them:

1. *Supply Side.* Use a wood-burning fireplace.
2. *Efficiency.* Put an insulating jacket on the water heater to reduce heat loss.
3. *Efficiency through Management over Time.* Install a clock set-back thermostat, which adjusts temperatures up and down according to time of day.

All of these are technical solutions but with differing behavioral components. Water heater insulation requires almost zero behavioral change, while operating a fireplace requires significant day-to-day attention.

TABLE 5.1   Vital Statistics of Incandescent and Compact Fluorescent Bulbs Providing the Same Light Level

	Incandescent	Compact Fluorescent
Initial cost ($)	0.75	12
Lifetime (hours)	700	10,000
Power (W)	75	17

(1 kW)(1.1)(1.2) = 1.32 kW of power plant. This costs (1.32)($5000 to $7000) = $6600 to $9200 to build.

First Cost of the Bulbs   Assume that we want the amount of light produced by 13.33 75-W incandescent bulbs, drawing a total power of 1 kW. The same amount of light is produced by 13.33 17-W fluorescent bulbs drawing a total power of 227 W = 0.227 kW. Assume that the bulbs are on continuously. Because incandescent bulbs last only 700 hours, we need to buy (24)(365)/700 = 12.5 bulbs per year to keep one incandescent lit continuously. Compact fluorescents last 10,000 hours, so we need to buy (24)(365)/10,000 = 0.876 bulbs per year to keep one compact fluorescent lit continuously.

Over the 30-year lifetime of the power plant, therefore, we need to spend (13.33 bulbs lit)(12.5 bulbs purchased per year/bulb lit)($0.75/bulb purchased)(30 years) = $3750 for incandescent bulbs. For fluorescent bulbs, we need to spend (13.33 bulbs lit)(0.876 bulbs purchased per year/bulb lit)($12/bulb purchased)(30 years) = $4205.

The costs and benefits are summarized in Table 5.2.

This rough analysis shows that the total societal capital cost of the fluorescent bulb option is about half that of the incandescent option. The capital cost of the consumer is roughly the same, but the cost of the power company is reduced by about 75%. The power company's capital costs are concentrated at the beginning of the 30-year plant lifetime, while the consumer's bulb purchases are spread out over the 30 years. Including the operating cost to the residential consumer, that is, the cost of electricity, will affect this balance as well. We deal with that later, after addressing the question of how people weigh expenditures now versus later (discounting) in making decisions.

DISCOUNTING THE FUTURE

Time:

Economists calculate.
Planners obsess.
Parents hope.

TABLE 5.2   Capital (Not Operating) Costs of Providing Light by Two Options

Option	1. Use incandescent bulbs, build new power plant to deliver 1 kW	2. Use more efficient fluorescent bulbs giving same light, build power plant to deliver 0.23 kW
Cost to:		
Residential customer	$3750 for 5000 incandescent bulbs purchased over 30 years	$4205 for 350 compact fluorescent bulbs purchased over 30 years
Power company	$6600–$9900 first cost for a deliverable 1.0 kW (likely passed on to customers in higher energy costs)	$1500–$2247 first cost for a deliverable 0.227 kW (likely passed on to customers in higher energy costs)
Society (sum of customer and power company)	Total: $10,350–$13,650 over 30 years	Total: $5700–6300 over 30 years

Young and old sometimes live at the edge (see the accompanying box and Figure 5.2).

Wilderness proponents rhapsodize.

Poets rage.

Time:

My kingdom for a horse.

Eat dessert first.

The grasshopper and the ant.

Get a good education.

Strike while the iron is hot.

Get a credit card.

You can't take it with you.

Americans don't save as much as Japanese.

The seventh generation.

He who dies with the most toys wins.

Seize the time.

Youth is wasted on the young.

I want it all, and I want it now.

Sweet bird of youth.

All paths lead to the grave.
My children's children.

Personal Discount Rate: Three Stages in the Life of Lester Germer, 1897–1971

Figure 5.2 Lester Germer (b. 1897) climbing the chimney on "Updraft" at the Shawangunks in the Hudson Valley, 1966. The rope is slack and is for safety only.

Stage 1 (1897–1920)

Walked from Ithaca to Syracuse, New York, nonstop (50 miles). Flew in World War I. Wore white scarf. Shot down twice in France.

Stage 2 (1920–1950)

Physicist. Columbia Ph.D. Worked at Bell Laboratories, Murray Hill, New Jersey. Family. Insurance policy. Pension plan. In 1927 collaborated with C. J. Davisson on pivotal electron diffraction experiment. Nobel Prize to Davisson and G. P. Thomson (England).

Stage 3 (1950–1971)

1950. Took up rock climbing seriously.

1952. Was on first ascent of the "Jackie," a climb at the Shawangunks climbing area in the Hudson Valley.

1956. Climbed Devils Tower, Wyoming. Was on a first ascent in Cirque of the Towers region, Wind River Range, Wyoming.

1962. Involved in disaster on the Grand Teton. Climbing party (inadequately led by someone else) pinned by bad weather. 21-year assistant leader died of hypothermia. Germer suffered frostbite. He and party rescued. Retired by Bell Labs. Research professor at Cornell University.

1962–1971. Slept in office, kept case of ale in file cabinet, ice-climbed frozen waterfalls in Cornell gorges, journeyed to rocks to climb, mentored young physicists and climbers, slept in woods.

1966. Hiked to Everest Base Camp in Nepal. 6 weeks trekking, 6 weeks recovering in Japan. Rejected a gift climbing helmet because it was too hot, continued to climb bareheaded.

1967. Walked from Binghamton to Ithaca, New York (50 miles) for 50th college reunion.

1968. Broke bone in foot while working out on granddaughter's balance beam.

1971. Died of heart attack while climbing "Double Chin" at the Shawangunks and was caught on the rope.

Lester Germer's behavior implies that he valued the future most during stage 2, midlife, when he pursued a career and raised a family. During stages 1 and 3, he was more of a daredevil and seemed to worry less about the future. (My great-aunt Edith lived a Victorian life in upstate New York and never smoked, yet took up cigarettes at age 75. She used to burn holes in her dress.)

Discounting, a formalization of how we value things separated by time, is a difficult concept, with an extensive literature. It is *not* inflation. It is based on human evaluation of real goods and opportunities. It is related to the interest rate on investments. Roughly speaking, it is summarized by the answer to this question.

Q: Would you rather be given $1000 today or in 10 years?

Most humans would respond in a way that favors the present. For example:

A: I want it now. If not, I want to be paid to defer the pleasure I could have by spending that money; hence I want interest on my savings.

or

A: I am willing to pay a premium to have the money now instead of later; hence I am willing to sacrifice the interest I could get if I saved the money.

In each case the interest is a consequence of valuing now more than later. I believe humans discount the future because of their perceived mortality, but that is a deep issue, and I am no expert. I will accept it as a revealed behavior of humans, myself included.

The most common form of discounting is geometrical (exponential). This says that today we value future consumption according to

$$\text{PV}(C_t) = \frac{C_t}{(1 + d)^{t-1}} \qquad (5.1)$$

where $\text{PV}(C_t)$ is the present value of consumption occurring t years from now. Note that d can be positive, negative, or zero. A positive (negative) d implies that the future is valued less (more) than the present. Can you think of practical examples for the three possibilities?

The almost-equivalent exponential form is

$$\text{PV}(C_t) = C_t e^{-dt}$$

For the geometric form, I have switched back to the common, but dimensionally sloppy, notation.

The following are important issues concerning discounting:

1. Discounting need not be geometric. Even if it is, the discount rate need not be constant over time or between groups. For example, Cropper and Portney (1992) inferred discount rates by asking people to compare medical measures to save X lives now versus Y lives T years in the future. They found (geometric) discount rates ranging from 17%/year for $T = 5$ years to 3.8% for $T = 100$ years. Parents had higher discount rates than nonparents for $T = 25$ years, but there was no difference for $T = 5$ to 10 years. Older people had higher discount rates than younger, blacks higher than whites. Income and education had no effect.
2. What numeraire should be used? ($, physical units, ...)
3. What is the system boundary (both in time and conceptually)?

Suppose you will have $1 10 years from now. What is it worth to you now? Assuming geometric discounting, we can use Equation 5.1 and the Rule of 70 to construct Table 5.3. Another interpretation of the negative discount rate is that one needs more now because what one has will deteriorate, rather than accrue, over time.

TABLE 5.3 Discount Rates Corresponding to Different Present Values of $1 10 Years in the Future

t (years)	Present Value ($)	Inferred d with Geometric Discounting (%/year)
10	1	0
10	0.50	+7
10	2	−7
10	0.74	+3
10	1.34	−3

BENEFIT–COST ANALYSIS

We do benefit–cost analysis informally every minute: Is it worthwhile do mow the lawn, to do homework, to invest our brains and hearts in the plight of starving or warring people half a globe away or next door, or to call Mom? Benefit–cost analysis is also a formal economic discipline, not without deserved controversy, yet fundamentally necessary.

Most activities have both benefits and costs, B and C. For a given time period, we want $B > C$. Or, assuming that $d > 0$, given that $B = C$, we want B early and C late. Often, however, C precedes B, as shown in Figure 5.3a. The result of a benefit–cost analysis can be expressed in absolute terms (benefits less costs) or in normalized terms, such as the ratio of benefits to costs. I prefer the latter. One formal statement of the benefit–cost ratio is

$$\frac{B}{C} = \frac{\sum_{t=1}^{N} \frac{B_t}{(1 + d)^{t-1}}}{\sum_{t=1}^{N} \frac{C_t}{(1 + d)^{t-1}}} \tag{5.2}$$

where the B_t and C_t are the benefits and costs in year t, respectively.

What discount rate should one use? In Table 5.4 I sketch a few typical discount rates "revealed" by human behavior.

EXAMPLE: VARYING THE DISCOUNT RATE. SOMETIMES WE LIKE IT LOW, SOMETIMES HIGH

A general statement about people who champion environmental issues is that they have a long-range view, which implies a low discount rate. However, there are times when promoting a *high* discount rate has served the environmental side of a debate. Consider the two benefit curves shown in Figure 5.3a and b.

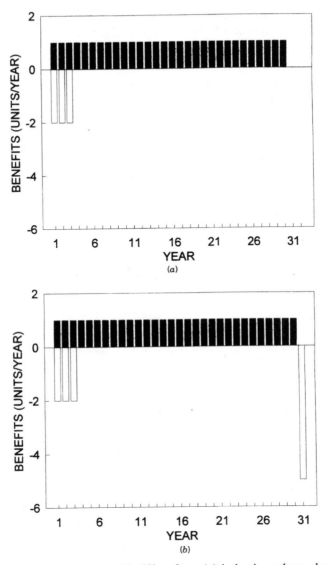

Figure 5.3 Two benefit curves. (*b*) differs from (*a*) in having a large decommissioning cost in year 30.

Figure 5.3*a* typifies the discussion of the proposed Grand Canyon dams in the mid-1960s. Proponents of the dams touted the benefits of hydroelectricity, water for irrigation and municipal water supplies, and lake recreation. All benefits came after the cost of building the dams, and no costs were envisioned afterwards.

Figure 5.3*b* typifies the discussion of a nuclear power plant. The benefit curve shares common elements with that of the dam: early cost, later benefits.

TABLE 5.4   Time Horizon and Corresponding Discount Rate, Assuming Time Horizon = Halving Time and Using the Rule of 70, Which Is Based on Geometric Discounting

Entity	Time Horizon	r (%/year)	Notes
Society	100 years	0.7	U.S. Constitution
Corporation	3 years	23	Promotion time scale for managers
Person			
Juvenile	1 week	3600	
Teenager	2 months	420	
Youth	2 years	35	
Midlife	35 years	2	
Old age	5 years	14	
Richard IV, cornered in battle	10 seconds	221×10^6	His frenzy to flee is the opposite of accepting death
Culture	30 years (human generation time)	2.3	Sexual revolution, rock and roll
Politician	1–3 years	70 to 23	Congressional elections are held every 2 years

However, there is an added element—the cost of decommissioning the plant at the end of its useful life. One could argue that a scrapping, recycle, cleanup cost should be associated with any facility. For a nuclear plant it is argued that this is relatively large.[2]

Opponents of the Grand Canyon dams had two disagreements with the benefits and costs as given by the proponents (the U.S. Bureau of Reclamation):

1. They thought the benefits were overstated, especially regarding lake recreation.
2. They thought that the costs were understated, especially regarding lost river recreation.

Dam opponents promoted objection 1 by using a discount rate argument: They claimed that the discount rate used by the Bureau of Reclamation (around 3%/year) was too low! Opponents argued for a higher discount rate, which reduced the numerator in B/C and made the project less desirable.

For a benefit curve like Figure 5.3b, however, the opposite is true. Nuclear proponents argue that even if decommissioning is expensive, it is 30 years

[2]Today XYZ Power Company's residential bill includes a decommissioning adjustment of 0.044¢/kWh, which increases the electricity cost by about 0.4%.

away and its present value is low with a reasonable discount rate. Opponents argue that 30 years is not very long, and the way to formalize that is to lower the discount rate.

These positions are summarized in Table 5.5.

In principle, discounting can be applied to any flow or stock, from dollars to barrels of oil to acres of trees to tons of CO_2 to numbers of condors. The essence of the argument is that *we* assign value to the flows or stocks in order to reach a decision. Discounting, it is said, institutionalizes a general, revealed human behavioral tendency. In a letter to the editor of *Science,* Kasting and Schultz (1996) argue for a zero discount rate for anything more than a generation. A response from economists disagrees.

Do you agree?

THE EFFICIENT LIGHT BULB AGAIN: BENEFIT–COST ANALYSIS

There are two generic problems with benefit–cost analysis. First, there is the difficult question of what to measure and whether to declare it a positive cost or a negative benefit. We will find that problematic in this calculation for the efficient light bulb. The second is in the use of a *B/C* ratio (or any other simplifying summary indicator) to convey information about the more detailed picture shown in the full graph of costs and benefits versus time. For example, there are infinitely many possible benefit curves tht will yield the same *B/C* ratio. Other summary indicators in benefit–cost analysis—payback time and internal rate of return—have the same problem.

B/C RATIO, PAYBACK TIME, AND INTERNAL RATE OF RETURN: THREE ATTEMPTS AT SUMMARIZING A BENEFIT CURVE (OPTIONAL DETAILS)

We illustrate by applying the definitions to the benefit curve in Figure 5.4.

B/C Ratio

For no discounting, that is, $d = 0$, $B/C = 30 * 1/(1 * 5 + 1 * 10) = 30/15 = 2.0$. For $d \neq 0$ we could evaluate the equation by tedious brute force. In this case, however, we can use Important Equation 2, as follows:

$$\frac{B}{C} = \frac{\sum_{t=1}^{30} \frac{1}{(1 + d)^{t-1}}}{5 + \frac{10}{(1 + d)^{30}}}$$

The numerator contains a familiar geometric series:

TABLE 5.5 Illustration of When High, and Sometimes Low, Discount Rates Are Promoted by Environmentalists

Issue	Proponents (Value for Discount Rate)	Opponents (Value for Discount Rate)	Notes
Grand Canyon dams	U.S. Bureau of Reclamation (low)	Sierra Club (high)	Costs precede benefits. Opponents wanted higher discount rate to deemphasize the touted benefits, which it considered costs.
Nuclear power plant	Nuclear industry (high)	Prairie Alliance (Midwest antinuclear group) (low)	Large decommissioning cost at end of facility life. Antinuclear groups wanted to assure that cost is weighted heavily.
Efficient light bulbs instead of new power plants	Environmentalists, life-cost minimizers (low)	Some power companies (high)	Costs precede benefits. Environmentalists want to assure that benefits are weighted heavily.

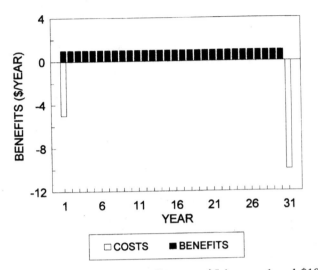

Figure 5.4 Hypothetical benefit curve. Costs are $5 in year 1 and $10 in year 31. Benefits of $1 occur yearly from year 1 through year 30.

$$\frac{B}{C} = \frac{1 + \dfrac{1}{(1 + d)^1} + \cdots + \dfrac{1}{(1 + d)^{29}}}{5 + \dfrac{10}{(1 + d)^{30}}}$$

Using Important Equation 2, noting that here $x = 1/(1 + d)$, this is rewritten as

$$\frac{B}{C} = \frac{\dfrac{(1 + d)^{30} - 1}{d(1 + d)^{29}}}{5 + \dfrac{10}{(1 + d)^{30}}} \tag{5.3}$$

In Table 5.6 we evaluate Equation 5.3 for various values of d. We see that B/C initially increases as d increases from 0 to 4%/year. This is because an increasing discount rate deemphasizes the large cost in year 31 relative to the benefits that are distributed over 30 years (as in the preceding nuclear decommissioning example). As d increases further these benefits are deemphasized relative to the cost of $5 in the first year, and B/C decreases, passing through the break-even point for $d = 25\%$/year. If d becomes very large, all years except the first are deemphasized, and B/C approaches a limit of 1/5.

TABLE 5.6   B/C versus Discount Rate d for the Benefit Curve in Figure 5.4

d (%/year)	B/C	d (%/year)	B/C	d (%/year)	B/C
0	2.000	20	1.185	40	0.700
1	2.099	21	1.141	50	0.600
2	2.171	22	1.101	60	0.533
3	2.214	23	1.063	80	0.450
4	2.225	24	1.028	100	0.400
5	2.207	25	0.996	∞	0.200
6	2.164	26	0.966		
7	2.103	27	0.939		
8	2.029	28	0.913		
9	1.946	29	0.888		
10	1.861	30	0.866		

Internal Rate of Return

The internal rate of return (IRR) is defined as the value of the discount rate for which $B/C = 1$. An equivalent statement is: "Costs are considered deposits into, and benefits are considered withdrawals from, a bank account which is empty at the start of the project. When the balance is positive, interest accrues at rate r; the balance is increased. When the balance is negative, interest is charged at the same rate r and the balance becomes more negative. At the end of the project the account is again empty. What value of r makes this possible?"

We saw in Table 5.6 that B/C passes through 1.0 for $d = 25\%$/year. This internal rate of return is considerably higher than the interest obtainable in a bank account.

Payback Time

This is the number of years from startup at which the accumulated benefits equal the accumulated costs. If no discounting is used, this is called *simple payback time*. Here the simple payback time is 5 years. With discounting the payback time is longer, for the same reason that high-interest mortgages take longer to pay back, given by the value of t for which

$$5 = 1 + \frac{1}{(1 + d)^1} + \cdots \frac{1}{(1 + d)^{t-1}} = \frac{1 - \dfrac{1}{(1 + d)^t}}{1 - \dfrac{1}{(1 + d)}} \tag{5.4}$$

Equation 5.4 can be solved exactly [compare Eq. 3.7 with $r = 1/(1 + d)$] or by trial and error. We expect t to be a bit more than 5 years for a small d

and to increase as d increases. For $d = 10\%/\text{year}$, for example, $t = 6.4$ years. For $d = 20\%/\text{year}$, $t = 9.8$ years.

This example illustrates a pitfall of the payback time approach, which implicitly assumes early costs and then consistent benefits, which is a common pattern. The implication is that once the payback year is reached, there will be only net benefits from that time on until the end. However, here the large cost in year 31 violates this view. We need more words than conveyed by payback time to communicate the complexity of this particular benefit curve.

THE EFFICIENT BULB: THE CONSUMER'S VIEW, INCLUDING THE SAVINGS ON ELECTRICITY

For 10,000 hours of light, one can buy a compact fluorescent bulb for $12, or one can purchase 14.3 incandescent bulbs at $0.75 per unit for a total cost of $10.71. There is little difference in the undiscounted capital cost of the two options. However, we have not yet accounted for the electricity savings.

Many people think this is a negligible cost. Let us make a quick estimate: How much does it cost to operate a 100 W bulb for a year? The energy is $(100 \text{ W})(24 * 365 \text{ hours})(1 \text{ kW}/1000 \text{ W}) = 876 \text{ kWh/year}$. Electricity costs about $0.10/kWh, so this amounts to $87.60/year—if the bulb is on all the time. If it is only on an average of 6 hours a day, the yearly electricity cost is about one-fourth of this, or about $22/year. It evidently is *not* negligible compared with the purchase cost.

The *life cost* of the two bulbs will include the electric energy to operate them:

$$\text{Life cost} = \text{Purchase cost} + \text{Operation cost} + \text{Maintenance cost}$$

Table 5.7 lists the life costs for the two bulbs.

The fluorescent's life cost is 34% of the incandescent's life cost, with a savings of about $57 per fluorescent bulb over its lifetime. This is a net benefit of $57 for a net investment of ($12 − $10.71) = $1.29, which appears to be a fabulous bargain.

Sales of these bulbs are increasing, but most residential bulbs are still incandescents. Why have fluorescents not penetrated the market more? One problem is time. If the light is on all the time, the savings occurs in a little over a year. However, if the bulb is used less, the savings are spread out over more time. Human time preference enters. Social scientists working in energy issues have calculated the apparent discount rate for people to refuse this offer, and it comes out amazingly high. We can perform the calculation for 5 years. Figure 5.5 shows the benefit curve.

We assume that the cost is that of the fluorescent bulb, $12. There are two benefits. The first is the avoided cost of 14.3 incandescent bulbs, which is $(10,000/700)(\$0.75/\text{bulb}) = \$10.71$, or $2.14/year. The second is the cost of

TABLE 5.7   Cost (Undiscounted) of Incandescent and Compact Fluorescent Bulbs for 10,000 Hours of Operation (the Fluorescent's Lifetime). Installation and Maintenance Cost Is Assumed Zero

	Bulb Type	
	Incandescent (75 W)	Compact Fluorescent (17 W)
Purchase cost of bulb(s)	(10,000/700)($0.75) = (14.3)($0.75) = $10.71	$12
Electricity cost	(10,000 hours)(75 W) = 750 kWh. At $0.10/kWh, this is $75.	(10,000 hours)(17 W) = 170 kWh. At $0.10/kWh, this is $17.
Total (undiscounted sum)	$85.71	$29

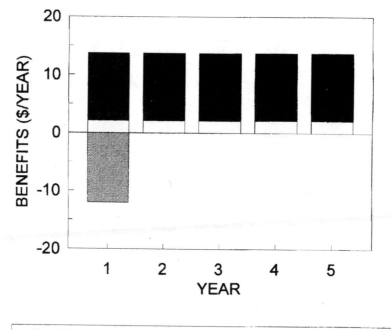

Figure 5.5   Benefit curve for efficient light bulbs. The cost ($12) is for the initial purchase of the efficient fluorescent bulb, which lasts 10,000 hours. The benefits are (1) the 14.3 incandescent bulbs not purchased ($2.14/year) and (2) the electricity saved ($11.60/year).

the saved electricity, which is (58 W)(2000 hours/year)(1 kW/1000 W) ($0.10/kWh) = $11.60/year. The two sum to $13.74/year.[3] Then the benefit–cost ratio is given by

$$\frac{B}{C} = \frac{\$13.74 \left(1 + \dfrac{1}{(1+d)^1} + \cdots + \dfrac{1}{(1+d)^4}\right)}{\$12}$$

$B/C > 1$ for any $d > 0$; analyzed this way for this use pattern, switching to a fluorescent bulb has a positive benefit–cost ratio, pays back in less than a year, and has an infinite internal rate of return. There are two more things to say about that:

1. We use 1 year as the time step. We could use a smaller period, say a month (as is done on home mortgages and car loans). We could even use continuous discounting (using the exponential factor e^{-dt}). Both of these would show that $B/C = 1$ for some period less than year, and hence that payback time is less than a year. The internal rate of return would be high, but finite.

2. The previous result is sensitive to assumptions on the cost of bulbs and electric energy. If the fluorescent costs $30 instead of $12, or if electricity costs $0.07/kWh instead of $0.10/kWh, or if the fluorescent bulb only lasts 5000 hours, or if incandescent bulbs cost only a nickel, or if the fluorescent bulb really uses 50 W, not 17 W, of power, B/C will pass through value 1 for a finite d. For example, B/C for a fluorescent cost of $30 is

$$\frac{B}{C} = \frac{\$13.74 \left(1 + \dfrac{1}{(1+d)^1} + \cdots + \dfrac{1}{(1+d)^4}\right)}{\$30} \tag{5.5}$$

Table 5.8 shows B/C using the initial cost of $30. $B/C > 1$ for $d < 75\%/$ year. Even if the compact fluorescent bulb costs $30 and is used only 2000 hours/year (about one-fourth of the time), it still is an investment that pays an effective interest rate of (and has an internal rate of return of) 75%/year. For $d \to \infty$, $B/C \to 0.458$.

Testing how results change as various input assumptions change is called sensitivity/uncertainty analysis. See Appendix 1.

---

[3]B/C can be changed by variations on the theme of considering benefits as negative costs, or the reverse. There is no totally unambiguous way to decide. The scheme here attempts to mimic what a person used to incandescents would feel when confronted with a $12 bulb purchase. It looks like an immediate investment with a long period of benefits later.

TABLE 5.8 B/C versus d when the Bulb Costs $30

d (%/year)	B/C
0	2.290
10	1.910
20	1.644
30	1.450
50	1.193
70	1.034
71	1.028
72	1.021
73	1.015
74	1.009
75	1.004
76	0.998
77	0.992
78	0.987
79	0.981
80	0.976

PROBLEMS

Level of difficulty is indicated as Easier/Moderate/Harder. Problems marked "(Spreadsheet?)" can be fruitfully approached using a spreadsheet. They need not be, however.

5.1. (Easier) Switching to compact fluorescent bulbs saves electric energy. If the energy comes from a fossil fuel power plant, it also reduces CO_2 emissions. Calculate how much less CO_2 from switching one 75-W in-candescent to a 17-W fluorescent, over the 10,000-hour lifetime. Is this a large number? Possibly useful information: In a coal burning plant, to produce 1 kWh requires about 0.8 lb coal. Assume coal is 100% carbon. Atomic weights: C, 12; O, 16.

5.2. (Easier) From a Real Goods Company catalog, August 1995: Table 5.9 presents data on three different types of light bulbs. All provide the light output equivalent of a 60-W incandescent bulb.

   (a) Calculate the (undiscounted) cost of providing 10,000 hours of light using each option. Assume a reasonable cost of electricity. Which is the better buy?

   (b) If the electricity is produced in a coal-burning power plant, calculate the CO_2 released over 10,000 hours using each option. See Problem 5.1 for additional information.

TABLE 5.9

	First Cost ($)	Lifetime (hours)	Power Use (watts)
Incandescent	0.75	700	60
Halogen	10.00	2,800	52
Compact fluorescent	25.00	10,000	15

5.3. (Moderate) How discount rate affects B/C: Assume you are deciding between two car models that are identical in all ways except that:

Car 1 gets 27 mpg.
Car 2 gets 40 mpg and costs $500 more.

Assume each is to be driven 10,000 miles/year for 10 years. These numbers are fairly realistic, though such cars may not be truly identical in all other ways. That you are buying a car and operating it as stated are givens. You are asked to perform a B/C analysis about spending the extra $500 to reduce fuel expenditures. Think of the $500 differential as the cost and the reduction in gasoline expenditures as the benefits.

(a) Calculate B/C for zero discounting.
(b) For what value of discount rate does $B/C = 1$?
(c) Which car would you buy? Why?

5.4. (Moderate) This is the exercise of Cropper and Portney (1992) mentioned in the text. Each year some people die as a result of exposure to chemical releases to the environment. Suppose you, as a government official, must choose between two programs, to be implemented now, to alleviate this. Program A will save 100 lives this year. Program B will save Y lives T years in the future. The two programs cost the same amount, and there is only enough money for one.

(a) In the following grid, for each T, enter the Y that makes Programs A and B equally desirable to you. *Fill in the personal column first, then confer and fill in the group column.*

T	Number of Deaths Prevented T Years from Now	
	Personal	Group
0	100	100
1		
2		
3		

(continued)

5		
10		
25		
50		
100		

(b) Calculate the exponential discount rate for each response. Comment on its magnitude and how it varies with T.

5.5. (Harder) As mentioned in the text, B/C, internal rate of return, and payback time each summarize the benefit curve but lose information. Different benefit curves can give the same B/C, internal rate of return, or payback time. Figure 5.6 shows examples. With discount rate $d = 0$, both (*a*) and (*b*) have $B/C = 1$ (so that the internal rate of return $= 0$) and payback time $= 6$ years. For $d = 14.87\%/$year (a halving time of 5 years), both (*c*) and (*d*) have $B/C = 2$ and payback time $= 6$ years. However, the internal rates of return are different.

(a) For each of the options given, in Table 5.10 design two different simple benefit curves that satisfy the given criteria. Specify the assumed discount rate used for B/C and payback time. Not all options may be possible.

(b) Calculate the internal rate of return for your answers for options 2 and 4–8.

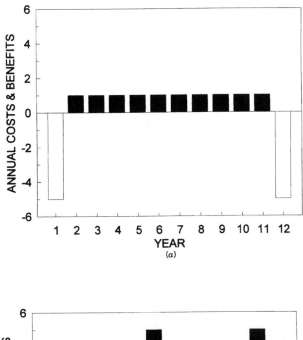

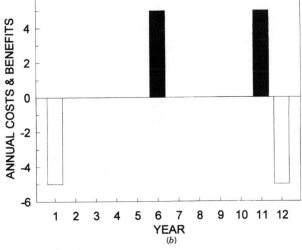

Figure 5.6

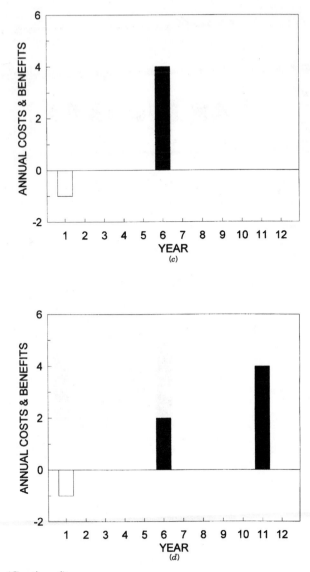

Figure 5.6   (Continued)

TABLE 5.10

Option	B/C	Payback Time	Internal Rate of Return	Notes
1	Same	Same	Same	Figure 5.6*a* and *b* does this for $d = 0$. IRR $= 0$.
2	Same	Same	Different	Figure 5.6*c* and *d* does this for $d = 14.87\%$/year (a halving time of 5 years). The IRR for Figure 5.6*c* is 31.95%/year (a halving time of 2.5 years). The IRR for Figure 5.6*d* is 26.47%/year.
3	Same	Different	Same	
4	Different	Same	Same	
5	Different	Different	Same	
6	Different	Same	Different	
7	Same	Different	Different	
8	Different	Different	Different	

6 Limits

Our children will enjoy in their homes electrical energy too cheap to meter.
—Lewis L. Strauss, chairman of the Atomic Energy Commission, speech at
the 20th anniversary of the National Association of Science Writers,
New York City, September 16, 1954, as reported by the *New York Times,*
September 17, 1954, p. 5

. . . Carpinteria [California] can soon expect a 100 per cent increase in water
fees . . . . Santa Barbara, Montecito, and Goleta will no doubt be experiencing
similar rate increases. What this will probably mean—besides higher bills for
homeowners—is that rental tenants can expect a rent hike so that landlords can
offset their increase. This is yet another nail in the coffin on the hopes that my
family, and those of everyone like me, will ever be able to afford a home here.
To everyone who is just struggling to survive here in paradise, take notice. It's
about to get harder.
—Letter to the editor, Santa Barbara *Independent,* July 25, 1996, p. 13

She told me the Yupik believe the more you share, the more you will catch the
next time. When I got back into my boat, I was carrying a salmon from her net
in each hand.
—D. Chadwick (1996). Sanctuary: U.S. national game refuges.
National Geographic (October), p. 22

1885, U.S. Geological Survey: "Little or no chance for oil in California."
1891, U.S. Geological Survey: Same prophecy by USGS for Kansas and Texas.
1914, U.S. Bureau of Mines: Total future production limit of 5.7 billion barrels,
perhaps ten-year supply.
1939, Department of the Interior: Reserves to last only 13 years.
1951, Department of the Interior, Oil and Gas Division: Reserves to last thirteen
years.
—J. Simon (1996). *The Ultimate Resource 2,* p. 165

1990, Ratio of world oil reserves to yearly extraction: 45.
—*World Resources, 1994–1995.* World Resources Institute, Table 9.2

1995, Ratio of U.S. oil reserves to yearly extraction: 10 years.
—My calculation from Energy Information Administration/U.S. Crude Oil,
Natural Gas, and Natural Gas Liquids Reserves (1995). Annual Report 19,
Table 6. (U.S. oil consumption is about ½ from domestic sources)

THE TOUGHEST CHAPTER

This has been the most difficult chapter of the book for me to write. The chapter will itself likely not convince you that limits should or should not affect your life . . . in a way other than already conveyed by "conventional economics," that is. I personally believe that the evidence for proximity to important biological and physical limits is compelling and justifies explicit planning as if they exist, and I originally thought I would deliver devastating proof here and now. The letter to the editor in paradisiacal California indicates a popular sense of limits.

However, I find it difficult to formulate a short argument that says this: that substitutes for even the "unsubstitutables" (like space, climate, water, biodiversity, natural capital, fossil fuels) cannot be found and developed in a way acceptable to you, if not to me. I hoped that my concerns are not in large part based on my value system, rather than on some (relatively speaking!) more absolute truth. But they *are* based on my values. And I do worry— some—that planning for limits will squelch human inventiveness and preclude certain better futures. Perhaps the Yupik statement given previously reflects optimism that encourages initiative.

On the other hand, if values are admittedly crucial to the debate, it is good to be explicit about them.

REALITY CHECK

The limits debate can be characterized, or caricatured, as essentially between two archetypes I call *entropy person* and *economic person.* (See Chapter 12 for a discussion of entropy.) Entropy person claims there are undeniable limits to (1) nonrenewable resources, (2) renewable resources that can be exploited so hard as to become nonrenewable, and (3) the earth's assimilative capacity for pollution. Entropy person believes:

1. *Explicit* attention should be paid to these biological/physical (called "biophysical") limits in planning and everyday activities.
2. The biophysical limits are so near that not paying explicit attention will lead to future problems we do not want and for which we are not prepared.

Economic person also believes in limits (after all, the phrase "limited resources" appears in the standard definition of economics), but believes:

1. Limits are properly revealed *implicitly* through the prices of things.
2. The economic system (almost always a free-enterprise system) is the best way to inform people and to elicit the proper response, at the proper

time. In particular, prices are the best way to stimulate human ingenuity in finding substitutes for limited resources of all types.

How the debate spirals is indicated by a famous wager between entropy person Paul Ehrlich, author of *The Population Bomb* (1968), and economic person Julian Simon, author of *The Ultimate Resource* (1981). See the accompanying box.

Simon's Bet

Julian Simon, bête noire of those he labels "doomsayer" environmentalists, insists that humankind's lot is getting ever better. And for the second time, he's offered to bet money on it.

Back in 1980 Simon, an economist at the University of Maryland, College Park, bet Stanford ecologist Paul Ehrlich and two colleagues that over 10 years the price of certain scarce metals [copper, chromium, nickel, tin, and tungsten] would fall as increased demand spurred production. Ehrlich said scarcity would boost prices. Simon won. Now he's issued a new challenge . . . in which he says he's willing to bet that "just about any trend pertaining to material human welfare will improve" with time.

Well, almost any. Ehrlich, and a Stanford colleague, atmospheric scientist Stephen Schneider, responded with a list of 15 trends they say will worsen in the next 10 years—including global warming, air pollution, and loss of species. They're willing to lay $1000 on each. But Simon's not playing. He told *Science* he will only gamble on "direct" measures of human welfare, such as life expectancy, leisure time, and purchasing power. Ehrlich and Schneider's list, he says, dwells on "aspects of our environment whose connection to human welfare is questionable." So for the moment, the betting window is closed.

—C. Holden (1995). Betting on the future. *Science* 268:1281. © 1995 American Association for the Advancement of Science. Reprinted with permission.

In the bet, perceived scarcity in a physical sense did not lead to economic scarcity. Even after paying up, however, entropy person has at least three counterarguments:

1. The economic system discounts the future (as discussed in Chapter 5). There will be serious scarcity at some future time, but it is hidden by time discounting. People have longer-term concerns than indicated by their apparent economic discount rate.

2. The economic price does not today adequately reflect many issues that really are a part of human welfare. These include basic life-support (e.g., climate's enabling of agriculture), human health (e.g., clean water), and quality-of-life issues such as open space and starry skies. These

formerly free biophysical benefits are deteriorating because their limits are being approached. The bet covered subjects not really important to Ehrlich. After the first bet, the differences in the value systems of the two bettors are clearer, and Simon and Ehrlich can find no common wagering ground. (See the discussion of other indicators of welfare in Chapter 11.)

3. Economic calculations do not cover a large-enough spatial extent and do not add things up in a global bookkeeping sense. Local scarcity is being bypassed today by global-reaching trade in which rich nations/ classes exploit poorer nations'/classes' resources. As poor nations develop they will attempt to do the same (and need to, if they emulate the U.S. consumption pattern), and eventually not all nations can borrow elsewhere. (See the discussion of ecological footprint in Chapter 8.)

Each of these elicits more counterarguments, and on it goes.

This book puts more weight on the entropy side ($I = PAT$, Chapter 2), exponential depletion of a finite resource (Chapter 3), human dependence on global net primary (biological) production (Chapter 8), depletion of open-access common resources (Chapter 9), and the thermodynamic basis for diminishing returns (Chapter 12). It puts less weight on the economic side (Chapter 5 on discounting and cost–benefit analysis and part of Chapter 11 on ecological economics).

DEFINITION IS A PROBLEM

The limits debate, which often starts with nonrenewable resources like oil, seems often to end up with quality-of-life issues about remembered rural scenes now paved over. That is, the discussion shifts from resources to quality of life, esthetics, and so on, and often contains an implicit statement like "you don't know what you are missing," in which an older person refers to some natural experience once easily accessible and now scarce or nonexistent. But sometimes the earnest response from a younger person is "I don't miss it."

I have gained a respect for the breadth of the task of identifying human needs and wants. Preferences do change, and if opportunities and possibilities change slowly enough, then preferences may change with them—in which case the change is acceptable. Even if we accept GDP and other economic variables as proper indicators, there is always the possibility of changing the market basket, the mix of goods and services, that goes into its definition. The possibility, and danger, of changed preference is suggested vividly by a Jules Feiffer cartoon in which Santa Claus asks a family what they want for Christmas. They state all kinds of high goals about a peaceful, just world full of opportunity, challenge, and beauty. He gives them a video game. As he is flying away they say "Thanks, Santa, this is the best Christmas ever!" Maybe biodiversity will not be missed, just as unfenced cattle range and buggy whips are not missed today.

SO ARE THERE LIMITS?

In my heart, I say yes. Here are several examples, without proof.

- The problem of storing nuclear waste is still not solved, and that is a contributor to nuclear electricity's not being cheap, contradicting Lewis Strauss' 1954 prediction at the beginning of the chapter.
- For electricity we now push north to the Arctic Circle with hydro projects.
- For oil we drill in the last wildernesses of the North American continent, in deep sea or where it is so cold a hammer thwack can shatter a tire, and even then U.S. domestic production is declining even as U.S. consumption is increasing. But I admit: Oil is cheap and its static lifetime is approximately the same as it was 50 years ago, as stated previously. See the accompanying box.
- 77% of the total water discharge of the 139 largest river systems in North America north of Mexico, in Europe, and in the former Soviet Union is severely or moderately regulated by reservoir operation, interbasin diversion, and irrigation (Dynesius and Nilsson, 1994).
- Two-thirds of the world's commercial fish species are fully or over-exploited (hence shrinking), or closed following collapse (Spurgeon, 1997).

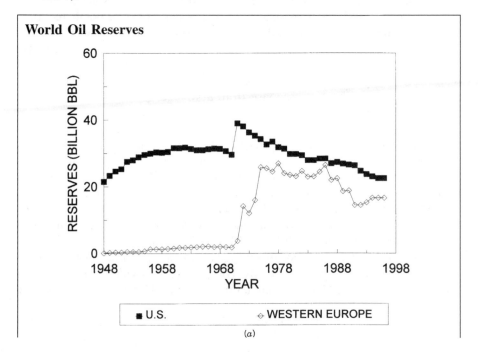

(a)

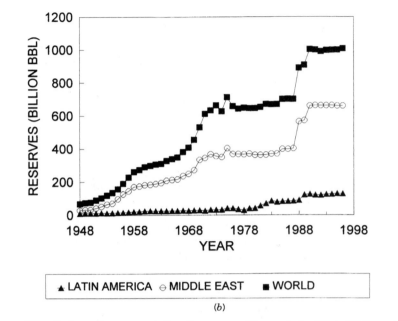

(b)

Figure 6.1 Estimated proven crude oil reserves. The scale in (*b*) is 20 times that in (*a*). (American Petroleum Institute, 1996, Section II, Table 1). From that source: Regions where reserves have increased 1991–1996: Latin America, Middle East, Africa; regions where reserves have decreased: United States, Canada, Western Europe; regions where reserves were essentially constant: Australasia, USSR/ eastern Europe. Current consumption: United States, 6.5 billion barrels/year; world, 26 billion barrels/year.

Figure 6.1*a* and *b* illustrates several issues about limits. World oil reserves have risen about 16-fold in 50 years, which argues against limits. However, several details imply limits. For example, U.S. and western European reserves are falling, despite increases for Alaskan (ca. 1970) and North Sea (ca. 1973) production. The increase in world reserves comes from Latin America, the Middle East, etc., areas that are less developed and less explored—and from which there are likely no similar areas to go to when their reserves start to fall. In addition, the world figure has been essentially constant since about 1991, which could imply that even those areas are approaching being fully explored. Again, arguing against limits is that reserves are about 40 times present annual use of 26 billion barrels and that world prices are low. Finally, there is the question of the details of the definition of reserves, especially the assumed price.

- It is likely that humankind is causing global warming (Schwartz and Andraea, 1996; Houghton et al., 1996).

• By 2020, seven developing countries with a combined population of 2.3 billion (China among them) will shift from grain self-sufficiency to grain import dependence as rising affluence allows them to shift their food preferences up the food chain. The remaining exporting nations will not be able to satisfy the demand (Brown and Kane, 1994; see also Kendall and Pimentel, 1994). But I admit: This is based on many assumptions about limits to yields, gains and losses of agricultural acreage, and so on. A likely consequence is increased grain prices (harsh on the remaining poor nations), which, economics says, should spur production.

Following is a very partial list of sources for the limits debate:

1. World Resources Institute, Washington, DC, notably "World Resources: A Guide to the Global Environment," published biennially in conjunction with the United Nations. The references lead one into rich data sources.
2. Worldwatch Institute, Washington, DC. Many publications, especially "Vital Signs," an annual publication of selected environmental trends.
3. These journals: *Science, Nature, Ecological Economics,* and *BioScience.*
4. Meadows et al. (1992), Chapter 3, has a clear exposition of the basic justification of limits.
5. Herman Daly's *Beyond Growth* (1996) offers no data, but is an excellent exposition of how to deal with limits. It also belongs in Chapter 11.
6. Julian Simon's *The Ultimate Resource 2* (1996), which argues against limits.

In this book we touch on many limits-related issues. Some of them are listed in Table 6.1, with an indication of how serious I think they are, in two ways. The first is at the micro level (personal, household, community, region). The second is global.

PROBLEMS

Level of difficulty is indicated as Easier/Moderate/Harder. Problems marked "(Spreadsheet?)" can be fruitfully approached using a spreadsheet. They need not be, however.

6.1. (Moderate) Do this for six possible combinations. Make the case for or against limits (assign three short, cogent points) assuming you are (pick one at a time):

TABLE 6.1 Some Limits Issues, with Portions of This Book That Address Techniques for Analyzing Them

Issue	Location in This Book	Seriousness		Comment
		Micro	Global	
Net energy of supply versus efficiency of use	Chapters 8, 12	7	10	Limits versus efficiency is always an issue ($I = PAT$)
Greenhouse gases → global warming	Chapters 7, 12	0	10	Four issues: 1. Is warming real? 2. Are we responsible? 3. Is it good or bad? 4. What is timing?
Biodiversity loss		5	10	Example of a currently non-costed factor with esthetic and potentially economic consequences
Depletion of fisheries	Chapter 9	7	7	Well documented, potentially reversible
Human dependence on global biological production, global water cycle	Chapter 8	3	8	Example of indirect effects
Fossil energy limits	Chapters 3, 12	7	7	Definition of "reserves" is crucial
Population growth versus food production	Chapters 3, 7, 8	5	10	Dynamics describes land use; indirect effects (e.g., food chain) important in grain demand as nations become richer
Fresh water	Chapter 4	8	5	End-use analysis has been used for water demand just as for electricity
Urbanization covering land	Chapter 3	8	5	
Size of whole human endeavor relative to natural system	Chapters 2, 8, 11	0	10	Large-scale bookkeeping, e.g., for fresh water, world grain production, energy, land
Thermodynamic limits	Chapter 12	6	6	Efficiency

Yourself	Worth $23
A U.S. farmer	Worth $300,000
A Chinese farmer	Worth $3,000,000
A Russian ex-factory worker	Entropy person
A U.S. ex-factory worker	Economic person
A Thai Nike factory worker	A car owner
10 years old	Not a car owner
25 years old	A resident of Bombay
50 years old	A resident of inner Detroit
75 years old	A resident of Marin County, California

and that you are talking to someone who is (pick one at a time):

Just like you	Worth $23
A U.S. farmer	Worth $300,000
A Chinese farmer	Worth $3,000,000
A Russian ex-factory worker	Entropy person
A U.S. ex-factory worker	Economic person
A Thai Nike factory worker	A car owner
10 years old	Not a car owner
25 years old	A resident of Bombay
50 years old	A resident of inner Detroit
75 years old	A resident of Marin County, California

6.2. (Moderate) Discuss whether Figure 6.1 justifies explicit concerns over limits to world oil.

7 Dynamics, Stocks and Flows, Age Class Effects

HUMAN SEWAGE IS BIODEGRADABLE, SO WHAT'S THE PROBLEM WITH IT?

In dynamics, *time* is again the issue.

- CO_2 in the atmosphere is entering the oceans, so what's the problem with it?
- Forests recover, so what's the problem with clear cutting?
- Joe the jeans magnate threw beer cans in Biscayne Bay with a clear conscience. See the accompanying box.

Beer Cans? No Problem

Miami, Florida. A recent college graduate meets an associate of his brother, a self-made millionaire trouser manufacturer, who invites them out on his yacht. They cruise out onto the Atlantic to fish. The mate baits the hook. The engine runs continuously and the gulls wheel and rake over the stern. Throughout the day the pants magnate and his friends throw their beer cans directly overboard. Finally the graduate summons his courage. "Joe, I've just met you but I've got to speak up. You're a millionaire, so how come you're a slob?" Joe replies, "Heck, I thought that everyone knows that in salt water an aluminum can disappears completely in less than a day. These will be gone tomorrow."

Things take time. We have already discussed how humans tend to deal psychologically/economically with that: time discounting. Now we deal with time delays physically and biologically. The first three points explicitly deal with lags; the recovery process occurs slowly compared with the damage process (Joe seriously underestimated the lifetime of beer cans).

- ". . . between 1982 and 2000, the number of people over 60 in China is expected to increase 72% while the total population grows by only

119

19%. . . ," yet the number of births per female has fallen below replacement (1.8 in 1996) (Holden, 1996).

- L.L. Bean offers three fits in its line of jeans (Fig. 7.1). The company did not do so 20 years ago. Why does it now?

- "By 2010, the state may have another 10 million people [current population is 27 million]. . . . At present, about 10% of California's general fund goes to higher education. That share will fall. The prison system, which now absorbs about 9% of State money, is admitting new felons so fast that by 2010 Mr. Shires reckons it will suck in 20% of all state revenues. At the same time, health and welfare services will have to expand for a growing and aging population."—California: Too poor for college. *The Economist,* July 20, 1996 pp. 26–27.

The last three points deal with age class structure. Because of previously large families, the Chinese population is young: There are many people of

Figure 7.1 Jeans in three fits. *Source:* L.L. Bean spring 1997 catalog, pp. 51–52. Reprinted with permission.

child-bearing age, and their modest per capita birthing still yields total births that exceed the deaths in the relatively sparse older age classes. Older adults tend to be shaped differently than younger adults, the American population is graying, and the assiduous marketer tailors the product line accordingly.

Lags and age-class effects are not completely independent, but we will approach them separately in this chapter.

GENERIC EXAMPLE OF LAGS: BIODEGRADABLE WATERMELON RINDS. IMPORTANT EQUATION 3

Watermelon rinds are often found in fireplaces in picnic areas in state parks, etc. They do eventually degrade and disappear, but at peak season they are being deposited at a rate that exceeds the rate of decay or of burning, and hence they accumulate. We sketch this process in Figure 7.2. Equation 7.1 summarizes Figure 7.2:

$$\frac{\Delta M}{\Delta t} = F_{in} - F_{out} \tag{7.1}$$

Equation 7.1 states the conservation of whatever stuff is flowing, and is explicitly the basis for much modeling. The reservoir question (Problem 1.6) is an application. In principle, the in- and outflows can depend on internal and/or external factors, including the stock itself. See Table 7.1.

We will concentrate on the particular case: when the outflow (units=gloof/time) is proportional to the stock (units=gloof). Because the constant of proportionality must have the dimensions of $1/time$, we therefore write

$$F_{out} = \frac{M}{\tau} \tag{7.2}$$

τ is variously called the lifetime, characteristic time, residence time, retention time, flushing time, and time constant, among other names. This particular dependence of F_{out} on M is called the residence time assumption. It often applies, but we need to remember that it is just one possible form. For ex-

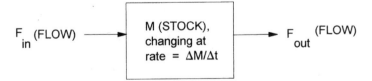

Figure 7.2   Stock accumulation as a function of in- and outflows.

TABLE 7.1   Factors Affecting Inflows and Outflows

	Inflow (F_{in})	Outflow (F_{out})
Possible dependence on internal factors	1. Eating, preying on other species 2. Giving birth 3. Gathering, stealing, taking food 4. "Diffusion"[a]	1. Excreting 2. Dying 3. Emigrating 4. "Diffusion"[a]
Possible dependence on external factors	1. Stocking (importing) 2. Immigrating 3. Emitting pollution 4. "Diffusion"[a]	1. Cropping (exporting) 2. Being preyed upon 3. "Diffusion"[a]

[a]"Diffusion" applies to all descriptions because it is dependent on a difference of concentrations across a boundary. For example, the ocean could be a sink, or source, of atmospheric CO_2, depending on the CO_2 concentration in each.

ample, on one hand, we can argue that the number of deaths per year in a human population is roughly proportional to the number of humans, so that the residence time assumption applies. On the other hand, the constant of proportionality will be different for a population of children versus a population of octogenarians. τ (the lifetime from now until death) for the children might be 60 years, while τ for the elderly might be 3 years . . . in a peaceful, affluent country, that is. Other τ's would apply to poorer countries or ones at war.

Another example is the drainage rate of a bathtub as a function of the volume. The pressure is proportional to the depth, and if (1) the tub has vertical sides so the volume is proportional to the depth and (2) the flow rate is proportional to the pressure, then the flow out is proportional to the volume and the residence time approximation applies. Conditions 1 and 2 are not exactly true, but for average bathtubs and everyday problems, they are close enough. On the other hand, the decay of radioactive isotopes follows the residence time approximation to extremely high accuracy.

Table 7.2 lists a number of characteristic times. These times are often approximate, and sometimes the residence time assumption (Eq. 7.2) applies only approximately. Nonetheless, keeping characteristic times like these in mind is important in understanding how systems respond to changing inputs.

Incorporating the residence time assumption into Equation 7.1 gives

---

IMPORTANT EQUATION 3

$$\frac{\Delta M}{\Delta t} = F_{in} - \frac{M}{\tau} \tag{7.3}$$

TABLE 7.2   Selected Characteristic Times

Entity	Process	τ
Plastic film container	Degrades	20–30 years
Aluminum can and tab	Degrades	80–100 years
Glass bottle	Degrades	1 million years
Plastic bag	Degrades	10–20 years
Plastic-coated paper	Degrades	5 years
Nylon fabric	Degrades	30–40 years
Rubber boot sole	Degrades	50–80 years
Leather	Degrades	Up to 50 years
Wool sock	Degrades	1–5 years
Cigarette butt	Degrades	1–5 years
Orange or banana peel	Degrades	2–5 weeks
CO_2 in atmosphere	Falls out to oceans	100 years
H_2O in atmosphere	Falls out	7 days
O_3 at ground level	Degrades to harmless products	Few hours
O_3 in stratosphere	Ditto	Few weeks
$CFCl_3$ in atmosphere	Degrades to products that do not increase stratospheric O_3	70 years
CF_2Cl_2 in atmosphere	Ditto	120 years
$C_2F_3Cl_3$ in atmosphere	Ditto	90 years
CH_4 in atmosphere	Degrades to products that are not as "greenhouse active"	10 years
CO in atmosphere	Ditto, though main product is CO_2	0.4 year
Human excrement in woods	Biodegrades	6 weeks
Graduate school	Student is awarded degree	5 years
Human	Reproduces	30 years
Building	Becomes unusable	50–75 years
Forest	Undergoes succession from clearcut to mature forest ecosystem	50–300 years
Fishery	Recovery from overfishing	5–10 years
Whales	Recover from overwhaling	50 years
Corporate middle manager	Accomplishes goals leading to promotion	3 years
Congressperson	Accomplishes goals leading to reelection	2 years
Senator	Ditto	6 years
Large appliance	Becomes unusable	15 years
Arable soil	Recovers from erosion	Centuries

Source: Data for plastic film container through orange and banana peels are from the U.S. Forest Service, quoted in G. Lepp, *Outdoor Photographer* (1989).

Equation 7.3 is for a finite time interval Δt; the corresponding continuous version merely replaces $\Delta M / \Delta t$ with dM / dt. Equation 7.3 describes the dynamics of accumulation with arbitrary inflow and with outflow governed by the residence time assumption. Steady state is defined by all quantities' being constant over time. Then $\Delta M / \Delta t = 0$ and

$$M = F_{in} \tau \qquad \text{(steady state)} \qquad (7.4)$$

Equation 7.4 again shows how the residence time τ is a bridge between stock and flow, dimensionally and numerically. A small flow does not necessarily imply a small steady-state stock; it depends on the residence time. In Problem 7.12, for example, we see that Lake Superior has a relatively small inflow (its drainage basin is surprisingly small), yet it has the world's second largest lake volume. This is possible because the residence time is about 200 years (whereas Lake Erie has a residence time of 2.6 years). Joe the jeans magnate implicitly understood Equation 7.4. If τ is small enough, the stock of beer cans will be small with any finite rate of can tossing. He was far from the mark on the lifetime of an aluminum can in salt water, however. It has been surprisingly difficult to get a solid answer, but comparison with some test data on aluminum plates in the ocean (Davis, 1993) gives a can lifetime of at least 5 years, and likely longer.

Table 7.3 lists some stocks and their corresponding flows.

For dynamics, we return to watermelon rinds. Suppose a rind disappears through predictable processes with $\tau = 5$ days. There are at least two ways to interpret this statement:

1. Every rind lasts exactly 5 days.
2. Different rinds last different times, but the average lifetime is 5 days. If all rinds are identical, then this can be stated that the probability that rind "dies" in a (short) time period Δt is $\Delta t / \tau$, independent of how long that rind has already been around.

The first interpretation is like a "queue": Rinds are produced, last exactly 5 days, and die. At steady state, one is produced just as a 5-day-old one dies, and there is an even age distribution. That is, there are equal numbers of 1-day, 2-day, 3-day, 4-day, and 5-day-old rinds.

The second interpretation is a probabilistic one. Rinds of all ages are possible, though ones much older than 5 days are relatively less likely. In this example, a new rind has a $1/5$ chance of dying on day 1, and a $(1 - 1/5)$ chance of surviving beyond that. The probability that a new rind will die on day 2 is the product of surviving through day 1 and dying on day 2, $(1 - 1/5)(1/5) = 4/25$. The probability of surviving beyond day 2 is the probability of surviving through day 1 minus the probability of dying on exactly day 2, $(1 - 1/5) - (1 - 1/5)(1/5) = (1 - 1/5)^2 = 16/25$. Table 7.4

TABLE 7.3   Stocks and Corresponding Flows

Entity	Flow In	Stock/Location	Flow Out	τ
Atmospheric CO_2	Fossil fuel burning, deforestation	Mass in atmosphere	Ocean absorption, uptake by afforestation	100 years
Atmospheric SO_2	Fossil fuel burning, ore smelting	Mass in atmosphere	Acid rain	1 week
Garbage	Production	Landfills, ocean dumping	Biological and physical degradation, burning, composting, recycling	10 years
Radioactive waste (e.g., Pu)	Power plants	Waste repositories, now almost wholly in interim storage in power reactors	Radioactive decay	24,000 years for Pu
Nutrients (nitrates, phosphates) in rivers, lakes, aquifers	Agricultural runoff	Water bodies	Flushing, plant uptake, burial in sediments, evaporation	(Depends on τ of lake) 1 year 100 years 3 months
Beverage cans	Discarding	Stock everywhere	Recycle, degrade	5 years?
College students	Matriculation, transferring in	Student body	Graduation, dropping out	4 years
Humans	Immigration, births	Population	Emigration, deaths	10 years?
Sewage	Production	Waterways	Biodegradation	1–3 years
Cars	Production, import	Car population	Junking, export	10 years
Housing	Construction	Housing stock	Burning, razing	50–75 years

illustrates this in general for a residence time of τ (days). Figure 7.3 illustrates this graphically for $\tau = 5$ days.

Under the probabilistic interpretation, the most likely lifetime is one day, with probabilities decreasing for larger lifetimes. Under the fixed assumption, the probability of dying on day 5 is 1, while under the probabilistic, it is only 0.08. By adding the probabilities, we see that there is a 0.33 probability that the lifetime will exceed 5 years.[1] One can show that the average lifetime is τ (see problems 7.4 and 7.5).

We emphasize the difference between fixed and probabilistic residence times because they produce different abruptness or sharpness of effects when

TABLE 7.4   Survival Probabilities Under Fixed and Probabilistic Residence Time Assumptions

	Fixed Residence Time		Probabilistic Residence Time	
Day	Probability of Dying This Day	Probability of Surviving Beyond This Day	Probability of Dying This Day	Probability of Surviving Beyond This Day
0	0	1	0	1
1	0	1	$1/\tau$	$1 - 1/\tau$
2	0	1	$(1 - 1/\tau)(1/\tau)$	$(1 - 1/\tau)^2$
3	0	1	$(1 - 1/\tau)^2(1/\tau)$	$(1 - 1/\tau)^3$
4	0	1	$(1 - 1/\tau)^3(1/\tau)$	$(1 - 1/\tau)^4)$
$\vdots$	0	1	$\vdots$	$\vdots$
τ	1	0	$(1 - 1/\tau)^{\tau-1}(1/\tau)$	$(1 - 1/\tau)^\tau$
$\vdots$	0	0	$\vdots$	$\vdots$
n	0	0	$(1 - 1/\tau)^{n-1}(1/\tau)$	$(1 - 1/\tau)^n$

Residence time = τ (days).

stocks are changing. To illustrate, assume that we start with no watermelon rinds and add 100 per day. How does the stock of watermelon rinds, the amount we see, vary over time?

Fixed Residence Time   The stock builds up: 100 after day 1, 200 after day 2, 300 after day 3, and so forth. At the end of day 5 the 100 added on day 1 die; these deaths just balance the new 100 added at the beginning of day

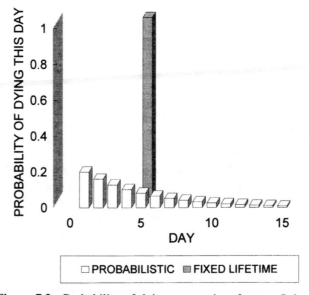

Figure 7.3   Probability of dying versus time for $\tau = 5$ days.

6, and the stock holds at 500 rinds. This continues forever. The system is at steady state and obeys Equation 7.2. Figure 7.4 shows how stock varies over time as the steady state is approached. There is a sharp corner at day 6 as the stock stops growing and settles in at its steady-state value.

Probabilistic Residence Time   Now we apply Equation 7.3, also known as Important Equation 3. On day 1, 100 rinds are added and the stock at the end of the day is 100 rinds. During day 2, another 100 rinds are added but $100/5 = 20$ die, so that the stock at day's end is $100 + 200 - 20 = 180$. On day 3, 100 rinds are added but $1/5$ of the stock of 180 die, so that the stock at day's end is $100 + 180 (1 - 1/5) = 244$. This process is repeated, yielding a geometric series to which we apply Important Equation 2:

$$M_t = 100 \left(1 + \frac{4}{5} + \left(\frac{4}{5}\right)^2 + \ldots + \left(\frac{4}{5}\right)^{t-1} \right) = 100 \left(\frac{1 - \left(\frac{4}{5}\right)^t}{1 - \left(\frac{4}{5}\right)} \right)$$

This result is also graphed in Figure 7.4. We see that the transition to the steady-state stock of 500 rinds occurs more smoothly, but necessarily more slowly. At the end of the fifth year, there are only 336 rinds, not 500 as given

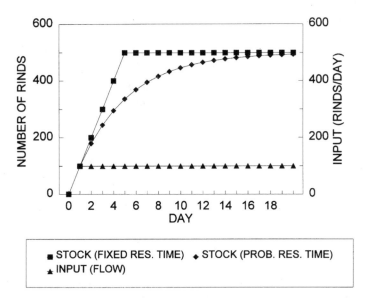

STOCK (FIXED RES. TIME) ◆ **STOCK (PROB. RES. TIME)**
▲ **INPUT (FLOW)**

Figure 7.4   Accumulation of watermelon rinds with a steady input of 100 rinds/day and a lifetime of 5 days.

[1]This is a finite-difference approach. For a continuous version, the probability of dying at time t is $(1/\tau)e^{-t/\tau}$.

using a fixed residence time. This occurs because here it is possible for rinds to die at ages less than 5 years. Strictly speaking, infinite time is required to reach the asymptotic value of 500 rinds.[2]

We have just predicted stock versus time using Important Equation 3 (which is a special case of the more general Eq. 7.1). This simple process is the basis for much of simulation modeling performed by computers. Figure 7.5 shows the process schematically. Table 7.5 lists the units of some representative stocks and flows.

AGE CLASS EFFECTS, APPLIED TO POPULATIONS OF MICE, HUMANS, AUTOMOBILES, AND SO ON

So far we have stressed stock–flow residence times to show how delays can occur, and how, even at steady state, flow and stock patterns can differ because of different residence times. We have seen how things accumulate when $F_{in} > M/\tau$. This approach has assumed that the gloof in question—CO_2, orange peels, radionuclides, automobiles—is composed of identical entities whose age structure is irrelevant. Now we turn to situations where age-dependent information is important to us. In Figure 7.1 we saw that a clothes seller differentiates its customers not just on height, but also on shape. The differing shape is fairly well correlated with age, and the age structure of the

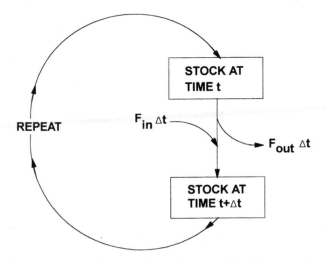

Figure 7.5 Schematic depiction of solving Equation 7.1. This is the basis for much of simulation modeling. In building a model, one connects stocks by flows and by time.

[2]Equation is in finite-difference form. The continuous form is $dM/dt = F_{in} - M/\tau$, which is integrated to give $M = F_{in}\tau(1 - e^{-t/\tau})$. M approaches $F_{in}\tau$ as $t \to \infty$.

TABLE 7.5   Units of Stocks and Flows

Entity	Stock or Flow?	Representive Units
Gross domestic product (GDP)	Flow	$/year
Wealth	Stock	$
Depreciation	Flow	$/year
Distance	Stock	feet
Speed	Flow	feet/second
Energy	Stock	kilowatt-hour
Power	Flow	kilowatt-hours/hour = kilowatt
CO_2 production	Flow	tons/year
CO_2 in atmosphere	Stock	tons
Birth rate	Flow	individuals/year
Population	Stock	individuals
Depositing of watermelon rinds	Flow	number/day
Watermelon rinds	Stock	number
Decay of watermelon rinds	Flow	number/day
Radioactive decay	Flow	disintegrations/second
Radioactive nuclei	Stock	number

customer base is relevant to splitting the blue jeans product line. Other age-dependent effects:

1. *Autos.* Older automobiles tend to pollute more and require more maintenance.
2. *Appliances.* New refrigerators are at least twice as energy efficient as ones sold 15 years ago.
3. *Highways.* Older highways require more maintenance.
4. *Yellow Perch in Lake Michigan.* Larval perch are susceptible to predation at hatch (length = 8 mm) until they are about 15 mm long, after which they are too large to be easily eaten.
5. *Chickens.* The percentage weight gain rate decreases with age, which dictates when to slaughter them.
6. *Underground Fuel Tanks.* Old tanks leak more often.
7. *Humans.* Older people need more medical care, but do not require maternity care.

Age class effects cause delays in the effectiveness of new programs, as well as over- or undershoots when some property of a particular age group is incorrectly assumed to characterize the whole population. We have already seen this in the introduction of more efficient refrigerators in Chapter 4. We further demonstrate by several examples:

- Hypothetical mouse population growth
- "Momentum" in human population growth

• Lags in auto fleet miles per gallon resulting from new car standards

Also, in Chapter 8 we will apply age class analysis to the net energy returns from building many power plants.

Hypothetical Organism "Musa"

We start with a hypothetical mouse I call "Musa", which lives exactly 4 years (fixed residence time) and reproduces only in the second year. To predict the Musa population over time, we must keep track of how many Musa are in each age class. This process is shown in Figure 7.6. The 1-year class in year 1 becomes the 2-year class in year 2, which, in turn, becomes the 3-year class in year 3. The 1-year class in any year is the offspring of last year's 2-year class. 4-year classes die. The progression is to the right (later) and down (older). Figure 7.6 could be amended to account for in- and out-migration, but we do not treat that complication here.

Let us run through the dynamics implied by Figure 7.6. We must specify the starting conditions; assume that there are (8, 4, 2, 1) Musa in age classes, 1, 2, 3, and 4, respectively—a population dominated by the young. Assume that second-year individuals just reproduce themselves. This year, the second-year class Musa will produce four young, the one fourth-year Musa will die, the 8 first-year class individuals will age a year, and so on. We represent this in Figure 7.7.

In Figure 7.7 the year 1 population ages while the second age class has four offspring, but only the single member of age class 4 dies. As a result the total population increases from 15 to 18 individuals. Going from year 2 to year 3, there are 2 deaths but 8 births, yielding a population of 24, which

YEAR 1   YEAR 2   YEAR 3   YEAR 4

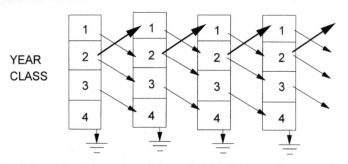

Figure 7.6 Schematic of dynamics of the hypothetical "Musa" population. The numbers represent the year class. Heavy arrows indicate birth, light arrows indicate aging, and ground symbols indicate death.

YEAR 1   YEAR 2   YEAR 3   YEAR 4

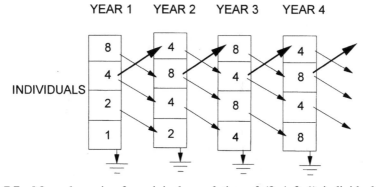

Figure 7.7 Musa dynamics for original population of $(8, 4, 2, 1)$ individuals. The numbers represent individuals in each age class. The initial population of 15 reaches a constant value of 24 after 2 years.

then holds constant, though the distribution alternates $(8, 4, 8, 4)$ and $(4, 8, 4, 8)$. This simple example demonstrates "population momentum," in which a population can grow, for a while, even though the child-bearing age class is just replacing itself. The population increase is a result of the initial population distribution, which is dominated by young and fertile age classes. If we had started with $(2, 2, 2, 2)$, the population and distribution would be constant indefinitely. The reader can also verify that starting with $(1, 2, 4, 8)$, which is an aged population, will result in a decline from 15 to a constant 6 individuals.

This process is a specific case of constant mortality and reproduction pattern. The most general model would have time- or density-dependent survival and reproduction, but that is beyond our scope here. Assuming the factors are constant, we can keep track of age class–specific dynamics with a worksheet such as in Table 7.6. This is shown with a starting distribution of $(2, 8, 8, 4)$, which produces an overshoot—an initial population of 22 increases to 26 and then decreases to a constant value of 20. In Table 7.6 we also calculate the average age, which starts at 2.14 years and settles down to alternating between 1.7 and 2.3, with an average of 2.0 years. The time necessary for the effects of the initial age distribution to pass through the population is 2 years, of order one Musa lifetime. These results are also shown graphically in Figure 7.8.

Population Momentum: China

Someone has said that half the people of the world have not started having children; they *are* children. Therefore population momentum is anticipated in many countries, even if the number of children per female of reproductive age were abruptly brought down to approximately two. This is true of mainland China.

TABLE 7.6 Example Age Class Analysis Worksheet for Musa Model

			Year						
			1[a]	2	3	4	5	6	7
Age Class (Average Age)	Survival Fraction	Reproduction Fraction	Number of Individuals						
1 (0.5)	1	0	2	8	2	8	2	8	2
2 (1.5)	1	1	8	2	8	2	8	2	8
3 (2.5)	1	0	8	8	2	8	2	8	2
4 (3.5)	0	0	4	8	8	2	8	2	8
Total population (number)			22	26	20	20	20	20	20
Births (number year^{-1})			8	2	8	2	8	2	8
Deaths (number year^{-1})			4	8	8	2	8	2	8
Birth rate (year^{-1})			0.36	0.077	0.4	0.1	0.4	0.1	0.4
Death rate (year^{-1})			0.18	0.31	0.4	0.1	0.4	0.1	0.4
Net growth rate (year^{-1})			0.18	−0.23	0	0	0	0	0
Average age (year)			2.14	2.12	2.3	1.7	2.3	1.7	2.3

[a]The initial distribution of (2, 8, 8, 4) results in a population increase, then a decrease to a constant number. This is also graphed in Figure 7.8.

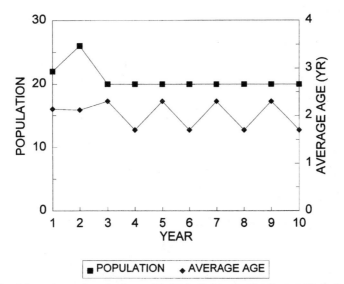

Figure 7.8 Musa dynamics starting with 22 individuals distributed (2, 8, 8, 4) among age classes 1–4. The data are given in Table 7.6.

Table 7.7 shows current data for China. The population data are quite accurate; the survival and reproduction factors less so, especially considering that we will assume them constant for a century. However, more accuracy is not needed to demonstrate the effect. We can use the Chinese data in a worksheet such as Table 7.6. The calculation is messier than the Musa example because the numbers are not simple zeros and ones, and four, not one, age

TABLE 7.7   Demographic Data for Mainland China

Age Class (year)	Population (10^3)	Survival Fraction	Reproduction Factor
0–9	218,457	0.9895	0
10–19	195,648	0.9868	0.0438
20–29	245,825	0.9822	0.7060
30–39	186,767	0.9696	0.1595
40–49	147,982	0.9327	0.0150
50–59	91,383	0.8316	0
60–69	68,627	0.6134	0
70–79	34,023	0.2761	0
80+	9,349	0	0

Population and reproduction fractions are for 1995. Survival fractions are for 1981, the latest available in this source: International Data Base, International Programs Center, U.S. Bureau of the Census, Washington, DC 20233. Available at Web site hhtp://www.census. gov/ipc/www/idbnew.html.

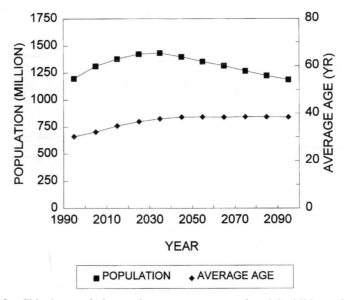

Figure 7.9 China's population and average age assuming 1.8 child per female and with the other assumptions given in the text.

classes can reproduce. A spreadsheet is well suited for this task, and it also allows easy graphing of results (Problem 7.15 covers an extension of the Chinese projection, and a spreadsheet helps considerably.) The result is graphed in Figure 7.9.

Even though the number of children per female is slightly below replacement,[3] the population overshoots its 1995 value of 1.20 billion to a high of 1.43 billion in 2035 and then begins to decline. This is a 19% overshoot (230 million people!), with a lag on the order of 40 years. With no change in the assumed reproduction factor, the population returns to its 1995 value in 2095 and eventually dies out. The average age is 30.2 in 1995, and reaches 37.7 in 2035, and 38.4 in 2095.

Figure 7.10 shows the age distribution in each decade. The large 20–29 age class in 1995 continues as a bump moving downward and to the right for 60 years, yielding the largest 80+ age class in 2055. Similarly, their children comprise a large 0–9 class in 2005 and continue as a lesser bump. The 1995 distribution is dominated by 20–29 year olds, and by 2095 the distribution is much flatter. The total population in 2095 is less than that in 1995. To remind us what all this may be used for, consider Figure 7.10. What does it say about the relative demand over time for diapers and loose fitting trousers, for elementary education teachers and social security services?

---

[3]In Table 7.7 the sum of the reproduction factors for all ages is 0.9243, which is below the replacement value of 1.000. Actual reproduction is even less because of deaths before females reach reproductive age. See Problem 7.3.

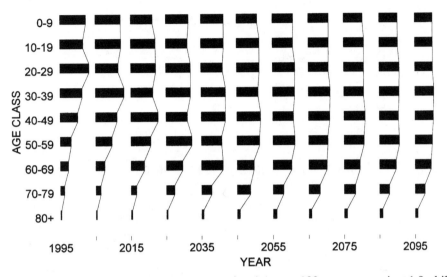

Figure 7.10 China's age class structure for the next 100 years assuming 1.8 child per female and with the other assumptions given in the text.

The U.S. Census Bureau's population forecast for China, which covers every year through 2050, predicts a peak population of 1.45 billion in 2034 (see Web site http://www.census.gov/ipc/www/idbnew.html). Our result shows excellent agreement with their more careful calculation, but that is a matter of our luck because their method uses survival and reproduction factors that change with time, they divide the population into more age classes, they use a yearly time step instead of a decade, and they account for the fact that there are more males than females.

The overshoot is also surprising considering that one hears that China has a strong one-child-per-couple program. The Census projection also assumes close to two children per female (1.92 in 1995, dropping to 1.7 in 2050). Three possible reasons that the one-child goal is not reached on average are: (1) the program is strongest in urban areas, but China is only 30% urban; (2) rural couples are allowed to have a second child if the first is a girl; and (3) couples themselves from single-child families will be allowed to have two children (Loraine A. West, U.S. Census Bureau, personal communication). Of course, this can change.

Lags: Auto Miles per Gallon

Figure 7.11 shows that the miles per gallon of new cars has increased over time, in large part in response to government standards. We would expect mpg for cars on the road to lag by a time comparable to a car's lifetime, 10

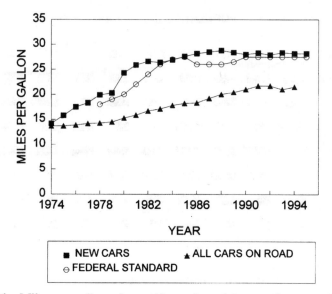

Figure 7.11 Miles per gallon of new (domestic and imported) cars and of cars on the road, 1974–1995. Federal new car standards went into effect in 1978.

years, while the older cars are retired. A lag of that order is seen, but the road mpg seems to be leveling off at about 20 even though the new car mpg has been between 26 and 28 since 1982. However, the new car standards are based on laboratory tests, which overstate mpg compared with actual road performance. Then Figure 7.11 shows that, since 1982, new cars have had about 20 mpg (road) corresponding to 26–28 mpg (test), and it has taken until about 1992 for the road fleet to reach the 20-mpg average.

Details of the average mpg depend on several other factors, such as driving habits, whether cars are living longer (they are), whether the ratio of road to test mpg is holding constant, overall growth rate of the car population, and what the age distribution was in 1974. Issues like these were treated in an analysis of cars after World War II by Kenneth Boulding (1955), who is known for coining the term "spaceship earth" and who pioneered the field of ecological economics discussed in Chapter 11. His interest was not fuel efficiency, but fluctuations in the demand for new cars, of interest to manufacturers and auto workers. The problem he anticipated was this: Because of the Great Depression of the 1930s and the war effort, in 1946 the U.S. auto fleet was old. In fact, Detroit had produced no private cars at all between 1942 and 1945. U.S. auto numbers had grown an average of only 1.1%/year from 1930 to 1946. One expected a large postwar pulse of demand for new cars dominated by replacement purchases. After several years of high demand, one could anticipate a drop in demand because most cars would be young and there would be few replacements required. The effect would be smaller if there was overall growth in auto numbers, so that new car purchases dominated sales. This largely happened; U.S. car numbers grew at an average of 92% between 1946 and 1956 (an exponential rate of about 6.7%/year). (Problem 7.8 covers a simple example of this type.) A similar example, the net energy returns from building many power plants, is discussed in Chapter 8.

SATURATION: PLANTING TREES TO SEQUESTER CO$_2$

Comments such as "forests are the lungs of the planet" beg us to investigate what the forests' digestive tract is doing as well. Photosynthesis and respiration are material mirror images of the same chemical reaction, $6H_2O + 6CO_2 \rightleftharpoons C_6H_{12}O_6 + 6O_2$. Photosynthesis proceeds to the right, respiration to the left. $C_6H_{12}O_6$ represents a generic carbohydrate molecule. A mature forest contains sequestered carbon (a stock), but shows a balance between biomass growth and biomass death and decay (flows), and hence is not a net absorber of CO_2 or a producer of O_2 (flows).[4] A previously unvegetated area undergoing forest succession has a positive CO_2 uptake rate, but that will slow and cease as the forest matures. This saturation of CO_2 uptake is often ignored or deemphasized in proposals for widespread afforestation to absorb CO_2.

In principle, there are ways to get around the saturation problem. If a forest grows, matures, is harvested, and the cut is prevented from decaying, then net CO_2 is sequestered. This could be done in at least three ways:

1. The wood could be used in durable goods such as buildings, which last longer than decaying litter on the forest floor.
2. The wood could, as one economist has put it, be "pickled" to prevent decay.
3. The wood could be deposited out of oxygen's reach in the deep ocean, mimicking the production of fossil fuel over geologic time.

Another option lets our industries be the gut for the forest, just as we are the gut for the corn field. We can use the wood as fuel, displacing fossil fuel burning. The long-term average net CO_2 uptake in a biomass plantation for fuel would be zero, but it would prevent CO_2 emissions, which otherwise would accumulate from burning coal, oil, and natural gas.

All of these possibilities are complicated, yet are approachable using simple stock–flow analyses. Let us look at logistic growth, which incorporates the basic elements of the problem and is a decent representation of forest succession.

---

[4]Increased CO_2 stimulates photosynthesis and can result in more stored biomass, but the effect is relatively small.

Logistic growth, mentioned briefly in the discussion of motivational graphs in Chapter 1 and in Problem 3.9, is an extension of exponential growth. Equation 7.5 shows the two. Exponential growth is defined by the time rate of change of gloof being proportional to the amount of gloof. Logistic growth multiplies this factor by a second factor that approaches zero as gloof approaches a limit, which saturates.

$$\text{Exponential: } \frac{dN}{dt} = rN, \text{ which integrates to } N = N_0 e^{rt} \qquad (7.5a)$$

$$\text{Logistic: } \frac{dN}{dt} = rN \left(1 - \frac{N}{K} \right), \text{ which integrates to} \qquad (7.5b)$$

$$N = \frac{N_0 e^{rt}}{1 + \frac{N_0}{K} (e^{rt} - 1)}$$

From the integrated forms in Equation 7.5, we can see that logistic growth looks like an exponential when $N \ll K$, yet approaches a zero growth steady state as $N \to K$. If N is the population, K is the carrying capacity. For a forest K represents the maximum biomass, the fixed carbon (which includes leaf litter, soil organic matter, etc., and is therefore significantly more than that found only in trees). Figure 7.12 shows the logistic curve for values roughly appropriate to a temperate forest, and Table 7.8 lists the numbers in detail.

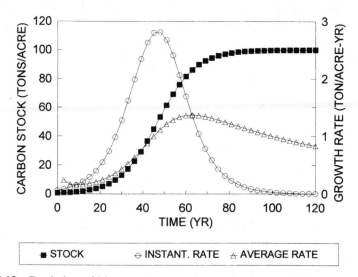

Figure 7.12 Depiction of biomass (expressed as carbon) accrual in temperate forest succession. Logistic curve with $N_0 = 0.5$ ton C/acre, $r = 0.113$ year^{-1}, and $K = 200$ tons C/acre. Instantaneous growth rate is the slope (derivative) of the stock curve. Average growth rate is stock/time. The data are given in Table 7.8.

Figure 7.12 and Table 7.8 show that the instantaneous growth rate peaks at 48 years (when $N = K/2$: Why?) and declines to zero as the forest matures. The average growth rate, which is what we would want to maximize if we are operating this forest on a continuing basis, peaks later, at 63 years (when $dN/dt = N/t$: Why?).

The main issue here is to anticipate how transient results may be misused to imply long-term results. In this case the maximum carbon uptake rate of 2.81 ton/acre-year occurs in year 48. In year 30 the uptake rate is less than half as much, and by year 60 it will be only 60% as much. Between years 30 and 70, a 40-year period, 80% of the uptake occurs, and for the rest of time only 25% more than that will occur, unless the forest is cut and replanted.

We have used the logistic to illustrate, but the general result is independent of the details. Any time we are interested in the cumulating flows associated

TABLE 7.8   Carbon Storage in Forest Succession

Year	N (tons/acre)	dN/dt (tons/acre-year)	N/t (tons/acre-year)	Year	N (tons/acre)	dN/dt (tons/acre-year)	N/t (tons/acre-year)
0	0.5	0.06					
3	0.7	0.08	0.23	63	86.2	1.35	1.37[a]
6	1.0	0.11	0.16	66	89.8	1.04	1.36
9	1.4	0.15	0.15	69	92.5	0.79	1.34
12	1.9	0.21	0.16	72	94.5	0.58	1.31
15	2.7	0.29	0.18	75	96.0	0.43	1.28
18	3.7	0.40	0.21	78	97.1	0.31	1.25
21	5.1	0.55	0.24	81	98.0	0.23	1.21
24	7.1	0.74	0.29	84	98.5	0.16	1.17
27	9.6	0.98	0.36	87	99.0	0.12	1.14
30	13.0	1.28	0.43	90	99.3	0.08	1.10
33	17.4	1.62	0.53	93	99.5	0.06	1.07
36	22.8	1.99	0.63	96	99.6	0.04	1.04
39	29.3	2.34	0.75	99	99.7	0.03	1.01
42	36.7	2.63	0.87	102	99.8	0.02	0.98
45	44.9	2.80	1.00	105	99.9	0.02	0.95
48	53.4	2.81[a]	1.11	108	99.9	0.01	0.93
51	61.7	2.67	1.21	111	99.9	0.01	0.90
54	69.3	2.41	1.28	114	99.9	0.01	0.88
57	76.0	2.06	1.33	117	100.0	0.00	0.85
60	81.6	1.69	1.36	120	100.0	0.00	0.83

Values for logistic curve with $N_0 = 0.5$ ton C/acre, $r = 0.113$ year^{-1}, and $K = 100$ tons C/acre, as shown in Figure 7.12. This forest reaches 80% of its maximum storage in 60 years. These are rough numbers for a temperate mixed hardwood forest. dN/dt is the instantaneous growth rate ($= rN_0 e^{rt}(1 - N_0/K)/[1 + (N_0/K)(e^{rt} - 1)]^2$ by manipulating Eq. 7.5b). N/t is the average growth rate.

[a]Maximum value.

Source: Estimates based on Harmon et al. (1990) and Herendeen and Brown (1987).

with a finite stock, we encounter a time limit. CO_2 sequestering is a resource depletion issue. The resource in this case is the environment's ability to absorb pollution.

PROBLEMS

Level of difficulty is indicated as Easier/Moderate/Harder. Problems marked "(Spreadsheet?)" can be fruitfully approached using a spreadsheet. They need not be, however.

7.1. (Easier) The Alaska pipeline is 800 miles long and currently (1996) delivers 1.45 million barrels of crude oil per day (Mitchell, 1997).

(a) How long does it take for a drop of oil to make the trip?

(b) What is the average speed?

(c) Are the answers to (a) and (b) reasonable?

7.2. (Easier) For the following production rates, estimate a characteristic time and then calculate the steady-state stock. Specify where the stock resides.

(a) Beer cans: 6/day.

(b) Ditto, but assume Joe the jeans maker's τ of 1 day.

(c) Garbage: 5 lb/person-day.

(d) CO_2: An average household uses 8000 kWh/year of electricity. A coal-fired power plant burns about 0.8 lb of coal to produce a kilowatt-hour.

7.3. (Easier) (Spreadsheet?) We want the number of live births expected from an infant female today over her lifetime. In Table 7.7 we could add the reproduction factors for all ages to obtain 0.9243, but this over-estimates because some females die before reaching reproductive age. Use all the data in Table 7.7 to obtain a better estimate.

7.4. (Moderate) The average lifetime is the sum of each possible lifetime times that lifetime's probability. If the probability of a lifetime is as given in Table 7.4, that is, $p(n) = (1 - 1/\tau)^{n-1}(1/\tau)$:

(a) Verify that the probability of dying sometime is 1, that is, that the sum of $p(n)$ from $n = 1$ to ∞ is 1.

(b) Show that the average lifetime is τ.

Important Equation 2 may be useful. Additional hint for (b):

$$(1 + x + x^2 + x^3 + \cdots + x^n + \cdots)(1 + x + x^2 + x^3 + \cdots + x^n + \cdots)$$
$$= 1 + 2x + 3x^2 + 4x^3 + \cdots + (n + 1)x^n + \cdots$$

7.5. (Moderate) As in Problem 7.4, but use integration for 0 to ∞ over the continuous form for the probability of dying at exactly at time t, which is $(1/\tau)e^{-t/\tau}$.

7.6. (Moderate) (Spreadsheet?) For the example of 100 watermelon rinds/day inflow, compare stock versus time obtained using the finite-difference approach (Eq. 7.3) and using a continuous approach (see footnote 2). One is always smaller than the other. Which, and why?

7.7. (Moderate) (Spreadsheet?) In the Musa example, the survival and reproduction factors were given as:

Age Class	Survival Factor	Reproduction Factor
1	1	0
2	1	1
3	1	0
4	0	0

(a) Using these same factors, specify an initial population distribution that will:

  1. Overshoot and eventually reach a steady population greater than the starting value.

  2. Overshoot and eventually reach a steady population smaller than the starting value.

  3. Undershoot and eventually reach a steady population smaller than the starting value.

  4. Undershoot and eventually reach a steady population greater than the starting value.

(b) Repeat (a) with the same survival fractions, but using these three different sets of reproduction factors:

Age Class	Reproduction Factor		
1	0	0	0
2	0.5	0.5	0
3	0	0.5	0.5
4	0.5	0.5	0

7.8. (Moderate) U.S. auto population:

1946	28,217,028
1947	30,849,353
1948	33,355,250
1949	36,457,943
1950	40,339,077
1951	42,688,309
1952	43,823,097

The cars in 1946 were old because of limited production during World War II. Assume there were equal numbers in age classes 6–10 years.

(a) If the fixed lifetime was 10 years, what was U.S. auto production for each year in 1946–1951? Neglect imports and exports.

(b) These assumptions lead to a large decrease in auto manufacturing in 1951. Do you believe it?

7.9. (Moderate) Atmospheric CO_2: Method 1, based on absolute numbers. Human activity causes the following CO_2 release to the atmosphere annually: 4 to 7 billion metric tons from deforestation and 18 billion metric tons from fossil fuel burning. About half remains in the atmosphere. Assume this release will hold at today's value indefinitely. Today the atmosphere is about 540 ppm (parts per million) by weight CO_2. The CO_2 residence time is 100 years. The weight of the atmosphere is 5.14×10^{18} kg (Harte, 1988, Appendix III).

(a) What is the eventual atmospheric concentration?

(b) Estimate how long it will take to achieve this.

7.10. (Harder) Atmospheric CO_2: Method 2, based on ratios. The preindustrial atmospheric CO_2 concentration was 380 ppm by weight (= 250 ppm by volume). It is now 540 ppm by weight (= 350 ppm by volume). About one-half of today's atmospheric anthropogenic CO_2 emissions (absolute value not known) are not removed and hence are accumulating.

(a) Assuming that atmospheric CO_2 in excess of the preindustrial level was and is governed by a residence time process with $\tau = 100$ years and that the emission rate remains constant at today's level forever, what is the eventual CO_2 concentration? How long will it take to achieve this?

(b) Starr (1993) argues that τ for atmospheric CO_2 is actually 5 years. Repeat (a) in these two cases: (1) $\tau = 5$ years for all atmospheric levels in excess of the preindustrial level; and (2) for all atmospheric levels in excess of the preindustrial level, $\tau = 100$ until today, but from here on changes abruptly to 5 years. Sketch the atmospheric concentration over time in each case.

7.11. (Moderate) The following is from an article in *Time* magazine, July 15, 1996 (Church, 1996):

> In a $7 trillion economy, what seems to be tiny differences in percentages is in fact enormous. Adding just half a percentage point to the growth rate over the next eight years would generate approximately 400,000 jobs per year, boost real wages by $7000 per family, and add around $200 billion (in tax collections) to the U.S. Treasury, says Jerry Jasinowski, president of the National Association of Manufacturers.

(a) This passage is sloppy about units of the numbers given (stocks or flows?). Modify the given units, if needed, so the statement makes dimensional sense.

(b) With the units assigned in part (a), perform simple calculations to justify, or debunk, the figures 400,000, $7000, and $200 billion.

(c) If the figures in part (b) do not make numerical sense, explain what might have gone wrong. Do you think it was intentional or accidental?

7.12. (Harder) (Spreadsheet?) Figure 7.13 gives volumes, retention times, and watershed areas for the Great Lakes (Colborn et al., 1990). The overall question to answer is: Are the precipitation rates that we infer from the flow pattern reasonable? Assume the Great Lakes are at hydrological steady state. The flow in the lakes is (Michigan + Superior) → Huron → Erie → Ontario → St. Lawrence River to the Atlantic Ocean, as shown. Ignore evaporation.

(a) At the outset, what is your estimate/guess for local average annual precipitation?

(b) What is the outflow for each of the lakes (five answers)?

(c) The inflow for a lake is the sum of precipitation on its drainage (including its own area) and flow from lakes "upstream." What is the precipitation inflow for each lake (five answers)?

(d) Assuming that precipitation is distributed evenly across at lake's drainage, what is the annual precipitation in each lake's drainage (five answers)?

(e) Comment on the reasonableness of your answers in part (d). Include a comparison with the result in part (a).

(f) Actually Chicago withdraws water from the southern end of Lake Michigan and releases it outside of the Great Lakes watershed into the Illinois River, which feeds the Mississippi to the Gulf of Mexico. Assume the withdrawal rate is 100 gallons/person/day. If we accounted for this, would we need to change our responses to parts (b)–(e)? *Note:* Even if the answer is yes, do not redo (b)–(e).

7.13. (Harder) (Spreadsheet?) Consider two lakes as shown in Figure 7.14. The only outlet of Lake A is the only inlet of Lake B. Ignore evaporation loss and assume steady-state water flow. Assume the water in each lake is always thoroughly mixed (say by wind-driven currents). The retention time of Lake A is 4 months and that of Lake B, 20 months.

(a) At steady state, what is the relationship between the volumes of the two lakes?

(b) Dynamic problem: Assume that before $t = 0$ there is no pollutant in either lake. At $t = 0$, a steady flow of water-soluble pollutant

Physical Characteristics of the Great Lakes

Lake	Area of Lake	Area of Drainage Basin	Average Depth	Volume	Retention Time
Superior	31,700 sq. mi. 82,100 sq. km.	49,300 sq. mi. 127,700 sq. km.	483 ft. 147 m.	2,900 cu. mi. 12,100 cu. km.	191 yr.
Michigan	22,300 sq. mi. 57,800 sq. km.	45,600 sq. mi. 118,000 sq. km.	279 ft. 85 m.	1,180 cu. mi. 4,920 cu. km.	99 yr.
Huron	23,000 sq. mi. 59,600 sq. km.	51,700 sq. mi. 134,000 sq. km.	195 ft. 59 m.	850 cu. mi. 3,540 cu. km.	22 yr.
Erie	9,910 sq. mi. 25,700 sq. km.	30,140 sq. mi. 78,000 sq. km.	62 ft. 19 m.	116 cu. mi. 484 cu. km.	2.6 yr.
Ontario	7,340 sq. mi. 18,960 sq. km.	24,720 sq. mi. 64,030 sq. km.	283 ft. 86 m.	393 cu. mi. 1,640 cu. km.	6 yr.

Depth Profile of the Great Lakes

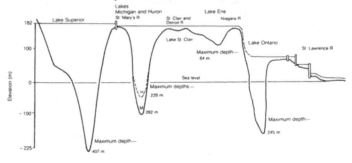

The Great Lakes Basin

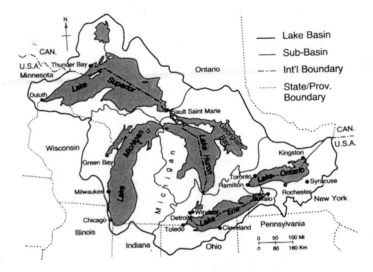

Figure 7.13 Great Lakes hydrological data. *Source:* T. Colborn, A. Davidson, S. Green, R. Hodge, et al. (1990). *Great Lakes, Great Legacy?* The Conservation Foundation. © 1990 World Wildlife Fund and Institute for Public Policy Research. Reprinted with permission.

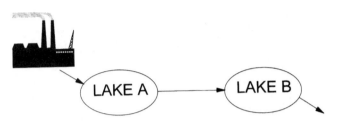

Figure 7.14   Pollution in a chain of lakes.

enters Lake A through its inlet, so that the pollution concentration of the inflow is 0.2 g/l. The pollutant does not degrade, settle out, or evaporate.

(c) Sketch a graph of pollutant stock versus time in each lake.

(d) Model the dynamic problem using a time step of 1 month from $t = 0$ to $t = 50$ months. Do this either by hand plus pocket calculator or by spreadsheet. *Caution:* Lake B does not start to fill with pollutant until Lake A starts to leak it.

(e) New dynamic problem: Assume that the pollutant has been incoming for so long that pollutant levels are at steady state and that at $t = 0$ the pollutant input is turned off. Repeat (c) and (d).

7.14. (Harder) The following is from *Ecology USA,* November 11, 1996:

> The Biomass for Rural Development program centers on a 2600 acre tract where officials hope to develop hybrid, faster-growing willows that will produce between 37–47 MW, or enough power to light 40,000 homes. Officials, who hope the willows will provide a viable energy source by 2000, project willow-based sales could be as much as $20 million per year, which could lead to $135 million worth of related energy sales .... A single planting can last up to 20 years, so there will be a significant reduction in erosion and land maintenance; and, the density of willows eliminates the need for herbicides.

(a) Are these numbers correct: 37–47 MW, 40,000 homes, $20 million/year? (Assume the other numbers are correct.)

(b) If not, change them so that the passage makes sense.
    Possibly useful numbers (which are correct): The best projected average yields from intensive biomass plantations is about 8 dry tons of wood per acre per year (Herendeen and Brown, 1987). Wood can be burned to provide about 10,000 Btu per pound. 10,000 Btu of heat in a power plant produces about 1 kWh of electricity. A typical single-family residence uses about 700 kWh/month for all uses and about 80 kWh/month for lighting.

7.15. (Harder) (Spreadsheet?)

 (a) Using the 1995 population and survival factors in the China example (Table 7.7), assume the one-child family is achieved immediately. Is there a population overshoot?

 (b) Make biologically reasonable modifications to the reproduction factors (assumed constant over time) to produce an eventual steady population. What is the smallest steady population you obtain?

 (c) Reproduction and survival factors do not remain constant over time as we have assumed so far. Assuming that survival factors do not change, qualitatively discuss how reproduction factors would need to vary over time for the Chinese population to hold constant at the 1995 value.

7.16. (Harder) For a system characterized by the residence time approximation, we have investigated how stock changes with time for F_{in} = constant. Investigate for:

 (a) $F_{in} = kt$, where t = time and k is a constant (this is linearly increasing input flow).

 (b) $F_{in} = Ae^{at}$, where A and a are constants (thus is exponentially increasing input flow).

This can be done by integration (challenging) or by simulation using a pocket calculator, a spreadsheet, or a computer simulation language such as STELLA.

8 Indirect Effects

INDIRECT EFFECTS IN TIME, SPACE, AND CONCEPT

- All flesh is grass.
- New York City gets its water from the Catskill Mountains, 100 miles distant.
- We eat potatoes made of oil.
- Humankind is now dependent on at least a quarter of the net primary productivity of the biosphere.
- Only 10% of the energy to manufacture a car is burned in the auto assembly plant.
- Increased return of bottles increases materials handling jobs and decreases container manufacturing jobs.

In this chapter we cover a wide range of indirect effects such as those listed previously. We will concentrate on the indirect effects that result from expanding the conceptual system boundary to the questions we ask. Often this also implies an expansion in space and, perhaps, in time. For example, let us ask how much energy is required to allow your car to travel 1 mile. Here are possible answers to the question:

1. The fuel burned
    2. plus the energy to extract, refine, and transport the fuel
        3. plus the energy to manufacture the car (prorated to 1 mile's use)
            4. plus the energy to produce tires, replacement parts, etc.
                5. plus the energy to build and maintain roads
                    6. plus the energy to maintain auto repair shops, government regulation and registration services, etc.
                        7. plus the energy to produce and maintain that portion of the health system used to care for the consequences of auto accidents and auto-related health problems.

This progression is by no means complete, and the cumulative result becomes larger at each step. Also, there are side steps: A similar expanding wave of concern and impact ripples out from, for example, the energy to make the car, which could include:

1. the energy consumed at the assembly plant
    2. plus the energy used to produce the steel, glass, rubber, and so on
        3. plus the energy used at the iron mine, sand pit, and sulfur mine
            ⋮
            ad infinitum

even including the cars used by the iron mine, so that the process runs in circles. (We will see later that, even though the process is circular, it converges mathematically to a finite result.)

Figure 8.1a shows the results of this calculation: Around 1970 the true energy cost of an automobile was about 60% higher than just the fuel to power it. Figure 8.1b also shows a recent estimate, in economic terms, of various impacts of auto use and disposal. These amount to an increment of about 40% over the conventional sticker price. Even given the high uncertainty of these numbers, they are significant. Figure 8.2 exemplifies how complicated it is to determine indirect effects.

Another example concerns the energy required to provide human food:

1. The caloric content of the food
    2. plus fuel used in field operations on the farm
        3. plus energy used to make agricultural chemicals
            4. plus energy to process food
                5. plus energy to transport to market
                    6. plus energy to store and prepare to home.

Figure 8.3 summarizes several studies on the energy required to produce food. Of particular note is the trend of increasing energy subsidies in U.S. agriculture. In 1970 to produce 1 Cal of food required about 8 Cal of fossil fuel to be burned.

A third example connects the demand for electric power and the distant inundation of large wilderness tracts, such as the James Bay Hydro Project in northern Quebec. See Figure 8.4.

It seems that most humans tend to think of, deal with, matters that are local, immediate, and relatively direct in their causation. Many environmental problems, however, are regional or global, involve lagged impacts from the past and delayed effects in the future, and have indirect causation. Figure 8.5 illustrates the range of concern in a three-dimensional framework covering space, time, and conceptual complexity. In this chapter we concentrate on indirect effects; in Chapters 5 and 7 we have concentrated on time. Spatial issues are generally beyond the scope of this book.

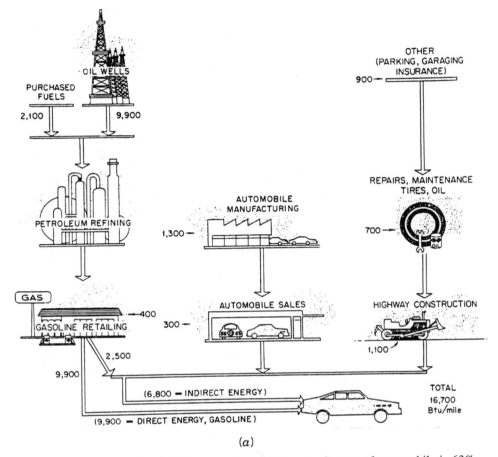

(a)

Figure 8.1 Examples of indirectness. (a) Total energy impact of automobile is 63% higher than direct fuel use (Hirst and Herendeen, 1973). (b) True economic cost of automobile is 39% than normal sticker price. *Source:* T. Prugh (1995). Natural capital and human economic survival. ISEE Press. © 1995 ISEE Press. Reprinted with permission.

In Figure 8.5 certain viewpoints are semiwhimsically assigned to specific professional groups. Politicians, and most people, tend to think in terms of local (20 miles, or perhaps to national borders), short-term (2 years), and conceptually direct issues. Population biologists study temporal variation (over several generations) but seldom extend their work to species far beyond the one of interest or to spatial variation (though this is changing). Diplomats are concerned with spatial distribution over longer time scales (5–10 years), but still tend to concentrate on fairly direct mechanisms. In this chapter we will stress conceptually indirect effects, but not temporal or spatial effects. The World 3 model of Meadows et al. (1992) covers dynamic effects over

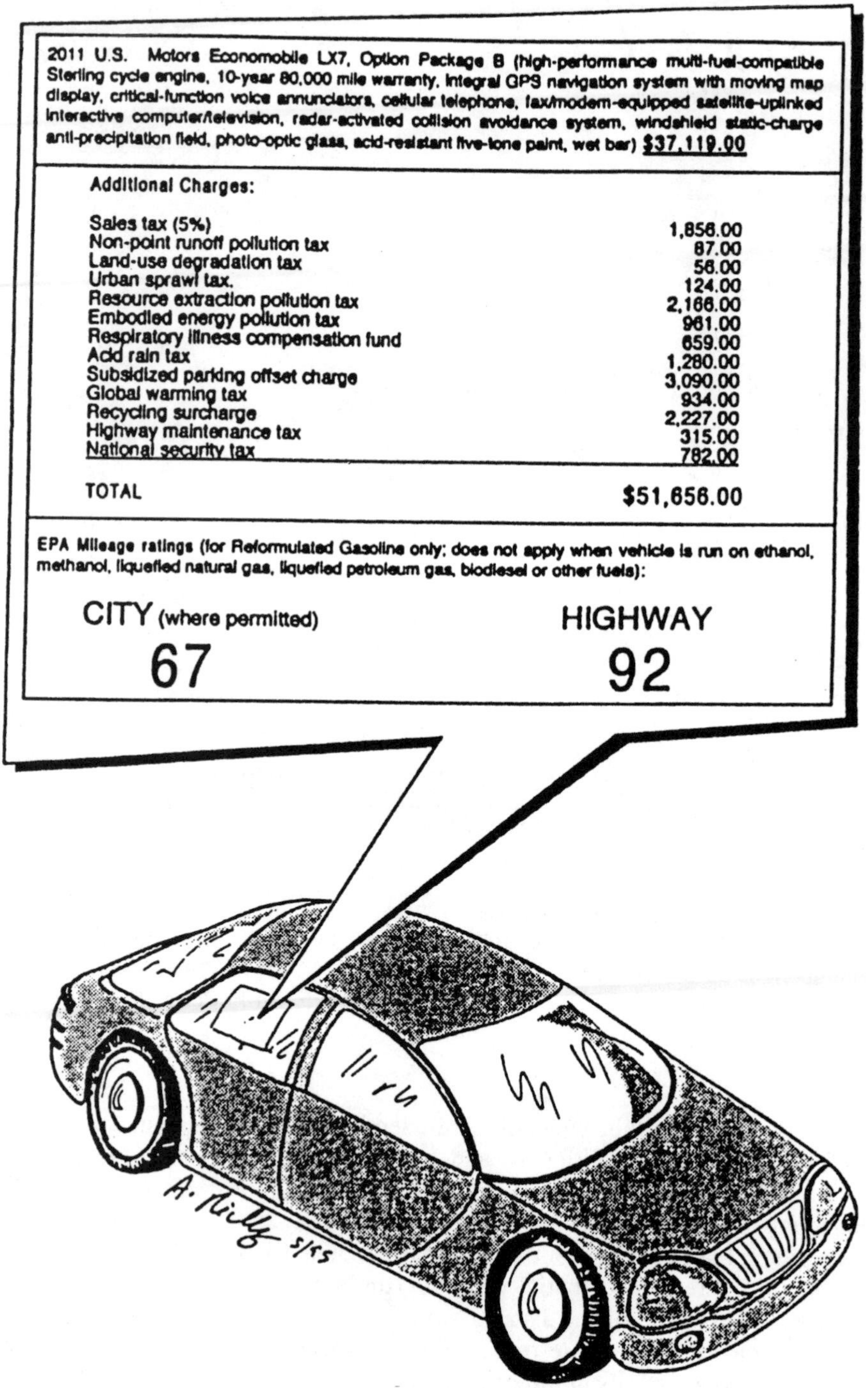

2011 U.S. Motors Economobile LX7, Option Package B (high-performance multi-fuel-compatible Sterling cycle engine, 10-year 80,000 mile warranty. Integral GPS navigation system with moving map display, critical-function voice annunciators, cellular telephone, fax/modem-equipped satellite-uplinked interactive computer/television, radar-activated collision avoidance system, windshield static-charge anti-precipitation field, photo-optic glass, acid-resistant five-tone paint, wet bar) **$37,119.00**

Additional Charges:

Sales tax (5%)	1,856.00
Non-point runoff pollution tax	87.00
Land-use degradation tax	56.00
Urban sprawl tax	124.00
Resource extraction pollution tax	2,166.00
Embodied energy pollution tax	961.00
Respiratory illness compensation fund	659.00
Acid rain tax	1,280.00
Subsidized parking offset charge	3,090.00
Global warming tax	934.00
Recycling surcharge	2,227.00
Highway maintenance tax	315.00
National security tax	782.00
TOTAL	$51,656.00

EPA Mileage ratings (for Reformulated Gasoline only; does not apply when vehicle is run on ethanol, methanol, liquefied natural gas, liquefied petroleum gas, biodiesel or other fuels):

CITY (where permitted)
67

HIGHWAY
92

(b)

Figure 8.1 (Continued)

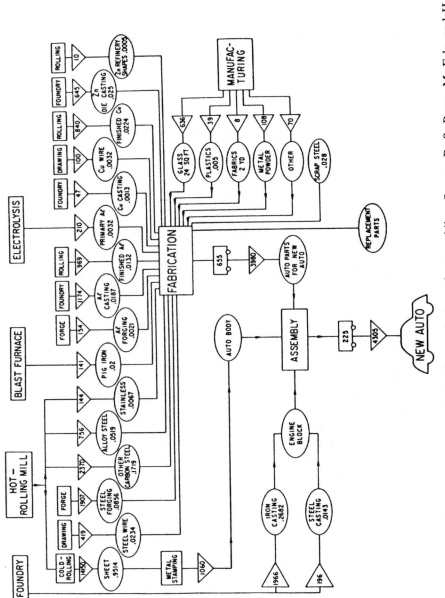

Figure 8.2 Example of detailed energy accounting in the production of automobiles. *Source:* R. S. Berry, M. Fels, and H. Makino (1974). A thermodynamic valuation of resource use: making automobiles and other processes. In *Energy: Demand, Conservation, and Institutional Problems* (M. Acrakis, ed.), pp. 499–515. © 1974 MIT Press. Reprinted with permission.

151

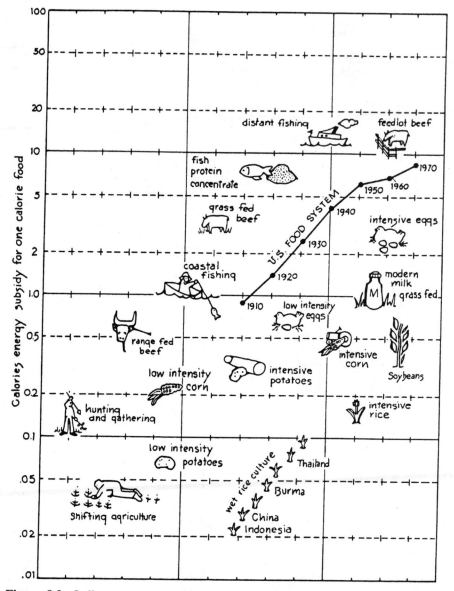

Figure 8.3 Indirect energy requirements in food production. Solar energy is not counted. Human energies are counted in subsistence systems. In developed countries human inputs are dominated by inputs in machinery, fuel, and agricultural chemicals. *Source:* C. Steinhart and J. Steinhart (1974). *Energy: Sources, Use, and Role in Human Affairs.* Duxbury Press. © 1974 Wadsworth Press. Reprinted with permission.

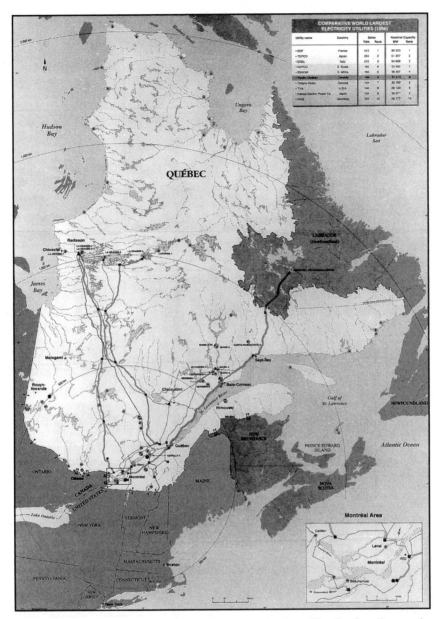

Figure 8.4 Main (765 Kv) power lines of Hydro Quebec. The line heading northeast goes 1200 km to Churchill Falls, Labrador, developed in the late 1960s. The two heading north are to stations on the LaGrande River, which is dammed into several reservoirs. The LaGrande project (1971–1996) also diverted the Opinaca and Eastmain Rivers into the LaGrande. 11,500 km^2 of new reservoir area were created. Eight of 9 planned stations have a combined peak power of 15,700 MW. Proposed but deferred projects are on the Great Whale River, 150 km north of the LaGrande; and on the Rupert/Nottaway/Broadback Rivers, 200–400 km south. The Churchill project is on the Atlantic drainage. All other rivers flow, or flowed, west into Hudson/James Bay. Interlinks through New York and Vermont allow power export to the U.S. *Source:* A World of Electricity (map), 2nd ed. (April). © 1997 Hydro Quebec International, Inc. Reprinted with permission.

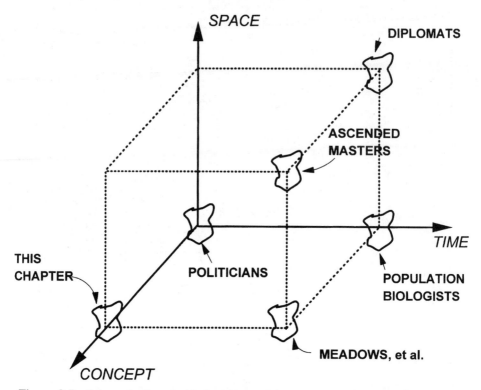

Figure 8.5   Schematic for considering the spatial, temporal, and conceptual scale of a problem. Most humans operate at the intersection of short times, small spaces, and simple explanations. A few achieve "ascended master" status by considering complex problems over wide spatial extent on a long time scale.

several decades in systems with many indirect linkages, but aggregates the globe into a single unit, effectively removing spatial concerns. The person or institution that truly looks at complex problems over wide spatial extent and with a long time perspective may be called an "ascended master."

A Surprising Disbenefit of Pollution Cleanup

Improved water quality may cause a marine organism population explosion in Manhattan's East River. Shipworms and gribbles have long been held in check by the toxic effects of pollution, but have recently begun to increase in numbers. They may have been responsible for the recent collapse of a 50-year-old wharf and deterioration of some of the pilings supporting Franklin D. Roosevelt Drive.

—*Water Newsletter* (1995). Water Information Center, Inc., Denver

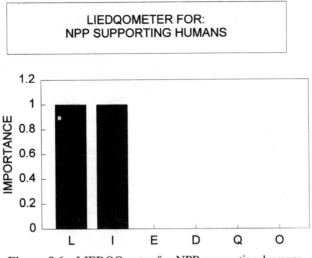

Figure 8.6 LIEDQOmeter for NPP supporting humans.

EXAMPLE: HUMAN USE OF BIOSPHERIC PRODUCTION

Vitousek et al. (1986) sought to quantify to what extent the human race depends on the "light of a star," the sun. (See Figure 8.6.) Green plants (producers) fix solar energy (gross primary production, GPP) via photosynthesis, then dissipate much of that via respiration. If we assume a steady state, the remaining fraction (net primary production, NPP) is consumed by other living things, as shown in Figure 8.7. Both GPP and NPP are thus measured in energy per unit time. This is expressed in grams of dry biomass per year.

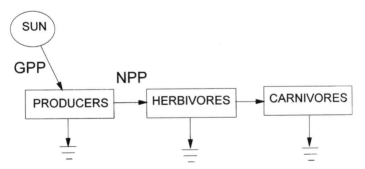

Figure 8.7 Energy flows in a hypothetical food chain. Gross primary production (GPP) is the solar energy fixed per year by producers. Dissipation is indicated by flows to the ground symbols. GPP minus the dissipation by producers is net primary production (NPP), which is available as input to consumers or could be exported from the system. Here herbivores are assumed to consume all NPP.

Roughly, 1 gram biomass = 4.5 kcal (also called Calories, the unit often used in human dietary discussions). The question is what fraction of global NPP supports humans. Vitousek et al. developed three responses, starting with direct use and expanding to indirect uses, as shown in Tables 8.1A and 8.1B.

In Table 8.1 two points are important. First, we see that the high estimate is over eight times the low, a vivid demonstration of indirect effects. The second is that the high estimate is about 25% of global NPP. Allowing for large uncertainties in the calculation of Vitousek et al., this is still a large fraction of global NPP. This is especially true given the anticipated growth in the human population compounded with a desired growth in per capita consumption.

TABLE 8.1A   World NPP in Petagrams per Year of Carbon Fixed by Photosynthesis

	Area (10⁶ km²)	NPP (Pg/year)[a]
Forest	31	48.7
Woodland, grassland, savannah	37	52.1
Deserts	30	3.1
Artic/alpine	25	2.1
Cultivated land	16	15.0
Human-occupied area	2	0.4
Chaparral, bogs, swamps, marshes	6	10.7
Already lost from conversion of forests and grasslands to agricultural land and pastures, desertification, etc., listed under high option in Table 8.1B	—	17.5
Terrestrial subtotal	147	149.6
Lake and streams	2	0.8
Marine	361	91.6
Aquatic subtotal	363	92.4
Total[b]	510	242.0 (100%)

[a]Pg/year = petagrams/year = 10¹⁵ grams/year.
[b]The total includes some potential already lost in conversion of natural systems to pasture and agriculture, desertification, and so on.

TABLE 8.1B   Low, Medium, and High Estimates of NPP to Support Human Activity

	NPP (Pg/year)
Low (mostly "direct" use)	
1. Energy of plant production consumed by humans	0.8
2. Energy of fodder consumed by livestock	2.2
3. Energy of forest wood consumed for timber, fiber, fuel	2.2
4. NPP of exploited aquatic ecosystems (= human consumption of fish, carried back to aquatic system NPP by multiplying by a factor of 10 ∗ 10 = 100)	2.0
Low subtotal	7.2 (3.0%)
Medium (including NPP "co-opted by humans"). Add to low:	
1. NPP of crop plants (stalks, etc., not consumed by humans)	14.2
2. NPP of pasture land (portion not consumed by pasture animals)	9.4
3. NPP of forests used for timber, fiber, fuel (portion not consumed for timber, fiber, fuel)	11.4
4. NPP of human-occupied areas (e.g., parks)	0.4
Medium subtotal	35.4
Low + medium total	42.6 (17.6%)
High (including NPP foregone because of human activities). Add to medium:	
1. NPP lost from converting natural vegetation to agricultural land	9.0
2. NPP lost from converting forest to pasture	1.4
3. NPP lost from desertification	4.5
4. NPP lost from converting natural vegetation to human-occupied areas.	2.6
High subtotal	17.5
Low + medium + high total	60.1 (24.8%)

THE INPUT–OUTPUT APPROACH APPLIED TO ECONOMIC AND ECOLOGICAL SYSTEMS: IMPORTANT EQUATION 4

The determination of direct plus indirect effects can be carried out in the same way for a wide range of issues. For example:

- the energy (or the copper, labor . . .) to make something
- the CO_2 (or wastewater . . .) released

• the land disrupted.

Later in this chapter we discuss several policy and scientific applications of this approach. First, we develop the ideas, starting with an example.

Figure 8.8 represents the flow of biomass energy, and heat from respiration, in a hypothetical two-compartment ecosystem. Photosynthesis by producers (green plants) fixes 100 solar energy flow units (say Calories/day). Of that 100 units, 90 is dissipated in respiration. Nine of the remaining 10 are eaten by consumers (animals), and 1 is removed (exported) from the system. The animals, in turn, dissipate 7 units, and finally 2 units of animals is removed from the system. This diagram describes the flows, not the stocks. The system is at steady state.

Figure 8.8 represents a trophic pyramid; at each level the major share of the energy flow into the compartment is dissipated and only 10 or 20% is available for the next level's consumption or for export. In Table 8.2 we consider several "direct and indirect" questions whose answers can be determined from Figure 8.8. It is important to be careful about units here. In each answer the first term is a dimensionless ratio obtained by dividing a flow by a flow. The ratio is often called the *energy intensity,* which is listed in detail in the last column of the table.

Energy intensity (units = energy/gloof) is the energy required at all steps for the system to produce one unit of output of gloof. Energy intensity is not necessarily actual energy that can be obtained by burning the gloof, usually much of that energy has already been dissipated. Rather, it is all the energy that must be dissipated or sequestered for the system to do the job. On one hand, most of that energy is no longer available; on the other hand, it is an absolutely essential requirement and connection between the gloof and the

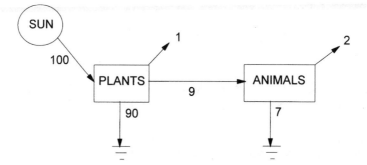

Figure 8.8   Energy flow (units = Cal/day) in hypothetical chain ecosystem. The flows to the ground symbols are dissipated as heat.

TABLE 8.2 Questions about Figure 8.8

Question	Answer	Appropriate Energy Intensity?
How much solar input is needed for plants to produce 1 Cal/day to be eaten by animals?	(100/10)(1 Cal/day) = 10 Cal/day	10 Cal solar/Cal plant output
How much input to animals is needed to allow 1 Cal of animal to be removed?	(9/2)(1 Cal) = 4.5 Cal	4.5 plant Cal eaten/ animal Cal removed
How much solar input is needed to allow the system to produce 1 Cal of animal for removal?	(100/10)(9 Cal)/2 = 45 Cal	45 Cal solar input/ animal Cal removed

system and environment that produced it.

From a bookkeeping standpoint there is nothing unique about energy. Figure 8.8 could represent a totally different system, say one producing automobiles from steel, as shown in Figure 8.9. In contrast to the energy flows in Figure 8.8, the flows in this system are lossless: No steel leaks out and all ends up in the cars. In Table 8.3 we ask similar direct and indirect questions regarding this system. Here the intensities are expressed in appropriate units. The indirectness is quantified; directly, no iron ore is used to make a car; indirectly, ore *is* required. In this example three different flow variables (tons ore/day, ingots/day, and cars/day) are used in the same diagram, and the intensities are not dimensionless . . . but it all makes dimensional sense.

The mathematical procedure we have used to track indirect connections has been so straightforward that we have not even specified it. It is easy because the process we have used is linear, or chainlike, and has no looping back, no feedback. Feedback converts a chain structure to a web and makes the bookkeeping much more complicated. In Figure 8.10 there is an energy flow from plants to animals. In a biological system this feedback for energy is somewhat uncommon, but possible: Consider, for example, the Venus flytrap. (Feedback is more likely in terms of nutrients, such as nitrogen cycling back from animals to plants. In the car example it is easy to imagine some cars being used by an iron mine.) The question is still: How much solar energy fixation needs to occur in plants in order for a calorie of animals to be produced? There are two ways to proceed.

IRON ORE: 200 TONS/DAY   STEEL   STEEL: 10 INGOTS/DAY   CARS   CARS: 2 CARS/DAY

Figure 8.9 Flows in a steel-to-car chain production system.

TABLE 8.3 Questions about the Steel–Car Production System in Figure 8.9

Question	Answer	What Is the Appropriate Intensity?
How much ore is required to produce 1 ingot of steel?	20 tons	20 tons ore/ingot
How much steel is required to produce a car?	5 ingots	5 ingots/car
How much ore is required to produce a car?	100 tons	100 tons ore/car

Vertical Analysis (Follow Your Nose, in Steps) Figure 8.11 indicates the stepwise process of producing a product such as a car. The auto factory is the box on the far left. To produce an auto, the factory receives inputs from three other sectors, say steel, glass, and rubber. Each of these receives inputs from three sectors and so on. Vertical analysis traces this web of inputs backward. At each node it evaluates the amount of the desired input (say energy) at that point and then traces still farther back. Let us do this for the plant–animal system with feedback in Figure 8.10.

Step 1. In Figure 8.10 we see that for 1 Cal removed from animals plants need to produce $9/3 = 3$ Cal.

Step 2. For plants to produce 3 Cal, they must input $(1/10)(3) = 0.3$ Cal of animals and *30 Cal of solar energy*.

Step 3. For animals to produce 0.3 Cal, they require $(9/3)(0.3) = 0.9$ Cal from plants.

Step 4. For plants to produce 0.9 Cal, they must input $(1/10)(0.9) = 0.09$ Cal of animals and *9 Cal of solar input*.

And so on.

ACTUAL ENERGY FLOW

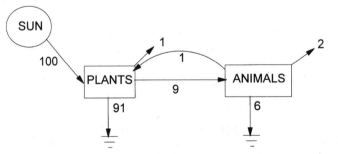

Figure 8.10 A web: Energy flows when feedback is added to the production chain in Figure 8.8 (units = Cal/day).

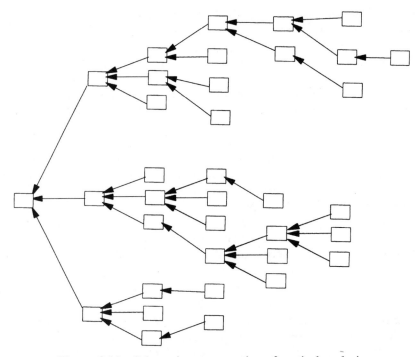

Figure 8.11   Schematic representation of vertical analysis.

In these steps the energy inputs have been italicized. The process continues indefinitely, but the terms are decreasing. Continuing in this fashion, we sum the energy inputs to find that to produce 1 Cal of consumer requires

$$30 + 9 + 2.7 + 0.81 + \cdots \text{Cal of solar input}$$

This is

$$(30)(1 + 0.3 + (0.3)^2 + (0.3)^3 + \cdots)$$

By Important Equation 2 the sum of the geometric series is $(1 - (0.3)^\infty)/(1 - 0.3) = 1/0.7$, and therefore to produce 1 Cal of consumer requires $(30)(1/0.7) = 42.86$ Cal of fixed solar input. This is different from the 45 Cal obtained with no feedback in Table 8.2.

This approach can be used for more than two compartments, in which case the mathematics is the same in principle but more involved in practice. It is used, for example, in determining the energy cost of cars (Berry and Fels, 1973). The process is stopped when the additional terms seem acceptably small.

Input–Output Analysis   Our method here is really nothing more than setting up and solving a set of simultaneous equations, but its historical connection with input–output economics is strong and instructive. We will see that the input–output (I–O) approach can answer indirectness questions covering economic systems (including labor and taxation questions), energy (and pollution) analysis, and trophic structure of ecosystems. The analogies between these systems are strong, and while analogies only infrequently lead to rigorous equivalences, in this case they do so.

The basis for this approach is three assumptions. We start with a system with N compartments, each with an output flow measured in gloof/time. Gloof need not be biomass energy (as it is in the ecosystem example, Fig. 8.8), and it can even vary from compartment to compartment (as in the car example, Fig. 8.9). The assumptions are:

1. Every flow in the system that we wish to count (units = gloof/time) has an associated energy intensity according to its source compartment (units = energy/gloof).
2. Embodied energy flows everywhere there are original flows, and the magnitude of the embodied energy flow (units = energy/time) is the product of the energy intensity (units = energy/gloof) times the original flow (units = gloof/time). This assumes that the flow variable is a good surrogate for embodied energy flow, which is a judgment call by the user.[1]
3. Assuming that the original gloof flows are at steady state, embodied energy is conserved in each compartment; that is, the amount "in" equals the amount "out." See Figure 8.12.

These assumptions are sufficient to set up equations to solve for the energy intensities. Mathematically, the assumptions are stated by Important Equation 4 as follows:

IMPORTANT EQUATION 4

$$\sum_{i=1}^{N} \epsilon_i X_{ij} + E_j = \epsilon_j X_j \tag{8.1}$$

---

[1] For example, in an economic example the food compartment might produce grain and meat, and we might use dry weight of output as the flow variable, thus aggregating grain and meat. Yet meat requires more energy per unit of dry weight, and if one consumer receives only meat, and another, only grain, we could argue that the use of weight does not adequately reflect that difference. At that point, we could either: (1) accept this imprecision as an inevitable consequence of the aggregation or (2) disaggregate the flows and make a more complicated flow table that maintains the identity of grain and meat.

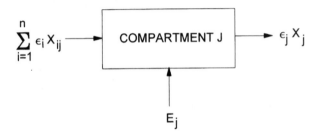

Figure 8.12 Embodied energy flows into and out of compartment j. The I–O assumption is that the sum of embodied energy inputs (the inflows) is equal to the sum of embodied energy outputs (the outflows).

where $X_{ij} \equiv$ actual gloof flow from compartment i to compartment j (units $=$ gloof$_i$/time)

$X_j \equiv$ sum of all output flows from compartment j (units $=$ gloof$_j$/time)

$E_j \equiv$ actual energy input flow to compartment j from outside the system (units $=$ energy/time)

$\epsilon_j \equiv$ energy intensity of output of compartment j (units $=$ energy/gloof$_j$).

Here the subscript on gloof indicates explicitly that there can be different flows from each compartment. Important Equation 4 represents the conservation of embodied energy (assumption 3), which is also shown in Figure 8.12.

Equation 8.1 is assumed to hold for each of the N compartments, yielding N equations in N unknowns. We know the X_{ij}'s and E_j's, so we can solve for the N ϵ_j's. Equation 8.1 is an important equation, first, because it formalizes the allocation of indirect effects in a self-consistent manner, and, second, because it represents a general approach that can be used to allocate indirect *anything,* not just energy.

Let us set up the equation for the feedback examples. Figure 8.13 shows schematically the embodied energy flows in the system with feedback of Figure 8.10. It is important to stress that in an embodied energy diagram such as Figure 8.13 the dissipation flows are removed. The point is to embody those losses in the flows that we (decide to) retain; the losses will become embodied in the actual flows. This is the crux of the embodied energy (or embodied anything) question, and one should think hard about this.

The balance equations are

$$\text{Plants:} \quad 100 + \epsilon_a = 10\epsilon_p$$

$$\text{Animals:} \quad 9\epsilon_p = 3\epsilon_a$$

These are solved to give

EMBODIED ENERGY FLOW

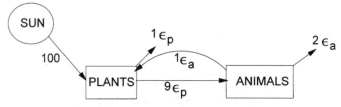

Figure 8.13 Embodied energy flows in the feedback example of Figure 8.10 (units = Cal/day).

$$\epsilon_p = 14.29 \text{ Cal solar input/Cal plant}$$

$$\epsilon_a = 42.86 \text{ Cal solar input/Cal animal}$$

The result for animals agrees with that from vertical analysis, and the result for plants is consistent with this. We could have obtained the latter by vertical analysis also.

We should step back and restate what we have done here. We have set up a self-consistent method of incorporating into a final product a quantitative measure of something used indirectly. This particular method conserves that indirectness: The plant is made of the light of a star; the animal is made of the plant and hence of the light of a star also. The I–O approach is mathematically equivalent to vertical analysis (see the accompanying box) and is much easier, though it can become computationally messy as the number of compartments increases. For example, the U.S. input–output economic accounts have about 350 compartments (U.S. Bureau of Economic Analysis, 1994a, b).

Leontief's Equation (Advanced Topic Requiring Matrix Algebra)

The N simultaneous equations to obtain gloof intensities can be written in matrix notation, in which case it is completely analogous to the economic input–output approach developed by Leontief (1973) to analyze indirect connections in economic systems (to answer questions such as "What will happen to the communications industry if households purchase more vegetables and less meat?"). Our equations

$$\sum_{i=1}^{N} \epsilon_i X_{ij} + E_j = \epsilon_j X_j$$

can be written in matrix form as

$$\epsilon X + E = \epsilon \hat{X}$$

$$\epsilon = E(\hat{X} - X)^{-1} \tag{8.2}$$

$$\epsilon = E\hat{X}^{-1}(I - X\hat{X}^{-1})^{-1}$$

where E is a vector of energy input flows, ϵ a vector of energy intensities, X a matrix of the flows X_{ij}, and $\hat{X}$ is a diagonal matrix of the total outputs X_j. For labor, pollution, and so on, intensities, E is replaced with labor inputs or pollution outputs.

This is the matrix statement of the equations we have already used to solve for the energy intensities. The term

$$X\hat{X}^{-1}$$

is a matrix obtained by dividing the column entries in X by the total outputs. In I–O economics this is called A. Then the energy intensities are given by

$$\epsilon = E\hat{X}^{-1}(I - A)^{-1} \tag{8.3}$$

Let us use this method to calculate energy intensities for the system in Figure 8.10, which we have already done using Important Equation 4 (Eq. 8.1). Using Figure 8.10,

$$X = \begin{pmatrix} 0 & 9 \\ 1 & 0 \end{pmatrix} \qquad \hat{X} = \begin{pmatrix} 10 & 0 \\ 0 & 3 \end{pmatrix} \qquad \hat{X}^{-1} = \begin{pmatrix} 1/10 & 0 \\ 0 & 0/3 \end{pmatrix}$$

$$A = \begin{pmatrix} 0 & 3 \\ 1/10 & 0 \end{pmatrix} \qquad E = (100 \quad 0) \qquad E\hat{X}^{-1} = (10 \quad 0)$$

$$\epsilon = E\hat{X}^{-1}(I - A)^{-1} = (10 \quad 0) \begin{pmatrix} 1 & -3 \\ -1/10 & 1 \end{pmatrix}^{-1}$$

$$= (10 \quad 0) \begin{pmatrix} 10/7 & 30/7 \\ 1/70 & 10/7 \end{pmatrix} = (14.29 \quad 42.86)$$

These energy intensities agree with what we found by solving Important Equation 4.

A further aspect of matrix algebra can be used to demonstrate the equivalence of vertical analysis: The crux of the method is inverting the matrix $(I - A)$, which can be expanded as an infinite series of powers of the matrix A:

$$(I - A)^{-1} = I + A + A^2 + A^3 + \cdots \qquad (8.4)$$

Each term represents another step in a vertical analysis, and by careful bookkeeping one can show that the terms are exactly equal to what we obtained in the vertical analysis given in the text.

Other aspects of this kind of analysis are as follows:

1. Embodied energy flows can exceed the energy flow into the system. Using the energy intensities we calculated, the embodied energy flows are given by the product of the actual energy flows times those intensities. Figure 8.14 shows the actual embodied energy flows for the system in Figure 8.10. Each compartment is in embodied energy balance, as it should be, and the flow of embodied energy from plants to animals exceeds the solar energy fixation flow into the system. The reason for this is feedback; without feedback this does not occur. This violates no physical laws, because embodied energy is not actual useful energy. (Problem 8.11 demonstrates that if the system input were not dissipatable, say nitrogen, interior flows would be measurably greater than the input flow.) It is a quantitative indication that feedback is occurring.

2. Embodied energy for the entire system is in balance. We can see this in Figure 8.14: the sum of the embodied energy leaving as exports of plants and animals exactly equals the solar input fixed. This is satisfying as the idea of tracing indirect effects is not to lose anything that we *decide* to keep. One can show rigorously that overall system balance is a consequence of individual compartment balances (Bullard and Herendeen, 1975). The proof is left as Problem 8.14. In analyzing systems for gloof intensities, one can, and should, check for the balances to verify that he/she has calculated the intensities correctly.

EMBODIED ENERGY FLOW

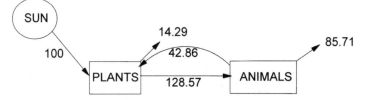

Figure 8.14 Embodied energy flows in feedback system. Each compartment, and the entire system, is in embodied energy balance (units = Cal/day).

3. The two methods we used—vertical analysis and I–O analysis—are completely equivalent if the same data are used and the vertical analysis is taken to an infinite number of steps (if feedback requires that). We demonstrated that in the food web example, but to show it in general for a many-compartment system involves matrix algebra. This is discussed in the box on page 164, but its level is beyond elementary calculus and hence it is an optional topic.

4. Increased feedback generally causes energy intensities to approach a common value. To demonstrate, let the feedback be variable, as shown in Figure 8.15. X can vary from 0 (no feedback) to a maximum of 7 Cal/day. The balance equations are now

$$\text{Plants:} \quad 100 + Z\epsilon_a = 10\epsilon_p$$

$$\text{Animals:} \quad 9\epsilon_p = (2 + Z)\epsilon_a$$

Solving gives

$$\epsilon_p = 100(2 + Z)/(20 + Z) \text{ Cal solar input/Cal plant}$$

$$\epsilon_a = 900/(20 + Z) \text{ Cal solar input/Cal animal}$$

Figure 8.16 shows the intensities as a function of Z. For $Z = 0$ (no feedback), the intensities are 10 and 45 Cal/Cal for plants and animals, respectively, as we found before. For $Z = 7$ Cal/day, the intensities attain the same value, 33.333 Cal/Cal. We can see why are identical in this case: The animals compartment now has no dissipation and is operationally a part of the plants. The combined compartment now has an export of 3 Cal/day and a solar input of 100 Cal/day, leading to an energy intensity of $100/3 = 33.33$ Cal/Cal.

ACTUAL ENERGY FLOW

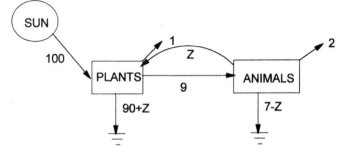

Figure 8.15 Energy flows in system with variable feedback. Z can vary from 0 to 7 Cal/day.

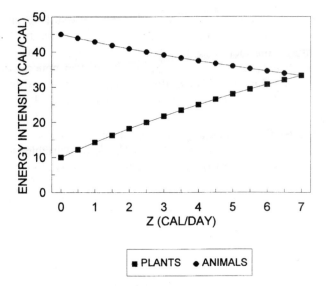

Figure 8.16 Energy intensities in Figure 8.15 as a function of feedback from animals to plants. $Z = 0$ is no feedback; $Z = 7$ Cal/day is maximum feedback.

Feedback thus has the effect of making the two system outputs more similar, which is intuitively reasonable.

5. The I–O approach can be used for labor, copper, pollution, or almost-anything intensity.[2] We have said that the flows X_{ij} can be anything; actual energy is just one possibility. The inputs E_j need not be energy either. They can be person-hours/time, in which case we have labor intensities (units = person-hours/gloof). They can be the amount of the pollutant SO_2 emitted/ time, in which case we obtain SO_2 intensities (units = SO_2/gloof). Figure 8.17 shows a hypothetical example that incorporates mixed units. In this diagram the car industry used steel, but some cars are used in the steel process. Each industry has energy inputs (coal, measured in tons/day) and labor inputs (measured in person-days/day). The flows between compartments are sometimes ingots of steel, sometimes cars. We want to answer two questions:

1. What are the energy (ϵ) and labor (λ) intensities of steel and cars?
2. What fraction of the total energy/labor to produce an ingot/a car is consumed on site?

[2]For example, indirect materials analysis is found in Adriaanse et al. (1997).

DAILY FLOWS

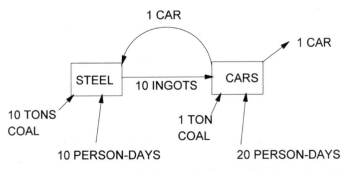

Figure 8.17 Mixed-flows hypothetical example for parallel calculation of energy and labor intensities.

To answer these questions, we set up the balance equations, being very careful to keep track of units.[3]

Energy	*Labor*
$10 + \epsilon_c = 10\epsilon_s$	$10 + \lambda_c = 10\lambda_s$
$1 + 10\epsilon_s = 2\epsilon_c$	$20 + 10\lambda_s = 2\lambda_c$

Solving the balance equations gives

$\epsilon_s = 2.1$ tons coal/ingot $\lambda_s = 4$ person-days/ingot

$\epsilon_c = 11$ tons coal/car $\lambda_c = 30$ person-days/car

Fraction of steel's total energy that is consumed onsite:

$10/(10 + (1)(11)) = 0.476$

Fraction of car's total energy that is consumed on site:

$1/(1 + (10)(2.1)) = 0.0455$

Fraction of steel's total labor that is used onsite:

$10/(10 + (1)(30)) = 0.250$

Fraction of car's total labor that is used on site:

$20/(20 + (10)(4)) = 0.333$

These input fractions are obtained by dividing the directly used gloof by the

[3]Example of keeping track of units: The first embodied energy equation is actually

100 tons coal/day + (1 car/day)(ϵ_c tons coal/car) = (10 ingots/day)(ϵ_s tons coal/ingot)

total embodied gloof (energy or labor). In this example we see that indirect effects skew our "normal" expectations. 75% of the labor to produce steel comes through the steel industry's use of cars. 95% of the energy to make a car is used in the steel industry. The latter result tells us that in attempting to reduce the energy used to make a car, larger savings will likely result from conservation in the steel industry than in the auto industry. This is not guaranteed, however; one needs to know the potential for improvement in each industry as well.

APPLICATIONS OF CALCULATING INDIRECT EFFECTS

The Energy Cost of Living

A useful and telling application of indirect effects is to link everyday personal consumption patterns with their impact on resource use:

$$\text{Gloof} = \sum_{i=1}^{N} (\text{Gloof intensity})_i (\text{Consumption})_i \qquad (8.5)$$

Consumption is measured for a range of familiar categories i, such as food, restaurants, furniture, auto fuel, clothing, and so forth. Then one needs gloof intensities, which are calculated exactly as we have done before, if we accept the simplifying assumptions and if data are available. In the 1970s this was done for energy (Herendeen et al., 1981), labor, and some forms of pollution. Energy intensities were obtained in Btu/$, and consumption data in $/year. See Figure 8.18.

Energy Intensities   A few vertical analyses have been performed on specific products such as automobiles (Berry and Fels, 1973). The remaining energy intensities were calculated for about 350 sectors covering the full range of economic expenditures in the U.S. input–output economic accounts (U.S. Bureau of Economic Analysis, 1994a,b). Data on flows between sectors (say steel → cars) were recorded in dollars per year. We assumed that dollars were a satisfactory numeraire for allocating embodied energy. Dollar flow data were combined with energy use data from the U.S. Department of Commerce. Such data are now routinely published by the Energy Information Administration of the U.S. Department of Energy. Solving the 350 simultaneous equations of Important Equation 4 was a major job for the mainframe computers of the day (Bullard and Herendeen, 1975).

One immediate question was whether the energy intensities (units = Btu/ $) *did* vary among sectors. If not, the energy consequences of spending a dollar for any good or service would be the same, and the details of expenditures would be irrelevant. We already knew that a primary metals industry

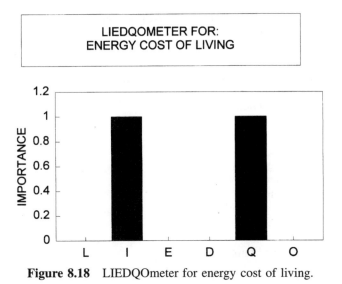

Figure 8.18 LIEDQOmeter for energy cost of living.

tended to be energy intensive compared with a service industry such as entertainment, but we were only interested in consumption options open to individuals and households, which generally covered finished products. Therefore we had to check before proceeding. The answer was yes; there was a significant variation, as shown in Table 8.4. For example, the energy intensity of gasoline was 443,000 Btu/$(1972), while that of private education was 35,000 Btu/$(1972), a variation of a factor of 13. Among nonenergy, nontransportation categories, there was a variation of a factor of 5, from rental dwellings [14,000 Btu/$(1972)] to floor coverings [71,000 Btu/$(1972)].

Detailed Consumption Data   Approximately once a decade the U.S. Bureau of Labor Statistics performs a detailed analysis of consumption "market baskets" of U.S. households (U.S. Bureau of Labor Statistics, 1978). Between 1972 and 1973, 19,000+ households were surveyed, with expenditures broken down into 61 categories as given in Table 8.4.

Combining expenditures and intensities using Equation 8.5 yielded results such as shown in Figure 8.19. Figures 8.19a–c show the energy impact, taken all the way back to the mouth of the mine or wellhead, of the market basket of average households in lowest and highest expenditure deciles and for the mean household. The 61 consumption categories have been aggregated into 13. Of these, two are what one would normally call direct energy expenditures (residential fuel and electricity, auto fuel). The direct energy requirements (including the "energy cost of energy") amount to approximately one-half of the total energy impact for the average household [expenditures = $11,493(1972)]. For the lowest decile, the direct energy requirement is about

TABLE 8.4 Energy Intensities for Personal Consumption Categories, 1972–1973

Consumption Category	Energy Intensity [10^3 Btu/$\$(1972)$]
1. Food at home	54
2. Food away from home	44
3. Alcoholic beverages	51
4. Tobacco	30
5. Rented dwelling	14
6. Owned dwelling	12
7. Other shelter, lodgings	21
8. Fuel oil and kerosene	89
9. Coal and wood	795
10. Other fuels	795
11. Gas main	915
12. Gas in bottles and tanks	999
13. Electricity	616
14. Water, sewage, trash	26
15. Telephone, telegraph, cable	24
16. Domestic service	0^a
17. Household textiles	59
18. Furniture	45
19. Floor coverings	71
20. Major appliances	66
21. Small appliances	65
22. Housewares	57
23. Misc. house furnishings	48
24. Dry cleaning, laundry	44
25. Clothing	44
26. Vehicle purchase	68
27. Vehicle purchase finance charges	27
28. Gasoline and oil	443
29. Tires and lubrication	69
30. Batteries	59

two-thirds of the total, and for the top decile, about one-third. For the average expenditure level and higher, one would miss at least one-half of total energy by looking only at direct energy.

Figure 8.19*d* shows this another way. It also shows that direct energy impact tends to saturate, that is, to level off as expenditure level increases; there seems to be some upper limit on auto use and residential fuel use. Indirect energy continues to increase with increasing expenditures; there is less likely to be a limit on football tickets, clothing, furniture, plane tickets, and condos in the Virgin Islands. Because the average energy intensity of these latter expenditures is lower than that of direct energy purchases (i.e., of energy itself), the overall graph of energy versus expenditures also bends down a bit.

TABLE 8.4   (Continued)

Consumption Category	Energy Intensity [10^3 Btu/$(1972)]
31. Auto repair and service	37
32. Auto insurance	19
33. Auto registration and fees	0[a]
34. Local bus and train—commuting	56
35. Local bus and train—school	56
36. Local bus and train—other	56
37. Transporation to school away from home	132
38. Plane—trip outside commuting area	167
39. Train and bus—trip outside commuting area	68
40. Ship—trip outside commuting area	129
41. Limousine and taxi—trip outside commuting area	56
42. Car rental	38
43. Health insurance	19
44. Health care	47
45. Personal care	48
46. Owned vacation home	12
47. Other transportation costs on vacation	91
48. All-expense tours, summer camps	31
49. Other vacation expenses	33
50. Boats, aircraft, motorcycles	65
51. Television	48
52. Other recreation	41
53. Reading	43
54. Private education	35
55. Public education	37
56. Misc. consumption expenditure	41
57. Personal insurance and pensions	20
58. Gifts and contributions	41
59. Increase in savings	47
60. Housing purchase and improvement	40
61. Increase in investment	47

[a]Labor and government services are assumed to have zero energy intensity relative to the consumer. For labor, this is done to avoid double-counting. For government, the energy requirement is not lost but rather charged against government expenditures.

Source: Herendeen et al. (1981).

Energy Tax and Rebate Program

The idea of a tax on energy has gone through several cycles in popularity in the past two decades, and a tiny energy tax was passed by the U.S. Congress early in the Clinton administration (1993). The standard rationale for a wellhead/mine-mouth tax and rebate is that, according to a long-term view, we are wasting energy (and other nonrenewable resources) because they are

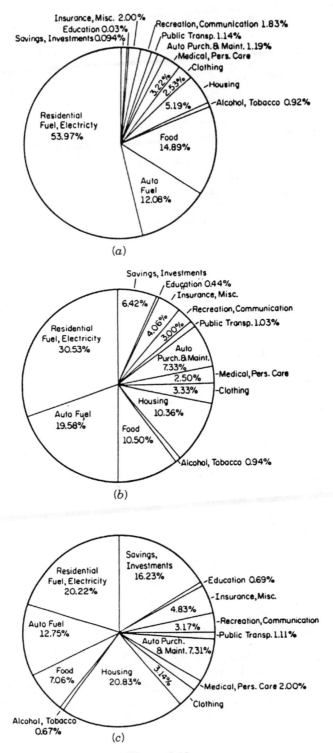

Figure 8.19

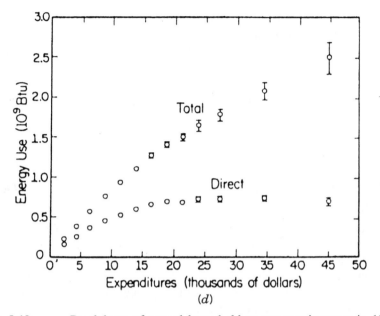

Figure 8.19   *a–c*. Breakdown of annual household energy requirements in 13 consumption categories for expenditures in lowest, average, and highest decile in 1972–1973: (*a*) expenditures = $2034, energy = 196 million Btu; (*b*) expenditures = $11,493, energy = 858 million Btu; (*c*) expenditures = $36,229, energy = 2112 million Btu. 1972 dollars. (*d*) Household annual energy requirements versus expenditures, 1972–1973. Direct covers residential energy and auto fuel, including energy used in producing energy. *Source:* R. Herendeen, C. Ford, and B. Hannon (1981). Energy cost of living, 1972–1973. *Energy* 6:1433–1450. © 1981 Elsevier Science Ltd. Reprinted with permission.

too cheap. Raising the energy price will raise the price of all goods, but more so for more energy-intensive goods, and consumers will shift purchases toward goods whose prices do not increase as much. This is true even if the tax is rebated to preserve real income, so that a household could purchase the old market basket—if it still wanted to. However, because of differential price changes, it will change that market basket.

A standard objection to an energy tax is that (without an involved rebate scheme) it is regressive: It hits the poor harder than the rich on a percentage basis. This is supported by Figure 8.19*d*, as long as we confine our attention to direct energy. The expenditure data used to obtain Figure 8.19*d* reinforce this: Both fractions

$$\frac{\text{Direct energy}}{\text{Total energy}} \quad \text{and} \quad \frac{\$ \text{ for direct energy}}{\$ \text{ for all purchases}}$$

are greater for poor than for rich. However, indirect energy increases as a fraction of the total for richer households. Indirect energy connections will cause the price of everything to increase when energy prices rise, implying a less regressive effect than that based solely on the direct effect. If the graph of total energy versus expenditures were a straight line and if all energy price increases were passed on by industries to consumers, there would be no regressivity at all; all expenditure classes would be affected equally on a percentage basis (Herendeen and Fazel, 1984). Problem 8.12 deals with this in more detail, including how to design a tax rebate to counteract the income-reducing impact of the tax.

Appliances: Energy to Produce and Maintain versus Energy to Operate

We have already seen that the energy impact of the car is about 60% greater than what goes into the fuel tank (Fig. 8.1). What fraction of the energy use for a toaster, say, is used to manufacture and market it, and what fraction issued to operate it? The answer is useful in evaluating different strategies to reduce energy use, such as increasing operational efficiency, decreasing energy use in manufacture, or increasing the device's lifetime. Consider all the energy associated with an appliance:

$$E_{\text{life}} = \text{Manufacturing energy} + \text{Maintenance energy}$$
$$+ \text{Disposal energy} + T * \text{Operational power}$$

where T is the lifetime. The total power is the lifetime energy divided by the lifetime, T:

$$P_{\text{tot}} = \frac{E_{\text{life}}}{T} = \frac{\text{Manufacturing} + \text{Maintenance} + \text{Disposal}}{T} + P_{\text{operation}}$$

$$= \left(\frac{1}{T} \frac{\text{Manufacturing} + \text{Maintenance} + \text{Disposal}}{P_{\text{operation}}} + 1 \right) P_{\text{operation}}$$

$$= \left(\frac{Q}{T} + 1 \right) P_{\text{operation}} \tag{8.6}$$

where $Q \equiv$ (manufacturing, maintenance, and disposal energy) divided by the power required to operate the device. Q has the units of time, the time it would take to provide the energy to do these things if we supplied that energy at a rate equal to the power required to operate the device. For electric appliances energy could be measured in kilowatt-hours and power in kilowatts. See Figure 8.20. Table 8.5 summarizes a number of household appliances.

We can see that most appliances tend to have high operation power and low Q/T or vice versa. The appliances usually considered large energy users—such as refrigerators, freezers, water heaters, and light bulbs—have

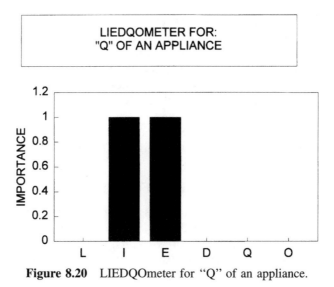

Figure 8.20 LIEDQOmeter for "Q" of an appliance.

TABLE 8.5 Energy to Operate versus Energy to Manufacture, Maintain, and Dispose of Selected Appliances

Electric Appliance	$P_{operation}$ (kWh/year)	Q (year)	T (year)	Q/T	Classification ($P_{operation}/Q/T$)[a]
Blender	17	7.2	14	0.15	Low/high
Garbage disposal	33	12	14	0.87	Low/high
Mixer	14	7.5	14	0.53	Low/high
Vacuum cleaner	51	6.4	14	0.45	Low/high
Freezer[b]	1900	0.73	14	0.05	High/low
Range	1333	1.2	14	0.08	High/low
Refrigerator[b]	1333	1.3	14	0.09	High/low
Clothes dryer	1080	0.97	14	0.07	High/low
Water heater	4700	0.11	8	0.01	High/low
75-W incandescent bulb[c]	657	0.00144	0.080	0.018	High/low
17-W compact fluorescent bulb[c]	146	0.103	1.14	0.09	High/low
Iron	158	0.48	8	0.06	High/low
Exhaust fan	48	2.5	14	0.18	Low/low
Coffee maker	83	0.61	8	0.08	Low/low
Toaster	43	1.9	8	0.23	Low/low
Personal computer (at work)[d]	160	7	7	1.0	High/high

[a]Classification: $P_{operation}$: <100 kWh/year ≡ low; ≥100 kWh/year ≡ high. Q/T: <0.25 ≡ low; ≥0.25 ≡ high.
[b]New freezers and refrigerators today use 40 to 50% less energy than those indicated here.
[c]Assumes bulbs are on continuously.
[d]Assumes computer is used 8 hours/day, 200 days/year.
Source: Most of the data are from Herendeen and Sebald (1975) and Meir et al. (1992).

$Q/T < 0.1$. Smaller appliances have $Q/T \geq = 0.5$. This implies, but does not prove, that to save energy one should likely concentrate on operational energy efficiency for the first group, while for the second there is likely potential in both operational and manufacturing efficiency. We can also see that because light bulbs have $Q/T < 0.1$ we need to make little correction to the energy conservation saving calculated for operation only. Problem 8.8 addresses this question further.

The personal computer, if used 8 hours a day, 5 days a week, has a high operation power (160 kWh/year) and a high Q/T (1.0).

Labor Versus Energy: Highway Trust Fund and Appliances Again

Energy policy issues quickly abut labor issues; this was especially important after the oil price increases in 1973 and 1979 to 1980. It was often claimed that saving energy put people out of work. This was often true directly, as some jobs were lost in the energy industry. However, the indirect effects often produced more jobs than were lost. This could happen in two ways— increased activity in, say, an industry producing energy efficiency equipment or products (such as insulation) or through respending of saved energy bills on a wide range of expenditures.

Alternatives to the Highway Trust Fund   The Highway Trust Fund was a federal program of directing road fuel taxes into the construction of roads, specifically prohibiting their use for anything else, such as railroad and mass-transit development, educational facilities construction, or water and waste treatment facility construction. Bezdek and Hannon (1974) used Equation 8.5 to obtain the energy and labor requirements generated by a federal expenditure of $5 billion (1975) in each of these and several other programs. See Figure 8.21. They needed detailed direct employment data in the 350 U.S. economic sectors to calculate labor intensities. Then they needed detailed "bills of goods" for each program: the amount spent for concrete, steel, and so on.

As shown in Table 8.6 all redirections increase jobs and all but one require less energy. One reason that this occurs is a general trend, not without exceptions, that energy-intensive industries tend to have lower direct labor inputs. Showing this to be true when indirect effects are included strengthened the argument for energy conservation, and this argument was, and continues to be, used in the political debate.

Such results must be used very carefully, however. First, there are questions of data age and quality and whether the linear assumptions implicit in this approach are valid (if a steel mill doubles its production, does it double its workforce?). When all sources of inaccuracy are included, are the results for different options really different from each other? Second, there is the extremely important question of the kind of job and what it pays. It is possible to destroy a skilled, unionized position paying $35,000/year and to create

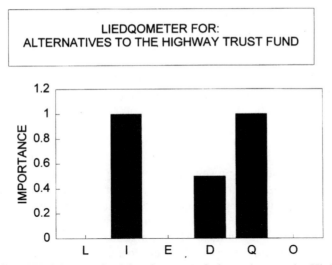

Figure 8.21 LIEDQOmeter for labor impacts of alternatives to the Highway Trust Fund.

TABLE 8.6   Energy and Labor Impact of Redirecting $5 Billion/Year of U.S. Government Expenditure from the Highway Trust Fund to Seven Other Possible Uses, Applying Equation 8.5

Federal Program	Energy Intensity [10^3 Btu/$(1963)]	Percentage Change in Energy Requirement	Labor Intensity [jobs/$100,000 (1975)/year]	Percentage Change in Labor Requirement
Highway construction	112	—	8.1	—
Railway and mass transit construction	43	−62	8.4	3
Water and waste treatment facility construction	65	−42	8.2	1
Educational facilities construction	71	−37	8.5	5
National health insurance	40	−64	13.4	65
Criminal justice and civilian safety	119	3	12.4	54
Return to consumers as tax relief	86	−23	8.7	7

Source: Bezdek and Hannon (1974).

two unskilled positions paying \$12,000/year. In Table 8.6 we can use the "Jobs per \$100,000/year" column to calculate average salaries. These range from \$12,300 (1975)/year for highway construction to \$7500 (1975)/year for national health insurance. Bezdek and Hannon went into some detail on the types of jobs created and destroyed. For the shift to health insurance, hospital and institutional attendants, nurses, janitors and sextons, and secretaries dominated the employment increase, while laborers, carpenters, drivers, and excavating machine operators were the big employment losers. One can guess that the losers (often unionized) were more highly paid than the winners (usually not unionized).

Third, there is the ever-present question of system boundaries. For example, are these results just for the construction of the facilities, or is there an accounting for the fuel to operate cars versus trains, say? This is not included in Table 8.6, but is covered elsewhere in the article. Fourth, this is a static analysis. What about dynamics: How long does it take for the calculated effects to occur? Is this long or short compared with the time scales of interest? For example, sometimes those industries/job types that are predicted to lose have a natural attrition rate (from retirement, job shifts) that exceeds the loss rate that actually would occur when the program is implemented at a realistic rate.

Appliances Again   My colleagues and I investigated the dollar cost, energy, and labor impacts of several consumer options centered on appliance use (Herendeen and Sebald, 1975). The results turned out to be fairly complicated because of the many combinations of type of energy used and a number of options (e.g., should we include the energy to drive if one does laundry in a laundromat?). Figure 8.22 shows the results of one comparison, paper versus cloth towels. One of the vexing questions was how many cloth towels are equivalent in use to a roll of paper towels. We obsessed about such things.

The figure indicates the complexity of the answer, but some general conclusions emerged: For an equivalent amount of drying "service":

1. Cloth towels are less expensive than paper towels.
2. Cloth towels are more energy intensive than paper towels, by as much as a factor of 2.3, depending on washing and drying options. Even if the wood energy is included, the hot water for washing cloth towels dominates.
3. Cloth towels are less labor intensive than paper towels. (Home labor is not included.)

Trophic Structure of Ecosystems (the Sunlight in an Eagle)

There are several indicator quantities that summarize indirect effects in ecosystems (Hannon, 1973; Finn, 1976; Patten, 1985; Ulanowicz, 1986). Two

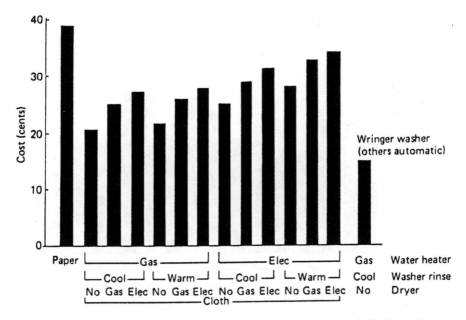

Dollar Cost of Paper vs. Cloth Towels (16 Cloth Towels, 1 Roll Paper)

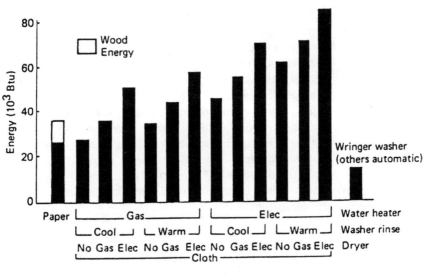

Energy Cost of Paper vs. Cloth Towels (16 Cloth Towels, 1 Roll Paper)

Figure 8.22 Dollar, energy, and labor costs of paper versus cloth towels (Herendeen and Sebald, 1975).

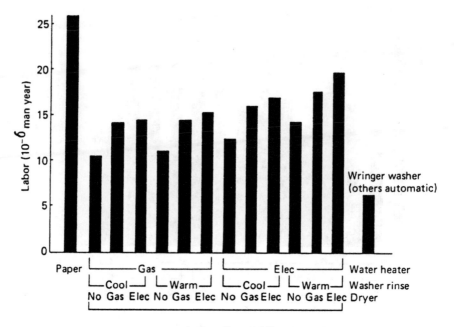

Labor Cost of Paper vs. Cloth Towels (16 Cloth Towels, 1 Roll Paper)

Figure 8.22   (Continued)

that are especially appropriate in quantifying the solar dependence of all life[4] are energy intensity and trophic position. We have already discussed energy intensity, which tends to increase multiplicatively in a linear food chain (see Fig. 8.23). The trophic position of a compartment is defined as the number of energy transfers between that compartment and the sun. Trophic position increases stepwise in a food chain, as also shown in Figure 8.23.

Historically, ecological thinking has often tended to concentrate on food chains, for which trophic positions (called trophic levels in this case) are integers. As we found with energy intensities, things are more complicated with a web. Then trophic position is not necessarily integral. The trophic position, TP, is (the weighted sum of TPs of inputs to j) + 1. Assume the weighting is proportional to the energy flows. Using the language we used for calculating energy intensities,

$$\text{TP}_j = \sum_{i=1}^{N} \left(\frac{X_{ij}}{\sum_{i=1}^{N} X_{ij}} \right) \text{TP}_i + 1 \qquad (8.7)$$

[4]There is an exception: Deep-sea vent communities are fueled by chemical energy deriving from volcanic action. No photosynthesis is involved.

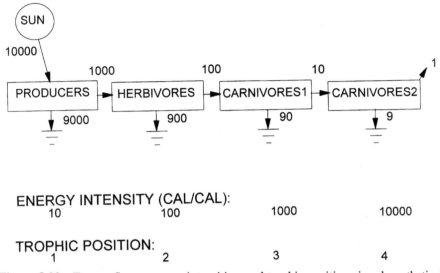

Figure 8.23 Energy flows, energy intensities, and trophic positions in a hypothetical food chain. Energy flows are in Calories/time. Implicitly, fixed sunlight has an energy intensity of 1 Cal/Cal and the sun has a trophic position of zero.

Equation 8.7 is similar to the energy intensity equation, Important Equation 4, but it has a significant difference. The factors in the parentheses sum to 1 because they are normalized with respect to the input flows, whereas in Important Equation 4 the normalization is with respect to total output and the factors X_{ij}/X_j usually sum to less than 1. Equation 8.7 represents N equations in N unknowns. For the food chain in Figure 8.23, the weighting factors are all 1, and Equation 8.7 gives the trophic positions 1, 2, 3, 4. Implicitly, TP_{sun} = 0. Now let us analyze the trophic structure of the system with feedback in Figure 8.15. Applying Equation 8.7,

Plants: $TP_p = (Z/(100 + Z))TP_a + 1$

Animals: $TP_a = (9/9)TP_p + 1$

Solving gives

$$TP_p = (100 + 2Z)/100$$

$$TP_a = TP_p + 1 = (200 + 2Z)/100$$

These results are graphed in Figure 8.24, which, for comparison, also contains the dependence of energy intensity on feedback previously shown in Figure 8.16. With no feedback, energy intensities are 10 and 45 Cal/Cal for plants and animals, respectively, a difference of a factor of 4.5, and TPs are 1 and 2. Feedback increases both trophic positions, but they always differ by 1

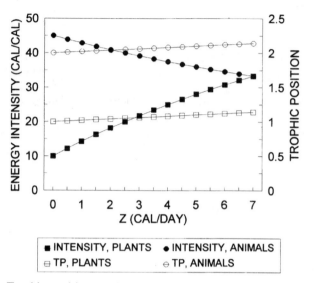

Figure 8.24 Trophic positions and energy intensities (the latter from Fig. 8.16) as a function of feedback from animals to plants. $Z = 0$ is no feedback; $Z = 7$ Cal/day is maximum feedback.

because animals receive their input from plants. Meanwhile, feedback causes the energy intensities to approach a common value.

There is a fascinating literature on network analysis of ecosystem flows that covers many indicators based on indirectness. Besides energy intensity and trophic position, there are path length (the number of compartments the energy passes through before it leaves the system), residence time (how long it stays in the system), and cycling indices of various types (Finn, 1976; Patten, 1985; Burns, 1989). Several problems address some of these aspects, including calculations for real ecosystems. An example for a food web is shown in Figure 8.25. In this bog food web the detritus compartment is important to trophic structure, and it is fairly hard to decide by inspection which compartment has the highest trophic position or energy intensity. Applying Important Equation 4 (Eq. 8.1) and Equation 8.7 yields the results shown in Table 8.7. Problem 8.6 asks the reader to perform the calculations.

Because plants get input only from the sun, $TP_{plants} = 1$. Because decomposers get all their input from detritus, $TP_{decomposers} = TP_{detritus} + 1$. Animals and detritus have more than one input, and their TPs are mixtures. In this accounting decomposers (e.g., bacteria) are on top of the energy pyramid and the food web.

Net Energy Analysis

It requires energy to make the equipment perform the activities needed to find and develop new energy sources. We know we are looking farther and

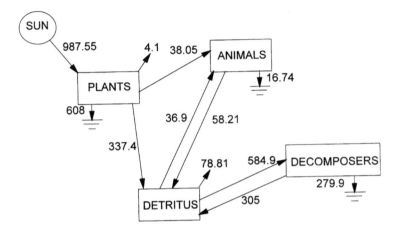

Figure 8.25   Energy flows for Taozhny Log Bog in Russia (Logofet and Alexandrov, 1983). Units are grams of fixed carbon per square meter per year. Detritus is dead material that is so broken down that its original type cannot easily be determined—it is analogous to shredded metal in a recycling facility. Animals eat almost as much detritus as they do plants. Being dead, detritus has no dissipation. Decomposers (e.g., bacteria) also consume detritus.

farther from home for energy, drilling deeper, working in harsher conditions and climates, and often dealing with (speaking of coal) thinner seams under deeper deposits of overburden. Somewhere, we think, there must be a point at which we use as much energy to obtain new energy, and the net energy yield from the whole endeavor is zero. We have a sense that if this is happening, the price of energy should tend to increase, but that the economic system may not convey the signal in time. Figure 8.26 shows the framework for discussion.

The fundamental assumption is that it is possible to separate the "energy industry (or facility)" from the rest of the economy that uses energy. In Figure 8.26, $E_{out, gross}$ is the energy supplied by the energy industry to the nonenergy sectors of the economy (e.g., the coal output of the coal mining industry). $E_{in, support}$ is the energy that is required for the economy to provide all the

TABLE 8.7   Energy Intensities and Trophic Positions for the Food Web of Taozhny Log Bog, Shown in Figure 8.25

Compartment	Energy Intensity (Cal/Cal)	Trophic Position
Plants	2.60	1.00
Animals	9.56	3.43
Detritus	12.4	3.90
Decomposers	23.8	4.90

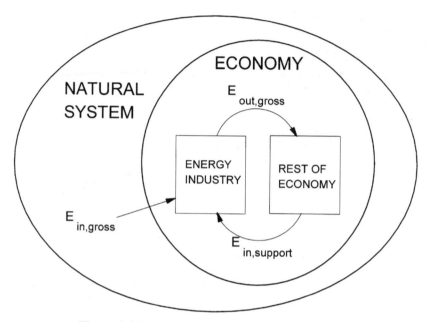

Figure 8.26 Framework for discussing net energy.

material and service inputs to the energy industry. $E_{in, gross}$ is the primary energy removed from the ground or from the sun by the energy industry (e.g., the coal actually dug from the ground or left in a way that it can never be removed—as for pillars to hold up the ceiling in deep mines—by the coal mining industry). We can define two dimensionless indicators of net energy:

Incremental Energy Ratio	Absolute Energy Ratio
$$IER = \frac{E_{out,\ gross}}{E_{in,\ support}}$$	$$AER = \frac{E_{out,\ gross}}{E_{in,\ gross} + E_{in,\ support}}$$
$IER \geq 0$	$AER \leq 1$

Incremental energy ratio (IER) reflects an economic view of the energy resource: The cost is what it costs *us*, and IER indicates the efficiency of converting our output to more useful inputs. Absolute energy ratio (AER) reflects a physical or environmental view of the energy resource: The cost is what it costs *nature*, and AER reflects a physical efficiency of converting primary resources to useful inputs. IER can have any value greater than 0, and the net energy break-even point occurs when IER = 1. AER can never be greater than 1, and there is no such thing as an energy break-even point; all energy extraction must dissipate resource energy. Most net energy discussions in the literature use some version of IER (also called EROI, "energy return on investment," by Hall et al., 1986).

Figure 8.27 uses two hypothetical coal mines to demonstrate how AER can vary while IER remains unchanged. Each mine has an IER of 10. However, mine (*b*) wastes a large amount of coal on site, while mine (*a*) does not, and (*b*) therefore has a lower AER. AER is more useful in addressing resource lifetime questions.

So far net energy analysis (NEA) appears to be a clean and attractive concept. In the 1970s federal legislation was passed to require a net energy analysis of federally supported energy development [Public Law 93-577, Sec. 5(a) (5)], to be applied, for example, to then-popular projects such as liquid fuel from coal, geothermal electricity, and solar energy in various forms (including biomass plantations, ethanol from grain, and the solar power satellite). In practice, net energy analysis turned out to be loaded with conceptual and procedural difficulties that make it much less useful than one would think based on the examples we have presented. A U.S. General Accounting Office Report in 1982 pointed out that the law was not being followed. In response, the U.S. Department of Energy said net energy analysis was so difficult and ambiguous that it would not perform it. Table 8.8 lists a number of the difficulties.

Many of these difficulties go beyond energy questions. What is especially frustrating for potential users is that they often expect that research will have

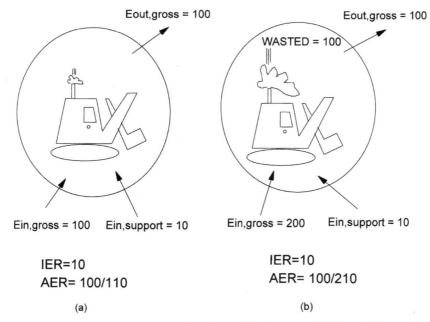

Figure 8.27 Two hypothetical coal mines with the same IER but different AERs. Energies are flows.

TABLE 8.8 Conceptual and Procedural Difficulties with Net Energy Analysis

Issue	Example, Solar	Example, Nonsolar or General	Remedied by Careful Statement of Problem?	Comments
1. Specification of system boundary				
a. Spatial	Is sunlight "free"? Is auxiliary heating energy included?	Are CO_2 mitigation effects included?	} Yes	Differences of opinion persist.
b. Temporal	Is soil quality maintained in biomass production?	Will nuclear plants require significant energy inputs for decommissioning?		
c. Conceptual	How much of passive solar retrofit is "redecorating"?	Should the energy required to support labor be included?		
2. End-use considerations (related to system boundary)	Is the fact that gasohol gets better mpg than expected allocable as an energy benefit to an NEA of ethanol from grain?	Should an NEA of an electric power plant depend on whether that electricity will be used in heat pumps?	No	Fundamental question is to what extent the energy system can really be separated from the rest of economy.
3. Opportunity cost (also related to system boundary)	Is the energy output ("benefit") of a solar facility just that energy, or is the energy *not needed* from another source?	If energy is diverted from society at large to build a power plant, what about the energy needed to provide substitute inputs to other industries?	Yes	Difficult to set ground rules that are not too situation specific.

4. Dynamic problem	Will a program of developing many energy facilities produce positive net energy for the first n years? Occurs when the doubling time for the building program approaches the single facility energy payback time. Always a potential problem even if single facility NEA is favorable.	Yes	Raised regarding nuclear energy in the mid-1970s but proved not to be significant. (One reason is that the projected rapid construction has not occurred.)
5. Existence of more than one kind of energy	How is electric output of a power plant compared with the coal inputs to produce the plant's steel components?	Not completely	A truly vexing problem.
6. Average versus marginal accounting	Going from 70% to 100% solar hot water heat requires more energy inputs than going from 0% to 30%. New oil has a lower IER than old oil	Yes	A general problem in resource analysis.
7. Dependences of NEA on some economic factors	Energy requirements for steel production are dependent on the price of energy.	No	Energy analysis, because it is based on real technologies, is simply not free of economic influences.

Source: Herendeen (1988). Net energy considerations. In *Economic Analysis of Solar Thermal Energy Systems* (R. West and F. Krieth, eds.), © 1988 MIT Press. Reprinted with permission.

removed the difficulties, resulting in one or a few "right" ways to perform NEA. However, the opposite is true. Research and serious thinking show that these issues do not have emergent correct ways to approach them; rather, the user must confront all this ambiguity and decide for him or herself what to do about it.

In spite of the difficulties, some useful net energy analyses have been done. Typically, these dealt with proposed technologies that, even given uncertainties such as in Table 8.8, are near the break-even point, IER = 1. We return to some examples after a sample calculation.

Net energy analysis closely parallels benefit–cost analysis, discussed in Chapter 5. In benefit–cost analysis we sum money flows (units = dollars/year), often discounted, to get benefits and costs in dollars. In NEA we sum energy flows, that is, power (units = energy/time), usually not discounted, to obtain benefits and costs in energy. The fundamental information is the power curve, as exemplified in Figure 8.28. From the power curve we can abstract energy analogs to the economic indicators (B/C ratio, internal rate of return, and payback time) that were discussed in Chapter 5. Assuming that the power costs are just $E_{\text{in, support}}$ in Figure 8.26, B/C with zero discount rate is the same as IER. In Figure 8.28 IER = $30(1)/(5(2) + 2(1)) = 30/12 = 2.5$. This energy facility returns 2.5 times as much energy as it requires. Internal rate of return and payback time are covered in Problem 8.9.

All the NEA and benefit–cost analysis we have done up to now have been static analyses, averaged over the lifetime of the facility. A dynamic problem is mentioned in Table 8.8. Benefits for a single facility come after (some of

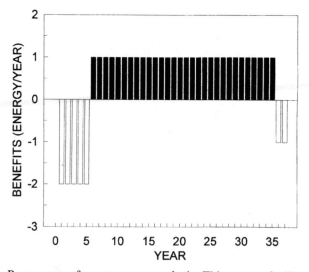

Figure 8.28 Power curve for net energy analysis. This energy facility is under construction for 5 years, produces energy output for 30, and requires 2 years to decommission. Construction and decommissioning require energy inputs.

the) costs. If one envisions an expanding program of building power plants, it is possible that the majority of the plants will be in early construction stages and hence the entire program could be a net power sink for many years. (This is another example of age class effects, which were discussed in Chapter 7. The problem is far more general than energy.) In the mid-1970s several nations had exponential plans (or perhaps sales goals) for constructing nuclear power plants, as shown in Table 8.9.

Such plans were unlikely to blossom for a number of reasons (and they did not), but one objection was dynamic net energy. It was acknowledged that a single nuclear plant had an IER greater than 1, but that only when the exponential growth slowed would the entire program produce net positive power. The construction period for the envisioned nuclear plants was around 3 to 5 years. Let us do a quick dynamic calculation for the example energy facility in Figure 8.28. Suppose we begin one facility in year 0, two in year 3, and four in year 6, Though this facility has only a 5-year construction period, the summed effect of the program does not produce net positive power until year 11, when all plants are complete and operating, as shown in Figure 8.29.

Examples of Net Energy Analysis

Conventional Energy Technology Table 8.10 shows IERs for conventional energy technologies in the mid-1970s. All are much greater than 1. The highest IER is for ceiling insulation, for which $E_{out, gross}$ is considered to be the energy saved. This extension of the NEA concept combines an end-use consideration (as in Chapter 4) with the supply-side-oriented separation of the energy industry and the rest of the economy in Figure 8.26.

Oil: How IER Is Changing with Time An important resource question is not only what IER is at the moment, but how it is changing over time. Figure 8.30 shows this for U.S. oil extraction. The cumulative effect of the increasing trend for IER from 1910 through 1970 was canceled completely by a steep decrease from about 1970 through 1982. Since then IER has risen steeply again. Interpretation is as follows (Cleveland, 1993). With relatively stable

TABLE 8.9 Exponential Nuclear Power Construction Plans in the Mid-1970s

Nuclear Power Construction Plans	Doubling Time (years)	Period of Program (years)
United States	≈5	25
United Kingdom	6	20
Common Market countries	3–4	12–15

Source: Chapman and Mortimer (1974).

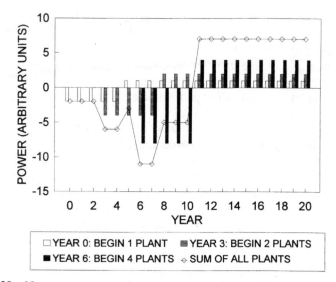

Figure 8.29 Net power output from an exponential building program for power plants. Each plant is characterized by Figure 8.28 and begins operation after a 5-year construction period.

world oil prices, especially after World War II, technical improvements in extraction came in an orderly way and the IER increased. In the 1970s the world oil price jumped roughly fourfold. This stimulated extraction from wells and regions that were previously marginal. The marginal sources were more expensive in terms of direct energy inputs and in equipment and infrastructure, which increased total energy inputs and decreased IER. When world oil prices stabilized (and hence dropped after correcting for inflation), the

TABLE 8.10   IERs for Nonsolar Technologies

Energy Type	IER
Coal, U.S. average	37
Eastern surface coal	43
Crude petroleum (delivered to refinery)	7
Natural gas (delivered through gas utility to user)	11
Geothermal electricity (vapor dominated)	13 ± 4
Geothermal electricity (liquid dominated)	4 ± 1
Coal mine–electric power plant	8
Natural gas well–electric power plant	2.3
Uranium mine–light water reactor	5
Conservation: ceiling insulation as energy displacer	136

Source: R. Herendeen (1988). Net energy considerations. In *Economic Analysis of Solar Thermal Energy Systems* (R. West and F. Kreith, eds.), pp. 255–273. © 1988 MIT Press. Reprinted with permission.

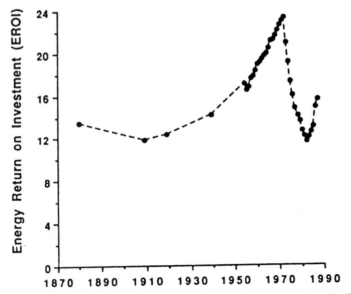

Figure 8.30   Incremental energy ratio (IER) for petroleum extraction in the United States, 1880–1989. *Source:* Reprinted from C. Cleveland (1993). An exploration of alternative measures of natural resource scarcity: the case of petroleum resources in the U.S. *Ecological Economics* 7:123–157. © 1993 Elsevier Science Ltd., with kind permission from Elsevier Science—XIL, Sara Burgerhartstraat 25, 1055 KV Amsterdam, The Netherlands.

United States bought more foreign oil and decreased domestic extraction. Producers first closed down the marginal wells with low IERs, and average IER went up. This occurred because oil was cheap, with a high IER, and available for import.

On one hand, Figure 8.30 reflects what economics would predict: When the world oil price increases, more oil will be extracted. On the other hand, Figure 8.30 reinforces the idea that even higher prices did not make oil easier to extract in a physical sense.

Solar Thermal Technologies   Table 8.11 shows IER for several solar thermal technologies—those that convert sunlight first to heat (hence excluding photovoltaic and wind electric power). These all have an IER greater than 1, but they are generally lower than IERs for the "conventional" energy sources listed in Table 8.10. Energy is harder to win this way than from East Texas oil gushers 80 years ago.

A Source with IER ≈ 1: Ethanol from Grain   Ethanol from grain is now a 10% additive to gasoline. Early on this mixture was called gasohol. From the beginning (ca. 1977) there were concerns about the net energy balance because grain production requires so many energy inputs, as shown in Figure

TABLE 8.11   Net Energy Results for Solar Thermal Technologies

Technology	IER[a] or EPT[b]	References and Comments
Thermal electric power		Electric output at 3413 Btu/kWh
160 MW ocean thermal	EPT = 4.7–6.2 years	
	IER = 6.6	
100 MW power tower	IER = 11	
	= 20	(For Barstow, CA)
	> 6	(For Barstow, CA)
	= 20–30	(For Barstow, CA)
	EPT = 3 years	
Biomass		
Direct combustion	IER = ~2.7	Agricultural residues
	< 15–23	Poplar, 6–14 dry ton/ha-yr
	= 10–22	Herendeen and Brown (1987), without fertilizer
	= 2.5–3.8	with fertilizer, several species
Liquefaction	= 2	methanol
	= 5.6	methanol, premium-fuel basis
	= 1–1.4	Chambers et al. (1979), ethanol from grain
	= 2.3–3.8	ethanol from grain, premium-fuel basis
Gasification	= 0.8	Manure digestion, gas used to generate electricity
Direct use of heat/space heat		
Solar pond	IER = 1.8	Single house (for Columbus, OH)
	= 2.7	20 houses (for Columbus, OH)
	= 13	Town size in western Massachusetts
Active	= 1.6	(For Sante Fe, NM) 60% solar
Passive	= 8–16	
Active	= 3–5	(For Toronto), 50% solar, "moderately" insulated, ~2 days storage
Active	= 1.7	(For Michigan and New York)
Passive	= 10–25	
Active	= 2.0	(For Denver, CO)
Passive	= 2.6	
Passive	EPT = 1.5–2 years	(For Germany)
Direct/hot water		
	IER = 5.2	(For Michigan)
	= 2.5	(For Albuquerque, NM)
	= 2.2	(For Finland)
	EPT < 5 years	
Direct/high temperature	IER = 2.5	250°C steam, trough collectors (for Madison, WI)

IER is incremental energy ratio; EPT is energy payback time.

Source: R. Herendeen (1988). Net energy considerations. In *Economic Analysis of Solar Thermal Energy Systems* (R. West and F. Kreith, eds.), pp. 255–273. © 1988 MIT Press. Reprinted with permission.

8.3, and distilling ethyl alcohol from the fermentation vat also requires significant energy. The process is sketched in Figure 8.31. Corn is dried on the farm, shipped to an ethanol plant, and fermented in a water mixture from which the product ethanol is distilled. The residual protein and solids comprise a high-quality livestock feed from which the water must be evaporated to prevent spoilage if the feed is not quickly consumed.

A quick estimate supports skepticism. A bushel of corn can produce 2.5 gallons of ethanol having a combustion energy of about 80,000 Btu/gallon. The agricultural inputs (fuel, fertilizers, herbicides, pesticides, wear and tear on equipment) amount to 130,000 to 180,000 Btu/bushel. With no other energy costs or benefits, this gives IER = 200/130 to 200/180, that is, 1.5 to 1.1. Fine-tuning these numbers by more careful study reveals many of the difficulties in applying NEA. A long list of possible interpretation issues arises, as shown in Table 8.12. Several that are particularly important and controversial are:

1. How to credit changed miles per gallon of gasohol versus gasoline (see Problem 8.13)
2. How to account for the animal feed byproduct
3. How to account for using spoiled corn or other otherwise-wasted products as inputs (One small ethanol producer, now defunct, used a spoiled shipment of Chuckles candy as input to fermentation. Local ethanol enthusiasts claimed the energy requirements for this were zero, because the Chuckles would have otherwise been discarded.)

Another example with an IER close to 1 is the solar power satellite (Herendeen et al., 1979), which we do not discuss here.

Indirect Area: Ecological Footprint

The earth has a surface area of 51 billion ha ($\approx$125 billion acres), of which 14.5 billion ha is land, of which 8.9 billion ha is ecologically productive. On average, each of the 5.7 billion humans can claim 1.5 ha. In the United States the average is about 3 ha per capita, while in the Netherlands it is 0.2 ha per capita. On the other hand, Wackernagel and Rees (1996) calculate that the total land supporting the consumption of a citizen of a rich nation is 3 to 5 ha. If all humans lived at that level, they would need two additional planet earths to sustain them with today's technology.

Wackernagel and Rees' method hinges on conversion factors for the areal impact of consumption of all consumer products and a share of the infrastructure that uses land. Using Equation 8.5 for land,

$$\text{Area required} = \sum_{i=1}^{N} (\text{Area intensity})_i \, (\text{Consumption})_i \qquad (8.8)$$

They identify four types of land:

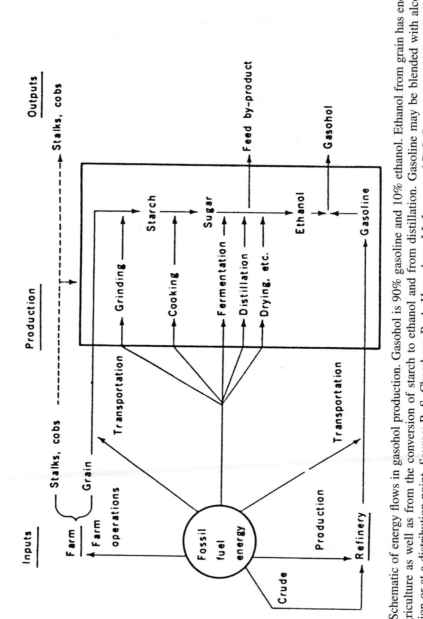

Figure 8.31 Schematic of energy flows in gasohol production. Gasohol is 90% gasoline and 10% ethanol. Ethanol from grain has energy inputs from agriculture as well as from the conversion of starch to ethanol and from distillation. Gasoline may be blended with alcohol during production or at a distribution point. *Source:* R. S. Chambers, R. A. Herendeen, J.J. Joyce, and P. S. Penner (1979). Gasohol: Does it or doesn't it . . . produce positive net energy? *Science* 206:789–795. © 1979 American Association for the Advancement of Science. Reprinted with permission.

TABLE 8.12   Options for Energy Analysis of Gasohol

Effect on Net Energy Balance Relative to Base Case of National Average Corn

Option		Comment
Input		
Use corn from corn belt, not national average	+ (decreases inputs)	Better than average crop yields
Do not dry corn on farm	+ (decreases inputs)	Requires rapid transit to ethanol plant to avoid spoilage
Use waste materials from other processes	Uncertain	Need to analyze specific case
Process		
Do not dry feed byproduct	+ (decreases inputs)	Requires rapid transit to feedlot to avoid spoilage
Burn corn cobs and stalks as boiler fuel in ethanol plant	+ (decreases inputs)	Removal from field may affect soil fertility
Improve distillation technology	+ (decreases inputs/increases outputs)	Obviously desirable, but feasible?
Output		
Sell excess cobs and stalks as fuel	+ (decreases inputs elsewhere)	Removal from field may affect soil fertility; may be a hard-to-use fuel
Correct for miles per gallon of gasohol	+ or −, depending on actual mpg	Energy balance is sensitive to this
Credit feed byproduct with energy required to grow corn for animals instead	− (decreases inputs)	Energy input to corn production is less than caloric content of crop

Source: Chambers et al. (1979).

1. *Energy Land.* Land impacted by energy use.
2. *Consumed Land.* Land covered by the built environment.
3. *Managed Productive Land.* Gardens, cropland, pastures, managed forests.
4. *Land of Limited Availability.* Productive natural ecosystems like rain forests, biologically nonproductive areas like icecaps.

In addition, five types of consumption were identified:

1. Food
2. Housing
3. Transportation
4. Consumer goods
5. Services

Their conversion factors are obtained by several approaches, none of which uses the input–output technique stressed here. The use of land to absorb wastes is not counted, though Wackernagel is currently working on including the areal impacts of fishing (ocean area) and composting wastes. There are a number of other issues (such as the dynamic versus static issue in biomass sequestering of CO_2 discussed in Chapter 7), but the magnitudes are reasonable and the approach useful. For the energy land impact for fossil fuel burning, Wackernagel and Rees use three approaches which all give similar answers: (1) planting vegetation to absorb the CO_2, (2) producing biomass-based ethanol, and (3) producing biomass for direct combustion. All three options give a footprint of about 1 ha per 1.8 metric tonne of carbon emitted/year (energetically equivalent to 1 ha per 2 tons of coal/year or approximately 1 ha per 400 gallons of gasoline/year).

The coefficients can be challenged, but the method is a powerful way to illustrate the approach to limits and the impacts of human beings. For example:

1. Of the industrialized countries, only two have an ecological footprint that fits inside their borders. Australia's footprint is about 12% of its ecologically productive land, and Canada's is about 29%. For the United States the footprint is about 1.8 times the productive area.
2. The footprint of the greater Vancouver, British Columbia, area is 19 times larger than the actual urban area. For the Netherlands the footprint is 15 times the country's area.
3. For a comparison of the ecological footprints of a poor and a rich person, see Table 8.13.

Another example of ecological footprint is a study of cities in countries that border on the Baltic Sea, which includes essentially all of Sweden, Poland, Finland, Latvia, Estonia, and Lithuania and portions of Denmark, Russia, Germany, and so on (Folke et al., 1997). The cities, the largest of which are St. Petersburg, Warsaw, Copenhagen, and Stockholm, contain 26% of the

TABLE 8.13   Average per Capita Ecological Footprint for India and Canada

	India (ha/capita)	Canada (ha/capita)
Food	0.20	1.14
Forest	0.13	0.59
Energy	0.05	2.34
Urban	Not given	0.20
Total	0.38 + urban contribution	4.27

Source: Wackernagel and Rees (1996), pp. 82, 98.

region's population and cover 0.1% of its total area, yet have a footprint estimated at 60 to 120% of that area. About 80% of the footprint is for pollution assimilation and 80% of that for carbon sequestration in biomass.

PROBLEMS

Level of difficulty is indicated as Easier/Moderate/Harder. Problems marked "(Spreadsheet?)" can be fruitfully approached using a spreadsheet. They need not be, however.

8.1. (Easier) In Tables 8.1A and 8.1B there is information on the direct food input to all humans. Does that figure agree with your sense of a human's caloric input?

8.2. (Easier) In Table 8.10 the IER was given for ceiling insulation. This application of NEA breaks down the separation of the energy industry and the rest of the economy as shown in Figure 8.26.

(a) Is this a valid application of NEA? Explain briefly.

(b) Give and briefly explain two other instances/possibilities in which this separation is impossible or inconsistent with the spirit of NEA.

8.3. (Easier) Discuss the Chuckles candy question: Should the energy inputs for spoiled products be included in calculating net energy?

8.4. (Moderate). Consider a three-level food chain represented by the steady-state flow in Table 8.14. All quantities are in Calories/day.

(a) Draw an appropriate flow diagram.

(b) Calculate the energy intensities (units = Cal/Cal).

(c) Label (a) with the embodied energy flows. Are there any internal embodied flows that exceed input flows?

8.5. (Moderate) Figure 8.32 shows flows and pollution generated in a hypothetical corn–tortilla production system. The goal is to calculate direct and indirect pollution intensities. In contrast to energy intensities

TABLE 8.14

| From | To | | | | | |
	Producers	Herbivores	Carnivores	Dissipation	Export	Total Output
Producers	0	100	0	900	0	1000
Herbivores	0	0	10	90	0	100
Carnivores	0	0	0	8	2	10
Energy input	1000	0	0			

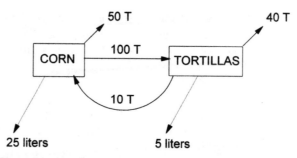

Figure 8.32 Daily flows in a corn–tortilla production system. Corn and tortilla flows are in tons/day. The dotted arrows are pollution production in liters/day. 50 tons of corn and 40 tons of tortillas are exported from the system daily.

(which represent energy sequestered), pollution intensities will represent pollution emitted.

(a) Fill in a flow table like Table 8.14. The energy inputs will be replaced by pollution outputs. Specify units.

(b) Set up and solve the pollution intensity equations.

(c) Verify sector embodied pollution balance and overall pollution balance.

(d) What fraction of the pollution generated to produce a tortilla is emitted in the tortilla sector? What fraction of the pollution generated to produce corn is emitted in the corn sector?

8.6. (Moderate) Table 8.7 lists energy intensities and trophic positions for a real four-compartment ecosystem with feedback, shown in Figure 8.25. Calculate them yourself and compare.

(a) Make a table of the flows, as in Problem 8.4.

(b) Set up the equations and solve for energy intensities.

(c) Set up and solve the trophic position equations (assume the sun has TP = 0).

(d) Discuss qualitatively: If the flow variable for the bog in Figure 8.25 were nitrogen instead of energy, so that there was a connection from decomposers back to plants, what would happen to energy intensities and trophic positions?

8.7. How much indirectness one sees in a system depends on the choice of flow variable, or numeraire. In this example we begin using energy (which here has no feedback; hence a chain structure) and then add nutrient flow (which has feedback; hence a web structure). See Figure 8.33. P = producer, C = consumer, D = detritus. All flows are in Calories/day except the quantity in parentheses, which is in grams/day. That is a flow of nitrogen from detritus to producers, shown as a dotted

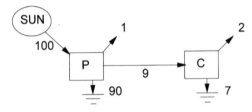

Case I. Biomass energy flow.

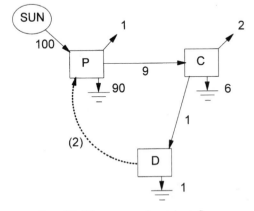

Case II. Biomass and nutrient flow.

Figure 8.33

line. Case I is a straight chain. In Case II we indicate that the dissipation of 7 Cal/day in Case I is actually made up of two parts: six units of metabolic loss and one unit of mortality. The latter becomes detritus and degrades, releasing nitrogen, which is recycled to producers. Thus the nutrient flow shows a connection that the energy flow did not show.

(a) For Case I calculate energy intensities and TPs. Give units.

(b) For Case I relabel the diagram, showing embodied energy flows.

(c) For Case II calculate energy intensities and TPs. Give units.

Caution: Keep track of units. Also, note that TP is based on actual energy flows only . . . it cannot use mixed units. Here nitrogen flow does not count in the calculation of TP.

(d) For Case II relabel the diagram, showing embodied energy flows.

(e) Comment on the similarities and differences between the results for Cases I and II.

8.8. (Moderate) Sensitivity/uncertainty analysis. Refer to Table 8.5 and Appendix 1. For these appliances—water heater, toaster, personal computer, blender—determine the percentage change of p_{tot} when $p_{operation}$,

Q, or T are independently changed by 10% in a direction that decreases p_{tot}. That is, change one at a time. Also give your impression as to how difficult these changes would be in practice.

8.9. (Moderate) Figure 8.28 shows an energy facility with an IER of 2.5. Calculate the simple payback time and the internal rate of return. Comment on the use of these two indices for this particular power curve.

8.10. (Moderate) (Spreadsheet?) Dynamic net energy. Assume the power curve shown in Figure 8.34 for an energy facility.

(a) What is the (undiscounted) IER for one facility?

(b) What is the energy payback time for one facility?

(c) Assume a building program of identical energy facilities of this type:

YEAR	NUMBER STARTED THAT YEAR
1	1
2	2
3	4
4	8
5	8
6	8
7 and following . . .	8

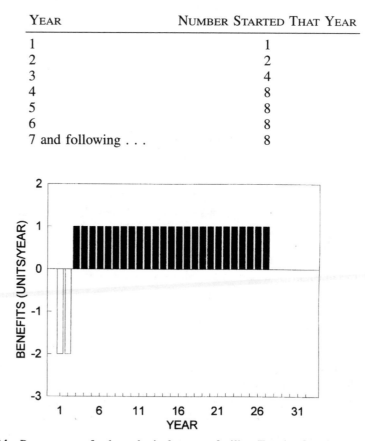

Figure 8.34 Power curve for hypothetical energy facility. For the first 2 years, it is an energy sink, requiring 2 energy units/year. Then for 25 years it produces energy at 1 unit/year. Then it is retired.

TABLE 8.15   Mercury Concentrations in Organisms in Lake Ontario

Approximate Trophic Level	Organism	Mercury per Wet Biomass (10^{-6} g/g)
5	Herring gull (bird)	51
4	Lake trout (fish)	5.7
3	Smelt (fish)	1.7
3	Sculpin (fish)	1.7
2	Pontoporeia (crustacean)	0.3
2	Mysis (shrimp)	0.1
1	Plankton	0.001

Source: Colborn et al. (1990).

Graphic the summed power curve for all facilities together for years 1–20.

(d) What is the energy payback time for the whole program?

8.11. (Harder) In Lake Ontario the concentrations of mercury given in Table 8.15 have been measured. This is bioaccumulation. Biomass is burned and dissipated, but the mercury is not excreted and is passed on. The ratio of mercury to biomass is therefore greater for biomass leaving a compartment than biomass entering that compartment. Very roughly, there is a 90% loss of biomass in each trophic level, and hence a factor of 10 increase of mercury/biomass in each trophic level in a chain.

In this problem we calculate nutrient intensity, which demonstrates bioaccumulation. We also use the results to justify the observation that embodied energy flows in a system can exceed actual energy inputs. Consider a three-level food chain represented by the steady-state flow in Table 8.16. All quantities are in Calories/day except for nutrient, which is in grams/day. Nutrient is not dissipated.

TABLE 8.16

From	To					
	Producers	Herbivores	Carnivores	Dissipation	Export	Total Output
Producers	0	100	0	900	0	1000
Herbivores	0	0	10	90	0	100
Carnivores	0	0	0	8	2	10
Energy input	1000	0	0			
Nutrient input	5	0	0			

(a) Draw an appropriate flow diagram.

(b) Calculate the energy intensities (units = Cal/Cal) and nutrient intensities (units = g/Cal).

(c) Label (a) with the embodied energy and embodied nutrient flows. Are there any internal embodied flows that exceed input flows?

(d) Comment: "Embodied energy flows are not experimentally measurable, as they account for dissipated inputs. Embodied nutrient flows in this case are measurable, as they account for nondissipated inputs. Here embodied nutrient flow *is* actual nutrient flow."

(e) Now assume feedback from carnivores to producers. Modify the flow table as follows: Increase carnivores → producers to 1 Cal/day, decrease carnivores → export to 1 Cal/day, increase producers → dissipation to 901 Cal/day, and increase producers' total output to 1001 Cal/day. Repeat steps (a)–(c).

(f) Comment: "In the feedback case internal embodied flows, including nutrient, do exceed system input flows. However, in part (d) we argued that in this case embodied nutrient flows are real and measurable. Therefore, for nutrient, this apparent imbalance actually occurs. Because it is measurable, we conclude that this type of bookkeeping is reasonable for embodied anything." *Hint:* Without feedback, an atom of nutrient passes from producers to herbivores just once. With feedback, however . . . .

8.12. (Harder) Figure 8.19*d* shows total household energy impact versus household expenditure.

(a) Show that if (1) the wellhead energy price increases, (2) no economic sector changes its pattern of using inputs to produce its output, and (3) the price increase is passed on by each sector, then the price increase of a product is proportional to its energy intensity: *Hint:* It is acceptable to demonstrate using a simple example.

(b) The "regressivity" of an economic policy measure refers to the differential impact on two different income (or expenditure) levels. Suppose a consequence of the measure is to increase the cost of a household's market basket by a fraction f. Then:

f is the same for all income levels: neutral.

$f_{poor} > f_{rich}$: regressive.

$f_{rich} > f_{poor}$: progressive.

Show how, under the assumptions in (a), comparing the shapes of the graphs in Figure 8.19*d* can be used to estimate the regressivity of an energy tax. Quantitatively compare the regressivity based on an analysis of (1) direct and (2) total energy.

(c) Explain how the results of (b) would be used to estimate an energy tax rebate that preserves a household's ability to purchase the same market basket.

8.13. (Harder) The miles-per-gallon (mpg) effect in the NEA of ethanol from grain. Gasoline has a combustion energy of 125,000 Btu/gallon; ethanol, 80,000 Btu/gallon.

(a) If mpg were proportional to combustion energy, compare the mpg of gasohol to pure gasoline.

(b) Suppose $(mpg_{gasohol}/mpg_{gasoline}) = x$ and credit all the extra or lost mileage to the ethanol. Determine an energy "credit" to be added to the ethanol energy in the NEA of ethanol from grain.

(c) One study reported no difference in mpg between gasohol and gasoline, that is, $x = 1$. Assume that without the energy credit in part (b) the IER $= 1$ for ethanol. If the credit is applied, what is the IER?

(d) Is this kind of bookkeeping fair?

8.14. (Harder)

(a) Prove that the energy embodied in system exports equals the energy inputs to the system. The general expression to prove is

$$\sum_{i=1}^{N} E_i = \sum_{i=1}^{N} \epsilon_i Y_i$$

where the total output X_j is the sum of flows from j to all other compartments plus the export Y_j. Figure 8.35 illustrates this for a two-compartment system, for which the statement is

$$E_1 + E_2 = \epsilon_1 Y_1 + \epsilon_2 Y_2$$

(b) Substitute reasonable numbers of your choice in Figure 8.35, solve for the intensities, and verify that the equation is satisfied. Be sure to specify the units of all quantities.

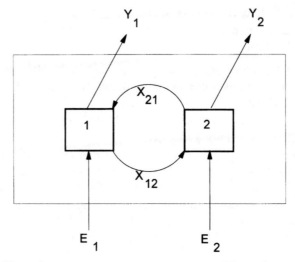

Figure 8.35 Flows in a two-compartment ecosystem. The only system inputs are energies E_1 and E_2; the only system outputs that are counted are product exports Y_1 and Y_2. Dissipated energy also leaves the system, but it is not counted; it is embodied in internal flows and in exports.

9 Shared Resources and the Tragedy of the Commons

There are more than a million fishing vessels worldwide now, a doubling since 1970.

> "The fish just get a little smaller each year", a Spanish shipowner with a Belize-registered ship tells me in Dakar. In the face of such declines neither traditional nor industrial fishermen can turn to voluntary conservation, because there's no profit in it. It just gives the fish to someone less scrupulous. Instead, everyone just fishes harder. (p. 21)
>
> One of the great problems with allowing unlimited numbers of fishermen is that no one owns the fish; they are a resource held in common. In that situation, it doesn't do anyone any good to conserve—the other guy will take the fish you leave. That's why Mbaye Diiop, Lazaro Larzabal, and so many others fish harder when stocks go downhill, instead of conserving. (p. 30)
>
> —Michael Parfit (1995). Diminishing returns. *National Geographic* (November):2–37

These quotes summarize a fundamental problem in resource use. In economics it is called "common property resources with unlimited entry." It was promoted to the larger environmental community in Garrett Hardin's now classic paper in *Science* in 1968, "The Tragedy of the Commons" (TOC). The problem is a combination of competition, dynamics, and instability. Competition and equity issues underlie the statement that if one voluntarily conserves, someone less altruistic grabs what is saved. Dynamics enters when competitive people realize this and push on anyway. Lastly, without complicated controls the system is unstable: Once a competitive battle begins the system is pushed to ruination. Given the (few) rules of the game, this process seems relentless and inexorable, leading to its description as a tragedy in the Greek sense of inevitability. Often the results are also tragic in the sense of human suffering.[1]

Our aim is not to discuss but rather to illustrate the TOC, by using numerical examples and games. We jump right in.

---

[1]Technically, a commons does have limited access, but Hardin's imprecision has become common terminology. We retain it here.

THE TRAGEDY OF THE COMMONS GAME/EXERCISE

The idea of the game is to become rich by grazing your cows on a common pasture that is shared by several neighbors' cows as well. The only managerial decision you and the other pasturers will make is how many cows to put on the pasture each spring; they remain on the pasture through fall. Your yearly profit is the weight gain of the cows you own. (Thus the cost of the cows and of managing and butchering them is assumed to be 0.) In this game we operate over K years; your score is the summed weight gain over K years. Each year you can put any number of cows on the pasture.

The problem is that the common pasture is finite and can be overgrazed, even to the point of killing off all the grass and destroying the pasture effectively forever. It is a potentially renewable resource whose rate of use is limited. You know about this quantitatively; each year the pasture (assuming it has not been killed off) has a total yield (= total weight gain of all n cows on it) given by

$$\text{Yield} = 100 - (10 - n)^2 = 20n - n^2$$

This function is 0 for no cows, is maximum (yield = 100 pounds per year) for 10 cows, and then decreases to 0 at $n = 20$, which kills the pasture. Unless the pasture is killed, it recovers completely by next year. Figure 9.1 and Table 9.1 show the yield function in detail. A humped curve of this sort

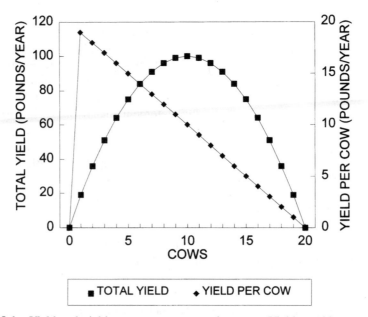

Figure 9.1   Yield and yield per cow on assumed pasture. Yield $= 100 - (n - 10)^2$.

TABLE 9.1 Yield and Yield per Cow on Assumed Pasture

Number of Cows	Total Yield = $100 - (n - 10)^2$	Yield per Cow	Number of Cows	Total Yield = $100 - (n - 10)^2$	Yield per Cow
0	0	0			
1	19	19	11	99	9
2	36	18	12	96	8
3	51	17	13	91	7
4	64	16	14	84	6
5	75	15	15	75	5
6	84	14	16	64	4
7	91	13	17	51	3
8	96	12	18	36	2
9	99	11	19	19	1
10	100	10	20	0	0

is typical of many renewable resources such as forests and fisheries. With no harvesting effort (e.g., no cows) there is no yield, and for a pasture jammed with rump-to-rump cows, there is no yield. Somewhere between these extremes there is yield; hence the humped curve.

The yield per cow is decreasing as the number of cows increases:

$$\text{Yield per cow} = \text{Yield}/n = 20 - n$$

Your yield is the number of cows you have times the yield per cow. If you are the sole controller of the pasture, you quickly realize that putting 10 cows out maximizes your annual profit, and you operate the pasture optimally and, quite likely, renewably forever. In this game, however, there are other pasturers, and there is open access: New entrants may put cows out in any year. Now your (personal) profit and the health of the pasture depend on the actions of all pasturers. It is the interaction of all pasturers that conveys the essence of the problem.

In the game each pasturer states how many cows she/he wants to put out in year 1. A person selected as gamemaster tallies and publicizes all entries, the total yield, and the individual yields for that year. You, as a player, are to keep track of your cumulating profit (and likely the other players' as well) in deciding how many cows to put out next time.

Players will want to discuss ground rules and roles:

Can players communicate?

Can they lie?

Do they act according to certain "personality" profiles/types (competitive, cooperative, impatient, patient, leader, follower, altruist, Ghengis Khan, etc.)?

What penalty should be assessed if the pasture is destroyed?

If the pasture represents a major global food source, the consequence of collapse is widespread famine. If the pasture represents a smaller part of life support, we can, for example, calculate thus: Your total profit is the sum of your yearly profits, for as along as the game lasts. If the pasture is operated at full yield, the sum of everyone's profits has a maximum of $100K$, where K is the number of seasons. Then let

Your actual profit =

$$\underbrace{(\Sigma \text{ Your profits for whole game})}_{\text{Competition Factor}} \underbrace{\left(\frac{\Sigma \text{ Everyone's profits for whole game}}{100K}\right)}_{\text{Total Yield Factor}}$$

The term in large parentheses is 1 only if the maximum yield is obtained for every one of the designated number of seasons. In this scheme every player is penalized for the collective inability to operate the pasture at full production. Another possibility is to time-discount *past* profits, thereby creating an incentive for continued high profits.

The question of different personalities/attitudes/motives is the crux of the fun, challenge, and anguish of this game and what it represents in life. As a start, consider the profiles in Table 9.2. Players will keep track of the games progress on a tally sheet as shown in Table 9.3. Experience with students has shown that in early years they tended to kill the commons. More recently, the commons has survived, but operating at approximately 75% of its poten-

TABLE 9.2 Sample Roles for the Tragedy of the Commons Game

A	You are smarter, leaner, and meaner than the rest. You will say and do anything to get it all.
B	You are not fatally altruistic, but you are willing to cooperate with reasonable people.
C	You are conservative and will not enter the game until everyone else has settled down. Once you enter you are willing to make deals.
D	You hate the person on your right; you want to do better than her/him so much that you will even accept declining yields for yourself as long as that person suffers even more.
E	You feel worn out with all this strategizing. The person on the left seems competent, so whatever she/he did last time, you will do this time.
F	It is not worth selling your soul to try to beat the system, and, anyway, people are basically sensible. You will put out your fair share ($1 - n$th of the total number of cows that maximizes yield).
G	You are unpredictable, even to yourself.

TABLE 9.3   Sample Tally Sheet

Tragedy of the Commons Game—Number of Cows				
	Player 1	Player 2	Player 3	Player 4	Total Yield
Round					
1					
2					
3					
4					
5					
6					
7					
8					

tial yield, with more than the optimum number of cows. Table 9.4 shows the results of one game of $K = 8$ seasons, with four players assigned roles from Table 9.2. In this game players could not talk or reveal their roles. The two players who were ruthless (role A) had much higher yields than the two who were "fair" (role F). Although the commons was not killed, it was operated at an average of 65% of maximum yield, in all cases with too many cows. In round 8, there were 18 cows; 2 more would have killed the commons.

Most recently, I have also experimented with tangible payoffs. So far I have used pennies, which the students leave in a pile in front of them (thus flaunting their affluence and inviting envy).

TEMPORAL INSTABILITY: THE RIGHT THING AT THE WRONG TIME LEADS TO COLLAPSE

There are at least two instability problems associated with the TOC. The first we have discussed: A cooperative equilibrium can be broken by one or more greedy people and especially by newcomers. If you already have some cows on the commons, you cannot be sure that adding a cow will increase your total yield; you have to calculate and make assumptions about the actions of the other pasturers, leading to interesting games (see the Problems). However, if you have nothing on the commons, you will always profit in putting out a cow unless the pasture is killed. Even if your action reduces total yield, you get more than zero. This latter situation has analogs in immigration policy.

TABLE 9.4 Results for a Game Played by Four Students Who Were Assigned Roles from Table 9.2

Round	Player 1 (F)		Player 2 (F)		Player 3 (A)		Player 4(A)		Total Cows	Total Yield
	Cows	Yield	Cows	Yield	Cows	Yield	Cows	Yield		
1	2	12	2	12	5	30	5	30	14	84
2	2	12	2	12	5	30	5	30	14	84
3	2	10	2	10	7	35	4	20	15	75
4	2	8	2	8	7	28	5	20	16	64
5	2	6	2	6	8	24	5	15	17	51
6	2	8	2	8	7	28	5	20	16	64
7	2	8	2	8	7	28	5	20	16	64
8	2	4	2	4	7	14	7	14	18	36
Total		68		68		217		169		522

A = ruthless, F = fair. Players were not allowed to communicate or reveal their roles. Maximum yield for each round was 100.

Immigrants from poor countries profit by moving to richer countries even if the overall richness of that country is diminished. This equity issue is fundamental, problematic, and wrenching.

The second instability is a temporal one. Strictly speaking, it is not part of the tragedy of the commons per se, because it can occur even if entry is limited and if the pasturers agree on who sets out how many cows. The problem occurs because of a time delay between changed conditions and human response, a vivid example of dynamics and lags. It is especially well illustrated by a system in which a time delay is a natural part—for example, a fishery. Roughgarden and Smith (1996) have applied it to the collapse, and potential recovery, of the fisheries off the coasts of the northeast United States (Georges Bank) and maritime Canada (Grand Banks).

We will need some preliminary mathematics first. The net number of surplus fish (i.e., those that can be harvested this year without depleting the fish stock next year) depends on the number of fish at the beginning of this year. A plot of this potential harvest (a flow, called "production," measured in fish/year) versus stock (measured in fish) often has the humped shape seen in Figure 9.1. Again this shape is anticipated on general grounds if the fish are limited by the carrying capacity of their environment.[2] Figure 9.2 shows a hypothetical production curve.

[2]This thinking could be applied to the pasture also, if we let the condition of the grass in the fall affect the condition the following spring. We ignored this in the TOC game, assuming that the pasture was in 100% good shape unless it had been killed completely. The fish example is easier to visualize.

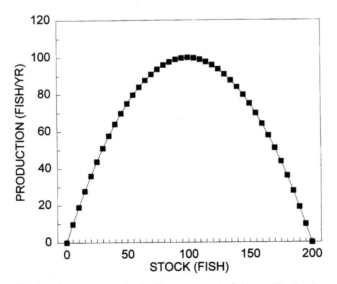

Figure 9.2 Production versus stock for assumed fishery. Production = 100 − (stock/10 − 10)².

Assume that we sharers of this fishery agree on quotas, gear limitation, and so forth, in an attempt to maintain the stock at 100 fish and hence allow maximum harvest (= 100 fish/year). We also prohibit new entrants. The political process to achieve the agreement was long and trying, and it will take a long time to change, but it appears that the TOC has been averted. Suppose, however, that in a single year, say year 5, something alters Figure 9.2, and even though stock = 100 fish, production is only 90 fish. This might be due to weather or other natural causes, to a pollution event, and so on. We might not realize that production is low, but even if we do, it takes years to change the quota. Instead of an immediate decision to reduce the harvest to 90 fish, the harvest is maintained at 100 fish. In all following years the production versus stock relation again is as shown in Figure 9.2; year 5 was a unique occurrence. What happens to the fishery? We apply Equation 7.1 or Figure 7.2:

$$\text{Stock}_{t+1} = \text{Stock}_t + \text{Production}_t - \text{Harvest}_t$$

$$\text{Stock in year 6} = 100 + 90 - 100 = 90 \text{ fish}$$

The production/stock relation returns to the original form:

$$\text{Production in year 6} = 100 - (90/10 - 10)^2 = 99 \text{ fish/year.}$$

$$\text{Stock in year 7} = 90 + 99 - 100 = 89 \text{ fish.}$$

Then

$$\text{Stock in year 8} = 89 + [100 - (89/10 - 10)^2 - 100$$
$$= 87.79 \text{ fish.}$$
$$\text{Stock in year 9} = 87.79 + [100 - (87.79/10 - 10)^2 - 100$$
$$= 86.30 \text{ fish.}$$

A pattern is clear: The stock is decreasing, production is decreasing, and there is no way to compensate unless there is a quick change in the harvest rate. Without that, the preceding trend continues, as shown in Figure 9.3, and the fishery collapses.

Alternatively, we can ask what happens if production is 110 fish/year in year 5. The stock in year 6 goes up, production drops, and harvest pulls the stock back toward the original value of 100 fish, as shown in Figure 9.4.

We have demonstrated that this system (with its rules and inertia) is stable against a fluctuation up but not against a fluctuation down in production. We could make an analogous statement about fluctuations in the harvest rate: A brief increase leads to a crash; a brief decrease leads to a return to the starting

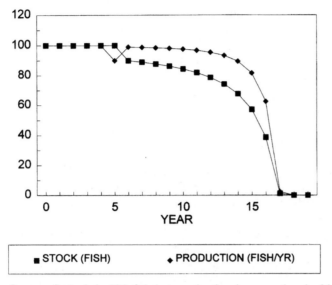

Figure 9.3 In year 5 stock is 100 fish but production is anomalously 90 instead of 100 fish/year. No adjustment is made to the harvest rate of 100 fish/year. Fishery collapses.

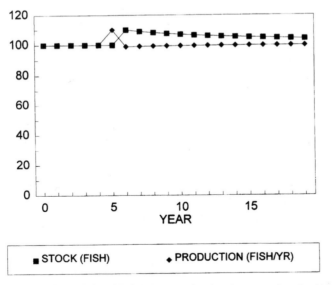

Figure 9.4 In year 5 stock is 100 fish but production is anomalously 110 instead of 100 fish/year. No adjustment is made to the harvest rate of 100 fish/year. Fishery returns to starting condition.

condition. These statements are based on an assumed inflexibility and delay in the system's ability to react. Certainly there are adaptive, quick responses that prevent crashes like these. For example, if we reduce the harvest to 90 fish in the year that production dropped to 90, the crash is avoided. However, we must act quickly.

Another example is even more surprising. Let the initial equilibrium be stock = 50 fish, harvest = 75 fish/year. If production drops to 65 fish/year in year 5 only, we expect a crash, since that is roughly just an intermediate point on the crash path we have already seen that started at the top of the curve. (The reader should verify this.) On the other hand, when production increases to 85 fish/year in year 5 only, as shown in Figure 9.5, the fishery moves through the top of the production curve and settles down at a new equilibrium with production at the original value, but with three times as much stock!

One might ask why it does not stop at the top of the curve. It cannot because there the harvest rate is only 75 fish/year, while production at the top is 100 fish/year, and system stock continues to increase until production drops to 75. The reader can experiment with different starting equilibrium situations and perturbations. The results are summarized in Table 9.5. We see that instability occurs on the left side of the production curve, and stability on the right side. The slope of the production curve is responsible. If the harvest level is held constant, then a change in production leads to a change of the same sign in stock. That stock change can lead to a production change

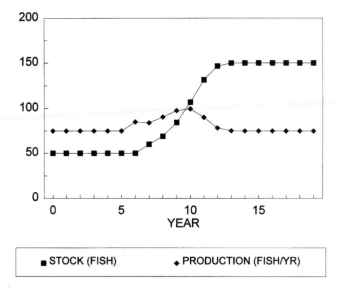

Figure 9.5 In year 5 stock is 50 fish but production is anomalously 85 instead of 75 fish/year. No adjustment is made to the harvest rate of 75 fish/year. Fishery moves to a new equilibrium with stock = 150 fish, production = 75 fish/year.

TABLE 9.5   Stability Properties of the Humped Production Curve, Figure 9.2. Harvest Rate Is Constant Throughout, and in One Year the Stock is Perturbed

Location of Initial Equilibrium on Production Curve	Sign of Stock Change (All Perturbations Can be Expressed as an Equivalent Stock Change)	Stable or Unstable?	Outcome
Left side	+	Unstable	Seeks new equilibrium on right side
Left side	−	Unstable	Crashes
Exact top	+	Stable	Returns to start
Exact top	−	Unstable	Crashes
Right side	+	Stable	Returns to start
Right side	−	Stable	Returns to start

of either sign, depending on where on the production curve we are situated. If the production change is the same sign as the original production change, we have positive feedback and instability. If the production change is of opposite sign, we have negative feedback and stability. These two conditions correspond to the slope of production versus stock being positive or negative. The argument is valid whether the original change is positive or negative, which agrees with what we have seen so far, except at the exact top of the production curve, where the sign does matter.[3] Figure 9.6 shows this schematically.

---

[3]Calculus digression: At the very top the production curve has zero slope (first derivative), and there stability depends on the signs of the stock change and the second derivative. Suppose production changes by ΔP_0 in year 0. Then

$$P_1 = f(S_1) = f(S_0 + \Delta P_0) \approx P_0 + df/dS(\Delta P_0) + d^2f/dS^2(\Delta P_0)^2/2 + \cdots$$

by a Taylor series expansion. Then

$$S_2 - S_1 = \Delta P_1 = P_1 - P_0 = df/dS(\Delta P_0) + d^2f/dS^2(\Delta P_0)^2/2 + \cdots$$

and

$$(S_2 - S_1)/(S_1 - S_0) = df/dS + d^2f/dS^2(\Delta P_0/2) + \cdots$$

$(S_2 - S_1)/(S_1 - S_0)$ is the ratio of successive stock changes. If the ratio is positive, there is instability. If it is negative, there is stability. If $df/dS \neq 0$, it dominates and there is no sign dependence of stability. If $df/dS = 0$, as it is at the top of the hump, then the second term dominates, and that depends on the sign of ΔP_0. For the standard humped production curve, $d^2f/dS^2 < 0$, and therefore at the top of the curve the system is stable against positive changes in stock and unstable against negative changes.

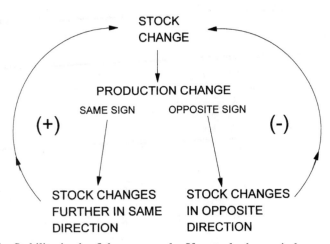

Figure 9.6 Stability in the fishery example. If a stock change induces a production change of the same sign [positive feedback, indicated (+), the stock continues to drift away from the initial value. It either attains another equilibrium or crashes. If the production change is of opposite sign [negative feedback, indicated (−)], the stock returns to its initial value.

As we have said, the problem here goes away if there is tight monitoring of fish populations, reproduction, and harvesting, and fast policy adjustment to the results. Neither of these requirements is satisfied here. However, if we were situated on the right side of the production curve, this would not matter, because of the inherent stability of that region. A position on the right has gained stability at a cost of less-than-maximum production. In class I have found that players of the TOC game tend to home in on that region. In many of the world's fisheries we are usually on the left side, which is unstable (Roughgarden and Smith, 1996). It is possible to move from a left-side equilibrium to a right-side equilibrium (which these authors recommend), but to do so we have to keep the harvest constant even as stocks begin to increase. Even with rules this is a hard temptation to resist in at least four ways:

1. Although we assume that the regulatory process is slow, it will likely move faster on apparent good news (stocks are increasing) than bad (stocks are decreasing). Then political pressure will be to increase harvest, thus stopping the move toward a right-side equilibrium.
2. Some regulations cover fishing effort rather than catch. With higher stocks the same effort will inadvertently result in a bigger catch.
3. Increasing stocks will tempt more fishers to cheat.
4. Economic theory favors the left side. The difference in right-side and left-side stock (100 fish in our example) is considered an investment,

which yields no additional production and which therefore should be harvested, with the proceeds invested in something that does return an income. Such thinking includes no consideration of stability, of course.

The Georges Bank (off New England) fishery was closed to fishing for cod, haddock, and yellowtail flounder in October 1994. The Grand Banks (off Newfoundland) were closed to fishing for selected groundfish in 1993. This was in spite of quotas set by the Canadian Department of Fisheries and Oceans annually since 1973. Data show that Newfoundland's fishers obeyed the quotas, yet the fishery collapsed, leading to the recent closures. Figure 9.7 shows the pattern of stocks, harvest, and quotas. In waiting for a fishery to recover, we must wait longer to reach the right-side equilibrium than the left-side equilibrium. Humans who discount the future will not want to wait, especially fishers who were put in dry dock by the moratorium. Roughgarden and Smith (1996) estimate that a proper wait for the Grand Bank is 9 years, whereas the Canadian Fisheries Resource Conservation Council recommends 5 to 7 years.

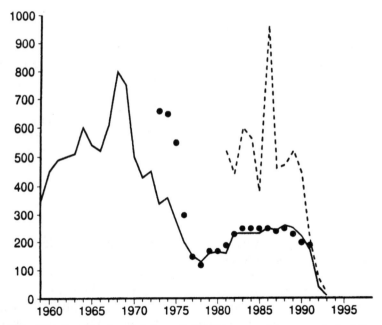

Figure 9.7   Newfoundland cod fishery. Solid line, annual harvest; dashed line, stock; dots, annual quota (units = thousand tons). Fishery shows three phases: 1960–1980, 1981–1990, and 1991–1993. These are respectively characterized by high harvest, low harvest, and collapse. *Source:* J. Roughgarden and F. Smith (1996). Why fisheries collapse and what to do about it. *Proceedings of the National Academy of Sciences* 93:5078–5083. © 1996 National Academy of Sciences. Reprinted with permission.

This example merely touches on a wide range of problems involving stability (one is how to *define* it; another concerns the size of the perturbation; here we have been a bit loose) and measures to increase it. See Problem 9.5.

PROBLEMS

Level of difficulty is indicated as Easier/Moderate/Harder. Problems marked "(Spreadsheet?)" can be fruitfully approached using a spreadsheet. They need not be, however.

9.1. (Easier) With at least four participants, play the tragedy of the commons game. You might want to use a bigger pasture, say one characterized by yield $= 400 - (n - 20)^2$. Role playing is especially recommended. For example,

- No communication, no roles assigned or required.
- No communication, everyone picks a role from a list such as Table 9.2.
- No communication, all assigned role B.
- No communication, two assigned role A, two assigned role F.
- Communication allowed, one assigned role D, three assigned role B.

9.2. (Easier) (Spreadsheet?) Tragedy of the commons exercise. Table 9.6 presents explicit yields for you, and for everyone else, on the example pasture in the text [for which yield $= 100 - (n - 10)^2$], and how these change when you add a cow and the other pasturers maintain their herds. The table thus contains the outcome of one possible future for the pasture when you add a cow.

   (a) Calculate similar tables for $n = 0, 10, 19$.

   (b) Contrast the "sanity" of these strategies: (1) keeping your herd small relative to the total and (2) owning all the cows.

9.3. (Moderate) Tragedy of the commons: payoff matrix (see Table 9.7). The TOC is an example of a noncooperative game, with four general possibilities based on whether I change my herd or not and whether "they" change their herds or not. Assuming specific numbers for each of these possibilities, I can calculate the change in yield for myself and for the other pasturers. This will help me decide what to do next, although the results are only as good as my guesses about what they will do. Assume yield $= 100 - (n - 10)^2$.

   (a) Calculate the entries in Table 9.7 for the following case: Initially there are five pasturers, each with one cow, and the possibilities are that I will add one cow or none, and that the others will add a total of four cows or none. Comment briefly on the results: Of the possible

TABLE 9.6

Total Cows	Your Cows	Total Yield	Your Yield	Total Yield if Add 1 Cow	Your Yield if the Added Cow is Yours	Change in Total Yield	Change in Your Yield	Change in Everyone Else's Yield
4	0	64	0	75	15	11	15	-4
4	1	64	16	75	30	11	14	-3
4	2	64	32	75	45	11	13	-2
4	3	64	48	75	60	11	12	-1
4	4	64	64	75	75	11	11	0
14	0	84	0	75	5	-9	5	-14
14	1	84	6	75	10	-9	4	-13
14	2	84	12	75	15	-9	3	-12
14	3	84	18	75	20	-9	2	-11
14	4	84	24	75	25	-9	1	-10
14	5	84	30	75	30	-9	0	-9
14	6	84	36	75	35	-9	-1	-8
14	7	84	42	75	40	-9	-2	-7
14	8	84	48	75	45	-9	-3	-6
14	9	84	54	75	50	-9	-4	-5
14	10	84	60	75	55	-9	-5	-4
14	11	84	66	75	60	-9	-6	-3
14	12	84	72	75	65	-9	-7	-2
14	13	84	78	75	70	-9	-8	-1
14	14	84	84	75	75	-9	-9	0

TABLE 9.7

Add Cows? I/They	Yes	No
Yes	Δ total yield, Δ my yield, Δ their yield	Ditto
No	Ditto	Ditto

combinations of results for Δ my yield/Δ their yield, how many occur in this example? Why?

(b) Repeat but with the initial situation of each pasturer having two cows.

9.4. (Moderate) (Spreadsheet?) For production $= 100 - (\text{stock}/10 - 10)^2$, using either a calculator or a spreadsheet, investigate these situations for stability:

(a) With fishery originally operating at steady state at a stock of 40 fish:

1. Increase catch in one year only by 5 fish.
2. Decrease catch in one year only by 5 fish.
3. Increase stock in one year only by 5 fish.
4. Decrease stock in one year only by 5 fish.

(b) Repeat 1–4 for fishery originally operating at steady state at a stock of 160 fish.

(c) The instability we see in this problem is a consequence of our keeping the catch constant except for a one-time perturbation. If we could adjust the catch every year, based on predictions following from the production curve, we could prevent a crash. However, there are often unavoidable delays in the response of social/economic systems. Pick one of the previous situations that resulted in a crash and design an adjustment to subsequent catches to prevent the crash . . . if it is implemented immediately. Then implement it with a delay of one round and see whether a crash is prevented. Example: To prevent a crash, you might decide: "Next round we need to reduce the catch to x." But make that correction two rounds from now.

9.5. (Harder)

(a) For the yield curves in Figure 9.8, indicate which regions are stable and which are unstable, against small fluctuations in "catch." Indicate what "small" means here.

(b) There are many specific definitions of stability, covering size, sign, and timing of perturbation, time to recover, whether the return is to the original condition or just to any, possibly different, equilibrium. For yield $= 100 - (\text{stock}/10 - 10)^2$:

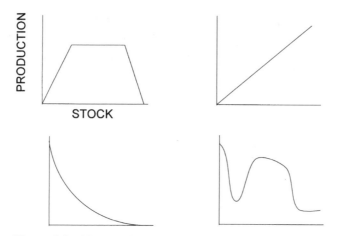

Figure 9.8   Hypothetical production versus stock relations.

1. Define stability as the ability to return to the original situation. Assume that harvest just equals production for stock = 20, that is, a steady state. Specify what one-time stock changes will allow a return to that point.

2. Do the same for stock = 50, 100, 130, 180. Example: For stock = 180 (with production = harvest = 36), changing the stock to anywhere in the range >20 to ≤200 will result in a return to stock = 180. Therefore −160 < Δstock ≤ 20 is the range of stability.

3. Now define stability as the ability to reach any equilibrium, not necessarily the starting point. Again specify allowable stock changes starting at stocks of 20, 50, 100, 130, 180.

9.6. (Harder) Economics and equilibrium fishing level. Neoclassical economics assumes that there is always an alternative, "backstop" investment that will pay a positive interest rate r. Entrepreneurs invest their capital hoping for a rate of return exceeding or at least equaling r. In the fishery example, we can think of the stock as capital investment, because (ignoring the cost of catching them) we have the option of harvesting all fish at any time and investing the proceeds somewhere else.

(a) Justify that this economic requirement has two parts: (1) The average rate of return (on all money invested) is greater than or equal to r and (2) the marginal rate of return (on the next dollar invested) is greater than or equal to r. In the fishery example, the average rate of return is equal to production/stock, while the marginal rate of return is Δproduction/Δstock, that is, the slope of the production curve.

(b) In Figure 9.2 estimate the average and marginal rates of return and plot them versus stock.

(c) Given that the backstop interest rate r is usually greater than 0, locate the region of Figure 9.2 that neoclassical economics says is profitable and comment on the stability in that region.

10 The Automobile: A Powerful Problem

Results of a poll of 4800 graduating college seniors: What would you like most as a gift?

New car or down payment on new car	47%
Money	45
Travel	27
A job	25

—News item on National Public Radio, June 8, 1996

. . . While some workers lost their jobs in the depression, the local sentiment, as heard over and over again, is that "People give up everything in the world but their car. . . . The depression hasn't changed materially the value Middletown people set on home ownership, but that's not their primary desire, as the automobile always comes first."

—R. Lynd and H. Lynd (1937). *Middletown in Transition: A Study in Cultural Conflict*, p. 265

A few years back I attended a public debate between the founder of a renowned world-saving organization and the CEO of a coal-mining company. The Bad Guy won the toss, took the mike, and said to the large crowd of obviously hostile adults. "Before we start, I'd like to know how many of you would be willing to give up your automobiles right now." A loud cheer went up, most hands waving madly in the affirmative. The miner stared for maybe a full minute, waiting for the tumult to subside. Then he said quietly, with just a hint of a sneer in his voice, "I'm not about to waste an evening talking to a roomful of liars." And then he walked out.

—J. Baldwin (1990). Eco-cars. *Whole Earth Review No. 68.* © 1990 Whole Earth Review. Reprinted with permission.

Robert Arnberger [Park superintendent] believes that the glory of his domain, Grand Canyon National Park, has been perverted by the automobile—not because of exhaust fumes but because of the mindset that autos create. "We don't have a people problem . . . . We have a car problem. We've created automobile-based recreation, which has spawned an entire way of looking at the parks."

—J. Margolis 1997. With solitude for all. *Audubon* (July–August), pp. 45–53

Should there be automobiles in the national parks? No, said James Bryce, a former British ambassador to the United States, who in 1912 warned . . . that

automobiles should be prohibited, especially from California's Yosemite Valley: "If . . . you were to realize what the result of the car will be in that wonderful, that incomparable valley," Bryce said, "you will keep it out." On the other hand, William Colby of the Sierra Club said yes, there should be automobiles. Both he and Club founder John Muir wanted to preserve the parks by popularizing them, and, he said, they hoped that automobiles "will be allowed to come in when the times comes, because we think the automobile adds a great zest to travel and we are primarily interested in the increase of travel to these parks."
—T. H. Watkins (1997). National parks, national paradox. *Audubon* (July–August), pp. 40–43

Every country that has developed the affluence to afford individual mobility opts for it. Even in countries that have good high-speed transportation systems, people love cars. They love that individual freedom of being able to do what they want when they want-the feeling of individual control. Even if that means going out and sitting in a gridlock traffic jam.
—D. Cole, quoted in S. Wilkinson (1993). Our next car? *Audubon* (May–June), pp. 57–67

Postcard ca. 1920: "Your photo in real autos." Randall's Postal Studios, Cincinnati

The forbidden city, Beijing. The car is the photographer's prop; people pay to have their picture taken beside it.
—Photo caption in O. Schell (1980). Hanging out in Beijing, *Mother Jones* (December), pp. 47–59

Many environmental discussions, regardless of the starting point, end up on cars. The automobile is the most challenging environmental problem facing developed countries, and could well be such for developing ones as they develop. There is no doubt that this is an extreme statement, but I believe it fervently. Most of the supporting points are aspects of LIEDQO:

1. The impacts of the automobile are deep and broad, ranging from air pollution to diminished social interactions (indirect, as well as direct, effects).
2. Humans are strongly attracted to automobiles, leading to rapid growth (dynamics) with many associated equity issues.
3. The dynamics of how autos penetrate a society, displace competing transportation modes, and influence spatial and community structure is universal and powerful. The auto's infrastructure has a characteristic lifetime of 10 years (autos themselves) to 75 years (urban structure, road networks) (dynamics and lags, marginal versus average analysis).
4. The auto is an individual benefit but often a collective mess (limits, tragedy of the commons).

5. Many auto issues can be dealt with, at least for a while, by efficiency improvements, particularly fuel use and number of passengers per vehicle.

This chapter cannot adequately cover the automobile and its alternatives. Instead it concentrates on several issues of the dynamics connecting cars and public transportation and a simple analysis of traffic congestion. First, we discuss the environmental impacts of cars and the growth of their numbers.

AUTOMOBILE IMPACTS

Most of us recognize the benefits, and likely have an inkling of the costs, of the private car. For example, Figure 8.1 showed Prugh's (1995) calculation of additional new-car charges to compensate for environmental impacts and hidden subsidies to auto traffic; they increased the sticker price by about 34%. On the other hand, we may not realize the extent to which cars shape our lives (see Problem 10.1). I will just mention a few brief points, appealing to the reader to add from experience, and finally to make his/her own decision on how serious they are. As with limits in Chapter 6, I feel the auto's costs are sufficiently important to discuss them. References on the car include Flink (1976, 1990), MacKenzie et al. (1992), Sachs (1992), MacKenzie (1994), and Lovins and Lovins (1995). The latter two discuss increased fuel efficiency and other environmental improvements.

About cars:

Urban smog caused by auto emissions: 50% (Conservation, 1990)

U.S. carbon monoxide emissions from cars and light trucks: 56% (AAMA, 1995)

U.S. nitrogen oxide emissions from cars and light trucks: 22% (AAMA, 1995)

U.S. volatile organic compound emissions from cars and light trucks: 23% (AAMA, 1995)

U.S. land area devoted to auto infrastructure: 2% (60,000 square miles) (Conservation, 1990)

Typical city land devoted to auto infrastructure: 1/3 (Conservation, 1990)

U.S. commuting trips via public transportation: 6% (Conservation, 1990)

U.S. commuting trips by single-occupant car: 64% (Conservation, 1990)

Average commuting vehicle occupancy: 1.1 person/car (Conservation, 1990)

U.S. CO_2 emissions from motor vehicles: 25% (MacKenzie, 1994)

U.S. oil use for transportation: 64% (Conservation, 1990)

Changes in U.S. oil consumption, 1973–1992:
  Electric utilities: −73%
  Residential/commercial buildings: −50%
  Industrial fuel: −33%
  Transportation: +22% (MacKenzie, 1994)
U.S. auto-related injuries and deaths: 4,000,000 and 47,000 per year, respectively (MacKenzie, 1994)
U.S. population growth rate, 1983–1990: 0.9%/year (U.S. Census Bureau website http://www.census.gov)
U.S. car miles growth rate, 1985–1993: 3.2%/year (AAMA, 1995)
1992 percentage modal split for commuting: private auto/public transportation/bike or foot:

Houston, Texas	93.9/3.3/2.8
Boston, Massachusetts	74.1/16.1/9.8
Toronto, Canada	62.9/31.3/5.7
Zurich, Switzerland	45.0/34.0/21.0
Tokyo, Japan	16.1/59.0/24.9

(Canadian Urban Institute, 1994)

AUTOMOBILE GROWTH

Figures 10.1 and 10.2 show the growth of auto numbers since 1930 or 1950 for the world, the United States, and Norway. In 1946 the world had about 40 million passenger cars, 80% of them in the United States. Fifty years later, the world has abut 500 million cars, 30% of them in the United States. The world car population has grown 12-fold (with a doubling time of about 14 years and equivalent growth rate of 5%/year), and the U.S. car population, 5-fold. Figures 10.2b and c indicates that the United States and Norway show some tendency for per capita car ownership to level out (at around 0.57 per person in the United States and about 0.4 in Norway). On a global scale, however, there is very large potential for growth, and Figure 10.2a shows no real leveling trend of per capita cars, which is currently at about 0.09 car per person. In 1995 more new cars were sold in Asia than in Europe and North America combined (Tunali, 1996). Table 10.1 gives more details on per capita cars around the globe. A quick calculation tells us that without any further human population growth, auto growth to current Norwegian or U.S. per capita levels will result in a world auto population of 2 or 3 billion.

DYNAMICS: WHY WE GOT A CAR IN NORWAY

My sensitivity to the impact and dynamics of cars came when I, a native American, lived in Trondheim, Norway, from 1975 to 1977. Looking back, I

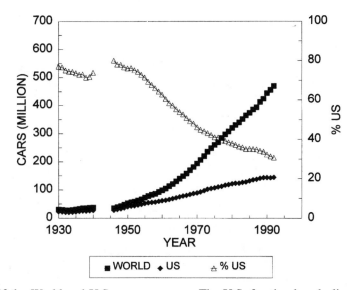

Figure 10.1   World and U.S. passenger cars. The U.S. fraction has declined steadily since 1930, except for the effect of World War II.

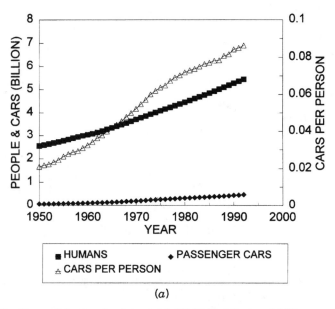

(a)

Figure 10.2   Car registration for (a) world, (b) United States, (c) Norway, 1950–1992 or 1995. The scale for cars per person varies. Current values for cars per capita: world, 0.09; United States, 0.57; and Norway, 0.39 (AAMA, 1995).

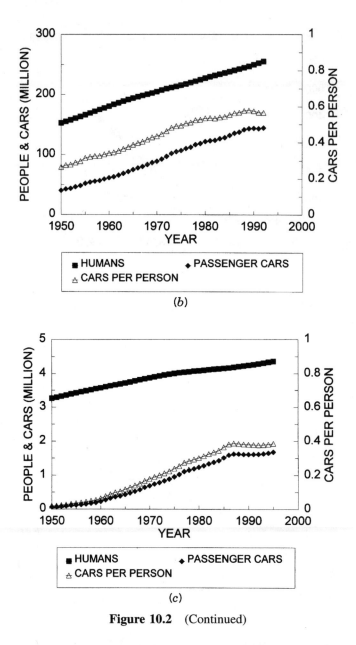

(*b*)

(*c*)

Figure 10.2   (Continued)

see what happened as indicative of several general principles, but I learned it first viscerally, there and then.

In 1975 Norway had about 0.24 car per person, as a well as healthy surface public transportation system of buses, trams, ferries, and railroads. The United States had 0.24 car per person around 1948, a time I could remember. A

TABLE 10.1   Persons per Car and per Vehicle around the World, 1992

	Population (million)	Persons/Car	Persons/Vehicle
Africa	656	65	42
Egypt	56	50	36
Kenya	26	166	90
Nigeria	89	111	62
South Africa	42	12	7.7
Zaire	39	372	195
Asia	3049	48	29
Bangladesh	119	1776	915
China	1170	616	183
India	886	316	170
Japan	124	3.2	2.0
Philippines	67	139	102
North and Central America	429	2.6	1.9
Canada	27	2.1	1.6
Guatemala	10	65	38
Mexico	92	13	8.5
United States	256	1.8	1.3
South America	309	14	12
Argentina	33	7.4	5.5
Brazil	158	12	11
Peru	23	54	34
Venezuela	21	13	10
Europe	854	4.3	3.7
France	58	2.4	2.0
Germany	80	2.1	1.9
Norway	4	2.7	2.2
Poland	38	5.9	4.9
Former Soviet Union	293	16	11
United Kingdom	58	2.5	2.2
Yugoslavia	24	7.8	6.4
Oceania	27	3	2
Australia	18	2.2	1.8
Papua New Guinea	4	348	97
World	5325	11	8.7

Source: AAMA (1994), pp. 25–27.

"snapshot" of Norway in 1975 would imply that many of the factors that led to auto problems in the United States were different:

1. Norwegian fuel and cars were taxed so as to cost at least two times as much as in the United States. Driving lessons costing $900 (1975) were

mandatory to obtain a driver's license. Drunk driving was strictly dealt with: 3 mandatory weeks in jail, and the legal blood alcohol limit was 0.05%, half of the then-typical U.S. limit.

2. Public transportation was cheap, efficient, well used, and subsidized; Norway had made a policy of extending transportation (and electric power) to remote fishing and farming districts. In 1975 the links were often ferries and trains. Fifty percent of Norwegian workers commuted by car versus 90% in the United States.

3. Norway was dedicated to providing services for the elderly, who had grown up in an essentially car-free Norway and were too set in their ways to change. Because of a low population growth rate, the percentage of aged was greater than in the United States.

4. Norway's culture was permeated by appreciation of nature and a vigorous life in the outdoors. No stores were open on Sunday, when it was a national pastime to go into the woods . . . on foot or on skis. The newspaper told of a bank robber in Oslo who escaped on skis into the spaghetti-tracked city forest.

5. Most Norwegians were only one generation away from fishing or farming and had strong ties to their relatives and home towns. Norwegians would joke that in the United States places are named after people, but in Norway people are named after places.

However, a single snapshot would not show the rate of change of these things and of other fundamental forces:

1. Norway was about to start pumping North Sea oil. There was no oil flowing in 1975; currently (1996) oil revenues amount to 13% of the gross domestic product. North Sea oil did not result in cheap gasoline, however, because Norway sold to itself at the world price and still taxed fuel heavily [today (1996) gasoline costs about $4/gallon versus $1.30/gallon in the United States]. However, the revenues from North Sea oil made Norwegians richer, with more disposable income.

2. On a percentage basis public transportation was losing ridership, and the prices for it were growing faster than for gasoline.

3. Norway was looking into ways to participate in the manufacturing of cars, which would make the auto industry more economically important and hence more powerful politically. In 1975 there were no cars produced in Norway. The only attempt at a Norwegian car had resulted in six units of the "Trollmobile" between 1956 and 1957, but the Swedes, having no oil themselves, then promoted a deal for Norway to be involved in the production of Volvos. [That deal did not jell, but Norway now produces many auto parts and some buses built on imported chassis. Plans for the production of a commuting car, the "CityBee," are currently underway.]

4. Young people wanted cars more than old people. Personal ads in the Trondheim paper literally said "You must have a car." The growth rate of auto registrations was 7%/year.
5. Larger, cheaper, centralized stores were starting up, neighborhood stores were closing, and the papers routinely ran public service announcements to "Support your local shop . . . so that it is there when you need it."
6. Women were entering the workforce, and larger stores were staying open longer.
7. Connections to distant districts, then largely complete for boat/train, were shifting to roads. In 1976 by wife and I worked for a week on a farm in Fjaerland, a valley 2 hours by ferry from the highway net. The name means the land of waterfalls. A plan had been approved for a 4-km tunnel through the mountains for direct road access. It is now complete.

In short, the forces of change were strongly at work, and over time they caused changes. Now, 20 years later, Norway has 0.39 car per person. Norway still has expensive gasoline, programs to keep cars out of central cities, and a reasonable, but diminished public transportation system.

In Norway my wife and I had no car for the first fall and winter. The following spring we bought a used car. We had environmental leanings, we appreciated the Norwegian lifestyle and the freedom that public transport sometimes offered (such as ski trips that ended 30, or 60, km from their start), but we were influenced by strong forces, thought conventionally, and reached the usual decision. In the end we acquired the car in large part because of the tragedy of the commons, and we used the car often as a consequence of average versus marginal costing, which will be discussed later in this chapter.

Of course, two other requirements underlay all of this. First, we could afford a car, and, second, we wanted one. We could afford a used car, in spite of the high prices in Norway. (Cars were twice as expensive and gasoline about 2.5 times as expensive as in the United States, and the average take-home pay was about 60% of the U.S. level.) We wanted a car because, with negligible exceptions, all humans want cars. There are many reasons, and to analyze them is interesting and even fun (see the accompanying box and Problem 10.2), but dilatory. People want cars, and we were no different.

Auto Advertisements

How on earth do you lose 5.6 billion people?

Some people have a habit of losing things. With the new Grand Cherokee Limited 4 × 4 the only "thing" you'll get in the habit of losing is the human race. Not to mention, all the headaches that go along with it

—Jeep advertisement, *Scientific American,* October 1995

> Ta bilen och stick! (Take the car and take off!)
>> —Auto tour catalog, Scandlines Ferry, Helsingborg, Sweden, Spring 1995
>
> Let your heart take the wheel . . . Live Without Limits℠
>> —Cadillac Eldorado advertisement, *Newsweek,* May 26, 1997
>
> In primitive times, it would've been a god.
>   It has the qualities man has revered and respected for thousands of years.
> The power to tame the forces of nature.
>> —Toyota Land Cruiser advertisement, *National Geographic,* February 1997
>
> It's not a car. It's an aphrodisiac.
>> —Nissan Infiniti advertisement, *Scientific American,* December 1992

The Car: Tragedy of the Commons

1. In Norway we stood almost as good a chance of getting killed by car if we had none as if we did. In 1975, 45% of the 537 auto-related deaths were pedestrians, cyclists, sledders, and skiers. (In the United States this was about 21%.) This high fraction was a result of the auto's rapid introduction in Norway, but in any case it was a fact.

2. The other disbenefits of cars—pollution, congestion, noise—were suffered as much by people out of cars as in. Atmospheric lead, hydrocarbons, and asphalt (ground out of the pavement by mandatory studded tires in winter months) were highest in the central city, where almost everyone shopped and many worked. Cyclists and pedestrians actually experienced these more, since they moved more slowly along the same corridors; there were no separate bikepaths or walkways. Buses were slowed by traffic jams caused primarily by cars; there were no special bus lanes.

We reasoned that if we got car in Trondheim, we would add one to a current auto population of 34,000, thus increasing pollution levels, congestion, and so on, approximately 1 part in 34,000. On the benefit side, we would make our own lives much cleaner, more mobile and spontaneous, and no less safe. After 8 months of walking and biking on icy roads through a tunnel of pollution, of standing in the dark at bus stops breathing fumes, we bought a car.

The Car: Average versus Marginal Analysis

Most people know the cost of gasoline and hence the approximate fuel cost per mile to operate a car. What about the total cost per mile? Take a guess and remember it in the following discussion.

In 1976 most Norwegian families had one car, which was naturally used for vacations, trips to the mountains, and so forth. Yet they, and we, were using the car in the city—an evening trip to a movie, for example—where the other modes of travel were relatively pleasant. One strong reason for this is simple economics, a consequence of the difference in the cost of owning (fixed cost) versus that of operating (variable cost) a car. For example, Figure 10.3 shows that in 1995, 80% of the cost of driving a U.S. car is fixed, that is, is a consequence of owning, registering, and insuring it, even if it never gets out on the road. The remaining 20% is a direct cost of operation, proportional to the miles driven. (This separation is approximately correct, but not perfect. Certainly depreciation increases some with driving, and insurance rates go up for high-mileage drivers.) In Norway we bought a 10-year-old Ford Taurus (a middle-aged car by local standards). Depreciation, registration, and insurance totaled around $800 (1976) a year, and we drove about 4000 miles per year, giving a fixed cost of 20 cents (1976) per mile. The marginal cost of operation was about 8 cents (1976) a mile, mostly for fuel, giving a total (average) cost of 28 cents (1976) per mile of which 71% was fixed. On the bus a five-mile round-trip downtown cost 90 cents (1976).

- When we did not own a car, we thought in terms of the *average* cost of car operation, 20 cents (1976) fixed + 8 cents (1976) variable per mile, and concluded that the trip downtown would cost 5 × $0.28 = $1.40 (1976). For one person, the bus was cheaper. We felt good about not having a car.

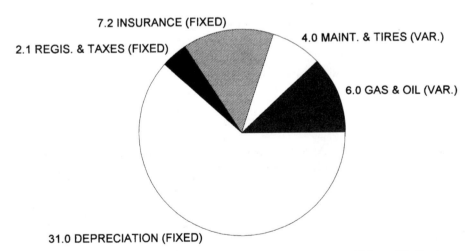

Figure 10.3 Passenger car operating costs per mile (AAMA, 1995, p. 58). Intermediate size car driven 10,000 miles per year for 6 years and then sold. Total = 50.3 cents (1995) per mile. Fixed and variable costs are indicated. Fixed costs are 80% of the total.

• When we already owned a car, we thought in terms of the *marginal* cost. The car trip would cost 5 × \$0.08 (1976) variable = \$0.40 (1976), which was cheaper than the bus. We felt good about driving. If more than one person was in the car, we felt even better.

The ratio of fixed-to-variable cost was approximately the same in Norway and the United States in 1976, and the ratio is comparable in the United States in 1995, Figure 10.3. The ratio in 1976 in the United States and Norway, and in the United States today, favors short trips. If the biggest problems of concern arise from ownership of cars (resource impacts from construction of cars, roads, parking, etc.), then the present "mix" of fixed and variable costs is appropriate. If the problems of concern (pollution, congestion, etc.) arise from operation rather than mere ownership, then the present mix is inappropriate. Changing the relative proportions would change the relative attractiveness of long and short trips. Consider what auto/public transport would look like if every citizen were given a car on his/her 18th birthday and fuel cost \$25.00 a gallon. Or, as is happening in many cities such as Oslo and Trondheim now, time-of-day and location tolls were levied for driving into the city center. Finally, parking costs, not even mentioned in Figure 10.3, raise marginal costs quickly. For a 30-mile round-trip commute, a typical (1996) Chicago parking charge of \$5.50 (1996)/day is the equivalent of \$5.50/30 = 18 cents (1996) per mile, which is a 36% increase in the per mile cost in Figure 10.3. Free parking has been called a fertility drug for cars.

The average cost per mile is related to fixed and variable costs as follows:

$$\text{Average cost per mile} = \frac{\text{Fixed cost per year}}{\text{Miles driven per year}} + \text{Variable cost per mile}$$

$$(10.1)$$

Table 10.2 shows how the average cost varies with miles driven for the data in Figure 10.3 using Equation 10.1. This is also shown graphically in Figure 10.4.

TABLE 10.2   Total per Mile Cost of Operating a Car versus Miles Driven per Year, Based on Data in Figure 10.3, Using Equation 10.1

Miles Driven/Year	Fixed Cost \$(1995)/Mile	Variable Cost \$(1995)/Mile	Total Cost \$(1995)/Mile
0	∞	0.10	∞
1	4030.00	0.10	4030.10
1,000	4.03	0.10	4.13
2,000	2.02	0.10	2.12
5,000	0.81	0.10	0.91
10,000	0.40	0.10	0.50

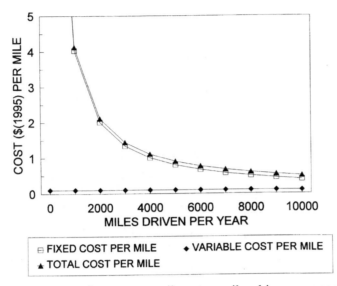

Figure 10.4 Auto operating cost per mile versus miles driven per year, also given in Table 10.2. Data are from Figure 10.3.

CARS AND PUBLIC TRANSPORTATION: POSITIVE FEEDBACK

Highways competed with parallel mass transit lines, luring away their customers. Pour public investment into the improvement of highways, while doing nothing to improve mass transit lines, and there could be only one outcome; those losses would make it more and more difficult for their owners to sustain service and maintenance; service and maintenance would decline; the declines would cost the lines more passengers; the loss in passengers would further accelerate the rate of decline; the rate of passenger loss would correspondingly accelerate—and the passengers lost would do their traveling instead by private car, further increasing highway congestion.

—R. Caro (1974). *The Power Broker: Robert Moses and the Fall of New York,* p. 888

This quote sums up a powerful positive feedback connection between the private automobile and mass transit. The connection is typically unstable, so that more car use means less bus use, which spirals; or less car use means more bus use, which spirals. In Chapter 9 we saw this type of instability in operating a fishery on the left side of the production curve. Figure 10.5 is an influence diagram summarizing several interactions. For what really happens we need to decide the strength of the interactions (as moderated by physical, economic, and social forces) and whether such a diagram is comprehensive and realistic. However, its broad aspects are correct. Problem 10.9 covers a simple example.

The way to slow down positive feedback is to weaken at least one segment. For example, it is cheap parking that stimulates cars, and expensive parking

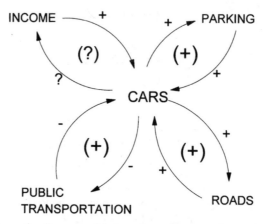

Figure 10.5 Schematic diagram of interaction of cars and associated factors. More cars produce pressure for more roads (a positive influence, shown as "+"), which encourage more cars (a positive influence, shown as "+"). These two influences produce a positive loop connecting cars and roads [shown as "(+)"]. This positive loop implies instability: Changing the number of cars will result in continued change in the same direction. There is a similar positive loop connecting cars and parking. The loop connecting cars and public transportation is also positive, the result of an even number of negative influences in sequence. More income produces pressure for more cars, but the effect of cars on income is less certain, so the cars–income loop has uncertain sign.

already creates backpressure against cars in many cities. It is cheap highways that stimulate cars, and high tolls and user fees make them less attractive. Figure 10.5 and other such influence diagrams usually do not explicitly include economic factors, but implicitly assume something about the factors. However, relative prices are just one factor and income is another. That something is cheaper than the alternative does not mean it will be preferred if the purchaser can afford either option. There are examples of public transport going unused even when it is free (Gordon and Suzuki, 1991, referring to Toronto).

THE AMOUNT OF TRAFFIC POSSIBLE: CONGESTION

In this section we use two everyday notions to get a quantitative insight on how congestion builds up as the number of vehicles, or the speed, increases. The notions are:

1. Distance traveled = (speed)(time) for constant speed.
2. For safety's sake, the distance between vehicles should increase at higher speed.

These are all we need to capture the basic elements of traffic jams, crowded roads, and drawbacks of unlimited speed as a solution to these problems.

Comparisons of walking, bicycling, various public transportation modes, and automobiles often tout the number of travelers per mile or the numbers passing a given point in an hour. Let us apply that thinking to a car traveling 60 mph. One driving rule of thumb states that cars should be separated by about 2 sec. Because 60 mph is exactly 88 ft/sec, 2 sec translates to $2 \times 88 = 176$ ft. For a 16-ft-long car, one car takes a space of $176 + 16 = 192$ ft. Then there are $5280/192 = 27$ cars per mile. This could be compared with pedestrians moving at 3 mph. This is 1/20th the speed of the car, so we assume the separation is $(1/20)(176) = 8.8$ ft. Assuming a walker with a vigorous arm swing is 6 ft long, he/she takes a space of $8.8 + 6 = 14.8$ ft. Then there are $5280/14.8 = 357$ walkers per mile. There are 13 times as many walkers per mile as there are 60-mph cars. The discrepancy is even greater when we account for the width of the traffic lane, say 30 ft for a car, 6 ft for a person. A 30-ft lane can carry 27 cars per mile at 60 mph or $5 \times 357 = 1785$ pedestrians per mile at 3 mph. These numbers seem to favor walking. Additionally, in terms of the number passing a point, the comparison still seems to favor walking. In 1 hour $60 \times 27 = 1620$ cars will pass in a 30-ft lane versus $3 \times 1785 = 5355$ walkers.

However, neither the number of travelers per mile nor the numbers passing a given point per unit time answers the most common question: How long does it take to move people over a given distance? To address this, we set up a small calculation. As usual, the task is to specify carefully what we want to know. Some possibilities are:

1. How many travelers can be contained by a lane (which we stated previously) (units = persons/distance)?
2. How many travelers can pass a given point in an hour (which we stated previously) (units = persons/time)?
3. How long does it take to get N travelers from point A to point B (units = time)?
4. What is the average speed for the entire trip (units = distance/time)? Call this the trip speed.
5. What is the travel capacity of the lane (units = persons * distance/time)?

To calculate these quantities, let us assume:

1. The vehicle's road speed is always v [units (say) = miles per hour] when it is traveling; it can accelerate instantaneously.
2. The vehicle's length is L (units = miles).
3. The proper separation in the direction of travel is τv, where τ is the human delay time in recognizing trouble and "hitting the brakes," typ-

ically stated as 2 to 4 sec in driver education classes. This is just one possible assumption for how separation should vary with speed.

4. The distance to travel is d (units = miles).
5. A vehicle carries λ people ($\lambda = 1$ for a walker or cyclist). λ is called the "load factor."

The process of moving N vehicles a distance d over a single lane has two parts. One is what we normally think of as travel, moving at speed v in orderly fashion. The second part is a consequence of congestion, the process of organizing traffic into the proper separation for the trip. Think of how cars come together at a red light and how long one waits after the light has turned green before the cars ahead have moved out and separated.

The organization step takes time, which can be calculated from two equivalent views. One is to assume that all vehicles are clustered at the start (Fig. 10.6a) and they leave one at a time, each waiting a time τ for the preceding one to get ahead by a distance τv. A second view assumes the vehicles are already queued up at the proper separation (Fig. 10.6b), but now the last vehicle must travel extra distance $(N - 1)(L + \tau v)$, which requires extra time for all vehicles to complete the trip. These two views give exactly the same results.

Now we need only apply the general idea that distance = speed ∗ time to derive these quantities:

$$\begin{array}{ll} \text{Number of vehicles} \\ \text{per length of lane} \end{array} = \frac{1}{L + \tau v} \qquad (10.2a)$$

$$\begin{array}{l} \text{Number of vehicles} \\ \quad \text{passing point} \\ \text{per unit time} \end{array} = \frac{v}{L + \tau v} \qquad (10.2b)$$

$$\begin{array}{l} \text{Time to transport } N \\ \text{vehicles distance } d \end{array} = \frac{d + (N - 1)(L + \tau v)}{v}$$

$$= \frac{d}{v}\left(1 + \frac{(N - 1)}{d}(L + \tau v)\right) \qquad (10.2c)$$

$$\begin{array}{l} \text{Trip speed of} \\ N \text{ vehicles over} \\ \text{distance } d \end{array} = \frac{v}{1 + \dfrac{(N - 1)}{d}(L + \tau v)} \qquad (10.2d)$$

$$\text{Vehicular travel capacity} = N * \text{trip speed}$$

$$= \frac{Nv}{1 + \dfrac{(N - 1)}{d}(L + \tau v)} \qquad (10.2e)$$

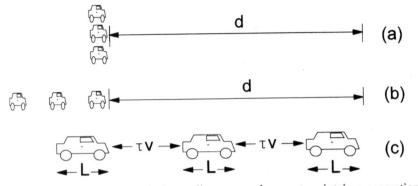

Figure 10.6 Vehicles of length L traveling at speed v must maintain a separation τ v. τ is the human reaction time to "hit the brakes." Trip length $= d$. (a) All vehicles are clustered at starting point, but must leave sequentially to establish separation while in motion. (b) Separation is established first, then all vehicles start simultaneously. (a) and (b) are equivalent for calculating travel time, etc. (c) Details of the separation between vehicles.

The "congestion factor" $(1 + (N - 1)(L + \tau v)/d)$ appears in Equation 10.2c–e. This factor is 1 if one or both of the following conditions is satisfied:

1. There is only one vehicle (the predominate depiction in media automobile advertisements).
2. The vehicle has zero length and the driver has infinitely fast reflexes (a common view among drivers I know).

For a congestion factor of 1, the trip speed is just v, the trip time is d/v, and the travel capacity is Nv. For more realistic assumptions about the number of vehicles, vehicle size, and human reaction times, the congestion factor exceeds 1, indicating slowed traffic, increased trip time, and diminished travel capacity. Increasing road speed does not increase trip speed indefinitely, and increasing N does not indefinitely increase travel capacity. Specifically: As N increases without limit (the commuter's nightmare),

Time to transport all vehicles a distance $d \rightarrow \infty$.

Trip speed $\rightarrow 0$.

Travel capacity $\rightarrow dv/(L + \tau v)$.

As v increases without limit (the ultimate autobahn fantasy!),

Maximum number of vehicles per length of lane $\rightarrow 0$.

Maximum number of vehicles passing a point per unit time $\rightarrow 1/\tau$.

Time to transport all vehicles a distance $d \rightarrow (N - 1)\tau$.

Trip speed $\rightarrow d/(\tau(N-1))$.

Travel capacity $\rightarrow Nd/(\tau(N-1))$.

In this high-speed limit everything occurs instantaneously except the passage of two successive vehicles, which must take time τ. The trip time does not depend on the distance, but only on the number of vehicles and the time required for the separated queue to pass. Travel is entirely dominated by the requirements of organizing the queue, that is, the requirements of separating to a proper traveling distance.

Figure 10.7 shows the trip speed for a 1-mile trip as a function of the road speed v for different values of N, assuming a 16-ft-long car and a reaction time of 2 sec. Only for $N=1$ is the average speed equal to the road speed. For $N=500$ vehicles a road speed of 60 mph gives a trip speed of only 3.1 mph! In this case 95% of the total travel time is spent waiting and positioning to enter the travel lane. Even if the road speed is infinite, the trip speed is only 3.6 mph. Approaching limits is a general characteristic of Equation 10.2, a consequence of simply maintaining an adequate distance between vehicles. Tailgating is one (risky) way to attempt to lift this limitation; see Problem 10.10.

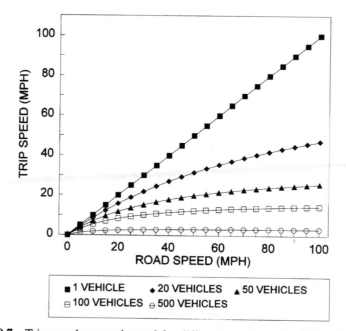

Figure 10.7   Trip speed vs. road speed for different numbers of vehicles for a 1-mile drive. Trip speed equals road speed only for a solo vehicle. Otherwise the time required for vehicles to separate to proper traveling distance results in reduced speed for the entire trip. Vehicle length $L=16$ ft, reaction time $\tau=2$ sec.

Travel capacity, which combines the number of vehicles and the actual trip speed, is probably the most useful single indicator of the desirability of a transportation mode. As we have seen, as N/d increases, the trip speed decreases, and the travel capacity approaches a limit of $dv/(L + \tau v)$ vehicle-miles/hour.

Now we return to the comparison of travel by bus, car, bicycle, and foot. Table 10.3 compares these modes for reasonable values of L, v, and τ for a 1-mile trip. In the table we also convert travel flow capacity to person-mile/hour by multiplying by λ, the number of persons per vehicle.

From Table 10.3 we can rank the four transportation modes according to four of the indicators, as shown in Table 10.4. Bike and foot are in the top two only for vehicles per length (a) or vehicles passing/hour (b), but generally are in the bottom two for the more useful indicators of trip speed (d) and travel capacity (e). Cars are faster, and fully loaded buses win for travel capacity.

PROBLEMS

Level of difficulty is indicated as Easier/Moderate/Harder. Problems marked "(Spreadsheet?)" can be fruitfully approached using a spreadsheet. They need not be, however.

10.1. (Easier) Do this experiment twice: While you are traveling by any mode anywhere in your town or neighborhood, record (estimates are okay) for a 10-minute period:

1. Number of pedestrians within 30 ft

2. Number of bicycles (moving or stationary) within 30 ft

3. Number of cars (moving or stationary) within 30 ft

List how you were traveling (i.e., mode) and where you were when you recorded these numbers, and graph the results (pie or bar).

10.2. (Easier) Watch at least five TV auto advertisements. For each:

(a) Record how often the following are mentioned or shown:

     1. Energy efficiency   6. Durability

     2. Safety   7. Comfort

     3. Speed   8. Freedom

     4. Acceleration   9. Sex

     5. Handling   10. Other attributes you find interesting (specify)

(b) When the car is shown moving, estimate the fraction of the time per ad it is shown:

     1. Alone

     2. With one or two other cars

TABLE 10.3   Trip Speed and Travel Capacity as a Function of Congestion *for One Lane* of Bus, Car, Bicycle, and Foot Travel

		Bus		
λ (persons/vehicle)	Road Speed (mph)	d (miles)	L (ft)	τ (sec)
40	30	1	35	2

Vehicles per Length (vehicles/mile)	Vehicles Passing Point (vehicles/hour)
43	1,288

N/d (vehicles/mile)	Trip Speed (mph)	Vehicle Travel Capacity (vehicle-miles/hour)	Person Travel Capacity (person-miles/hour)
1	30.00	30.0	1,200.0
20	20.80	415.9	16,636.5
50	14.01	700.5	28,018.0
100	9.07	907.4	36,294.9
500	2.38	1,188.2	47,526.9
1,000	1.24	1,236.0	49,439.4

		Car		
λ (persons/vehicle)	Road Speed (mph)	d (miles)	L (ft)	τ (sec)
5	50	1	16	2

Vehicles per Length (vehicles/mile)	Vehicles Passing Point (vehicles/hour)
32	1,623

N/d (vehicles/mile)	Trip Speed (mph)	Vehicle Travel Capacity (vehicle-miles/hour)	Person Travel Capacity (person-miles/hour)
1	50.00	50.0	250.0
20	31.50	630.8	3,153.9
50	19.92	996.2	4,980.9
100	12.35	1,234.6	6,172.8
500	3.05	1,526.9	7,634.4
1,000	1.57	1,573.5	7,867.3

TABLE 10.3 **(Continued)**

	Bicycle			
λ (persons/vehicle)	Road Speed (mph)	d (miles)	L (ft)	τ (sec)
1	10	1	6	2

Vehicles per Length (vehicles/mile)	Vehicles Passing Point (vehicles/hour)
149	1,494

N/d (vehicles/mile)	Trip Speed (mph)	Vehicle Travel Capacity (vehicle-miles/hour)	Person Travel Capacity (person-miles/hour)
1	10.00	10.0	10.0
20	8.87	177.4	177.4
50	7.53	376.5	376.5
100	6.02	601.5	601.5
500	2.30	1,152.3	1,152.3
1,000	1.30	1,301.2	1,301.2

	Foot			
λ (persons/vehicle)	Road speed (mph)	d (miles)	L (ft)	τ (sec)
1	3	1	6	2

Vehicles per Length (vehicles/mile)	Vehicles Passing Point (vehicles/hour)
357	1,070

N/d (vehicles/mile)	Trip Speed (mph)	Vehicle Travel Capacity (vehicle-miles/hour)	Person Travel Capacity (person-miles/hour)
1	3.00	3.0	3.0
20	2.85	57.0	57.0
50	2.64	131.9	131.9
100	2.35	234.8	234.8
500	1.25	625.3	625.3
1,000	0.79	789.4	789.4

The effect of different lane widths for different modes is not included in this table. λ = number of persons/vehicle, N = number of vehicles to be transported, d = distance, τ = human reaction time. Road speed = assumed speed whe actually on road. Trip speed = (distance traveled)/(total time required).

TABLE 10.4 Four Surface Transport Modes Ranked According to Four of the Indicators in Equation 10.2, Each for One Traffic Lane, based on Table 10.3

Indicator	N/d	Ranking	Ratio Largest/Smallest
a. Vehicles per length	Any > 1	Foot > bike > bus > car	9
b. Vehicles passing/hour	Any > 1	Car > bike > bus > foot	1.5
d. Trip speed	1	Car > bus > bike > foot	17 (by assumption)
d. Trip speed	100	Car > bus > bike > foot	5
d. Trip speed	1000	Car > bike > bus > foot	2
e. Vehicle travel capacity	1	Car > bus > bike > foot	17 (by assumption)
e. Vehicle travel capacity	100	Car > bus > bike > foot	5
e. Vehicle travel capacity	1000	Car > bike > bus > foot	2
e. Full vehicle: person travel capacity	1	Bus > car > bike > foot	400
e. Full vehicle: person travel capacity	100	Bus > car > bike > foot	154
e. Full vehicle: person travel capacity	1000	Bus > car > bike > foot	67

3. In light traffic
4. In heavy traffic

10.3. (Easier) Estimate the fraction of the area in your town/city that is dedicated to cars.

10.4. (Easier)
(a) Estimate your average annual speed in mph relative to the earth's surface. (This has been called the Celebrity Index.) That is, estimate all your motion/travel for a year and divide by the number of hours in a year.
(b) Roughly estimate the index for a highly traveled public person like President Bill Clinton or basketball star Michael Jordan. Compare yours.

10.5. (Moderate) For the following data, discuss quantitatively the changes in U.S. average energy efficiency and ridership of buses and autos between 1980 and 1993. Units = 10^3 Btu per passenger mile/per seat mile (per passenger mile only for train)

	Auto	*Bus*	*Train*
1980	8.13/4.78	36.6/2.81	3.00
1993	5.75/3.59	39.08/4.37	3.69

Source: Sarimiento (1996).

10.6. (Easier) Current (1996) world auto production is about 35 million per year.
(a) Assuming this holds constant indefinitely, what is the eventual world stock of automobiles?
(b) If today's human population holds constant and if the world per capita car registration rose to the current U.S. level, there would be about 3 billion cars. What annual world production is needed to maintain this stock?

10.7. (Moderate) The President Clinton–sponsored energy bill placed a $0.043/gallon additional tax on gasoline.
(a) Using Figure 10.3 as a starting point, estimate the fraction by which this increases the total money cost of owning and operating a car.
(b) Compare this fraction with that from (1) adding a parking cost of $245/year (1996 permit charge at the University of Illinois), (2) doubling of initial cost of car, and (3) taxing gasoline until it costs $4/gallon. The last two measures are in effect in most of Europe.

10.8. (Moderate)

> The typical American male [sic] devotes more than 1600 hours a year to his car. He sits in it while it goes and while it stands idling. He parks it and searches for it. He earns the money to put down on it and to meet the monthly installments. He works to pay for petrol, tolls, insurance, taxes, and tickets. He spends four of his sixteen waking hours on the road or gathering resources for it. And this figure does not take into account the time consumed by other activities dictated by transport: time spent in hospitals, traffic courts, and garages . . . the model American puts in 1600 hours to get his 7500 miles; less than five miles an hour.
>
> —Ivan Illich (1974). *Energy and Equity,* pp. 18–19

(a) Perform this calculation for a car, yours if you have one.

(b) Do it again for a bicycle, and compare.

(c) Is this a "fair" calculation?

10.9. (Moderate) (Spreadsheet?) Assume an interaction between cars and buses as indicated in Figure 10.5. Initially, ridership is 50:50 cars:buses. The total number of riders is constant over time. Buses must maintain revenues, so that the price of a trip is inversely proportional to ridership. The cost of a car trip does not change. When the price of a bus trip increases 1%, $x\%$ of the current ridership switches to cars. Assume it takes 6 months for this adjustment to occur.

(a) In the first half of year 1, for some reason, car:bus ridership goes to 52:48. Calculate and plot car:bus ridership for the next 20 years for x = 0.5, 0.7, and 1.0 (0%).

(b) Criticize this calculation.

(c) Suppose instead the car:bus ridership goes to 48:52 in the first half of year 1. Describe what will happen for the three values of x. Is it the mirror image of the answer to part (a)?

10.10. (Moderate) City drivers tend to leave less than 2 sec between them and the car ahead, often resulting in multiple collisions. Table 10.3 lists trip speed for v = 50 mph, L = 16 ft, τ = 2 sec, and N/d = 1, 20, 50, 100, 500, and 1000 vehicles/mile.

(a) Repeat for τ = 1 and 0.5 sec.

(b) Does tailgating like this result in significantly higher trip speed?

10.11. (Moderate) Stickler's correction to the congestion equations (Eq. 10.2): The equations are based on the time to transport N vehicles. This is the time for the last vehicle, the worst case. The vehicle at the head of the queue encounters the best case, no congestion at all. Rewrite Equation 10.2 for the average case.

10.12. (Harder) (Spreadsheet?) Suppose you are a planner making a presentation to a city council meeting. The issue is the commuter car traffic jam. Currently there is only the driver in each car. There are three proposals:

   1. Spread out the quitting times so that N is effectively divided by 2.
   2. Require strict car pooling that results in three people in a car.
   3. Increase the speed limit by one-third.

Assume that initially $N = 1000$, $d = 10$ miles, $L = 16$ ft, $\tau = 2$ sec, and $v = 30$ mph. Calculate the changes in trip time for each option, and work the results into a short narration that explains the reason for the results to a nonnumerate council member. A graph may be useful.

10.13. (Harder) U.S. auto fuel efficiency has roughly doubled since 1974, but the improvement has leveled recently, as shown in Figure 10.8. Figure 10.8 also shows the U.S. standard for mile per gallon for new cars. The standard refers to each manufacturer's sales-averaged miles per gallon, as determined in specified tests. This is called corporate average fuel economy (CAFE).

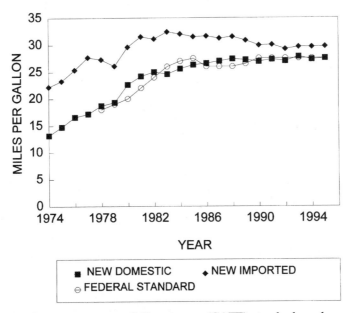

Figure 10.8 Corporate average fuel economy (CAFE) standards and average miles per gallon for new domestic and imported cars, 1974–1995. There was no standard before 1978 (AAMA, 1995, p. 85).

(a) One criticism of standards is that they effectively become a ceiling: No one tries to do better than the standard, even if the technological means exist. Criticize this view, using Figure 10.8.

(b) There is also a CAFE standard for new light trucks. This has varied between 20.2 and 20.7 miles per gallon between 1990 and 1995. Light trucks (including pickup trucks, vans, four-wheel drive machines, and sports utility vehicles) are predominantly used for personal transportation like cars. They are a growing fraction of new vehicle sales. There are currently (early 1996) no plans for changing the standards for cars or light trucks. Given all of this, what is the expected trend in average miles per gallon of new vehicles?

11 Ecological Economics and Sustainability

The self-organizing principles of markets that have emerged in human cultures over the past 10,000 years are inherently in conflict with the self-organizing principles of ecosystems that have evolved over the past 3.5 billion years. . . . The conflict . . . is illustrated by the fact that economic indicators have shown vigorous growth during the last century while a variety of environmental indicators have exhibited negative trends.
> —J. Gowdy and C. McDaniel (1995). One world, one experiment: addressing the biodiversity–economics conflict. *Ecological Economics* 15:181–192

. . . various lines of evidence suggest that [economic] inequities are . . . unsustainable for two reasons. First, the inequities themselves help perpetuate poverty, which generates vicious cycles involving deleterious and sometimes irreversible impacts on biophysical components of the Earth's life-support systems. Second, they hinder cooperation among parties of differing socioeconomic status—cooperation purportedly required for averting potentially disastrous population–environmental problems.
> —G. Daily and P. Ehrlich (1996). Socioeconomic equity, sustainability, and earth's carrying capacity. *Ecological Applications* 6:991–1001

. . . my major concern about my profession today is that our disciplinary preference for logically beautiful results over factually grounded policies has reached such fanatical proportions that we economists have become dangerous to earth and its inhabitants.
> —H. Daly (1993). The perils of free trade. *Scientific American* 269:50–57

These three statements and Figure 11.1 reflect two realities addressed by the field of ecological economics (EE):

1. Economics is established and is powerful in its influence in gauging progress and welfare.
2. Economics does not tell us all we need to know about how we are and where we are headed. Sometimes it gives wrong signals.

What can be done to bring together the physical/environmental/social concerns that go beyond what economics currently deals with? Because economics is in place and influential and because many human decisions can be

251

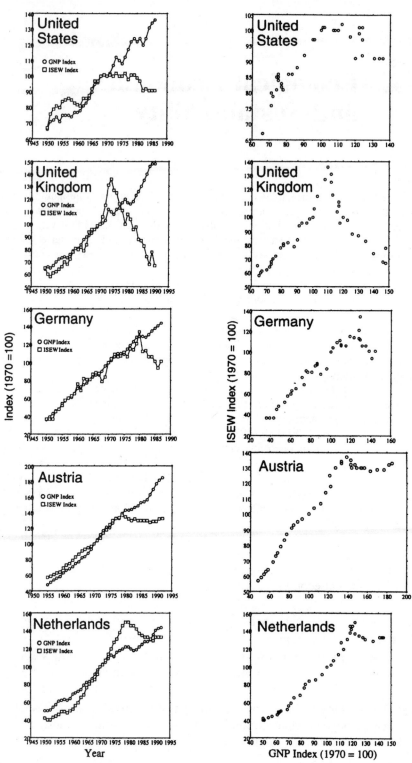

United States

O GNP Index
□ ISEW Index

United Kingdom

O GNP Index
□ ISEW Index

Germany

O GNP Index
□ ISEW Index

Austria

O GNP Index
□ ISEW Index

Netherlands

O GNP Index
□ ISEW Index

Index (1970 = 100)

Year

United States

United Kingdom

Germany

Austria

Netherlands

ISEW Index (1970 = 100)

GNP Index (1970 = 100)

252

described in economic terms, the answer to this question should also be couched in economics-like terms. A new field (ecological economics), society (International Society for Ecological Economics), and journal (*Ecological Economics*) have arisen to tackle this.

Dealing with all the issues in the ecology–economics interface is the final exam, the holy grail, in ecological literacy, numeracy, or sanity. The items are usually incommensurate—tons of lead, numbers of species, acres of old-growth forest, numbers of lung cancers, and dollars of income—and synthesizing them into useful form is the fundamental aim of ecological economics (EE).

Several of the central issues of EE overlap with what we have covered so far. Three of the concepts in LIEDQO are from Daly's (1992) formulation of EE. According to Daly, EE is:

1. Conventional economics [which concerns itself chiefly with the (economically) efficient allocation of resources]
   plus
2. Explicit treatment of how wealth and income are distributed across people (equity)
   plus
3. Explicit consideration of physical and biological scale (limits).

Daly says that today economics deals with these three issues in the following order:

1. (Most important). Economically efficient allocation is the center of neo-classical economics.
2. Welfare economics is concerned to some degree with the distribution of income and wealth.
3. Limits are hardly touched by economics, except as revealed by changing prices.[1]

Daly favors reversing this ordering.

---

[1]Economics does use the term "limited resources" as well as "unlimited human wants" (see Gowdy and O'Hara, 1995). However, limits are inferred by human behavior, especially how people price resources. Limits are revealed reactively, rather than anticipated and incorporated into actions proactively.

Figure 11.1   Per capita gross national product (GNP) and Index of Sustainable Economic Welfare (ISEW) for selected countries. In the last 15 to 25 years, per capita ISEW has held constant or dropped while GNP has increased. ISEW is discussed later in this chapter. *Source:* M. Max-Neef (1995). Economic growth and quality of life: a threshold hypothesis. *Ecological Economics* 15:115–118. © 1995 Elsevier Science Ltd. Reprinted with permission.

Many specific EE issues have already been touched in this book: indirect effects (Chapter 8), impacts of changing discount rates (Chapter 5), the cost of environmental services and damages, average versus marginal thinking (Chapter 10), and equity and stability in exploiting a common-property renewable resource (Chapter 9). How far we have come is indicated in Table 11.1, which lists ways ecosystems benefit humans and the extent to which each is incorporated into standard economic evaluation today.

This book cannot cover all of EE, which is a rapidly developing new field. We will look at three aspects which are important and numerically straightforward:

1. Income versus wealth: satellite accounts versus "green" GDP.
2. Sustainable resource management: the El Serafy method.
3. Other indicators of welfare and progress toward sustainability (Index of Social Health, Human Development Index, Index of Sustainable Economic Welfare, Four Principles of the Natural Step Foundation).

INCOME VERSUS WEALTH AND SATELLITE ACCOUNTS VERSUS GREEN GDP

These two pairings are two theoretically distinct, but practically entwined, dichotomies.

TABLE 11.1   Ecological Benefits to Economic Activity

Benefit	Degree to Which Covered in Current Economic Evaluation
Food, fiber	High
Wild medicinals	Low
Water purification	Low
Flood control	Low
Erosion control	Low
Carbon sequestration in vegetation	Nil
Wildlife habitat	Low–medium
Biological diversity	Nil
Nutrient recycling	Nil
Detoxification of chemicals	Low
Recreation	Medium
Aesthetics, spiritual fulfillment	Low

Source: Bingham et al. (1995).

Income/Wealth   Income is a flow, whereas wealth is a stock. Gross domestic production (GDP) is production, or consumption, per·unit time (usually a year), and thus a flow. GDP is not what we have or own, but what we produce from what we own. GDP is effectuated through the use of our stock of things, our wealth. If that use is dissipative, we have the paradoxical result that increasing GDP will accelerate the depletion of productive stock and hasten the approach of the time when we cannot produce. A popular term for this is "eating the seed corn." This can happen both for nonrenewable resources (say oil) or those renewable resources that are exploited beyond their sustainable levels (say fisheries, aquifers, forests, or seed-producing agriculture). See the accompanying box.

Three Types of Sustainability

Social Sustainability (SS)	*Economic Sustainability (EcS)*	*Environmental Sustainability (ES)*
SS is maintained by strong community participation. Social cohesion, cultural identity, tolerance, fellowship, and law abidingness are parts of social capital. Human capital investments in education and health are recognized as a part of economic development, but the creation of social capital is not adequately recognized.	EcS is defined as maintenance of capital, of which there are four types: 1. Human made (e.g., steel plant). 2. Natural (e.g., Amazon rain forest). See column 3. 3. Social (e.g., universal suffrage). See column 1. 4. Human (e.g., literate populace). See column 1.	ES is defined as maintenance of natural capital—the environment's ability to furnish raw materials, to process wastes, and to provide other services. See Table 11.1.

Four degrees of environmental sustainability:

1. *Weak Sustainability.* Maintain the sum of all capital, without regard to type. Assumes perfect substitutability of the four types (e.g., sewage treatment plant substitutes for forested watershed to cleanse water).

2. *Intermediate Sustainability.* Maintain the sum of all capital, assuming substitutability only to a point (e.g., tree farms can replace some, but not all, old-growth forests). A major difficulty is to define the threshold where substitution fails.
3. *Strong Sustainability.* Maintain each type of natural capital separately (e.g., assure that oil depletion is compensated by the development of other, sustainable energy sources). Assumes no substitutability.
4. *Absurdly Strong Sustainability.* Never deplete anything: no depletion of nonrenewable resources.

—Goodland and Daly (1996)

Satellite Accounts/Green GDP   Issues outside of conventional economics affect our lives and ultimately affect our economy. The first task is to identify the issues (e.g., CFCs and ozone depletion) and then to collect information about them. The second issue is how to incorporate the information into making decisions. Do we keep distinct sets of books on economics, ozone, soil loss, species counts, CO_2 release, timber cut and grown, coal removed, and so forth, almost all with their own units and unique measurement problems? Or do we use this information to create summary indicators that simplify making decisions, but inevitably lose details? The use of dollars for much of what we do tells us that we have implicitly accepted this "summarizing" for many things, but not all. Satellite accounts for resources, which are parallel to, and more recent than, standard economic accounts are increasingly used (United Nations, 1991, 1993; Landefeld and Carson, 1994). At the same time, there is a literature on "greening" GDP calculations (Pearce et al. 1989, 1991), in which information on changes in resource stocks is used to modify GDP.[2] Here we will apply both perspectives to the example of coal in Illinois. First, we look at satellite accounts and then show two ways (of many) that these can be used to modify the Illinois gross state domestic product (GSP). At the outset we should realize that there will need to be human decisions about how to convert between the two views (satellite accounts versus GDP modification); we cannot escape that necessity. In the end, human preference will matter, just as it does in economics.

Illinois, a state with 70% of its land in row crops, also has large coal deposits. As we have calculated previously in Chapter 3, the coal static lifetime is on the order of 500 years. Figure 11.2 shows how Illinois' reserves have varied over time. Figure 11.2 contains the stock, the inflow (discoveries),

---

[2]A recent bold step is to assign a monetary price to all natural services from the world's ecosystems (Costanza et al., 1997). The authors assign a value of $33 trillion/year to natural services, while the GWP is about $25 trillion/year. The $33 trillion/year figure is obtained by multiplying area times per area values obtained from a variety of methods, themselves very rough and justifiably controversial. However, the magnitude is significant: The unpriced free services from nature are at least as important as the activities we do price.

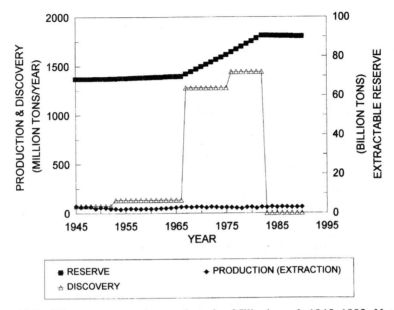

Figure 11.2   Discovery, extraction, and stock of Illinois coal, 1945–1992. Note different scales for flows and stock.

and the outflow (extraction, called "production" in economics). Applying Equation 7.1 to the flows will give the stocks. How much coal is really there (at what price) and what new discoveries may come are, of course, uncertain, but we will accept Figure 11.2 as accurate. Surveys in the 1960s and 1970s showed more coal, and the stock increased. Since 1982 there have been no more discoveries, and the stock has decreased only slightly with extraction. Figure 11.2 can be compared with a graph of GSP versus time, Figure 11.3.

On one hand, Figures 11.2 and 11.3 give all the information. If we wish to maintain that detail, a discussion of coal depletion and its short- and long-term consequences on state economic product might be carried on in two languages, tons and dollars. On the other hand, if a decision needs to be made, there will be an explicit or implicit weighting, summing-up, and coalescing of all information into one decision variable. Given that, why not be explicit about it? Let us bring the two approaches together using one of several approaches (Landefeld and Carson, 1994). One method is the current rent method, which just means weighting the annual stock changes (tons/year) from Figure 11.2 with some price ($/ton) and then comparing the resulting dollar figures with some aspect of GSP in Figure 11.3. The process is basically bookkeeping, as expressed by the flowchart in Figure 11.4. In a time period, say a year, physical processes change the stock of a resource. Simultaneously, economic forces change the price. The value of the resource, which is the product of its stock and its price, can also change.

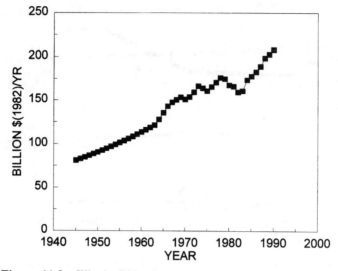

Figure 11.3   Illinois GSP, 1945–1993, in constant 1982 dollars.

Example   Suppose that in year t nation "Landet" produces a GDP of $100/year. In that year it is noted that Landet's stock of resources increases from 4 to 5 tons, while the world resource price decreases from 3 to 2 dollars per ton. We have these two pictures:

> *Parallel Accounts.* In year t, GDP = $100; change in amount of resource = +1 ton.

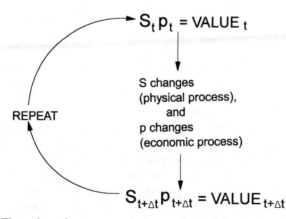

Figure 11.4   The value of a resource is the product of the stock and the price. Both can change over time Δt.

Modified GDP. In year t, the unmodified GDP = \$100. The value of the resource changed by $(4)(3) - (5)(2) = -\$2$. Therefore GSP (modified) = \$100 - \$2 = \$98.

In this case the physical amount of resource increased, yet its value dropped because the current price dropped. This calculation involves simple arithmetic, but the choice of price is very complicated. One problem is that because GDP is production, the price should be a net price—not the price of the resource as sold, but the profit remaining after the costs of extraction and processing are subtracted. For a raw material this price is approximately the "economic rent," the payment to nature for an extractive good. Of course, this payment accrues to the miners, extractors, and so on. Thus for coal selling at \$40(1995) per ton, the price to use in Figure 11.4 is approximately \$2/ton. Landet might encounter other problems:

1. If Landet is a tiny nation, the (world) price is not affected by Landet's production, but if Landet has a monopoly on the resource, then Landet does affect the price, which will be higher than otherwise.
2. The current price is applied to the entire stock of resource, even though we might anticipate that the price will increase as the resource is depleted.

Figure 11.5 shows the selling price and the calculated economic rent for Illinois coal. The rent more than doubled in the 1970s, in large part because of the rise in the price of oil following the 1973 embargo; all energy types became more expensive, as consumers sought a substitute for oil. The true rent used here does not reflect that peak; there are arguments pro and con for including such short-term changes, and the source of these data admits that the actual numbers here are somewhat arbitrary. While the selling price has dropped since 1945 (except for the postembargo period in the mid-1970s), the rent is here assumed to have roughly quintupled in 45 years, which is equivalent to an exponential growth rate of about 3.5%/year. Figure 11.2 shows that the coal stock grew between 1945 and 1982. Since 1982 it has been decreasing by roughly 0.2% per year (corresponding to a static lifetime of 500 years). On average, we expect value to have grown every year, and hence expect a positive correction to GSP. Figure 11.6 shows this to be true. Especially large corrections, on the order of 10%/year, are seen in the 1970s and 1980s, when the reserves were growing, that is, when more coal was being discovered than extracted.

We can also make a quick estimate to justify the magnitude of the GSP correction, which is on the order of a few percent. Consider the years 1988 and 1989. From Figure 11.3 we can read directly or estimate that Illinois had a GSP of about \$200 billion (1982)/year. Figure 11.2 shows that the coal

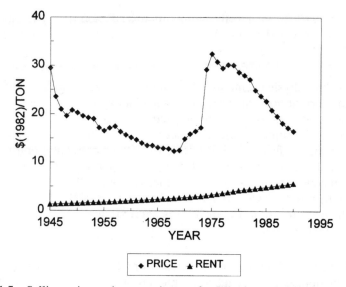

Figure 11.5 Selling price and economic rent for Illinois coal, in constant 1982 dollars. The rent is the "true profit" after production costs are accounted for (Herendeen and Mukherjee, 1996).

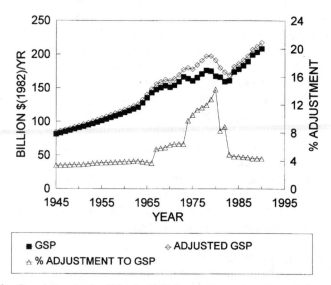

Figure 11.6 Correction to the Illinois GSP from change in value of the coal in state. This graph is calculated from the information in Figures 11.2 (coal stock), 11.5 (coal economic rent), and 11.3 (Illinois GSP).

stock of about 90 billion tons was being drawn down at a rate of about 100 million tons/year. The economic rent was about \$4(1982)/year and was increasing at about \$0.10(1982)/year. Table 11.2 shows the comparison of the coal's value in the years 1988 and 1989. The calculated change in coal value is 8.6/200 = 4.3% of the GSP. This approximate value agrees well with the value of about 4% in Figure 11.6.

This method has been applied to several developing countries [e.g., Indonesia (Repetto, et al., 1989), accounting for the depletion of forests and fisheries] and the state of Louisiana [(Foy, 1991), accounting for the depletion of natural gas and oil] (see Problem 11.4). The work has mostly been carried out by academics or researchers working for nongovernmental organizations (such as the World Resources Institute in Washington, DC). It is not accepted by most policy-makers to correct GDP in this way. We must again remember how limited the approach is:

1. Estimates of a resource are not independent of the anticipated price, so there is a potential interaction between S and p in Figure 11.3, even though we treat them as independent.
2. Even in isolation, S and p depend on estimates and are subject to political adjustment, as well as the conceptual problems mentioned previously.

EL SERAFY METHOD

This method of correcting GDP incorporates the idea that it is possible to invest in sustainable systems and that revenues obtained from drawing down unsustainable ones should be counted only after subtracting the portion to be used for sustainable investment. Whether that is possible (i.e., whether that portion is less than 100% of the revenue) depends on how long the depletable resource will last and how high the interest is on alternative investments. This correction is expected to be large for a nation whose economy is dominated by resource-intensive industries such as fishing, forestry, and mining. Many developing countries are in this situation.

TABLE 11.2   An Estimate to Justify the Size of the Coal Correction to Illinois GSP in 1989

Year	1988	1989
Approx. GSP [billion \$(1982)]	200	200
Approx. coal stock (billion tons)	90	90–0.1
Approx. coal price [\$(1982)/ton]	4.00	4.20
Approx. coal value [billion \$(1982)]	360.0	368.6

Figure 11.7 shows the standard picture of revenue versus time from exploiting a depletable resource. We assume it has a static lifetime of N years at a depletion rate C_0. El Serafy (1991) argues that because all revenue is from the depletion of the resource, which reduces future income-producing potential, the revenue is not "true" income. True (sustainable) income is that which flows without compromising the basis of future income, that which maintains capital. The only way to accomplish that goal with a depletable resource is to find a nondepletable substitute. The cost of investing in that sustainable resource (assumed to be a fraction β of C_0) should not be in GDP. The total revenue is counted in conventional gross product, so the capital fraction βC_0 would be subtracted from conventional GDP. Thus we have:

Conventional Depletion. N years' revenues at rate C_0, followed by nothing.
El Serafy Scheme. A fraction β of C_0 invested each year at interest rate r. At the end of N years this principal can yield a steady, perpetual revenue of r times the principal, that is,

Perpetual income
$$= r\beta C_0(1 + (1 + r) + (1 + r)^2 + (1 + r)^3 + \cdots + (1 + r)^{N-1})$$
$$= \beta C_0((1 + r)^N - 1)$$

where we have used Important Equation 2 for the sum of a geometric series. This is shown in Figure 11.8.

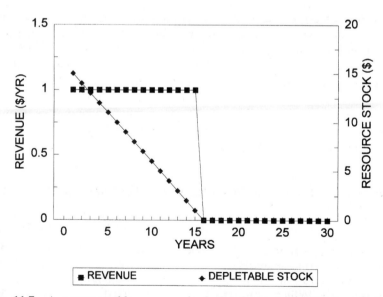

Figure 11.7   A nonrenewable resource is depleted at a constant rate and lasts 15 years. Revenue is constant for 15 years and then drops to zero.

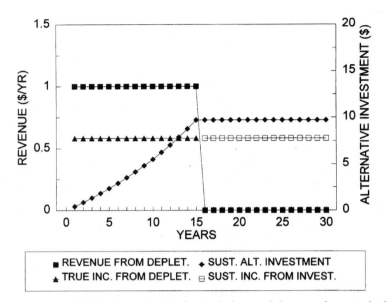

Figure 11.8 The El Serafy method of calculating real income from a depletable resource, illustrated for $r = 6\%$/year and $N = 15$ years. In the standard depletion approach (Fig. 11.7), all revenues are counted as income until they stop. El Serafy says first to subtract from the revenues enough to invest in a sustainable technology producing perpetual revenues. Only the fraction of the original revenue stream that is not required for this investment is true income and should be counted in GDP. In this case about 58% of the 15-year revenue stream is true income. The other 42% is invested to assure a perpetual income of the same value after the finite resource is depleted.

We can set the sustainable revenue to any desired value and see if a solution is possible with our values of r and N. Here let us assume that the sustainable revenue is equal to that part of C_0 that was not needed for the investment. For N years we have revenues of C_0, of which $(1 - \beta)C_0$ is true sustainable income and βC_0 must be invested, followed by an infinite period with true sustainable income [also equal to $(1 - \beta)C_0$]. Then

$$\beta C_0((1 + r)^N - 1) = (1 - \beta)C_0 \tag{11.1}$$

$$\text{True income fraction} = 1 - \beta = 1 - \frac{1}{(1 + r)^N}$$

The true income fraction is 0 for $r = 0$. Without the assumption of a "backstop" system that can pay interest indefinitely, there is no way to convert a finite resource into a infinite one.

The El Serafy approach is a true blend of physical and economic thinking: It is physical because it is explicit about depletion, and it is economic because it assumes substitution. It is physical in referring to solar-based technologies as sustainable, and it is economic in subsuming this idea under the concept of an interest rate that is obtainable (assumedly forever) on investments. Critics might object that such an interest rate assumption is unwarranted technological optimism: It assumes that we can experiment and maneuver with our technologies, but these are embedded in a larger system that continues to function and grow and nurture us forever. This criticism is well founded, yet the El Serafy method is a real advance in analysis.

For $r > 0$ the true income fraction $(1 - \beta) > 0$; that is, some part of the revenue is true income. For large r and N the fraction approaches 1: All revenue is true income. Again this says what we expect: If a resource will last a very long time and/or a high interest rate is available on alternative investments, the revenue is effectively perpetual. Table 11.3 contains representative values for β as a function of r and N.

Table 11.3 shows that there are combinations of r and N for which conversion to a sustainable resource (yielding the same nonzero revenues) is impossible. Such conversion is always impossible if $r = 0$, independent of N, again pointing out that to assume interest forever is to assume sustainability. The El Serafy method allows calculating quantities relevant to sustainability, but the possibility of sustainability is an implicit assumption used in this calculation, rather than a result of it. Table 11.3 shows that with r of a few percent per year and $N = 500$ years (the order of the static lifetime of Illinois' coal), the capital fraction is tiny, usually less than 0.1%. With life-

TABLE 11.3   Capital and Income Fractions Using the El Serafy Method (Eq. 11.1)

N (year)	r (%/year)	Capital Fraction β	True Income Fraction $1 - \beta$
10	0	Impossible to attain perpetual income	
10	1	0.905	0.095
10	3	0.744	0.256
10	6	0.558	0.442
10	10	0.386	0.614
100	0	Impossible to attain perpetual income	
100	1	0.370	0.630
100	3	0.052	0.948
100	6	0.003	0.997
100	10	0.00007	0.99993
500	0	Impossible to attain perpetual income	
500	1	0.007	0.993
500	3	0.0000004	0.9999996
500	6	0.0000000000002	0.9999999999998
500	10	0.000000000000000	1.000000000000000

times and discount rates that high, the El Serafy correction is negligible, and essentially all revenues are true income.

A Real Example.   Winter-Nelson (1996) has applied the El Serafy approach to the GDP of 18 African nations and expressed the correction (for petroleum and minerals only) as a percentage of the annual GDP growth. That is, apparent GDP growth is reduced when we account for the fact that the growth is partly based on the growth in the rate of depletion of petroleum and minerals. In Table 11.4 $r = 0$ corresponds to no true income from depleting a resource, and hence we should subtract 100% of income in that resource industry from GDP. For nations with resource-intensive economies, the resulting corrections are large. For example, Botswana's GDP average growth rate for 1980–1989 is reduced from 10.0 to 6.4%/year for $r = 0$. For nations with less dependence on resource industries, such as Kenya, the corrections are negligible.

OTHER MEASURES OF WELFARE

These run the gamut from further modifications of GDP, to social indicators with little or no economic content, to physical indicators.

Index of Social Health

Figure 11.9 shows this index for 1970 to 1993 in the United States (Miringoff, 1995). It is based on the following data:

Children:	Infant mortality
	Child abuse
	Children in poverty
Youth:	Teen suicide
	Drug abuse
	High school dropouts
Adults:	Unemployment
	Average weekly earnings
	Health insurance coverage
Aging:	Poverty among those over 65
	Out-of-pocket health care costs for those over 65
All ages:	Homicides
	Alcohol-related traffic fatalities
	Food stamp coverage
	Access to affordable housing
	Gap between rich and poor

Almost all of these are not explicitly included in GDP. The choice of issues

TABLE 11.4 Effect of the El Serafy Correction on GDP Growth for Five African Nations

Nation	Time Period	Percentage GDP from Petroleum and Minerals	Percentage National Income That Is True Income			Average GDP Growth Rate During Time Period (%/year)		
			With $r = 5\%$/year	With $r = 0\%$/year	As Normally Stated	Corrected, with $r = 5\%$/year	Corrected, with $r = 0\%$/year
Nations with Relatively Large Petroleum and Minerals Industries								
Botswana	1980–1989	53	89	47	10.01	9.13	6.42
Gabon	1973–1989	26	91	74	0.37	−0.38	−1.77
Nigeria	1973–1989	23	96	79	0.62	0.65	0.67
Nations with Relatively Small Petroleum and Minerals Industries								
Kenya	1973–1989	0	100	99	4.81	4.82	4.82
Zimbabwe	1973–1989	6	99	99	2.90	2.89	3.03

Source: Winter-Nelson (1996).

266

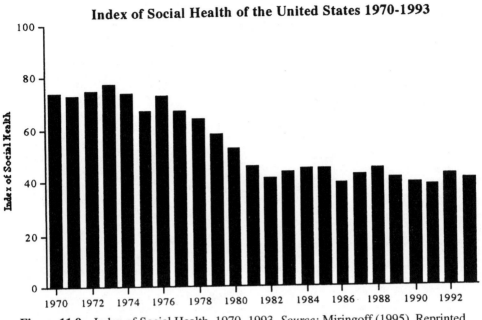

Figure 11.9 Index of Social Health, 1970–1993. *Source:* Miringoff (1995). Reprinted with permission.

and how they are weighted in calculating the index are, of course, subject to argument. This particular index was roughly constant from 1970 to 1976, then dropped steadily until about 1980, and has remained roughly constant since. In contrast, U.S. per capita GDP increased about 50% (an average of 1.8%/year) between 1970 and 1993.

Human Development Index

The Human Development Index (HDI) is one of several indices used by the United Nations Development Program. It combines life expectancy at birth, literacy fraction plus school enrollment fraction, and per capita GDP. It is less subtle than the other indices discussed in this section, but appropriate for comparing developed and developing countries. Table 11.5 lists recent values of the HDI.

Index of Sustainable Economic Welfare

So far we have criticized GDP because it measures income, not wealth, and we have discussed two corrections for this problem. Another criticism of GDP is that it counts as benefits things that are really costs (such as medical care for crime victims and pollution control) and that it neglects things that are

TABLE 11.5   Human Development Index

Rank (of 175)	Nation	Life Expectancy at Birth (years)	Percentage Literacy	Percentage School-Aged Children Enrolled	GDP per Capita [$(1994)]	HDI[a]
1	Canada	79.0	99.0	100	21,459	0.960
4	United States	76.2	99.0	96	26,397	0.942
19	Germany	76.3	99.0	81	19,675	0.924
68	Brazil	66.4	82.7	72	5,362	0.783
69	Bulgaria	71.1	93.0	66	4,533	0.780
108	China	68.9	80.9	58	2,604	0.626
129	Zimbabwe	49.0	84.7	68	2,196	0.513
138	India	61.3	51.2	56	1,348	0.446
155	Bhutan	51.5	44.1	31	1,289	0.338
156	Haiti	54.4	44.1	29	896	0.338
175	Sierra Leone	33.6	30.3	28	643	0.176

[a]The index is the average of three scores: (1) life expectancy, with 25 years given score 0 and 85 years given score 100%, (2) the average of the literacy and school enrollment fractions, and (3) GDP per capita, with $100/year given score 0 and $40,000/year given score 100%. (1) and (2) are scored proportionally: A life expectancy of 65 years gets score = 40/60 = 66.7%. (3) is scored disproportionately: A GDP above the world average is given relatively little extra score. *Source*: HDRO (1997).

true benefits (such as labor in the household). As Daly points out in *Beyond Growth* (1996), "[We celebrate] the increase in GNP that results as formerly free goods become scarce and receive a price." Table 11.6 lists more problems with GDP. The Index of Sustainable Economic Welfare (ISEW), which is shown in Figure 11.1, is one attempt to include these things (Daly and Cobb, 1989).

Figure 11.10 shows the ISEW per capita for the United States for 1950 to 1986, as compared with GNP per capita. During that period GNP per capita doubled (in constant dollars). The ISEW per capita increased about 28% during the period, but actually decreased after about 1978. Table 11.7 lists the components of the ISEW and their weightings. From Table 11.7 we can get an idea of the magnitudes of the corrections promoted by Daly and Cobb, but this is shown better in Table 11.8, in which we normalize everything with respect to personal consumption expenditures. Then all corrections are expressed as percentages of that base number. The ISEW was 128% of the PCE in 1951 and decreased steadily to 71% of PCE in 1987. We can see what trends contributed to this change from Table 11.8. Listing items that changed by at least 3% of PCE:

Things that got worse: corrections that decreased between 1951 and 1987:

C'.	Income distribution correction	−11%
E.	Household labor	−50

TABLE 11.6   Possible Corrections to GDP

Item	Correction to Conventional GDP
Conventional GDP counts these as benefits, but they are really costs:	
Medical care for accident victims	(−)
Medical care for pollution-caused conditions	(−)
Crime prevention costs	(−)
Communting costs	(−)
National advertising	(−)
Conventional GDP does not include these, but should include them as benefits	
Household labor	(+)
Conventional GDP does not include these, but should count them as costs:	
Resource depletion	(−)
Long-term environmental damage	(−)
Deviation from flat income distribution	(−)

I.	Expenditures on consumer durables	− 7
M.	Density costs	− 3
W.	Change in international position	− 6
Sum of these decreases		−77%

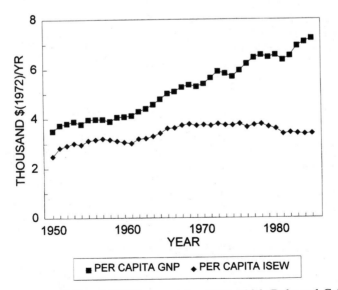

Figure 11.10 U.S. GNP and ISEW per capita, 1950–1986 (Daly and Cobb, 1989).

TABLE 11.7   Details of Calculating the ISEW

A	Year	1951	1960	1970	1980	1986
B	Personal consumption (billion $/year)	341.6	452.0	672.1	931.8	1155.5
C	Index of distributional [income] inequality	100.0	101.3	95.0	100.1	112.8
D	Modified personal consumption (= 100 * B/C) (billion $/year)	341.6	446.3	707.8	930.9	1024.4
E	Household labor (billion $/year)	315.4	354.0	402.4	457.3	493.9
F	Services from consumer durables (billion $/year)	14.6	21.7	37.3	61.3	79.8
G	Services from streets and highways (billion $/year)	6.6	9.6	14.6	17.5	18.5
H	Public health and education (billion $/year)	1.2	4.0	18.7	32.2	34.9
I	Expenditures on consumer durables (billion $/year)	−39.1	−51.4	−89.1	−137.5	−212.0
J	Private defensive, health, and education (billion $/year)	−3.3	−10.0	−23.4	−35.1	−44.2
K	National advertising (billion $/year)	−7.4	−10.8	−12.7	−16.7	−20.9
L	Commuting (billion $/year)	−8.5	−11.3	−17.4	−28.6	−33.5
M	Density costs (billion $/year)	−6.2	−11.6	−20.1	−41.4	−51.5
N	Auto accidents (billion $/year)	−13.2	−14.4	−25.3	−29.0	−30.5
O	Water pollution (billion $/year)	−9.2	−11.5	−14.9	−15.3	−15.3
P	Air pollution (billion $/year)	−25.2	−25.1	−30.0	−24.3	−22.4
Q	Noise pollution (billion $/year)	−2.1	−2.8	−3.8	−4.3	−4.6
R	Loss of wetlands (billion $/year)	−10.4	−13.6	−17.2	−19.5	20.6
S	Loss of farmland (billion $/year)	−7.8	−13.7	−20.9	−28.6	−33.3
T	Depletion of nonrenewable resources (billion $/year)	−21.8	−25.5	−30.9	−74.5	−62.4
U	Long-term environmental damage (billion $/year)	−86.9	−116.2	−161.8	−223.0	−258.7
V	Net capital growth (billion $/year)	0.1	31.4	51.1	8.4	44.0
W	Change in international position (billion $/year)	0.2	2.2	−0.7	6.4	−63.4
X	ISEW (= sum of D–W) (billion $/year)	438.5	551.4	763.4	836.3	822.1
Y	Per capita ISEW ($/year)	2831.2	3051.9	3723.1	3672.0	3402.8
Z	GNP, as normally reckoned (billion $/year)	579.4	737.2	1085.6	1475.0	1745.9
AA	Per capita GNP ($/year)	3741.0	4080.3	5294.3	6476.7	7226.4

Signs indicate whether contributions are added to or subtracted from the ISEW. All in constant 1972 dollars.

Source: From Daly and Cobb (1989), Table A.1, using their notation.

Things that got better: corrections that increased between 1951 and 1987:

F.	Services from consumer durables	+ 3%
H.	Public health and education	+ 3
P.	Air pollution	+ 5
U.	Long-term environmental damage	+ 3
V.	Net capital growth	+ 4
	Sum of these increases	+18%

The sum of increases and decreases is $18 - 77 = -59\%$, which shows that

TABLE 11.8   Details of Calculating the ISEW, but Normalized so That Personal Consumption (PCE) = 100.0. All Corrections Are Thus in Percentage of PCE.[3]

A	Year	1951	1960	1970	1980	1986
B	Personal consumption (PCE)	100.0	100.0	100.0	100.0	100.0
C'	Correction to PCE for income distribution	0.0	−1.3	5.3	−0.1	−11.3
E	Household labor	92.3	78.3	59.9	49.1	42.7
F	Services from consumer durables	4.3	4.8	5.5	6.6	6.9
G	Services from streets and highways	1.9	2.1	2.2	1.9	1.6
H	Public health and education	0.4	0.9	2.8	3.5	3.0
I	Expenditures on consumer durables	−11.4	−11.4	−13.3	−14.8	−18.3
J	Private defensive, health and education	−1.0	−2.2	−3.5	−3.8	−3.8
K	National advertising	−2.2	−2.4	−1.9	−1.8	−1.8
L	Commuting	−2.5	−2.5	−2.6	−3.1	−2.9
M	Density costs	−1.8	−2.6	−3.0	−4.4	−4.5
N	Auto accidents	−3.9	−3.2	−3.8	−3.1	−2.6
O	Water pollution	−2.7	−2.5	−2.2	−1.6	−1.3
P	Air pollution	−7.4	−5.6	−4.5	−2.6	−1.9
Q	Noise pollution	−0.6	−0.6	−0.6	−0.5	−0.4
R	Loss of wetlands	−3.0	−3.0	−2.6	−2.1	−1.8
S	Loss of farmland	−2.3	−3.0	−3.1	−3.1	−2.9
T	Depletion of nonrenewable resources	−6.4	−5.6	−4.6	−8.0	−5.4
U	Long-term environmental damage	−25.4	−25.7	−24.1	−23.9	−22.4
V	Net capital growth	0.0	6.9	7.6	0.9	3.8
W	Change in international position	0.1	0.5	−0.1	0.7	−5.5
Y	ISEW (= sum of B–W)	128.4	122.0	113.6	89.8	71.1

Source: From Daly and Cobb (1989), Table A.1, using their notation.

[3]Gross domestic product (GDP) is the sum of personal consumption expenditures, gross investment, government expenditures, net exports, and changes in inventory. Daly and Cobb start by assuming that personal consumption expenditures are basically beneficial (though subject to some corrections) and that government expenditures must be justified before being counted in the ISEW. In the United States in 1995, PCE was 68% of GDP.

these selected changes account for almost all of the 57% decrease in the corrections to PCE to obtain ISEW. It is noteworthy that the contribution of most types of pollution, including long-term environmental damage, changed very little (as a fraction of PCE; in absolute terms they did increase). Almost all of the change in the ratio of ISEW to PCE is from the change in household labor; it did not grow as fast as PCE. This is likely because of more home-makers in the commercial workforce, so that household labor dropped relative to commercial wage earnings.

In deciding whether to use the ISEW, one must evaluate how each correction is made and whether the weighting scheme to combine these is satisfactory. The details of the Daly–Cobb method can be found in their book *For the Common Good* (1989), but we mention several here:

1. Long-term environmental damage (flow, per year) is assumed proportional to cumulative U.S. nonrenewable energy consumption (stock) since 1900, using a factor of $0.50(1972)/year per barrel of oil equivalent. The authors admit this is a rough calculation. For comparison, a barrel of crude oil today (1996) costs about $4(1972).

2. Wetlands are assumed to provide services worth $600/year per acre.

3. For consumer durable products (e.g., washing machines), Daly and Cobb attempt to calculate the value of the service from the device rather than its purchase cost. They point out that if washing machines lasted 100 years, we would buy fewer of them. This would lower personal consumption expenses, but yield no change in welfare, as the same number of washes would be occurring. Therefore they subtract purchases of durables from GNP and then add back in a value for the services. Typically, consumer durables have lifetimes of 10 to 20 years, so that services per year are approximately 10 to 5% of purchase costs.

4. Daly and Cobb's method for correcting for nonuniform income distribution is discussed in Problem 11.7.

The Natural Step Foundation

The Natural Step Foundation (TNS) helps industries to bring their manufacturing and operations in general into line with environmental and social justice guidelines. Founded in Sweden in 1989, it expanded to the United States in 1995 and is active in several other countries. The foundation was successful in forging a coalition of academics, particularly ecologists and physicists, and businesspeople in formulating and applying four principles for guiding specific industries. The principles are as follows (Azar et al., 1996). Refer also to Figure 11.11:

1. Substances (e.g., lead) in the earth's crust (the lithosphere) must not be systematically released into the ecosphere.

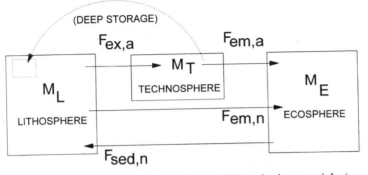

Figure 11.11 Schematic for tracing the flow of lithospheric materials (e.g., sulfur, cadmium, lead) used in principle 1 of the Natural Step Foundation. The F's are flows and the M's are stocks, as used in Chapter 7. $F_{ex, a}$ is anthropogenic extraction. $F_{em, a}$ is anthropogenic emission to the ecosphere. $F_{em, n}$ is natural emission by the lithosphere to the ecosphere via weathering, volcanic eruptions, etc. $F_{sed, n}$ is natural return from the ecosphere to the lithosphere via sedimentation. The dotted line represents anthropogenic return to the lithosphere, as with contemplated deep burial of radioactive waste. Principle 1 says that $F_{em, a}$ should equal 0.

2. Man-made substances, both those also occurring naturally (e.g., CO_2) and those not occurring naturally (e.g., synthetic pesticides), must not be systematically released into the ecosphere.

3. There must be no systematic deterioration of the physical conditions for biospheric diversity and production. This is also called maintaining natural capital, the long-term capability of (potentially) renewable resources.

4. There must be efficient and just use of resources to meet human needs.

Although these principles seem so general as to be difficult to implement, TNS has obtained strong cooperation from industry. Our purpose here is to look at several quantitative indicators to be used in evaluating progress toward applying the four principles, described in Table 11.9.

Most of the indicators are self-explanatory. $I_{2, 2}$, $I_{2, 4}$, and $I_{4, 3}$ make use of stock–flow thinking and the residence time approximation we used in Chapter 7. For example, $I_{2, 2}$ is calculated assuming that today's release rate continues indefinitely and that the removal rate from the ecosphere is equal to the stock/characteristic time. Then the eventual asymptotic stock resulting from anthropogenic sources is $F_{em, a}\tau$ (by Eq. 7.4). Assuming that the same characteristic time applies to preindustrial natural emissions, the steady-state natural stock is $F_{em, n}\tau$. Then the ratio of the future stock to the preindustrial stock is

$$I_{2, 2} = \frac{F_{em, n}\tau + F_{em, a}\tau}{F_{em, n}\tau} = 1 + \frac{F_{em, a}}{F_{em, n}} \tag{11.2}$$

TABLE 11.9 Indicators for the Four Principles from the Natural Step Foundation

Principle 1. Crustal (lithospheric) material should not accumulate in the ecosphere.	Principle 2. Anthropogenic materials should not accumulate in the ecosphere.	Principle 3. There should be no deterioration of the physical conditions for ecospheric production and diversity.	Principle 4. Resource use must be efficient and just in meeting human needs.
$I_{1,1}$ = anthropogenic lithospheric extraction rate/natural release rate (for natural materials such as copper) = $F_{ex,a}/F_{em,n}$.	$I_{2,1}$ = anthropogenic release rate of naturally occurring material/natural production rate (say SO_2 from coal burning versus that from volcanoes) = $F_{em,a}/F_{em,n}$.	$I_{3,1}$: indicators of transformation rates of land from one use to another, especially into and out of agricultural production.	$I_{4,1}$ (overall efficiency) = service per unit of substance extracted from nature now/service per unit of substance extracted from nature in a reference year.
$I_{1,2}$ = cumulative lithospheric extraction from a chosen date (say the start of industrialization), compared with prior cumulative extraction.	$I_{2,2}$ = the steady-state concentration factor for naturally occurring substances (the long-term stock implication of anthropogenic production = final concentration/concentration preindustrially), assuming today's production rate continues indefinitely, using the residence time approximation for removal (see Eq. 7.2), and assuming steady state before industrialization = $1 + F_{em,a}/F_{em\,n}$.	$I_{3,2}$ = agricultural land area with tolerable erosion/all agricultural land area.	$I_{4,2}$ (INTRAgenerational justice, "equity," as used in this book) = services per capita in a given region/services per capita in a reference region.
$I_{1,3}$ = nonrenewable power/total power.	$I_{2,3}$ = production rate of substances foreign to nature (e.g., plutonium, PCBs)*.	$I_{3,3}$ = agricultural or forest land area in which nutrients are being depleted (through leaching or burning, or through removal of crops or trees)/total agricultural or forest land.	$I_{4,3}$ (INTERgenerational justice) = annual dissipation of nonrenewable resource/(amount available in the crust and in the economic system) = $F_{ex,\,a}/(M_T + M_E)$. This is the inverse of static lifetime, how long the substance will last at current rates of dissipation (see Chapter 3)*.
	$I_{2,4}$ = the steady-state concentration factor for substances not found naturally (the long-term stock implication of anthropogenic production) = final concentration/concentration today, assuming production rate continues indefinitely and using the residence time approximation for removal (see Eq. 7.2) = $F_{em,a}\tau/M_E$.	$I_{3,4}$ = harvest or removal rate/growth or recharge rate (for forests, fisheries, aquifers).	$I_{4,4}$ = the fraction of the human population whose basic needs are not met (food, health, education).

Formulas refer to Figure 11.11. Except for two indicators marked with an asterisk, all are dimensionless. *Source:* Azar et al. (1996).

For materials that did not exist in nature before industrialization, $F_{em, n} = 0$ and the comparison is instead made to today's ecospheric stock, the amount we have already put there:

$$I_{2, 4} = \frac{F_{em, a} T}{M_E} \qquad (11.3)$$

These indicators are idealizations, assuming the residence time approximation applies. They also assume that today's emission rate will hold constant indefinitely. More careful calculation is needed for more complicated dynamics.

Table 11.10 shows indicators for principle 1. For most industrial metals and for carbon, sulfur, and phosphorus, today's anthropogenic extraction rate well exceeds the natural release rate, that is, $I_{1, 1} > 1$. Likewise, the cumulative anthropogenic extraction usually exceeds the preindustrial releases. Exceptions are aluminum and iron, both very common in the earth's crust. Note also that more aluminum, mercury, and sulfur are released as a byproduct of fossil fuel burning (the trace elements in coal, for example) than by mining.

Table 11.11 shows indicators for principle 2. Table 11.12 shows several physical efficiency indicators (principle 4). They are tracked over time and refer to a base year of 1970. For food, we see that the trend is toward using more phosphate fertilizer and less land per unit of food. For energy, we are more energy efficient in heating buildings and producing economic output. We see little change in the energy efficiency of transportation services.

Table 11.13 shows an attempt at intragenerational justice indicators, comparing Sweden and the entire world for food and energy. Sweden has more

TABLE 11.10   Indicators for Principle 1: Lithospheric Extraction

Element	Concentration in Soil (10^{-3} g per kg)	$F_{em, n}$ (Weathering and Vulcanism) (10^3 metric ton/year)	$F_{em, a}$ (Anthropogenic Release) From Mining (10^3 metric ton/year)	$F_{em, a}$ (Anthropogenic Release) From Burning Fossil Fuels (10^3 metric ton/year)	$I_{1, 1}$	$I_{1, 2}$
Al	72,000	1,100,000	18,000	34,000	0.048	0.01
Fe	26,000	390,000	540,000	34,000	1.4	1
Cu	25	380	9,000	55	24	23
Pb	19	290	3,300	85	12	19
Hg	0.09	1.4	5.2	10	6.5	17
C	25,000	780,000		5,400,000	6.4	
S	1,600	33,000	58,000	100,000	3.7	
P	430	6,500	21,000	1,700	3.5	

Data are for the world. *Source*: Azar et al (1996).

TABLE 11.11 Indicators for Principle 2: Anthropogenic Materials

Substance	$I_{2,1}$	$I_{2,2}$	$I_{2,4}$
Anthropogenic materials that also occur naturally:			
CO_2	0.07	1.8	—
CH_4 (methane, primary component of natural gas)	1.4–4.1	2.7	—
N_2O	0.5–1	1.5	—
SO_2	0.7–6		—
Anthropogenic materials that do not also occur naturally:			
CFC-12	—	—	7.5
CCl_4	—	—	14

By definition, $I_{2,2} = 1 + I_{2,1}$, so that for CO_2, $I_{2,2}$ should be 1.07. It is actually 1.8 because the residence time approximation does not apply to both preindustrial and industrial CO_2.
Source: Azar et al. (1996).

calorie, protein, and fat consumption per capita than the rest of the world, and the ratio has been fairly constant from 1970 through 1990. Sweden has a much higher energy use per capita than the world as a whole (as discussed in Chapter 4), but the ratio between the two has dropped from 7.8 to 3.8 in 20 years, almost entirely due to the increase in energy use by developing countries.

Indicators pertaining to basic needs require distinguishing needs from wants. Some are physical, such as per capita calorie intake or access to safe

TABLE 11.12 Indicators for Principle 4: Physical Efficiency

Efficiency Indicator (Normalized to 1970)	1970	1980	(1987) 1990
Food (All for the World)			
Calories/phosphate fertilizer	1	0.67	(0.61)
Proteins/phosphate fertilizer	1	0.66	(0.60)
Fats/phosphate fertilizer	1	0.69	(0.67)
Calories/land area	1	1.03	(1.08)
Proteins/land area	1	1.01	(1.03)
Fats/land area	1	1.07	(1.18)
Energy			
GDP/energy	1	1.07	1.21
GDP/energy	1	1.06	1.12
Housing space/energy	1	1.11	1.14
Person transport/energy	1	0.91	0.99
Goods transport/energy	1	1.06	0.93

Source: Azar et al. (1996).

TABLE 11.13   Indicators for Principle 4: Intragenerational Justice

Indicator	1970	1980	(1987) 1990
Food			
Per capita calories in Sweden/per capita calories in world	1.18	1.17	(1.13)
Per capita protein in Sweden/per capita protein in world	1.35	1.43	(1.37)
Per capita fat in Sweden/per capita fat in world	2.11	2.14	(1.98)
Energy			
Per capita energy in Sweden/per capita energy in world	7.8	5.8	3.8

Source: Azar et al. (1996).

drinking water. Others blend into the social indicators we began this chapter with. Defining, calculating, and making good use of indicators is a continuing challenge and an active research area.

PROBLEMS

Level of difficulty is indicated as Easier/Moderate/Harder. Problems marked "(Spreadsheet?)" can be fruitfully approached using a spreadsheet. They need not be, however.

11.1. (Easier) Are automobile commuting expenses a valid part of GDP?

11.2. (Easier) Daly and Cobb (1989) considered energy consumption only since 1900, rather than the start of industrialization, say 1750. If energy use has been growing exponentially since 1750, with a doubling time of 25 years, how large is the error in the Daly–Cobb calculation?

11.3. (Easier) For each of TNS principles, identify one aspect of your life that satisfies the principle, and one that does not.

11.4. (Moderate) Foy (1991) used the El Serafy method to correct the Louisiana GSP for oil and gas depletion. He found that for 1963–1986 the Louisiana GSP should be reduced 13.8% and 8.7% using interest rates of 5%/year and 10%/year, respectively.

(a) What is the assumed resource lifetime?

(b) What fraction of the uncorrected GSP was from oil and gas revenues?

11.5. (Moderate) Effect of resource depletion on GNP growth rate.

(a) For the Illinois data in Figures 11.2, 11.3, and 11.5, estimate the GSP growth rate conventionally, and corrected for the value of the coal resource, for 1973–1974, 1975–1976, and 1988–1989. Be careful with units: The GNP growth rate is the time rate of change of a flow.

(b) Are the differences large?

11.6. (Moderate) Sometimes it pays to sell off a renewable resource if a better investment can be found elsewhere; economics can tell one to kill and sell the golden goose, if it can garner the right price. Suppose the goose provides a perpetual, constant annual income of p dollars per year, and it could be sold for C dollars. The interest rate on investments is r per year.

(a) State the condition on p, C, and r for the sale to make economic sense.

(b) More complicated variation on the same theme from Fife (1977), pp. 76–81. Suppose the goose can be stimulated to produce more per year (say a total of q $ per year), but in that case it dies after N years. The comparison is between the perpetual income p and the perpetual income that could be obtained from an account formed by investing the excess income $q - p$ for N years. Derive an expression relating p, q, N, and r.

(c) In words, compare these calculations with the El Serafy method.

(d) What makes more economic sense:

1. $100/year forever

2. $200/year for 10 years

3. $700 right now
for $r = 0, 5, 10, 15\%$/year?

11.7. (Moderate) In ISEW and some other indicators, deviation from a uniform income distribution (everyone receiving the same) is considered undesirable. Daly and Cobb's index of income inequality is obtained by dividing the income recipients into quintiles. The first quintile contains the 20% of recipients with lowest income, the second quintile contains the next higher 20%, and so on.

(a) Briefly comment on the equity of these four hypothetical income distributions for a total of $50/year distributed over five recipients:
Distribution 1: 10, 10, 10, 10, 10 $/year for quintiles 1–5, respectively (base case)
Distribution 2: 4, 4, 4, 4, 34

Distribution 3: 2, 12, 12, 12, 12
Distribution 4: 8, 8, 8, 8, 18

(b) Daly and Cobb's index is calculated as

$$\frac{1}{5}\left(\frac{I_5}{I_1} + \frac{I_5}{I_2} + \frac{I_5}{I_3} + \frac{I_5}{I_4} + \frac{I_5}{I_5}\right)$$

where I_n is the total income to all recipients in the nth quintile. Additionally, they renormalize so that the base year's index is defined as 100. Calculate Daly and Cobb's index for distributions 2–4, defining the index as 100 for the base case, distribution 1.

(c) Do the indices you obtain convey the same sense of inequity you discussed qualitatively in (a)?

(d) Daly and Cobb's data for several years are listed in Table 11.14. Calculate the index for 1960, 1970, 1980, and 1987, using 1951 as the base case with an index renormalized to 100.

(e) Do the indices you obtain convey the same sense of inequity you get from just looking at the Daly and Cobb data?

11.8. (Moderate) Assume (1) the world is made up of two kinds of land, natural and human altered, and (2) human economic production is proportional to the product of the two types of land.

(a) Sketch human-controlled production as the fraction of land that is human altered goes from 0 to 1.

(b) Explain how if we knew the coefficients in the relationship we could deal quantitatively with the question of the proper scale of human activity.

11.9. (Moderate) Daly and Cobb's ISEW adds together many factors with weightings they have chosen. Assume that you agree with the adding (rather than multiplying or some other scheme) and with the individual factors, but that you disagree with the weightings. (For example, you may feel that long-term environmental damage is only half as important.)

TABLE 11.14

| Year | Percentage of Total Income by Quintile | | | | |
	I_1	I_2	I_3	I_4	I_5
1951	5.0	12.4	17.6	23.4	41.6
1960	4.8	12.2	17.8	24.0	41.3
1970	5.4	12.2	17.6	23.8	40.9
1980	5.1	11.6	17.5	24.3	41.6
1987	4.6	10.8	16.8	24.0	43.7

(a) Working from either Table 11.7 or Table 11.8, modify the weightings to suit your preferences and calculate "your" index for the years 1952, 1960, 1970, 1980, and 1987.

(b) Compare the behavior over time of the ISEW and your index.

11.10. (Harder) The effect of long-lived pollutants. Set up (but do not evaluate) using sums or integrals, the cumulative effect of releasing a pollutant that causes damage and also dissipates over time. Assume:

1. The emission rate over time is $f(t)$.

2. The stock of pollutant decays according to the residence time assumption with characteristic time τ years.

3. The damages per year are proportional to the stock.

4. Future damages are discounted with discount rate d per year.

11.11. (Harder) The effect of soil erosion on crop production can be thought of as a sum of a stock effect and a flow effect. The stock (depth) effect reflects the fact that thin soil has low productivity. The flow effect (rate of change of depth) reflects the fact that productivity is less on soil being disturbed (seeds face difficult germination if soil is literally being washed away). In Illinois the depth effect today is usually negligible because the soil is so deep, but the erosion rate effect is significant:

$$\text{Fractional decrease in yield} = bE$$

where E is the erosion rate in tons per acre per year and b is 0.01 per (ton acre^{-1} year^{-1}) (Herendeen and Mukherjee, 1996). In 1987 the average erosion rate was 6.2 ton acre^{-1} year^{-1}.

(a) Assuming that soil is 1.25 times as dense as water, express the erosion rate as a depth change rate.

(b) By how much was crop production depressed?

(c) Estimate the economic consequence for Illinois. Assume 25 million acres of cropland planted exclusively to corn with a typical yield of 130 bushels per acre per year and a selling price of $3/ bushel.

(d) Is this large?

12 Thermodynamics and Energy Efficiency

. . . or like the snow falls in the river.

A moment white—then melts for ever.

—Robert Burns, *Tam O' Shanter*

THERMODYNAMICS: FROM COSMIC TO PRACTICAL ASPECTS

The impact of this fundamental, difficult subject in environmental issues can be summarized at several levels:

1. *Broad, even Cosmic Perspective.* Living and economic systems are striving to create and maintain order relative to their less-ordered environs and can only do so by exploiting a necessary flow and degradation of free energy. Without that flow, order proceeds to disorder, as expressed by the Robert Burns quotation and Figure 12.1
2. *Detached, Academic View.* There are fundamental limits to the efficiency:
    a. of extracting useful work from energy flows,
    b. of concentrating disseminated resources from the environment,
    c. of the environment's processing of our wastes.
3. *Concerned, Limits-Oriented View.* The consequence of these limits is that there must be diminishing returns and depletability in the extraction and use of energy and resources and in the ability of the environment to absorb pollution.
4. *Soberly Hopeful View.* Although point 3 indicates ultimate limits to the efficiency of processes and technology, often efficiencies today are significantly lower than the theoretical maximum, indicating (often, but not always) the potential for significant increases in the near- and medium-term future, say the next 30 years.

Thermodynamics makes hard, scientifically testable, and tested, statements about the limits implied previously. While all science has a subjective element, thermodynamics is a very hard science that describes a "physical re-

Figure 12.1   Disorder happens. © 1981 King Features Syndicate.

ality" basis for environmental discussion. On top of that basis comes a long chain of technological, economic, behavioral, psychological, and humanistic issues involved in human decisions and actions. But under it all, free energy is flowing, subject to natural constraints.

In this chapter we will stress the device-oriented practical aspects[1] of efficiency questions but refer first to the broader perspective.

A compelling comparison of the economic and thermodynamic views of an economic system is conveyed by Figure 12.2. The economic view shows cyclic flows in which household members, as workers, produce consumer goods and, as consumers, purchase them. Economic goods move in one direction, and money in the other direction. This notion is strengthened by the existence of material cycles—from carbon in the biosphere to aluminum in the container industry (when recycling occurs). However, free energy—the ability to do work—does not cycle. It is truly dissipatable (unavoidably so, by the second law of thermodynamics). Thus an economic system, or an ecosystem, could be in perfect material and monetary balance, with no material or money crossing its boundary. However, there must be a cross-boundary flow of energy undergoing a transition from high quality (as in mechanical motion, concentrated fuels, or a hot flame) to low quality (as in the lower-temperature waste heat from a furnace). This view of an economic system as two cycles turning in opposite directions on an axis of energy flow, as shown in Figure 12.2, has been developed and made vivid by the ecologist Howard T. Odum (1971, 1983) and the economist Nicholas Georgescu-Roegen (1971).

There are a number of ways to quantify the degree of recycling, and they depend on the issues discussed in Chapter 8 such as system boundaries, choice of numeraire, and so forth.

---

[1]See Harte (1988) for a somewhat more technical discussion, which includes earth's radiation balance and chemical reactions.

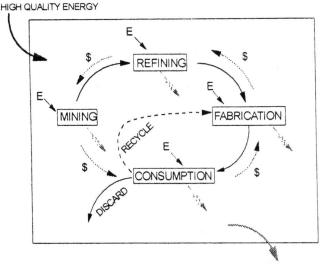

HIGH QUALITY ENERGY

LOW QUALITY ENERGY (LOW TEMPERATURE HEAT)

Figure 12.2 Material, monetary, and energy flows in an economy such as in the production of a knife, starting from iron ore. The flows labeled E are (high quality) energy consumption in each compartment; the wiggly arrows represent energy dissipation (i.e., release of low-quality energy). Materials and money can recirculate, but dissipated energy cannot. The figure is still simplified: If the consumption sector is households, there will be money flows (wages) to it from mining and fabrication as well.

FREE ENERGY: A QUICK TOUR

The practical impact of this chapter will mostly rely on point 4 given previously, the real potential for energy efficiency improvement, but we will spend additional time on the general thermodynamic view of systems functioning for our benefit. This section is a quick pass through the connection between energy and order and the ability to do work.

We start by asking: What things are of value to us? These fall into two general categories:

1. The ability to accomplish work (i.e., energy), for example, carbohydrate food, gasoline.
2. Order and structure, for example, protein food, buildings, art, medicines.

Georgescu-Roegen (1971) states that economic value and order usually go together (though there are exceptions, such as the highly ordered chemicals in poisonous mushrooms). From this thought we can speculate loosely that value (a human construct) is some function of energy and order, perhaps a sum of terms depending on each:

TABLE 12.1   Energy and Order in Familiar Materials

Examples	Energy	Order
Lump of coal	High	High (it is pure carbon)
Coal dust and dirt mixture	High	Low
Cracker box	Medium (it burns)	Medium
Swiss watch	Low	High
Carbohydrate food	High	Medium
Protein	High	High
Computer chip	Low	High

$$\text{Value} \approx \text{Energy} + \text{Order}$$

Units seem to be a problem in this definition, but we are bolstered by experience, which says that work (energy) can produce ordered things (consider any manufacturing process). There is hope that the two quantities can be expressed commensurably. Table 12.1 indicates qualitatively how these factors vary for different materials.

Energy and order are measured with respect to reference levels. Coal is useful as an energy source because there is available oxygen to burn it; the energy is measured with respect to that of the product CO_2. Similarly, concentrated silver atoms are useful relative to silver atoms disseminated in bedrock.

"Order" can have many subjective elements. Nonetheless we can try to discuss its fundamental basis. There are such quantities in thermodynamics, as well as quantities that combine energy and order, called "free energy." We want to demonstrate that a precise quantity used by thermodynamicists—free energy—shares many of the properties of our "value."

First, some comments on order: There are many ways to make a disordered system, but only a few to make an ordered one. If the probability of every arrangement is the same, then the probability is high that the system will be in a disordered state. To demonstrate, assume as a system $2n$ balls arranged in a row. The balls are indistinguishable except for color: n are red, n are green. There are $(2n)!/n!n!$ distinguishable ways to arrange them.[2]

On the other hand, we might want all the red balls on the left and all the green on the right—a well-ordered arrangement. There is only *one* way to make that arrangement, and therefore this perfectly ordered state has a probability of $n!n!/2n!$. As n increases, $(2n)!/n!n!$ increases astronomically, as shown in Table 2.2.

The probability of disorder becomes very close to 1 as the size of the system increases. For example, a shot glass of sea water contains about 6 $\times$

---

[2] $x!$ is called "x factorial" and defined by $x! \equiv x(x-1)(x-2) \cdots (2)(1)$. For example, $4! = (4)(3)(2)(1) = 24$. There are $(2n)!$ permutations of $2n$ objects, but in this case $(n!)(n!)$ are not distinguishable because all red, and all green, balls are identical.

TABLE 12.2 Number of Distinguishable Ways n Red and n Green Balls Can Be Arranged in a Line

$2n$	$(2n)!/n!n!$
2	2
4	6
10	252
20	184,756
50	1.27×10^{14}
100	1.01×10^{29}
200	9.07×10^{58}
500	1.17×10^{149}
2×10^{23}	$10^{60,000,000,000,000,000,000,000}$

10^{23} water molecules and 6×10^{22} salt molecules, so spontaneous separation into fresh water and pure salt is very unlikely.

When dealing with large systems, thermodynamicists use more familiar "macro" quantities such as temperature, pressure, and so on. In particular, they define entropy, S, by

$$\Delta S = \Delta Q/T$$

Where ΔQ is the amount of heat added to a system and T is the temperature. The equation holds if the process is done slowly enough. Thermodynamicists can also show that entropy is directly related to the disorder on the microscopic level we talked about; that is, the left-hand side of the equation refers to the increased disorder associated with the addition of heat, with that disorder being defined as before. This also makes sense from experience: Adding heat energy to a system does tend to disorder it (compare a smelting process when heat is added and then removed).

The consequence is that $T\Delta S$ is a plausible measure of increased disorder, and it has units of heat (energy). Therefore

$$\text{Value} = \text{Energy} + \text{Order} = \text{Energy} - \text{Disorder}$$

could have the form

$$\text{Value} = \text{Energy} - TS$$

Thermodynamicists have such a quantity: $F \equiv$ Helmholtz free energy $\equiv E - TS$ (Morse, 1964).

The Helmholtz free energy F can be specified for a substance (E can be determined relative to reference levels; so can S). What is of interest is F

relative to another state of the substance, for example, reactants and products in a chemical reaction (or a nuclear reaction). It can be shown that:

$$F \text{ (Reactants)} - F \text{ (Products)} = \text{Maximum work available}$$

It is difficult to attain the maximum. Alternately, the change in free energy is the minimum work needed to separate the products into the original reactants. Again, it is difficult to attain the minimum.

There is a symmetry between E and S in the expression for free energy. From a theoretical standpoint, low S can be just as much a resource for doing work as high E, although technologically this may not be true. We know it takes work/energy/expense to extract minerals, so we search the globe for concentrated deposits. Table 12.3 presents the results of a calculation for coal mixed to different dilutions in sand. Calculating entropy is beyond the scope of this book, so we just examine the results.

Thermodynamics thus says the *minimum* work required to collect very fine coal dust mixed 1 part in a million with dirt is only about 9% of the energy that could be recovered when it is burned. However, it is the *minimum.* Could one process a million pounds of dirt to get a pound of coal for less than 13,000 Btu, which is the energy in less than a pint of gasoline? That is doubtful. Real-life technology seldom reaches theoretical limits.

Do we ever, in practice, accept lower E in return for lower S energy resources? Yes. Montana coal is poor quality (only 8000 Btu/lb versus 13,000 Btu/lb for Appalachian bituminous). However, Montana coal is in 50-ft seams versus 3-ft seams in Appalachia; it is more concentrated and easier to mine. (Montana coal also has a relatively low sulfur content; see Problem 12.1.)

Is there a practical example of low entropy as a work-producing resource? Here is one proposed: At the mouth of the Amazon River there is a mass of fresh water encountering the salt water of the Atlantic Ocean. A gallon of fresh water sitting next to a gallon of salt water has lower S (more order) than after they are mixed (see Problem 12.6). Mixing the two liquids increases S and hence lowers F, which can do work. How can this be done? Recall the high school biology osmosis experiment, in which a tube of salt water with

TABLE 12.3   Helmholtz Free Energy of Coal in Pure State and Mixed with Sand

	1 lb Lump of Coal	1 lb Powdered Coal Mixed in Sand (1 part in 10)	1 lb Powered Coal Mixed in Sand (1 part in 10^6)
E (Btu/lb)	13,000	13,000 (same)	13,000 (same)
S (Btu $(K)^{-1}$ lb^{-1})	Low	Medium	High
TS (Btu/lb)	~0	201	1,205
$F = E - TS$ (Btu/lb)	13,000	12,799	11,795

[a] Assume T = room temperature = 20° C = 293 K.

a membrane over the end is immersed in fresh water. Initially, the water level in the tube is the same as that outside, but in a few minutes the level in the tube increases above the surrounding liquid, against gravity. Build this on a large scale and let the water tumble back over a turbine blade, and we have useful work. Theoretically, the salinity gradient at the Amazon's mouth (ocean water about 3% salt by weight) could drive the water to a height of approximately 225 m! (Norman, 1974; Levenspiel and de Nevers, 1974). Further, theoretically, a flow of 1 m^3/s could provide a power of 2.25 MW, or 1/440 of the output of a 1000-MW power plant (see Problem 12.5). The Mississippi River's average outflow to the Gulf of Mexico is about 17,000 m^3/s, which could theoretically provide 38,000 MW, roughly one-sixth the electrical output of the United States. However, there are many serious technical "ifs" separating this theoretical potential and the practical product (one being how to build a suitable membrane in large volume). In addition, the hydrological reworking of river deltas and estuaries would have large ecological impact.

Using a salinity gradient to accomplish work will cool the water a bit, the lost thermal energy balancing the potential energy gain by the water in the tube. However, the point is that this conversion of thermal energy into work would not have occurred if the order/disorder part of the free energy had not "driven" it by virtue of the tendency for the fresh water to mix with the salt.

Today we concentrate on low S when looking for energy sources (we look for high concentrations), but we often do not capitalize on it when using the energy. That is because the entropy contribution is fairly small. For example, in burning coal, $C + O_2 \rightarrow CO_2$: Theoretically, the diffusion of the CO_2 into the air (until it reaches an atmospheric concentration of 0.03% by volume) could be harnessed to do work, but at best that extra work would be equivalent to an increase of only about 5% in the work we derive from burning coal (APS, 1975). Similar figures apply to natural gas or oil. An even much smaller figure applies from distributing nuclear power fission products across the environment—and that is undesirable from an environmental perspective.

To achieve the maximum work from a reduction in free energy (or to produce an increase in free energy for the minimum work input) requires that reaction occur "quasistatically," which means very slowly compared with the microscopic mechanisms of heat transfer in real materials. Any reasonable speed requires more free energy (or work) expenditure than the minimum, and there are also potential energy "hills" to get over (e.g., wood is oxidized by decay bacteria over a period of years, but if you want a fire now you need a match), which also requires more energy. Similar problems exist in industry, and the science of catalysis tries to find shortcuts that will substitute clever technology for more time. Here are two simple examples of the free-energy cost of haste:

1. A steel plant puts hot ingots outdoors to cool rather than keeping them inside to heat water or space. Then additional energy must be used for these latter tasks.

2. A reaction proceeds faster at higher temperature, but at higher temperature more heat leaks through the reaction chamber's walls and is lost.

As shown in Table 12.4 there are large gaps between the real and ideal limits. On the other hand, we cannot get there if we want the process to proceed at nonzero speed. There is a growing field of nonequilibrium thermodynamics that addresses this problem.

THE HARSH NEWS: DIMINISHING RETURNS AND THERMODYNAMIC LIMITS

Even if we accept the idea of limits, we still wonder how we will approach the limits, and what will happen to the monetary and other costs of things as we approach them. The other side of this argument is to infer from the prices of resources that limits are being approached, which is a controversial issue, as discussed in Chapter 6. In this section we give some simple examples indicating that the cost of pollution control tends to increase exponentially with the degree of pollution removal.

Wet Scrubber for Removing Particles from Stack Gases

Basically smoke is passed through a shower, as shown in Figure 12.3a. Figure 12.3b shows an idealized top view. If the stream of shower drops is constant and the smoke passes through at a fixed rate (hence requiring a fixed time), the number of smoke particles captured will be proportional to the number present:

$$\frac{dC}{dt} = -kC \tag{12.1}$$

This is exponential decay of the pollutant concentration over time and gives

TABLE 12.4   Theoretical Minimum and Actual Free Energy (ΔF) Required for Several Primary Metals and for a Complete Automobile

Process	ΔF_{ideal} (Btu/lb)	ΔF_{real} (Btu/lb)	$\Delta F_{real}/\Delta F_{ideal}$
Blast furnace (iron)	876	9,191	10.5
Aluminum smelting	7,153	94,585	13
Copper smelting	−659[a]	18,197	−27.6[a]
Total car manufacture	1,606	57,827	36

[a] A negative sign indicates that the process should ideally release free energy.
Source: Berry et al. (1974).

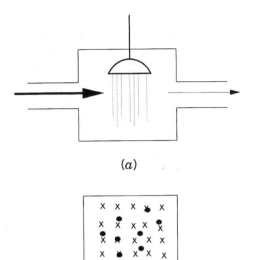

Figure 12.3 Schematic diagram of a wet scrubber. (a) Side view. Smoke is passed through a shower. (b) Top view. Crosses are water drops; circles are smoke particles.

$$C = C_0 e^{-kt} = C_0(1/2)^{t/\tau} \qquad (12.2)$$

To remove all pollution therefore takes infinite time (and hence infinite equipment, energy, and money) with a halving time of $\tau = \ln 2/k$. Other types of pollution control devices roughly follow the same pattern (Stairmand, 1965):

- Catalytic converters (where pollutants must collide with the catalyst surface)
- Electrostatic precipitators (where particles must acquire an electric charge in a manner similar to being struck by a water droplet in Fig. 12.3)
- Solution by dilution (where the tendency of material to diffuse is proportional to the concentration gradient)

The Compounding of Pollution Control Costs from Many Sources

Technology seeks to increase k in Equations 12.1 and 12.2, and advances occur, but they too have limits. The practical consequence comes when the desired pollution level (i.e., the desired level of removal) is set not by the cost of the control technology, but by limits on the environmental concentrations of pollutants. One consequence is that the total cost of control may rise faster than the amount of pollution being produced. Consider this example: In a confined airshed, in order to maintain ambient pollution concentration below a set level, legislation requires that the total atmospheric emission rate of a pollutant not exceed a fixed amount per day (C_{max} tons per day, say). Suppose one source already exists that emits just that amount per day. Now another, identical source is proposed: How much will all pollution control now cost? It will not be just twice as much, because that would produce twice as much pollution as with one plant and exceed the set limit of the airshed. The cost could be infinite: If the first source continues as before, the second must emit nothing, which requires infinite cost. The lowest cost is achieved if both new and old control to the same degree and emit half of the total. In that case the pollution control costs are related by

$$C_{max} = C_0 e^{-kS_0} \qquad \text{(one source)}$$

$$C_{max} = 2C_0 e^{-kS} \qquad \text{(two sources)}$$
(12.3)

Where S_0 is the cost of pollution control for the single source, and S for each of the two sources. The question is how S and S_0 are related. Setting the two equal gives $ks = kS_0 + \ln 2$, $S = S_0(1 + \ln 2/kS_0)$. The per source cost exceeds that for a solitary plant; the second term in the parentheses is the added cost of source density. For n identical sources the expressions are

$$S = S_0(1 + \ln n/kS_0) \qquad \text{(per source cost, } n \text{ sources)}$$

$$nS = nS_0(1 + \ln n/kS_0) \qquad \text{(total cost, } n \text{ sources)}$$
(12.4)

The total cost of pollution control grows faster than the number of sources.

This is an example of an interaction between P and T in $I = PAT$, occasioned by limits. Here kS_0 is related to the initial level of pollution reduction: $kS_0 = \ln(C_0/C_{max})$. Suppose that the first source initially removes 90% from its pollution stream, so that $C_{max}/C_0 = 0.1$ and $kS_0 = \ln 10$ by Equation 12.2. Then $S = S_0(1 + \ln n/\ln 10)$. The per source cost will be double the original value if there are 10 sources. This makes sense, because with 10 sources each must emit only 1% of its pollution, that is, 10% of what it did originally, which by Equation 12.2 requires additional cost S_0. Figure 12.4 shows this.

As more sources—plants, cars, septic systems, smelters, parking lots (runoff), and so forth—enter or are placed in an airshed, watershed, or region, the pollution control level must increase to maintain ambient pollution levels. For minimum total cost all plants should theoretically adjust their emissions, but, in practice, how to distribute these costs is a vexing equity issue. In the example if the original plant is not required to clean up, the burden accrues to the newcomers, who now must be infinitely clean, which is infinitely costly, which means the subsequent plants cannot enter at all. This argues for spreading the cost of abatement around, even to those who were there first. On the other hand, perhaps there should be some benefit of being first.

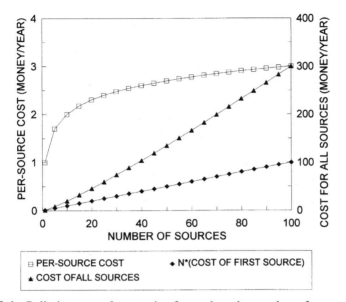

Figure 12.4 Pollution control costs rise faster than the number of sources because each source must become cleaner to avoid increasing total emissions. Here the first source achieves 90% reduction, but 10 sources must each achieve 99% reduction, and 100 sources, 99.9% reduction. The corresponding per source emission control costs are in the ratio 1:2:3.

ENERGY EFFICIENCY: TWO DEFINITIONS

First-Law Efficiency

Devices and processes that convert energy into useful services have limits. If the service is work in the physical sense (mechanical, electrical, chemical), the first law of thermodynamics (conservation of energy) states that no more than 100% of the energy can be converted to another energy type. We already mentioned the 95+ % efficiency of electrical turbines in converting mechanical energy of moving water to electrical energy, and, similarly, good motors can have 85% efficiency in making the opposite conversion of electrical energy into mechanical energy. Often, however, efficiencies are lower. Fossil fuel–burning power plants typically convert no more than 40% of the fuel's combustion energy to electrical energy, most of the rest necessarily being released as relatively low-temperature heat. Typically, only around 15% of the energy from burning road fuel goes to overcoming road friction and propelling a car, the other 85% being lost in imperfect combustion, overcoming air friction, and many mechanical losses inside the car. Similarly, incandescent light bulbs convert only about 5% of their energy input to visible light energy, while fluorescents convert about 20%. A typical older residential gas furnace gets only 50 to 60% of the combustion energy into the target space. The rest goes up the chimney (some necessarily so to transport combustion products), some through heating duct walls in uninhabited spaces, and so on. However, newer models can improve this to 95%. Table 12.5 gives typical first-law efficiencies for common processes.

However, it is possible to obtain a first-law efficiency greater than 1 if, for example, the objective is to transfer heat from one place to another. An air conditioner or, equivalently, a heat pump can transfer more heat from a colder place to a warmer place than the heat equivalent of the electrical energy needed to run it. Thus this definition:

First-law efficiency (η) = Energy transfer of desired kind/Energy input

which we have applied before. In principle η can have any value.

Second-Law Efficiency

Given that a heat pump can have a first-law efficiency greater than 1, how "good" is one with an observed η of 3? The second law of thermodynamics places limits on the first-law efficiencies, thus motivating this definition.

TABLE 12.5   First- and Second-Law Efficiences

Use	First-Law Efficiency	Ambient Temperature [°F (°C)]	Task Temperature [°F (°C)]	Carnot Factor[a]	Second-Law Efficiency
Residential					
Space heat (via combustion)	0.6	40 (4)	70 (21)	(294−277)/294 = 0.06	0.04
Water heat (via combustion)	0.6	55 (13)	120 (49)	(322−286)/322 = 0.11	0.06
Air conditioning	2.5 (0.8)[b]	90 (32)	55 (13)	(305−286)/305 = 0.06	0.15 (0.05)[b]
Refrigeration	2 (.07)[b]	70 (21)	0 (−18)	(294−255)/294 = 0.13	0.26 (0.09)[b]
Industrial					
Process steam					0.2
Direct Heat					0.3
Electric drive					0.3[b]
Transportation					
Auto	0.1				0.1
Truck	0.1				0.1

[a]The Carnot factor applies to a cyclical process moving heat energy such as refrigerators and air conditioners.
[b]Corrected for the first-law efficiency of a typical electric power plant, which is about 0.33.
Source: Data from APS (1975), Tables 2.2, 2.8, and 3.5.

Second-law efficiency (ϵ) = Heat or work usefully transferred/ Theoretical maximum heat or work usefully transferable using same inputs[3]

Second-law efficiencies are always less than or equal to 1.

Both first- and second-law efficiencies have limits, and in that sense the news is not good: A given amount of energy resource cannot provide infinite services, even if we are clever. On the other hand, efficiencies, especially the second-law efficiency, are often far from their theoretical limits. For example, a residential space can be heated to 20°C by burning natural gas in a furnace at 500°C with a first-law efficiency less than 1. It can also be heated by using a heat pump to transfer energy from outside (where the temperature is, say 5°C) to inside, and a heat pump can have a first-law efficiency greater than 1. In a second-law sense, we can see that something is lost using the furnace only for space heat because we know that we might *first* use that high-temperature heat to drive a chemical process, solder a joint, or forge a casting, and *then* use the leftover lower-temperature heat to warm the space. Table 12.5 compares first-and second-law efficiencies.

The Carnot Factor

Heat is one form of energy, and typically the greater the temperature difference between the hot and cold materials, the more work a given amount of heat can accomplish. Many of our technologies use some type of cyclical heat engine to convert chemical energy to heat to mechanical motion (e.g., auto, steam or gas turbine) or electric current (fossil fuel and nuclear power plants[4]). Other technologies work in reverse and use mechanical motion to effect transfers of heat—out of cold places (refrigerators, air conditioners) or into warm places (heat pumps). These depend on a cyclical heat engine, a device that relies on heating and cooling, and are therefore subject to a fundamental limitation discovered 200 years ago by S. Carnot. To justify it requires discussing the second law of thermodynamics and is beyond our scope here. For our purposes, we state the conclusion in two equivalent ways:

1. For a heat engine operating between two temperatures T_{hot} and T_{cold} (say a steam turbine), the *maximum* fraction of the heat flowing from the hot reservoir that can be converted to work is $(T_{hot} - T_{cold})/T_{hot}$. This fraction is less than 1; we cannot convert all the heat to work.

[3]An equivalent definition is the least free energy to accomplish task/actual free energy to accomplish task.

[4]This does not apply to hydropower plants, however. There is no fluid being heated and cooled; rather, the mechanical motion of water is converted to the mechanical motion of a turbine directly. There are some friction losses, but they are not limited as much as the thermal ones, and the conversion efficiency is typically greater than 95%. Direct conversion of solar light into electric current (as in photo cells) is also not subject to the Carnot constraint.

2. For a heat engine running backwards to move heat from the cold reservoir to the hot one (say an air conditioner), the maximum ratio of the amount of heat that can be made to flow uphill out of the cold reservoir to the work input is $T_{cold}/(T_{hot} - T_{cold})$. This fraction can have any value greater than 0; for a small temperature difference it is relatively easy to move heat uphill, but for a large temperature difference it approaches impossibility.

The temperature is measured from absolute zero, $-273°C$. Thus in Table 12.5 the Carnot factor for a refrigerator working between -18 and $21°C$ is $(273 - 18)/(273 + 21 - (273 - 18)) = 255/39 = 6.5$. Similarly, the Carnot factor for a steam turbine operating between $T_{hot} = 300°C$ (superheated steam) and $T_{cold} = 27°C$ (a cooling pond, say) is $((273 + 300) - (273 + 27))/(273 + 300) = 273/573 = 0.48$. These Carnot factors are the best that any heat engine can do; real machines can only approach these efficiencies. In addition, a power plant has a boiler, power train, generator, and so forth, so that the efficiency of the entire process of converting fossil fuel to electricity will be less than the Carnot factor. In fact, the efficiency of the entire process is around 40% in best practice today, and older plants are around 33%. Second-law efficiency compares actual performance to these Carnot limits, however elusive they are. For more discussions of the Carnot factor, see APS (1975) and Shonle (1975).

THE HEARTENING NEWS: EFFICIENCY IMPROVEMENTS

Theoretical limits to energy efficiency are indeed limiting, and so are practical issues that make the theoretical limits unreachable. Yet there are outstanding opportunities in the medium term (say several decades) for energy efficiency improvements to soften energy demand and the resulting environmental impacts. Table 12.5 is an example of the potentials. In the medium-term future, there is something that can be done with T in $I = PAT$ when I is energy. We have already discussed specific examples in Chapter 5, especially more efficient light bulbs. There we mentioned that often, though definitely not always, energy efficiency costs more (in material, technology, and money) early, but pays off later as the device is operated.

One need not be a theoretician to justify this position and to formulate environmental policy based on it. As Kenneth Boulding has said, "If something exists, it is possible." Thus we can look to the products on the market to see the range of efficiencies that are available, from cars to houses to water heaters to airplanes. For example, the American Council for an Energy-Efficient Economy publishes a listing of the energy requirements for the most efficient American-made household appliances[5]. The federal government requires an energy label containing energy use information on all new major appliances, as well as fuel usage for automobiles, and it has promulgated standards for appliances and new cars. In Chapter 2 we referred to the global energy-efficient future envisioned by Goldemberg et al. (1988). A comparable recent scenario can be found in von Weizsäker et al. (1996).

In Chapters 4, 7, and 10 we have calculated the dynamics of energy demand as such products enter the pool of existing models. There is evidence that in the last 20 years the U.S. economy has become approximately 30% more efficient in converting energy use per year into GDP, a concept supported by the international comparisons discussed in Chapter 4. Today 50-, 70-, and 100-mpg cars are feasible.

The Refrigerator: An Encouraging Example

In the early 1970s the average 16-cu-ft frost-free refrigerator used about 1800 kWh of electric energy per year in a typical household situation. Today the most efficient models on the mass market use 520 to 580 kWh/year. Thus today's models use about 1200 kWh/year less energy, cost approximately $100/year less to operate, and result in the emission of approximately 3000 lb less CO_2/year if the electricity comes from a coal-fired plant.

In an economic sense, the change is a consequence of government standards and information programs and of electricity price increases. In a technical sense, the change is a consequence of several factors:

1. Today's units are better insulated, so that the refrigeration system needs to remove less heat from within. They are better insulated because the insulating materials are more efficient and thicker. In the 1970s refrigerator external dimensions remained the same (standardization to make house building easier) while the interior volumes increased—factors that together imply thinner walls. This trend has partially turned around. In addition, doors seal better than 20 years ago.

2. The cooling systems are better: (i) larger, more efficient compressors and heat exchangers (which increases second-law efficiency of the refrigeration cycle); and (ii) more efficient (i.e., higher first-law efficiency) electric motors to turn them.

3. The refrigerators are better designed, with less outright contradictions. The contradictions included: (i) minimal insulation and isolation between the heat rejected from the refrigerator cycle and the interior, made

---

[5]American Council for an Energy-Efficiency Economy, 1001 Connecticut Avenue, NW, Washington, DC 20039. Another prime source is Rocky Mountain Institute, 1739 Snowmass Creek Road, Snowmass, CO 81654.

especially problematic by placing the compressor under the cooled space; and (ii) deliberate use of heat in, or next to, cooled space, especially to prevent condensation. (These practices have not been entirely eliminated. For example, a frostfree refrigerator often applies heat to interior cooling coils to "flash" off the ice. This speeds up the melting, but injects extra heat, which must then be removed.)

Further, there are energy-saving synergies that are difficult to assign to a particular end use. For example, a more efficient refrigerator puts less heat (from the electricity to run it) into the residence and therefore reduces the air-conditioning heat load, saving energy there as well. The same is true for more efficient light bulbs.

Efficiency proponents rightly point with pleasure to the refrigerator example. Detractors point out that the improvements are so spectacular because the base case is so egregious; those early 1970's refrigerators seem, in hindsight, to be technical jokes. However, this example, one of many, shows that we are far from the theoretical limit, and that recent practical experience shows solid potential. Energy efficiency,

- factored into $I = PAT$ thinking (Chapter 2),
- embedded in growth issues (Chapters 3, 7),
- combined with end-use analysis (Chapter 4) and economics (Chapters 5, 11),
- leavened by diminishing returns (Chapter 12), and
- complicated by indirect effects (Chapter 8),

will continue to be important in environmental issues.

PROBLEMS

Level of difficulty is indicated as Easier/Moderate/Harder. Problems marked "(Spreadsheet?)" can be fruitfully approached using a spreadsheet. They need not be, however.

12.1. (Easier) Midwest coal provides about 13,000 Btu/lb when burned; Montana coal, about 8000. Midwest coal is 3.2 to 4.5% sulfur by weight; Montana, 0.7% (Ayres and Simonis, 1994, p. 243). Compare the amount of sulfur per useful Btu for the two coals.

12.2. (Easier) A fossil fuel or nuclear power plant converts a fraction η of its heat to electricity and sends the rest into bodies of water and the atmosphere. In both cases, but especially in water, the heat is an environmental disrupter.

   (a) For a given electrical production, plot the waste heat versus η.

(b) Older fossil fuel power plants have $\eta \approx 0.33$, while new ones have $\eta \approx 0.40$. Compare the waste heat from the old and new plants.

12.3. (Moderate) For air conditioners, the energy efficiency ratio (EER) is defined as (heat-moving capacity in Btu/hour)/(input in watts). Typical "best" values for new units are 10 for room air conditioners, and 15 for central. How does this compare with the Carnot efficiency? (If 1 kWh is converted to heat, it yields 3413 Btu.) You will need to estimate the indoor and ambient temperature, in absolute temperature (kelvins).

12.4. (Moderate) Figure 12.5 contains a "conservation supply curve", which shows the cost of saved (something) on the y axis and the amount of (something) that could be saved at that cost on the x axis. Such curves are frequently used in water and energy debates. This particular curve is for residential energy.

   (a) Explain how you would use this in the determination of whether to authorize a new power plant.

   (b) What is a reasonable price of residential electricity today?

   (c) Given the price in (b), how much energy could be *cost effectively* saved annually in the residence typified in Figure 12.5?

   (d) In Chapter 5 a problem compares two cars. One gets 27 miles per gallon. The other, which costs $500 more, gets 40 miles per gallon. The cars are each driven 100,000 miles over their lifetimes. What is the cost of saved gasoline? Is it a bargain?

12.5. (Harder) The text claims:

   1. The salinity gradient at a river's mouth could theoretically drive the water to a height of approximately 225 m.

   2. Therefore a flow of 1 m^3/s could provide power of 2.25 MW, or 1/440 of the output of a 1000-MW power plant.

   3. The Mississippi River's average outflow to the Gulf of Mexico is about 17,000 m^3/s, which could therefore provide 38,000 MW, roughly 1/6 of America's electrical output.

   (a) Verify the calculation. The potential energy (in joules) of a mass m at a height h is mgh, where m is in kilograms, g is the acceleration of gravity $= 9.8$ m/s^2, and h is the height in meters. 1 J/s $=$ 1 W.

   (b) Do you believe it?

12.6. (Harder) Idealized fresh water–salt water mixing problem. Assume salt water is a mixture of water and salt molecules in the ratio 1:1.

   (a) Suppose equal volumes of fresh and salt water are allowed to mix, and then the mixture is separated into two equal volumes labeled A and B. What is the probability that volume A is pure water:

   1. When the original volumes are 2 and 2 molecules, respectively.

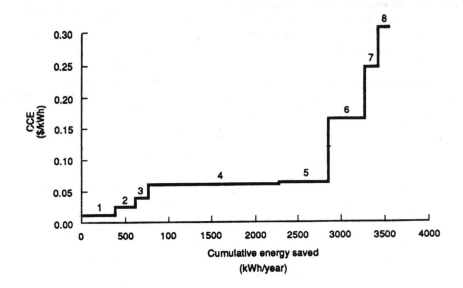

Measure	CCE ($/kWh)	Incremental Cost ($)	Measure Lifetime (years)	Measure Energy Savings (kWh/year)	Cumulative Savings (kWh/year)
Water heater blanket	0.009	25	10	400	400
High efficiency washing machine	0.023	50	15	240	640
Thermal traps on pipes	0.036	35	10	140	780
Average heat pump	0.055	750	15	1500	2280
Best heat pump available	0.059	300	15	560	2840
Hot water pipe drain system	0.16	225	15	150	3260
De-superheater on air conditioner	0.24	700	15	420	3410
Shower bath economizer	0.30	300	10	140	3550

Figure 12.5 Conservation supply curve for electricity for a single residence. CCE is cost of conserved energy. Measures are ordered by increasing CCE. *Source*: E. Vine and J. Harris (1990). Evaluating energy and non-energy impacts of energy conservation programs: a supply curve framework of analysis. *Energy* 15:11–22. © 1990 Elsevier Science Ltd. Reprinted with permission.

2. When the original volumes are 4 and 4 molecules, respectively.

(b) Are the answers to cases 1 and 2 the same? Explain.

(c) General expression. *Prove*: If brackish water is w molecules water and s molecules salt and if we divide it into two volumes containing a molecules and $w + s - a$ molecules, respectively, then the probability that a is pure water is

$$\frac{w!(w + s - a)!}{(w - a)!(w + s)!}$$

Show that when $w = s = a$, this reduces to the expression used in the text for the separation into equal numbers. (*Note*: 0! is defined as 1.)

APPENDIX 1
Sensitivity and
Uncertainty Analysis

Sensitivity analysis is the determination of how something changes with an infinitesimal change in one input only. Uncertainty analysis is the determination of how something changes (or is uncertain) with finite changes (or uncertainty) in one or more inputs. We see in the discussion of $I = PAT$ (Chapter 2) how changes in two or more of the factors compound to give a change different from summing the results of changing one factor at a time. Here we illustrate with another application of $I = PAT$.

Suppose P, A, and T all equal 1, with uncertainties (or changes) of -25%, -25%, and -50%, respectively. Sensitivity is defined in dimensionless terms:

$$\text{Sensitivity of } I \text{ with respect to } P \equiv \lim_{\Delta P/P \to 0} \left(\frac{\frac{\Delta I}{I}}{\frac{\Delta P}{P}} \right)$$

In words, the sensitivity of I with respect to P is the fractional change in I resulting from a very small fractional change in P. In calculus terms, the sensitivity is the partial derivative of I with respect to P: sensitivity = $(\partial I / \partial P)/(I/P)$. Sensitivity is independent of the actual changes, as it is defined in the limiting case. For $I = PAT$,

$$\frac{\Delta I}{I} = \frac{(P + \Delta P)AT - PAT}{PAT} = \frac{\Delta P}{P}$$

and the sensitivity of I with respect to P is 1. The same is true for A and T, by the symmetry of $I = PAT$.

Calculated sensitivities are often incorrectly used to perform uncertainty analysis by saying that the total change (uncertainty) is a simple sum of terms using the sensitivities to each independent variable. In our case the sum would be

$$\frac{\Delta I}{I} \approx (\text{Sensitivity})_P \left(\frac{\Delta P}{P}\right) + (\text{Sensitivity})_A \left(\frac{\Delta A}{A}\right) + (\text{Sensitivity})_T \left(\frac{\Delta T}{T}\right)$$

$$(\text{A1.1})$$

This is an approximation that holds for infinitesimal changes in P, A, and T, but is generally not correct for larger changes. Using Equation A1.1 for our example gives

$$\frac{\Delta I}{I} = 1(-0.25) + 1(-0.25) + 1(-0.5) = -1.0$$

which says that with these changes I is reduced 100% and has disappeared, which we know is wrong.

Uncertainty analysis, correctly done, uses no approximations:

$$\frac{\Delta I}{I} = \frac{(P + \Delta P)(A + \Delta A)(T + \Delta T) - PAT}{PAT} \qquad (\text{A1.2})$$

Using Equation A1.2 gives

$$\frac{\Delta I}{I} = [(1 - 0.25)(1 - 0.25)(1 - 0.5) - 1]/1 = -0.72$$

I has been reduced 72%, not 100%.

APPENDIX 2
Conversion Factors and Useful Numbers

This is a selected list, stressing especially stocks versus flows and energy units. More complete listings are found in Harte (1988), Halliday and Resnick (1978), and *The Handbook of Chemistry and Physics,* 77th ed. (1996).

Length

1 inch = 2.54 centimeters
1 foot = 0.3048 meter
1 mile = 5280 feet = 1.609 kilometers

Speed

60 miles/hour = 88 feet/second

= 96.56 kilometers/hour

= 26.82 meters/second

Area

1 square foot = 0.09290 square meter
1 square mile = 640 acres
1 acre is equivalent to a square 208.7 feet on a side
1 square kilometer = 100 hectares
1 hectare is equivalent to a square 100 meters on a side
1 square mile = 2.59 square kilometers
1 hectare = 2.47 acres

Volume

1 cubic meter = 35.31 cubic feet
1 cubic meter = 10^6 cubic centimeters
1 liter = 1000 cubic centimeters = 1.057 quarts
1 gallon = 4 quarts = 128 ounces (volume) = 231 cubic inches

1 cubic foot = 7.48 gallons
1 barrel = 42 gallons

Weight

1 kilogram = 2.209 pounds
1 pound = 16 ounces (weight)
1 ton ("short ton") = 2000 pounds
1 tonne ("metric ton") = 1000 kilograms = 2209 pounds

Density

Density of fresh water = 1 gram/cubic centimeter

= 1 tonne/cubic meter

= 62.4 pounds/cubic foot

Energy

1 joule = watt-second
1 kWh = kilowatt-hour = 3413 Btu
1 Btu (British thermal unit) = 1055 joules
1 kilocalorie (also called "Calorie" in dietary issues) = 4.186×10^3 joules
Food: 1 gram protein or carbohydrate = 4.5 Calories

1 gram fat = 9 Calories

Daily human diet = ca. 2500 Calories
1 barrel crude oil = 5.8×10^6 Btu
1 gallon gasoline = 124,000 Btu
1 ton coal = 25×10^6 Btu
1 foot pound = 1.356 joules
1 therm = 100,000 Btu = approximately 100 cubic feet of natural gas
1 quad = 10^{15} Btu

Power

1 watt = 1 joule/second
1 watt = 3.413 Btu/hour
1 horsepower = 550 foot-pounds/second = 746 watts

Temperature

Temperature (absolute, measured in kelvins)
    = temperature (degrees Celsius) + 273
"Room temperature" (= 20 degrees Celsius) = 293 kelvins

Prefixes and their abbreviations

10^3	kilo	(k)	10^{-3}	milli	(m)
10^6	mega	(M)	10^{-6}	micro	(μ)
10^9	giga	(G)	10^{-9}	nano	(n)
10^{12}	tera	(T)	10^{-12}	pico	(p)
10^{15}	peta	(P)	10^{-15}	femto	(f)
10^{18}	exa	(E)	10^{-18}	atto	(a)

CO_2 emissions from energy sources (Wilson and Morrill, 1996, Appendix 1).

All figures refer to the site where burned. Total emissions may be larger from energy burned in extracting, refining, and transporting energy. Total emissions from wood may be less if it comes from a sustainable rotation, as discussed in Chapter 7.

Source	lb CO_2/Unit	lb CO_2/million Btu
Fuel oil	26.4/gallon	190
Natural gas	12.1/therm	118
Gasoline	23.8/gallon	190
Coal	2.48/lb	210
Wood	2.59/lb	216
Electricity (from coal)	2.37/kWh	694
(from oil)	2.14/kWh	628
(from natural gas)	1.32/kWh	388
(national average of all electricity production, including hydro and nuclear)	1.54 lb CO_2/kWh	450

Weight CO_2/weight C = 44/12.

Greenhouse gas data (Houghton et al., 1996).

From Tables 1 and 4:

Substance	Preindustrial Concentration	1994 Concentration	1994 Rate of Change (%/year)	Residence Time (year)	Relative Warming Potential per Unit Mass for 20/100/500 Years
CO_2	280 ppmv	358 ppmv	0.4	50–200 (different mechanisms)	1/1/1
CH_4	700 ppbv	1700 ppbv	0.6	12 (nonlinear)	56/12/6.5
N_2O	275 ppbv	312 ppbv	0.25	120	280/310/170
CFC-11	0	110 pptv	0	50	
HCFC-22	0	110 pptv	5	12	
CF_4	0	72 pptv	2	50,000	4400/6500/10000

"ppmv" means parts per million by volume, etc. HFC-22 is a substitute for CFCs.

From Table 2: Average annual world CO_2 flows, 1980–1989. Units = Gtonnes (10^9 tonnes) carbon/year.

Fossil fuel combustion, cement production	5.5 ± 0.5
Net from tropical land use change	1.6 ± 1.0
Stored in atmosphere	3.3 ± 0.2
Ocean uptake	2.0 ± 0.8
Northern hemisphere forest regrowth	0.5 ± 0.5
Inferred sink	1.3 ± 1.5

APPENDIX 3
Selected Answers to Selected Problems

Chapter 1

1.1. ~7000 round trips per year.

1.3. (a) ~$88 to light a 100-W bulb continuously for a year.

(b) This room uses 1800 W and costs 18 times the answer to (a), $1584/year if on continuously.

(c) It costs $100,000 to replace 8000 bulbs, or an average of $12.50 per bulb. Compact fluorescent bulbs cost around $12 apiece, so this is reasonable. Assuming the bulbs are on for 6 hours per day, the savings per year is $80,000/year. This is in reasonable agreement with the annual savings of $50,000/year (the university likely pays less than $0.10/kWh).

1.4. Human diet releases ~200 g/day of C. An average car uses about 1 gallon of fuel/day, which releases about 3 kg. Note that this is only CO_2 on site. Indirect effects, such as CO_2 emitted in producing agricultural chemicals or in refining petroleum, are not included.

1.5. (a) 800 years.

(b) 74.3 years at 5%/year exponential growth. Forever at 5%/year exponential decline.

1.6. (a) Maximum volume at about July 1, 1993. Minimum volume at the very end of 1993.

(b) Maximum drawdown rate at about October 1, 1993.

1.10. United States: ~70 people/square mile.

1.11. 438,000 years. That long ago hominids in Europe, considered by some archaeologists to be preliminary Homo sapiens, used wooden spears on game, but are considered by most to have lacked higher cognitive stills. Neanderthal man would not appear for another 200,000 years.

1.12. Chicago–Amsterdam: 44.2 seat-miles/gallon. A 4-seat car getting 25 miles per gallon gets 100 seat-miles per gallon. This plane was almost full (284/297 seats filled) and therefore got about 40 passengers-miles per gallon.

1.13. The first question is 90% less pollution per what? If it is per unit of energy released, we can use the information in Appendix 2, which shows that natural gas produces 118/190 as much CO_2 as fuel oil (a good approximation for gasoline) per unit of energy released. For CO_2 Kane should have used 40%. His 90% likely refers to volatile hydrocarbons and other "traditional" air pollutants.

1.14. **(a)** Assume there are 100 million households, of which all have dryers and half are electric. If they are operated randomly, the average power from one is (4000 W)(hours in use per week/168). If used ~2 hours per week, the average power is (4000 W)(2/168) = ~50 W per dryer. (50 × 10⁶ dryers)(50 W) = 2500 × 10⁶ W = 2500 MW. A large nuclear plant at full capacity is typically ~1000 MW. If the plants are operating at 100% efficiency, we need 2.5 large nuclear plants to power the dryers. This is far fewer than the 110 plants claimed.

(b) **1.** Suppose all dryers are electric, doubling the number of electric dryers. This would reduce R by one-half.

2. If all dryers are on at 8 P.M., the power is 4000 W per dryer, not the average of 50 W we calculated previously. R would be reduced by a factor of 4000/50 = 80! This would bring R into the vicinity of 1, which then supports Caldicott's statement. One suspects that Caldicott assumed all dryers are on at once, which seems unlikely. On the other hand, there is no doubt some peakedness in dryer operation.

3. If capacity is less, so too is R.

4. This reduces R by 40%.

5. This reduces R by 10%.

These responses assume that each possibility/factor occurs alone.

1.15. **(a)** Requiring 40-mpg cars would save 3 to 5 times the 290,000 barrels/day expected from the ANWR. The savings is indeed about 10% of current oil use.

(b) Criticisms:

1. 40 mpg, 27 mpg are government test results. Actually, road mileage is lower.

2. Lags: It will take ~10 years for old cars to die and be fully replaced by 40-mpg cars.

3. Growth: Because the U.S. auto population is growing, it is improper to base the calculation on an assumed constant auto population.

4. Indirect effects: What about energy losses in refining and transporting oil?

1.16. The article's numbers are internally consistent, but the language is sloppy. It should read ". . . increase your chance of a fatal crash *to* 1 in 855,000."

Chapter 2

2.2. **(a)** Technology must become 75% cleaner.

(b) Per capita consumption must decrease by 75%.

2.3. **(b)** In the period 1950 to 1967, bottles per year increased by a factor of 6.9. Population and beer per capita increased only by factors of 1.3 and 1.05. The change was heavily dominated by the factor of 5.04 growth in bottles consumed per gallon of beer. Using the logarithmic approach: population growth, beer consumption growth, and change in bottle type contributed 13.6%, 2.6%, and 83.7%, respectively, to beer bottle growth in 1950–1967.

(c) This was a period when throwaway containers seriously penetrated a market previously held by returnables.

2.6. "pkm" means "passenger-kilometers."

(a) MJ/km ("energy intensity").

United States: Overall this dropped 12%. The average intensity of air and autos decreased by 53% and 9%, and these together held a nearly constant 95% of the kilometers traveled, so average intensity was dominated by the reduction in energy intensity.

Germany: Overall there was a 25% increase. Only air had a decrease in energy intensity, and this maintained only about a 0.8% share of kilometers traveled. Auto and bus both had increases in energy intensity ($\sim$20% and $\sim$50%, respectively), and these two uses account for $\sim$90% of all kilometers traveled. Intensities therefore dominated.

Sweden: Overall MJ/km increased by only 3%. Intensities for cars, buses, and trains increased by $\sim$3 to 11%. Intensity for air decreased dramatically, but it is still a small fraction of the total. Intensities therefore denominated; they changed relatively little for the dominant modes.

(b) Total MJ/year ("total energy"). Ratio of 1987 to 1970:

	KM	MJ/KM	MJ
United States	1.46	0.88	1.28
Germany	1.40	1.25	1.75
Sweden	1.48	1.03	1.52

In all three countries, the total transportation energy change 1970–1987 was positive, dominated by kilometers traveled. Changes in MJ/km were secondary, though significant in the United States (-12%) and Germany ($+25\%$).

Chapter 3

3.1. **(a)** Linear: 13.3%/year. Exponential: 7.32%/year.

3.3. The growth rates are 0, 1, 2, 3, 5, and 7%/year. (a), (c), and (d) are answered in Table A3.1. The answer to (b) is $r \leq -1.52\%$/year with $M = 1400$ billion barrels.

3.5. **(a)** $p = rM/(1 - (1 + r)^{-N})$
(d) For $r = 10\%$/year and $N = 360$ months, $p/M = 0.00878$.

3.8. Assume a generation time is 30 years.
(a) 1. Mrs. Dorsey's parents' generation: Doubling time ≈ 10 years.

TABLE A3.1

r (%/year)	τ (year)
$M = 1400.0$ billion barrels $C_0 = 21.3$ billion barrels/year	
0.00	65.73
1.00	50.52
2.00	41.96
3.00	36.31
5.00	29.11
7.00	24.61
$M = 922$ billion barrels $C_0 = 21.3$ billion barrels/year	
0.00	43.29
1.00	35.97
2.00	31.18
3.00	27.74
5.00	23.04
7.00	19.91
$M = 1867$ billion barrels $C_0 = 21.3$ billion barrels/year	
0.00	87.65
1.00	62.94
2.00	50.64
3.00	42.97
5.00	33.66
7.00	28.07

2. Mrs. Dorsey's generation: Doubling time ≈ 12 years.

3. Mrs. Dorsey's children's generation (age now ≈ 75): Doubling time ≈ 17 years.

4. Mrs Dorsey's grandchildren's generation (age now ≈ 45): Halving time ≈ 100 years.

5. Overall: Doubling time ≈ 15 years.

(b)

$$\text{gloof} = \frac{\text{gloof}_0 e^{rt}}{1 + \dfrac{\text{gloof}_0}{K}(e^{rt} - 1)}$$

Chapter 4

4.1. **(a)** 1 quad/year = 0.0335 TW.

(b) United States/world = 0.276.

4.3. **(a)** The graphical results for case 6 are shown in Figure A3.1.

(b) Power saved at point of use, assuming refrigerators operate randomly over time, = 29,000 KW = 29 MW. Distribution losses (averaging 10%) and a required power margin of ~15% would increase this result another 25%. Thus 36 MW of installed capacity is not needed. In addition, refrigerators tend to work harder in hot weather, so that their summer power requirements exceed the

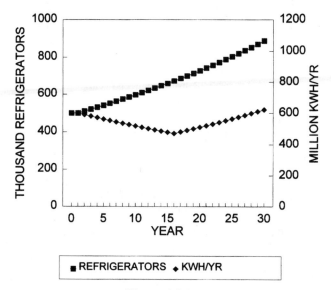

Figure A3.1

average, increasing the 36 MW still further. For a naked refrigerator in a non-air-conditioned location, this could double summer power requirements. Most refrigerators are in an air-conditioned space, so the effect is diminished.

Chapter 5

5.1. 1700 lb CO_2/bulb. This ignores electricity distribution losses.

5.2. **(a)** and **(b)** Assume electricity costs $0.10/kWh, an incandescent bulb costs $0.75, and a compact fluorescent bulb costs $12.

	TOTAL COST OF 10,000 HOURS LIGHT ($)	CO_2 EMITTED (LB)
Incandescent	$71	~1760
Halogen	$88	~1525
Compact fluorescent	$40	~440

5.3. Assume that gasoline costs $1.25/gallon and that the car travels 10,000 miles/year for 10 years.
  (a) $B/C = 3$ for zero discounting.
  (b) 41%/year.

Chapter 7

7.1. The outer diameter is exactly 4 ft. The thickness is 0.462 and 0.502 in. (Alyeska Pipeline Service Company Web site http://www.cais.com/alyeska/).
  (a) Transit time = 6.5 days.
  (b) Average speed = 5.1 miles per hour.
  (c) A few mph is typical (Robert Curry, personal communication). I originally estimated the diameter at 8 ft and obtained a speed 4 times slower.

7.2. **(a)** In salt water, τ is at least 5 years. Then stock = 10,950 cans. On land, cans last much longer, say 15 years. Then stock is 3 times what it was with $\tau = 5$ years, or about 33,000.
  (d) Assume $\tau = 100$ years. Then stock = 2.3×10^6 lb CO_2.

7.3. Reproduction factor = 0.8809.

7.7. **(a)** **1.** Overshoot and eventually reach a steady population greater than the starting value.

Age Class	Year	1	2	3	4	
1		2	2	2	2	
2		2	2	2	2	etc.
3		3	2	2	2	
4		0	3	2	2	
Total Population		7	9	8	8	

7.9. **(a)** 770 ppm (weight).

(b) Concentration (ppm by weight) = $540 + 230 (1 - e^{-t/\tau})$, with τ = 100 years.

7.10. **(a)** 760 ppm.

7.11. **(b)** Regarding the $7000: Average family income is about $40,000/ year. The 1/2%/year growth yields extra income of $200/year in year 1, $400/year in year 2, . . . , $1600/year in year 8. These sum to $7200. The $7000 is not the increase in income (a flow), but the cumulated sum of the increases over 8 years (a stock).

7.12. **(d)** Calculated precipitation in meters/year: Superior, 0.50; Michigan, 0.42; Huron, 0.36; Erie, 0.32; Ontario, 1.36.

7.14. **(a)** 2600 acres could provide about one-tenth of the stated power of 47 MW. 47 MW is roughly the total electric load of 40,000 houses, not just the lighting load. At $0.10/kWh, the electricity would sell for a total of ~$34 million/year. For the utilities to pay $20 million of that for their fuel seems a bit high, but not outrageously so. Therefore 37–47 MW, 40,000 homes, and $20 million/year are self-consistent, but 2600 acres seems 10 times too small.

Chapter 8

8.4. **(b)** $\epsilon_{prod} = 10$
$\epsilon_{cons} = 100$
$\epsilon_{pred} = 500$, all in Cal/Cal.

8.5. **(b)** $p_{corn} = 0.2$ l pollution/ton corn
$p_{tort} = 0.5$ l pollution/ton tortillas.

(d) 20% of the total pollution to produce a tortilla is emitted in the tortilla factory.

8.7. **(a)** $\epsilon_P = 10$ Cal/Cal
$\epsilon_C = 45$ Cal/Cal

$\text{TP}_P = 1.0$
$\text{TP}_C = 2.0$

(b) $\epsilon_P = 100/7 \text{ Cal/Cal}$
$\epsilon_C = 300/7 \text{ Cal/Cal}$
$\epsilon_D = 150/7 \text{ Cal/g}$
$\text{TP}_P = 1.0$
$\text{TP}_C = 2.0$
$\text{TP}_D = 3.0.$

8.9. Simple payback time = 15 years (after construction begins). IRR = 5.15%/year.

8.11. (b)

	ϵ (CAL/CAL)	η (g/CAL)
Producers	10	1/20
Herbivores	100	1/2
Carnivores	500	5/2

8.13. (c) IER is now 1.56.

Chapter 9

9.3. (a)

Add Cows?

I/They	Yes	No
Yes	Δ total yield, Δ my yield, Δ their yield = 25, 5, 20	9, 13, −4
No	24, −4, 28	0, 0, 0

9.4. (a) 1. Fishery crashes.
     2. When the catch is decreased by 5 fish in one year only, the fishery moves to stock = 160 fish.

9.6. (b) Rate of return (units = year^{-1}): Average, 2 − stock/100. Marginal, 2 − stock/50.

Chapter 10

10.5. Example: In 1980–1993 energy use per passenger-mile changed as follows:

Bus	+9%
Train	+23%
Auto	−29%.

Ratio 1993/1980:

	Energy/Passenger-mile	Energy/Seat-mile	Passenger/Seat
Auto	0.71	0.75	1.06
Bus	1.09	1.56	1.43

The 29% reduction in auto energy per passenger-mile was almost entirely due to increased physical energy efficiency. For buses, there was a 43% increase in riders per seat, but a countervailing 56% increase in energy use per seat resulted in a 9% increase in energy/passenger-mile.

10.6. (a) With an average car lifetime of 15 years, 525 million cars.

(b) With an average car lifetime of 15 years, production = 200 million/year.

10.7. (a) ~0.34%.

(b) **1.** ~5%.

2. ~60%.

3. ~24%.

10.9. (a) The graphical result for $x = 1.0$ (%) is shown in Figure A3.2.

10.10. (a) Trip speed (mph): See Table A3.2.

Chapter 11

11.2. Daly and Cobb's estimate is about 8% too low.

11.4. (a) 9.9 years.

(b) 22%.

11.6. (a) $rC > p$.

(b) It is profitable to kill the goose if $\dfrac{q}{p} > \dfrac{1}{1 - (1 + r)^{-N}}$.

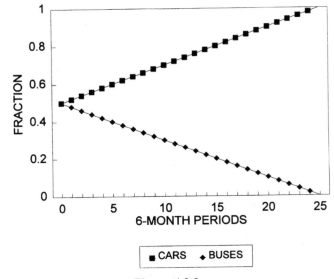

Figure A3.2

11.7.   (b)

DISTRIBUTION	INDEX
1	100
2	—
3	200
4	—

TABLE A3.2

	τ (sec)		
N/d (vehicles/mile)	2	1	0.5
1	50.0	50.0	50.0
20	31.5	37.8	42.0
50	19.9	27.3	33.6
100	12.4	18.7	25.2
500	3.05	5.3	8.36
1000	1.57	2.79	4.56

(d)

YEAR	INDEX
1951	100.0
1960	—
1970	95.0
1980	—
1987	—

11.11. (a) 0.0437 inch/year.

   (b) 6%.

   (c) $585 million/year.

Chapter 12

12.1. $(Sulfur/Energy)_{Midwest}/(Sulfur/Energy)_{Montana} = 2.8$ to 4.0.

12.2. Heat lost/Electricity $= (1 - \eta)/\eta$.

12.3. For an air conditioner operating between an indoor temperature of 77°F (= 25°C) and an outdoor temperature of 95°F (= 35°C), EER = 15 Btu/hour per watt is about one-seventh as efficient as the Carnot factor indicates.

12.4. (d) The undiscounted cost of saved energy is about $0.42/gallon.

12.6. (a) 1. 1/6.

   2. 1/70.

REFERENCES (WITH ANNOTATIONS)

(AAMA) American Association of Automobile Manufacturers. 1994. *World Motor Vehicle Data, 1994 Edition.* American Association of Automobile Manufacturers, Detroit, MI.

(AAMA) American Association of Automobile Manufacturers. 1995. *Automobile Facts and Figures, 1995 Edition.* American Association of Automobile Manufacturers, Detroit, MI.

Adriaanse, A. et al. 1997. Resource flows: the material basis of industrial economics. Report. World Resources Institute, Washington, DC.

(API) American Petroleum Institute. 1996. *Basic Petroleum Data Book: Petroleum Industry Statistics.* American Petroleum Institute, Washington, DC. Table 1 of Section II has world reserves broken down by region annually since 1948.

(APS). American Physical Society. 1975. *Efficient Use of Energy: A Physics Perspectives.*

Ayres, R., and U. Simonis, eds. 1994. *Industrial Metabolism.* United Nations University Press. Dominated by mass-balance studies. Comparison of neolithic and modern people's total material consumption.

Azar, C., J. Holmberg, and K. Lindgren. 1996. Socio-ecological indicators for sustainability. *Ecological Economics* 18:89–112. Indicators based on the four principles of the Natural Step Foundation.

Berry, R. S., and M. Fels. 1973. The energy cost of automobiles. *Science and Public Affairs* (December):11–60. Detailed vertical analysis.

Berry, R. S., and M. Fels, and H. Makino. 1974. A thermodynamic valuation of resource use: making automobiles and other processes. In *Energy: Demand, Conservation, and Institutional Problems* (M. Macrakis, ed.), pp. 499–515. MIT Press. Contains the auto results and free energy for industrial processes.

Bezdek, R., and B. Hannon. 1974. Energy, manpower, and the highway trust fund. *Science* 85:669–675. Use of input–output economics to determine energy and labor impacts of highway construction for comparison with alternatives.

Bingham, G., R. Bishop, M. Brody, D. Bromley, et al. 1995. Issues in ecosystem valuation: improving information for decision making. *Ecological Economics* 14: 73–90.

Boulding, K. 1955. An application of population analysis to the automobile population of the United States. *Kyklos* 8:109–124. An economist used biological population analysis techniques.

Brown, L., and H. Kane. 1994. *Full House.* Norton, New York. Claim that we cannot raise world grain production by very much because several past trends (in land, water, fertilization) are now saturating.

Brown, L., H. Kane, and E. Ayres. 1993. *Vital Signs 1993: The Trends That Are Shaping Our Future.* Norton, New York.

Bullard, C., and R. Herendeen. 1975. The energy costs of goods and services. *Energy Policy* 3:268–278. Input–output based energy intensities for 350 sectors spanning the U.S. economy.

Burns, T. 1989. Lindeman's contradiction and the trophic structure of ecosystems. *Ecology* 70:1355–1362.

Canadian Urban Institute. 1994. Cities without cars, report on phase 1, focus on land use and transportation. Report. Canadian Urban Institute, Toronto.

Caro, R. 1974. *The Power Broker: Robert Moses and the Fall of New York.* A. Knopf, New York.

Chambers, R. S., R. A. Herendeen, J. J. Joyce, and P. S. Penner. 1979. Gasohol: does it or doesn't it . . . produce positive net energy? *Science* 206:789–795.

Chapman, P., and X. Mortimer. 1974. Energy inputs and outputs for nuclear power stations. Report 005. Energy Research Group, Open University, Milton Keynes, UK.

Church, G. 1996. How fast can we grow? *Time* 148(July 15):40–42.

Cleveland, C. 1993. An exploration of alternative measures of natural resource scarcity: the case of petroleum resources in the U.S. *Ecological Economics* 7:123–157. Shows how net energy yield for oil has changed over the last 80 years.

Colborn, T., A. Davidson, S. Green, R. Hodge, et al. 1990. *Great Lakes, Great Legacy?* The Conservation Foundation.

Commoner, B. 1971. *The Closing Circle; Nature, Man, and Technology.* Knopf, New York.

Conservation Law Foundation of New England. 1990. *The automobile index.* Conservation Law Foundation of New England, Boston.

Costanza, R., R. d'Arge, R. de Groot, S. Farber, et al. 1997. The value of the world's ecosystem services and natural capital. *Nature* 387:253–260. Natural services not covered by conventional economic reckoning are worth ca. $33 trillion/year (very rough number). Conventional world economic product = $25 trillion/year.

Cropper, M., and P. Portney. 1992. Discounting human lives. *Resources* 108:1–4. Resources for the Future, Washington, DC. Results of questionnaire study to infer personal discount rates.

Daily, G., and P. Ehrlich. 1996. Socioeconomic equity, sustainability, and earth's carrying capacity. *Ecological Applications* 6:991–1001.

Daly, H. 1992. Allocation, distribution, and scale: towards an economics that is efficient, just, and sustainable. *Ecological Economics* 6:185–193. Beautiful summary of the need to address scale (i.e., limits) as well as allocation and equity.

Daly, H. 1993. The perils of free trade. *Scientific American* 269:50–57. Addressing scale/distribution/efficiency properly is thwarted by the mobility of capital.

Daly, H. 1996. *Beyond Growth.* Beacon. An eloquent summary of Daly's vision of ecological economics.

Daly, H., and J. Cobb. 1989. *For the Common Good.* Beacon. Introduces Index of Sustainable Economic Welfare (ISEW).

David, J., ed. 1993. *Aluminum and Aluminum Alloys.* ASM Specialty Handbook. American Society of Metals, Materials Park, OH. Has section on corrosion of aluminum in seawater.

Dincer. I. 1994. Unsteady heat-transfer analysis of spherical fruit to air flow. *Energy* 19:117–123.

Dynesius, M., and C. Nilsson. 1994. Fragmentation and flow regulation of river systems in the northern third of the world. *Science* 266:753–762.

Economist. 1996. California: Too poor for college. *The Economist* 340 (July 20): 26–27.

Ehrlich, P. 1968. *The Population Bomb,* Ballantine.

Ehrlich, P., J. Holdren, and B. Commoner. 1972. Review by Ehrlich and Holdren of B. Commoner's "The Closing Circle," and response by Commoner. *Environment* 14(3):24–52. Classic debate using *I = PAT.*

Ekins, P. 1993. "Limits to Growth" and "Sustainable Development": grappling with ecological realities. *Ecological Economics* 8:269–288. Reality check about economic growth and pollution control using *I = PAT.*

El Serafy, S. 1991. The proper calculation of income from depletable natural resources. In *Accounting for Sustainable Development* (E. Lutz and S. El Serafy, eds.). World Bank, Washington, DC.

Fife, D. 1977. Killing the goose. In *Managing the Commons* (G. Hardin and J. Baden, eds.), pp. 76–81. Freeman, New York. When good economics says to exhaust a potentially renewable resource.

Finn, J. T. 1976. Measures of ecosystem structure and function derived from an analysis of flows. *Journal of Theoretical Biology* 56:115–124.

Flink, J. 1976. *The Car Culture.* MIT Press.

Flink, J. 1990. *The Automobile Age.* MIT Press.

Folke, C., A. Jansson, J. Larsson, and R. Costanza. 1997. Ecosystem appropriation by cities. *Ambio* 26:167–172. Estimates ecological footprint of the 29 largest cities in Baltic Sea drainage and of 774 world cities with a total population of 1.1 billion.

Foy, G. 1991. Accounting for nonrenewable natural resources in Louisiana's gross state product. *Ecological Economics* 3:25–41.

Georgescu-Roegen, N. 1971. *The Entropy Law and the Economic Process.* Harvard University Press. Many pages to say that free energy that runs economies is depletable, but he was the first economist to say it loudly.

Gibbons, J., P. Blair, and H. Gwinn. 1989. Strategies for energy use. *Scientific American* 261 (September):136–143. End-use efficiency.

Goldemberg, J., T. Johansson, A. Reddy, and R. Williams. 1988. *Energy for a Sustainable World.* Wiley Eastern, New Delhi. Classic application of end-use analysis to project a feasible low-energy global future.

Goodland, R., and H. Daly. 1996. Environmental sustainability: universal and nonnegotiable. *Ecological Applications* 6:1002–1017. Explores three types of sustainability: environmental, social, and economic.

Gordon, A., and D. Suzuki. 1991. *It's a Matter of Survival.* Harvard University Press. Forceful quotes about how, in Toronto, people said they would not use public transportation even if it were free.

Gowdy, J., and C. McDaniel. 1995. One world, one experiment: addressing the biodiversity–economics conflict. *Ecological Economics* 15:181–192. Review article. Good footnote on discounting.

Gowdy, J., and S. O'Hara. 1995. *Economic Theory for Environmentalists.* St. Lucie.

Hall, C., C. Cleveland, and R. Kaufmann. 1986. *Energy and Resource Quality: The Ecology of the Economic Process.* Wiley, New York.

Halliday, D., and R. Resnick. 1978. *Physics* (Parts I and II, combined third edition). Wiley, New York.

Hannon, B. 1973. The structure of ecosystems. *Journal of Theoretical Biology* 41: 535–546. First application of input–output approach to ecosystems.

Hannon, B., and M. Ruth. 1994. *Dynamic Modeling.* Springer, New York. Includes STELLA version and stresses that language exclusively.

Hardin, G. 1968. The tragedy of the commons. *Science* 162:1243–1248.

Hardin, G. 1985. *Filters Against Folly.* Viking, New York. The three filters: literacy, numeracy, ecolacy.

Harmon, Ferrell, and Franklin. 1990. Effects on carbon storage of conversion of old-growth forests to young forests. *Science* 27:699–702.

Harte, J. 1988. *Consider a Spherical Cow: A Course in Environmental Problem Solving.* University Science Books, Mill Valley, CA. Good book, deeper and narrower than *Ecological Numeracy.* Extensive useful data and conversion factors in appendix.

HDRO. 1997. *Human Development Report 1997.* Human Development Report Office, United Nations Development Program. Oxford University Press. See also Website http://www.undp.org/undp/hdro/.

Herendeen, R. 1988. Net energy considerations. In *Economic Analysis of Solar Thermal Energy Systems* (R. West and F. Kreith, eds.), pp. 255–273. MIT Press.

Herendeen, R., and S. Brown. 1987. A comparative analysis of net energy from woody biomass. *Energy* 12:75–84.

Herendeen, R., and F. Fazel. 1984. Distributional aspects of an energy-conserving tax and rebate. *Resources and Energy* 6:1433–1450. The results of this hit the limelight very briefly in 1993 with discussion of Clinton's energy tax.

Herendeen, R., and J. Mukherjee. 1996. Natural capital of Illinois. Report 96/4. Center for Aquatic Ecology, Illinois Natural History Survey.

Herendeen, R., and A. Sebald. 1975. Energy, employment, and dollar impacts of certain consumer options. In *The Energy Conservation Papers* (R. Williams, ed.), pp. 131–170. Ballinger. Detailed comparisons of cloth versus paper towels, and so on.

Herendeen, R., C. Ford, and B. Hannon. 1981. Energy cost of living, 1972–1973. *Energy* 6:1433–1450. Detailed conversion of household expenditures to their energy impact.

Herendeen, R., T. Kary, and J. Rebitzer. 1979. Energy analysis of the solar power satellite. *Science* 205:451–454. Incremental energy ratio (IER) was less than 2.

Hirst, E., and R. Herendeen. 1973. Total energy demand for automobiles. *International Automotive Engineering Congress, Detroit, MI.* Society of Automotive Engineers, New York. Total energy/direct energy is approximately 1.6.

Holden, C. 1995. Betting on the future. *Science* 268:1281. The Paul Ehrlich–Julian Simon bet.

Holden, C. 1996. New populations of old add to poor nations' burdens. *Science* 273: 46–48. News article. Age class problem when population growth slows. Old people need as much care as children because they are living longer.

Houghton, J., L. M. Filho, B. Callender, N. Harris, et al., eds. 1996. *Climate Change 1995: The Science of Climate Change.* Contribution of Working Group I to the Second Assessment Report of the Intergovernmental Panel on Climate Change. Cambridge University Press. The full IPCC report, quoted to justify measurable climate change due to human activity. Some data on atmospheric greenhouse gases and global carbon balance are used in Appendix 2 of this book.

Hubbert, M. K. 1971. The energy resources of the earth. *Scientific American* 225. (3): 60–70. Stresses that oil extraction will peak and drop.

IIASA. 1996. Where science comes to life: IIASA at AAAS '96. *IIASA Options* (Spring):9.

Jenkins, T. 1996. Democratising the global economy by ecologicalising economics: the example of global warming. *Ecological Economics* 16:227–238. Good statement of the unfairness of CO_2 impacts relative to CO_2 producers.

Kasting, J., and P. Schultz. 1996. Letter to the editor: benefit–cost analysis and the environment (with a response from Arrow et al.). *Science* 272:1571–1572. Authors respond to Policy Forum in April 12, 1996 issue. They say that discount rate should be zero for issues with latency times of more than 1 generation. Arrow et al. say no. Discount rate is made up of two parts: (1) pure rate of time preference (which is normally >0) and (2) wealth effect (two-step argument: (a) the wealthier you are, the less additional consumption means to you and (b) wealth is likely to increase in future).

Kendall, H., and D. Pimentel. 1994. Constraints on the expansion of the global food supply. *Ambio* 23:198–205.

Kerr, R. 1995. Greenhouse report sees growing global stress. *Science* 270:731.

Kinsley, M. 1996. Less cost, more risk. *Time* 148(July 15):46.

Laitner, S. 1995. Calvert–Henderson quality of life indicators: tracking U.S. energy intensity. Report. Economic Research Associates, Alexandria, VA.

Landefeld, J., and C. S. Carson. 1994. Integrated economic and environmental satellite accounts. *Survey of Current Business* (April):33–49. Lays out the framework well.

Lapp, R. 1973. *The Logarithmic Century.* Prentice-Hall, Englewood Cliffs, NJ. Just before the oil embargo, and now almost quaint. The previous century was exponential and that cannot be repeated . . . for the United States. The word efficiency is not in the index. In 20 years, energy crisis and efficiency battles have come and settled down. The United States is not so exponential; the world seems to be.

Leontief, W. 1973. *Input–Output Economics.* Oxford University Press, New York.

Levenspiel, O., and N. de Nevers. 1974. The osmotic pump. *Science* 183:157–160.

Logofet, D. O., and G. A. Alexandrov. 1983. Modelling of matter cycle in a mesotrophic bog I. Linear analysis of carbon environs. *Ecological Modelling* 21: 247–258.

Lovins, A., and L. H. Lovins, 1995. Reinventing the wheels. *Atlantic Monthly* 275 (January):75–85.
"Hypercars," designed like airplanes of composite materials, far better than "supercars." Cars and light trucks now use 37% of oil, of which approximately 50% is imported. Military tanks get 0.56 mpg and aircraft carriers get 17 feet per gallon. Promotes "feebate" as superior to fuel taxes (which have not increased fuel efficiency in Germany and Japan, though they have reduced miles driven) and mpg standards, which are hard to administer and put upper limits on best effort. The last four paragraphs talk briefly about how hypercars will not solve all problems.
"Then we would discover that hypercars cannot solve the problem of too many people driving too many miles in too many cars; indeed, they could intensify it by

making driving even more attractive, cheaper, and nearly free per extra mile driven. Having clean, roomy, safe, recyclable, renewably fueled 300 mpg cars doesn't mean that eight million New Yorkers or a billion still-carless Chinese can drive them. Drivers would no longer run out of fuel or clean air but would surely run out of roads, time, and patience." Solution here is honest, equally subsidized pricing of competing modes.

Lynd, R., and H. Lynd. 1937. *Middletown in Transition: A Study in Cultural Conflicts.* Harcourt, Brace, New York.

MacKenzie, J. 1994. *The Keys to the Car: Electric and Hydrogen Vehicles in the 21st Century.* World Resources Institute, Washington, DC. Useful figures on air pollution, oil consumption. Then it's about alternative vehicles.

MacKenzie, J., R. Dower, and D. Chen. 1992. *The Going Rate: What It Really Costs to Drive.* World Resources Institute, Washington, DC. Data on actual subsidies to driving.

Max-Neef, M. 1995. Economic growth and quality of life: a threshold hypothesis. *Ecological Economics* 15:115–118. Some empirical evidence that for every society there is a period in which economic growth brings an improvement in quality of life, up to a threshold point beyond which quality of life begins to deteriorate. I worry that this statement confounds the effect of time with that of economic growth. Graph of GNP and ISEW per capita for five developed countries: United States, UK, Germany, Austria, Netherlands.

Meadows, D. 1995. Who causes environmental pollution? *Newsletter, International Society for Ecological Economics* 6 (July):1, 8. Meadows was challenged by women for using $I = PAT$, without referring to equity issues and important nonlinear effects. The critics said to distinguish household needs from luxuries and to note the disproportionate pollution by the military.

Meadows, D., D. Meadows, and J. Randers. 1992. *Beyond the Limits.* Chelsea Green, White River Junction, VT. Excellent book on limits and, especially, on the dynamics of growth and impacts. It is a follow-up to their *The Limits to Growth,* 20 years later. Same world model with slightly changed coefficients. Still aggregated over entire world.

Meadows, D. H., D. L. Meadows, J. Randers, and W. Behrens. 1972. *The Limits to Growth.* Universe Books.

Meier, A., L. Rainer, and S. Greenberg. 1992. Miscellaneous electrical energy use in homes. *Energy* 17:509–518.

Menzel, P. 1994. *Material World: A Global Family Portrait.* Sierra Club Books. Photos of families and their possessions around the world. Richest are Iceland, Kuwait, United States . . . but the sampling is not random. The description of the shoots by the photographers are excellent; they often lived for approximately 1 week with the families.

Miringoff, M. 1995. 1995 index of social health: monitoring the social well-being of the nation. Special section: comparing social health and economic growth. Report. Fordham Institute for Innovation in Social Policy, Fordham Graduate Center, Tarrytown, NY.

Mitchell, J. 1997. Oil on ice. *National Geographic* 191 (April):104–131.

Mlynski, M. 1994. University turning conservative. Better bulbs: New lights could save UI thousands. *Daily Illini* (January 10).

Morse, P. 1964. *Thermal Physics.* Benjamin, New York.

National Academy of Sciences. 1980. *Energy in Transition 1985–2010: Final Report of the Committee on Nuclear and Alternative Energy Systems.* Freeman, New York. Legitimatized the idea of widely differing energy demand for the same economic future.

Noam, E. 1995. Electronics and the dim future of the university. *Science* 270:247–249.

Norman, R. 1974. Water salination: a source of energy. *Science* 186:350–352.

Odum, H. 1971. *Environment, Power, and Society.* Wiley, New York. A hard book to read but suffused with deep insights about energy's fundamental role. Used the term "potatoes partly made out of oil."

Odum, H. T. 1983. *Systems Ecology.* Wiley, New York.

Parfit, M. 1995. Diminishing returns. *National Geographic* 188 (November):2–37. Popular article claiming depletion of world fisheries is now an accepted fact.

Patten, B. C. 1985. Energy cycling in the ecosystem. *Ecological Modelling* 28:1–71.

Pearce, D., E. Barbier, A. Markandya, S. Barrett, et al. 1991. *Blueprint 2: Greening the World Economy.* Earthscan, London.

Pearce, D., A. Markandya, and E. Barbier. 1989. *Blueprint for a Green Economy.* Earthscan, London.

Pimentel, D., C. Harvey, P. Resosudarmo, et al. 1995. Environmental and economic costs of soil erosion and conservation benefits. *Science* 267:1117–1123. See also July 28, 1995 *Science* for long critical letter from economist Pierre Crosson, and response by Pimentel and coauthors.

Prugh, T. 1995. *Natural Capital and Human Economic Survival.* Chelsea Green, White River Junction, VT.

Raskin, P. 1995. Methods for estimating the population contribution to environmental change. *Ecological Economics* 15:225–233. One way to deal with cross terms in *I = PAT* analysis.

Repetto, R., W. Magrath, M. Wells, C. Beer, and F. Rossini. 1989. Wasting assets: natural resources in the natural income accounts. Report. World Resources Institute, Washington, DC. Accounting for depletion of oil, forest, and soil, they get Indonesian GNP growth of 4.0% for 1971–1984. Standard calculation gives 7.1%. Also see "Wasted Assets" in *Technology Review* (January 1990):39–44.

Reutter, M. 1995. Illinois economy to experience "steady growth" in 1996, '97. *Inside Illinois* 15(5):1.

Roughgarden, J., and F. Smith. 1996. Why fisheries collapse and what to do about it. *Proceedings of the National Academy of Sciences* 93:5078–5083. Simple application of stability properties of humped curve of harvest versus stock.

Sachs, W. 1992. *For Love of the Automobile.* University of California Press. Translated from German edition, 1984. Subtitled *Looking Back into the History of Our Desires.* Many poignant ads, cartoons, vignettes, showing the strength of the attraction and relative weakness of resistance.

Sarmiento, S. 1996. Autos save energy. *Access* (Spring):41. Because cars are more energy efficient and bus and train ridership is down, Btu per passenger-mile is comparable for all three modes, and in 1993 auto was actually lowest (versus highest in 1980).

Schell, O. 1980. Hanging out in Beijing. *Mother Jones* 44–57.

Schipper, L., and A. Lichtenberg. 1976. Efficient energy use and well-being: the Swedish example. *Science* 194:1001–1013. Pivotal international comparison article.

Schipper, L., R. Steiner, P. Duerr, F. An, and S. Strom. 1992. Energy use in passenger transport in OECD countries: changes since 1970. *Transportation* 19:25–42.

Schwartz, S., and M. Andreae. 1996. Uncertainty in climate change caused by aerosols. *Science* 272:1121–1122. Perspectives article, quoting IPCC (1996). Aerosols are the reason for uncertainty in the question of whether climate change is real, they say. Aerosols whiten the otherwise blue sky. Backscatter from aerosols is now about twice preanthropogenic level. But aerosol effect is very uncertain.

Shonle, J. 1975. *Environmental Applications of General Physics.* Addison-Wesley, Reading, MA. Good discussion of energy efficiency of power plant in Unit 14.

Simon, J. 1981. *The Ultimate Resource.* Princeton University Press. The ultimate resource is population, he says. Everyone's cornucopian target, but hard to hit.

Simon, J. 1996. *The Ultimate Resource 2.* Princeton University Press.

Spurgeon, D. 1997. Canada's cod leaves science in hot water. *Nature* 386:107. News article. Part of a section (pp. 105–110) on fisheries science versus politics. Grand Banks cod fishery was closed in 1992 and is still closed. 40,000 jobs lost. Recovery is taking longer than expected. In a sidebar: FAO says world fish harvest will remain constant through 2010 (90 million tonnes/year). More than two-thirds of world's species (including cod, lobster, prawn, and shrimp) are being fished to capacity, overfished, or recovering from overfishing. 1992 production: China, 15 million tonnes/year, much for export; Japan, 8.5; Peru, 8.5; Chile, 6; European Union, 9.5; United States and Canada, 7.

Stairmand, C. 1965. Removal of grit, dust, and fumes from exhaust gases from chemical engineering processes. *The Chemical Engineer* (December):CE310–CE324.

Starr, C. 1993. Atmospheric CO_2 residence time and the carbon cycle. *Energy* 18: 1297–1310. Claims evidence supports residence time of 5 years, not the 50+ used by most. Makes a good case. One justification is that seasonal swing has not changed in amplitude, which one would expect because even proponents of the 50- to 100-year time now agree that preindustrial value was approximately 5 years.

Steinhart, C., and J. Steinhart. 1974. *Energy: Sources, Use, and Role in Human Affairs.* Duxbury, North Scituate, MA.

Stokey, E., and R. Zeckhauser. 1978. *A Primer for Policy Analysis.* Some stocks and flows, discounting, both well handled. On pp. 54–55 they derive the sum of a geometric series.

Swisher, J. 1994. Dynamics of appliance energy efficiency in Sweden. *Energy* 19: 1131–1142. Standard age class end-use analysis shows almost a factor of 2 difference in energy use in residential refrigerators and freezers and laundry and dish washing in Sweden in year 2010 depending on standards.

Tunali, O. 1996. The billion car accident waiting to happen. *World Watch* 9 (January–February):24–33. China is the big market for the world to go from the present 500 million cars to 1 billion. World car population has gone from 50 million to 500 million since 1950. For individual countries, the growth has been, or will be, far more spectacular (see graph). China had 30,000 in 1960, now has 1.8 million, and hopes to increase 20 times by 2010. In same period 1960–1990, Brazil went from 50,000 to 12.1 million. World car production now about 35 million/

year and has tended to level off in last 5 years. Misses boat on marginal/average question . . . still claiming that someone in Prague will use the car for long trips but use public transportation or bicycle for commuting. Quotes WRI (presumably MacKenzie's book) that U.S. car actually costs $2000/year more because of lost economic production from congestion, disease from emissions, and 2 million accidents (45,000 fatal)/year. Ford is about to build a $102 million plant in Vietnam, which requires a variance on the rule prohibiting building on rice-producing land.

Ulanowicz, R. 1986. *Growth and Development: Ecosystems Phenomenology.* Springer, New York.

United Nations. 1991. Concepts and methods of environment statistics: statistics of the natural environment. Report Series F, No. 57. United Nations, New York.

United Nations. 1993. *Integrated Environmental and Economic Accounting* (Interim Version). United Nations, New York.

U.S. Bureau of Labor Statistics. 1978. Consumer expenditure survey: integrated diary and interview survey data 1971–73. Report Bulletin 1992. U.S. Bureau of Labor Statistics, Washington, DC.

U.S. Bureau of Economic Analysis. 1994a. Benchmark input–output accounts for the U.S. economy, 1987. *Survey of Current Business* 74(4):73–119. Transactions, make and use tables.

U.S. Bureau of Economic Analysis. 1994b. Benchmark input–output accounts for the U.S. economy, 1987: requirements tables. *Survey of Current Business* 74(5):62–86. A matrix and inverse.

U.S. General Accounting Office. 1982. DOE funds new energy technologies without estimating potential net energy yields. Report GAO/IPE-82-1. U.S. General Accounting Office, Washington, DC. Criticizes the U.S. Department of Energy for not performing net energy analysis, as required by law.

Vine, E., and J. Harris. 1990. Evaluating energy and non-energy impacts of energy conservation programs: a supply curve framework of analysis. *Energy* 15:11–22. A nice tutorial, with a nice example for residential electricity.

Vitousek, P., P. Ehrlich, A. Ehrlich, and P. Matson. 1986. Human appropriation of the products of photosynthesis. *Bioscience* 36:368–373. They responded well to critics in a letter to *Science* in February 1987 (235:730).

von Weizsäker, E., A. Lovins, and H. Lovins. 1996. *Factor Four: Doubling Wealth-Halving Resource Use.* Earthscan, London.

Wackernagel, M., and W. Rees. 1996. *Our Ecological Footprint.* New Society Publishers.

Water Newsletter. 1995. Improved water quality may cause a marine organism population explosion. *Water Newsletter* 37:3. Water Information Center, Denver.

Watson, R., M. Zinyowera, R. Moss, and D. Dokken, eds. 1996. *Climate Change 1995: Impacts, Adaptations and Mitigation of Climate Change: Scientific-Technical Analyses.* Contribution of Working Group II to the Second Assessment Report of the Intergovernmental Panel on Climate Change. Cambridge University Press. Vegetation response to changed climate, ways to reduce greenhouse gas emissions from transportation, and so on. A wide spectrum.

Wilkinson, S. 1993. Our next car? Audubon (May–June):57–67. Lightweight article, but does point out that all cars pollute, that electric cars have to get their power somewhere, and that efficiency will not cure congestion. Cars have gotten so much cleaner that, in spite of growth, there should be less air pollution in California, say, but the car culture and the climate allow the old wrecks to stay on the road, and they pollute much more. People opting for big cars and no public transportation are being totally rational given cheap fuel.

Wilson, A., and J. Morrill. 1996. *Consumer Guide to Home Energy Savings.* American Council for an Energy Efficient Economy, Washington, DC. Good, popular summary of their efficiency publications. Good advice. They include most efficient appliances from their publication. Thanks to government standards, efficiency is up, and there is little difference between what is available at the upper end. This also likely means that standards tend to hinder improvement beyond them.

Winter-Nelson, A. 1996. Discount rates, natural resources, and the measurement of aggregate economic growth in Africa. *Ecological Economics* 17:21–32. Applies El Serafy and other corrective approaches to the GNP growth in African nations.

World Resources Institute. 1996. *World Resources 1996–1997.* World Resources Institute, Washington, DC.

Yuskavage, R. 1996. Improved estimates of gross product by industry, 1959–94. *Survey of Current Business* 76 (8):133–155.

INDEX

1